W9-ARF-384

National Security
for a New Era

National Security for a New Era

GLOBALIZATION AND GEOPOLITICS

Second Edition

Donald M. Snow

University of Alabama

PEARSON

Longman

New York   San Francisco   Boston
London   Toronto   Sydney   Tokyo   Singapore   Madrid
Mexico City   Munich   Paris   Cape Town   Hong Kong   Montreal

Editor in Chief: Eric Stano
Senior Marketing Manager: Elizabeth Fogarty
Production Manager: Denise Phillip
Project Coordination, Text Design,
   and Electronic Page Makeup: Stratford Publishing Services
Cover Design Manager: John Callahan
Cover Designer: Maria Ilardi
Cover Images: Courtesy of Getty Images
Senior Manufacturing Buyer: Alfred C. Dorsey
Printed and Binder: R.R. Donnelley and Sons
Cover Printer: Pheonix Color Corporation

Library of Congress Cataloging-in-Publication Data

Snow, Donald M., 1943–
   National security for a new era: globalization and geopolitics / Donald
M. Snow. —2nd ed.
      p. cm.
   Includes bibliographical references and index.
   ISBN 0-321-38393-1
   1.   National security—United States.   2. United States—Military policy.
3. World politics—1995–2005.   I. Title.
   UA23.S5253 2006
   355'.033073—dc22   2006006714

Copyright © 2007 Pearson Education, Inc.

All rights reserved. No part of this publication may be reproduced, stored in a
retrieval system, or transmitted, in any form or by any means, electronic, mechanical,
photocopying, recording, or otherwise, without the prior written permission
of the publisher. Printed in the United States.

Please visit us at www.ablongman.com

ISBN 0-321-38393-1

1 2 3 4 5 6 7 8 9 10—DOC—09 08 07 06

Contents

Preface

Between 1985 and 1998, I published four editions of the book *National Security*. During that period, the environment in which national security matters are considered changed radically with the collapse of Soviet Communism and the consequent artifice of the Cold War that had provided the framework for national security. The end of the Cold War provided a traumatic event, what I call in this text a *fault line*. The perfidious attacks on the World Trade Center towers and the Pentagon on September 11, 2001, represented the second great trauma for national security analysis.

Times have changed sufficiently that the old ways of looking at issues discussed in the earlier text seem woefully inadequate to understand current and future realities. It seemed to me that it was time to construct a new, fresh way to look at, so to speak, "national security for a new era." The pages that follow represent my attempt to provide such a fresh look.

The many recent changes in today's world are reflected in this edition of *National Security for a New Era*. One way in which change is manifest is in thinking about basic paradigms about how the international system works: as the subtitle *Globalization and Geopolitics* suggests, the alternative models are the globalization of the 1990s and the geopolitics of the Cold War and the period since 2001. The question is which will be dominant in a future national security environment that contains elements of both. Another way in which the environment is different is that national security concerns have broadened from a strictly military base to include elements that are semimilitary (terrorism, for instance) and nonmilitary (economic security, for example). National security is a more nuanced, subtle phenomenon than it once was.

This new text is, in some sense, a lineal descendent of my original work on national security. Readers familiar with that work will find some familiar materials the chapter on the American military experience, for instance. At the same time, there is a great deal of change. Reflecting the expanded American place in the world, there is considerable emphasis on problems that were much more muted during the Cold War—asymmetrical warfare, terrorism, the extension of the campaign against terrorism to places like Afghanistan and Iraq. There is even a chapter on peacekeeping and state-building that might have been handy to those designing the postwar phase of the Iraqi campaign. Recognizing that many of the students who will read this book lack much historical perspective on the material, I have tried wherever possible to point directly to the relevance of material to the present, both in the text and the accompanying Amplification and Challenge! boxes.

The second edition reflects these environmental changes. Most prominently and obviously, the new edition reflects the two most dramatic national security events of contemporary times, the campaign against terrorism following September 11, and the war in Iraq. Chapter 10 is now devoted exclusively to terrorism, and Chapter 9 has a much more expanded discussion of asymmetrical warfare of the kind the United States faces in Iraq. At the same time, Chapter 7 has a greatly expanded discussion of homeland security, the principal government organizational response to the new environment. Because some of this reemphasis has come at the expense of a focus on globalization, the discussion has been amended to incorporate changes in how we look at the prospects of globalization (notably Thomas L. Friedman's notion of a "flat world"). To accommodate these expanded emphases, other parts of the text have been condensed to keep the book near its original length. Thus, sections on the Cold War, competing images of the international system, and peacekeeping have been condensed as their centrality has declined, and the section on the war on drugs has been eliminated.

No work of this magnitude is accomplished alone. During the drafting and redrafting of the text, I have benefited from the useful comments and suggestions of a number of reviewers whose suggestions have strengthened the effort. They include: Chris Van Aller, *Winthrop University*; Valentine J. Belfiglio, *Texas Woman's University*; David Benjamin, *University of Bridgeport*; Patrick Haney, *Miami University*; Christopher Jones, *Northern Illinois University*; Richard J. Kilroy, Jr., *East Carolina University*; Lawrence Korb, *Center for American Progress*; Edward G. Moore, *University of Texas at Brownsville*; Linda Petrou, *High Point University*; J. Patrick Plumlee, *University of North Florida*; Philip Schrodt, *University of Kansas*; and Michael E. Smith, *Georgia State University*. Any remaining errors are, of course, my own.

Donald M. Snow
Tuscaloosa, Alabama and Hilton Head Island, South Carolina

National Security
for a New Era

INTRODUCTION

Framing the Problem of National Security

Since the tragic events of September 11, 2001, American concern for national security has been almost totally focused on, some might argue transfixed by, the problem of international terrorism and its likely recurrence on American soil. In the immediate wake of the airplane hijackings that ended with those airplanes being used as missiles against highly visible and symbolic American economic (the World Trade Center towers) and military (the Pentagon) targets, the reaction was of an astonished world fundamentally transformed by the acts of Usama bin Laden and his terrorist organization, Al Qaeda. The United States launched a military campaign to overthrow the Afghani government, which had provided the terrorists sanctuary, and began a manhunt for the elusive bin Laden and his cohorts that continues to this day. The national security establishment reoriented itself to a primary emphasis on suppressing terrorism and preventing its recurrence. The invasion and conquest of Iraq by the United States and its "coalition partners" in 2003 was largely justified as part of the terrorist campaign as well.

The transition has been difficult. Partly, the reason has to do with the nature of the new challenge: *terrorism*. Although terrorism is certainly nothing very new, its application by foreigners on American soil is novel. Domestic terrorist acts have certainly occurred sporadically during American history—the assassination of American presidents, for instance, and the bombing of the Murrah Federal Building in Oklahoma City in 1995 come to mind. At the same time, Americans overseas have been the victims of terrorist attacks; during the 1990s, the same Al Qaeda network that committed the September 11 acts was implicated in attacks against the American embassies in Dar es Salaam, Tanzania, and Nairobi, Kenya, in 1998 and against an American warship, the USS *Cole*, moored in a Yemeni port, for instance. The September 11 attacks dwarfed these previous actions physically and conceptually: three thousand people were killed in the shocking events, which were committed by foreigners acting on our own soil.

Part of the ensuing confusion was conceptual as well. Although a small community of analysts has studied the problem and likelihood of terrorist activity for years, the subject of terrorism had not previously caught the public attention. There is, for instance, a high degree of disagreement about what exactly constitutes terrorism; after

1

September 11, definitions became expansive, with more and more phenomena defined as acts of terrorism. Part of the problem was there is little agreement on what is and is not terrorism. In the near hysteria of the post–September 11 environment, policy became both riveted to and grounded around the global war on terrorism (GWOT), which became a centerpiece of national security policy.

Although we analyze the problem of terrorism later in this volume, our basic interest is broader. Our primary problem and focus is the national security situation that faces the United States and what policies the United States has and should adopt to confront that situation. Clearly, international terrorism is an element in that equation, arguably the predominant influence in the contemporary environment. But it is not the entire problem.

To look at the national security problem—to begin thinking about national security—two directions, outlined here, recur as primary emphases in the chapters that follow. One of these emphases is the theme of change, and it has two aspects in light of the September 11 events. The first is the extent and depth of change that the terrorist attacks introduce into the calculus of national security. The second regards changed dynamics of the environment in light of critical events in the past decade or more. Chief among those influences is the changing nature and profundity of threat. The other emphasis is on the basic nature of the national security environment, and this book introduces and examines two fundamental depictions: an environment dominated by international economic growth and expansion (globalization) and one dominated by military threats and what to do about them (geopolitics). As a preview, the geopolitical viewpoint predominated during the Cold War, which is the backdrop of the current period, and it has returned to dominance since September 11, 2001. The roots of that return entered the White House with George W. Bush in the form of a series of advisors known as the neoconservatives (or neocons) in January 2001. The globalization viewpoint dominated the decade between the two most traumatic, environment-altering experiences—the end of the Cold War and September 11.

THE NATURE OF CHANGE

The question of change is really two questions: How much has the environment truly been altered by events such as those of September 11, and what dominant characteristics of the national security environment have resulted from those changes? Because of the proximity of some of the events, there is no consensus on either of these matters. In these introductory pages, we introduce perspectives that will be elaborated in the body of the text and are intended to assist readers in reaching personal judgments on these matters.

How Much Has Changed?

Immediately after the trauma of September 11, the almost universal reaction of Americans and many overseas was that the change wreaked by the suicide air bombers was profound: that everything (at least figuratively) had changed. But was such a radical interpretation correct? The other way to think about September 11 was that the roots of change were present before the bombers struck and that those influences remain as prominent aspects of an environment. From this perspective, the underlying dynamics have not so much changed as have the vivid demonstrations of some of the most dramatic, traumatic implications of those dynamics. Each perspective deserves at least brief elaboration.

The popular view of the impact of September 11 on the national security environment is that it represents a fundamental, encompassing alteration of the problems facing the United States in the world and how these problems must be confronted. Partially born of the sheer magnitude and audacity of the attacks on the World Trade Center and the Pentagon and their vivid, relentless depiction on television, the initial reaction was that everything had changed, a perception largely reinforced by the volume and emphasis of the news media and reinforced by political figures. The terrorist acts were so dramatic that it was easy to view this as a "new kind of war," one which Americans had difficulty understanding.

Two related elements stood out from the initial shock. The first was the realization of physical vulnerability facing Americans. As pointed out in Chapter 3, one of the unique and favorable parts of the American historical experience has been the virtual invulnerability of American soil to foreign attack. The last time there was an organized physical assault on American soil was during the War of 1812. Granted that Soviet nuclear forces were capable of destroying the United States physically during the Cold War (see Chapter 4), American soil has seldom been threatened, and the integrity of the American homeland has rarely been a source of major concern. The terrorist breach of American invulnerability was thus particularly shocking. Although international terrorists did not (and do not) threaten American existence in the way that Soviet rockets did, our vulnerability to harm (if not extinction) was established by the events of September 11.

The second, related aspect was the continuing nature of vulnerability and the realization that the problem would not dissipate soon. This "new kind of war" would not be climactically decided on some major battlefield where the perpetrators would be decisively vanquished. Rather, the "war on terrorism" would be a long and difficult *campaign* (to borrow the description of French President Jacques Chirac) that would take considerable time and vigilance.

The contending interpretation suggests that less has really changed than was presumed immediately after the tragedy. The assertion that not a great deal has changed emphasizes continuities in the pre– and post–September 11 environments. It suggests, for instance, that the basic sources of instability in the international system before the event came from the most unstable countries of the developing world and that they still do. During the 1990s, the manifestations of this instability were largely chaotic civil conflicts that I call new internal wars (discussed in some depth in Chapter 11), where the policy question was whether these were important enough for our involvement. Contemporary conflicts continue in some of these states, and those states are the same kinds of places that provide the apparent breeding grounds for terrorism, the eradication of which is the current underlying policy rationale. In the 1990s, the

United States joined an international humanitarian effort in Kosovo; in 2001, the United States assisted in the overthrow of the Taliban government on the grounds of denying sanctuary for terrorists, followed by "regime change" in Iraq in 2003. For these efforts ultimately to succeed, we will have to engage in state-building activities so that the target countries will emerge as stable places that eschew violence and terrorists (also discussed in Chapter 11). Is that a sign of change?

At the same time, terrorism was a problem before September 11, and it continues to be a problem. Usama bin Laden had attacked Americans before his most spectacular foray, and he remains a potential menace. The antiterrorism community had been warning of possible terrorist attacks directly against the United Sates for years, but their warnings had largely gone unheeded (at least partly because those previous warnings had proven false). While it is true that essentially no one had predicted the scale, exact nature, or audacity of the attacks that did occur, it is equally true that terrorism did not come into existence on September 11.

New Dynamics in the Environment?

The last fifteen years have been an especially dynamic period in the evolution of American national security. As argued primarily in Chapter 3, the first two hundred years of the republic was marked by two major periods in national security terms. The first was what I call the formative period, lasting from the birth of the republic to World War II. This period was distinguished by a relatively low order of priority for national security concerns and relatively low commitments to defense matters, with "spikes" of concern when the country was thrust into war situations, followed by a return to the normalcy of peacetime. The second was the Cold War, from the latter 1940s until the implosion of Soviet communism in 1991 (discussed in Chapter 4). This period was distinguished from its predecessor because it was the first major American sustained involvement in national security affairs, when the United States developed and maintained large-standing armed forces in peacetime, and when the prevailing paradigm was the national security state (the situation in which preserving the integrity of the state is a major defining purpose of government). It was also the first time the existence of the United States became a matter of concern because Soviet nuclear weapons could physically destroy the United States as a functioning society, admittedly with terrible likely consequences for the Soviet Union as well.

The period from the beginning of the downfall of Communist regimes in Europe in 1989 until the terrorist events of 2001 produced large changes in the American national security problems. Two major events—fault lines—have largely defined those perceived changes. As a result of the second change in particular, there has also been a growing belief that the nature of warfare itself may be changing.

Fault Lines. What is a *fault line* as used in this text? The main idea of the analogy is that fault lines represent traumatic events—akin to the rupture of physical fault lines on the earth's surface accompanying earthquakes—that alter the environment and require an adjustment in the posttraumatic period. The notion is fundamentally compatible with the concept of tectonic shifts that Graham T. Allison Jr. introduced over a decade ago to describe the impact of the implosion of communist rule.

Two of these fault lines have emerged since 1989 and altered the national security environment in more or less fundamental ways. Both are discussed extensively in Chapter 1 and elsewhere throughout the text, but briefly introduced here. The first fault line was the end of the Cold War, symbolized by the peaceful demise of the Soviet Union and the fall, in most cases peacefully, of Communist regimes there and elsewhere. The net result was the end of both the military and ideological competition between the Communist states, led by the Soviet Union and to some extent China, and the West, led by the United States. Only four states in the world remain technically Communist today, and two of those—China and Vietnam—have renounced Marxist economics, a major underpinning of the ideology. (Only North Korea and Cuba remain staunchly communist.) In systemic terms, this fault line is the more consequential of the two because it affects the very nature of the operation of the international system and the basic threats to that system's existence.

The second fault line, of course, is the emergence of international terrorism through the events of September 11, 2001. As noted, those events and their aftermath have had their main impact on the United States (many other states had already experienced this phenomenon and made whatever adjustments they could to it). The impact of this traumatic event has been to raise awareness of vulnerabilities not previously acknowledged and to mobilize government and society to try to reduce that vulnerability.

A comparison of the two fault lines is not without irony, particularly when the measure is the impact of the two on threats, which are the major concern of national security planning. Threats (promises to do harm in the absence of compliance with some demand) can be usefully viewed on two criteria: their likelihood of being carried out and the consequences of their actualization. Likelihood can range from virtually zero (when threats are false—bluffs—or the threatener cannot carry them out) to virtual certainty. Consequences, on the other hand, range from the ability of a threatening party to do more or less great *harm* by carrying out a threat to being able to imperil the *physical existence* of the state by carrying out the threat.

National security environments and the impact of lacerations of the fault lines can usefully be categorized in these terms. During the Cold War, the stakes were exceedingly high, certainly much higher than they are now. The reason was that the potential consequences of war between the superpowers and their allies (planning for which was the central national security problem of the era) included an all-out nuclear exchange that could culminate such a war. That the Cold War could escalate to a nuclear hot war was plausible in an environment of ideological and political competition for predominance in the world.

As the Cold War evolved, however, those very consequences contributed to a gradually lowering likelihood of war. As time passed and arsenal sizes and deadliness increased, both sides increasingly realized that a hot war could effectively destroy them both, leaving no winner. The result was a *necessary peace* in which both sides avoided war not because of any mutual empathy but because of fear of the consequences of war.

As argued in Chapter 4, that realization contributed to the perceptions leading to the end of the Cold War.

Exposure of the first fault line—the end of the Cold War—obviously changed the nature of the threat environment. Russia, as the major successor state of the defunct Soviet Union, maintained the nuclear power to destroy the United States, but the death of Communism left it without any plausible ideological reason to use such weapons against a former adversary that was gradually becoming a friend and even ally. Although the arsenal sizes remain formidable, arms control agreements culminating in 2002 have reduced their size on both sides, as noted in Chapter 8. Thus, the period ushered in by the end of the Cold War (roughly the 1990s) saw both a reduction in the likelihood of major threats being carried out and a gradual lowering of the consequences.

Exposure of the second fault line further changes the threat calculus in different ways. Al Qaeda, and probably other groups in the future, show a very high level of willingness to carry out threats that, as argued in Chapter 10, probably cannot all be eliminated in advance: some will succeed. Thus, the likelihood of threats being carried out, in this case by international terrorists, has increased from the Cold War and post–Cold War periods, although it is impossible to specify how much in quantitative terms. While the drama and scope of the September 11 attacks serve as stark testimony to the willingness to do as much harm as possible, the consequences of terrorist threats are considerably less great than would have been the case had the Soviet Union launched a nuclear strike during the Cold War. The threat posed by terrorists, in other words, is to do harm, not to threaten the basic integrity of the American state. Should terrorists come into possession of some of the weapons of mass destruction (WMD, including nuclear, biological, and chemical weapons), as many fear and predict, the amount of harm they could do would increase; it is hard to imagine their development of a capability that threatens the integrity of the United States.

The quality of the threat environment has thus evolved. The Cold War—the memory of which is slipping from our conscousness—created a very deadly threat environment (enormous consequences of war) but one that became less dangerous (lower likelihood threats would be carried out) as time passed. The end of the Cold War gradually reduced the deadliness of threats both psychologically (the reduction of motivation) and physically (arms control; reductions of arsenal sizes) and reduced dangerousness as well, since threats gradually dissipated. The exception to the absence of plausible threats came from international terrorism, specifically from the threats of Usama bin Laden and his Al Qaeda adherents. Unless his capacity to do physical harm increases dramatically, however, such threats will remain at a much lower level of deadliness than was the case during the Cold War. These dynamics suggest several other changes in the environment as well.

The Changing Nature of War? Reaction to the terrorist attacks and subsequent analyses, which include the ongoing American campaigns in Afghanistan and Iraq, have raised a popular notion that warfare may be changing, both in the sense that the terrorists are practicing a new kind of war and that, in the future, traditional, conventional forms of warfare may have to be altered or may become obsolete.

These arguments are treated in some detail elsewhere: traditional forms of warfare in Chapter 8, the new kind of war in Chapter 9, terrorism in Chapter 10, and the Afghan experience in Chapter 11. They are introduced here as part of the general introduction of themes of the volume.

The term *asymmetrical warfare*, which has previously been used more or less interchangeably with several other terms to describe irregular warfare, is newer than the dynamic it purports to capture. In fact, the term refers to a form and approach to warfare as old as war itself.

At its base, asymmetrical warfare is defined as the situation in which both (or all) sides do not accept or practice the same methods of warfare. Asymmetry can extend both to the methods opposing sides use to conduct military operations and to the rules of warfare to which they adhere. Guerrilla warfare, which the United States encountered in Vietnam through the use of irregular enemy soldiers engaging in tactics such as ambushes, is one form of asymmetrical warfare. Terrorism is another. Those fighting asymmetrically may also reject the rules of war favored by their opponents; consciously targeting civilians is an example.

The concept of asymmetrical warfare implies its opposite, symmetrical warfare. Symmetrical warfare occurs when both sides adopt and fight in the same basic ways and follow the same basic rules. In the contemporary environment, symmetrical warfare generally refers to fighting between traditional, European-style armed forces (armies, navies, air forces) where both sides agree to be bound by the same rules of engagement, basically as specified in the various Geneva Conventions on war. A synonym for symmetrical warfare is *traditional western war* (western in the sense that it is warfare fought along the lines of European-style combat that evolved over time). World War II was the epitome of symmetrical warfare (even if some isolated combatants fought asymmetrically). In the American and European tradition, it is the acceptable, "honorable" way of war.

Why would someone in effect break the accepted conventions and rules on war and fight asymmetrically (a synonym for which is *dishonorably*)? The historical answer is clear: what we now call asymmetrical warfare is the approach of a weaker foe trying to overcome the advantages of a force that is superior in whatever the accepted, conventional forms of warfare of the time prescribes. If you know that you will lose if you play by the opponent's rules, then it only makes sense to reject those rules in ways that may turn your weakness into strength and negate your opponent's strengths. There is certainly nothing new or novel about this; in fact, it may be the only thing that makes sense for a weaker party.

Those who are stronger by conventional standards will always decry the resort to asymmetrical means. The United States Army would always prefer that its opponents face it in massed formations on conventional battlefield where overwhelming American firepower can be brought to bear to destroy the opponent. An inferior opponent would be foolhardy to cooperate in its own destruction by fighting the way the Americans prefer to fight. Thus, they adopt other means.

Those who argue that asymmetrical warfare is becoming the norm may have a point, although they seldom recognize the irony of why they are correct. Since the end of the Cold War, the gap between American conventional (symmetrical) military capability and that of any conceivable foes has progressively widened. This gap was first demonstrated in the Persian Gulf War of 1990–1991, and it has since increased. In 2002, for instance, the defense budget of the United States stood at about $350 billion out of a worldwide total of about $800 billion (including the American total). American military expenditures for 2002 were greater than the expenditures of the next fourteen largest spending states combined. The budget increases for 2003 pushed the U.S. portion to over one-half of the global total, meaning the United States spent more on defense *than the rest of the world combined*—a proportion that continues to hold.

The result is a conventional, symmetrical military situation in which, effectively, *no state or probable combination of states can successfully confront and fight the United States symmetrically*, using conventional methods and rules. The very success of the American military machine is to negate its own advantage. Any potential adversaries contemplating fighting the Americans can only conclude that the only chance they have of winning is to change the rules to negate the American advantage. In an act that amounts to an unconscious self-fulfilling prophecy, the United States has created the situation in which its future will almost certainly be in opposition to opponents fighting asymmetrically.

The American experiences in Afghanistan and Iraq reinforce this situation, if in slightly different ways. U.S. interest in Afghanistan arose because the Taliban government of Afghanistan was providing physical sanctuary for Al Qaeda (with whom they were allied in the 1980s effort to expel the Soviet Union from the country) and refused to relinquish the leadership to U.S. custody. Intent on destroying Al Qaeda, the United States thus found common cause with insurgents (the Northern Alliance) who were engaged in a conventional civil war to overthrow the Taliban. Although largely a guerrilla war, the campaign was symmetrical in the sense that both sides fought by the same rules.

The United States entered the fray with strategic air power and special forces (largely used as target spotters) against the Taliban. The Taliban were forced to stand and fight, incurring devastating losses, because to flee and avoid the bombers would also have ceded the field to the Northern Alliance. Overwhelming American conventional force was thus demonstrated as the Taliban were routed from power. After the overthrow, however, the remaining elements of the Taliban and their Al Qaeda allies reverted to mountain-based asymmetrical warfare and had, as of mid-2005, continued to evade capture or destruction by Afghan and American forces.

The situation in Iraq was similar. Based on their experience in the Persian Gulf War of 1991, the Iraqis knew a conventional, symmetrical defense against an American invasion was suicidal. Thus, they offered only a token resistance that allowed the Americans to sweep through the country with ease. Once the American occupation began, however, elements of the Iraqi armed forces began an asymmetrical campaign against the invaders and their Iraqi collaborators that, once again as of mid-2006, frustrated the American attempt to pacify the country. Future possible opponents of the United States have undoubtedly taken solace and possible inspiration from the Iraqi and Afghan asymmetrical efforts.

New Visions. A final element of change in the contemporary defense picture is the emergence of a group of analysts called the neoconservatives as close advisors and influencers of defense policy under Bush. Led intellectually by figures such as Paul Wolfowitz and Richard Perle and politically by Vice President Dick Cheney and Defense Secretary Donald Rumsfeld, this group had its original roots in government in the staff of the late Washington Senator Henry M. "Scoop" Jackson and the administration of Ronald Reagan (calling themselves first Jackson Democrats, then Reagan Democrats). They offer a very different view of the role of American military power in the world than previous administrations have held.

The neocon position is developed as the analysis continues, but its basic point can be made. The neocons see the current power balance that is overwhelmingly in favor of the United States as a distinct opportunity that should be maintained for as long as possible. Their argument is that the United States can use its power to force change in countries around the world to foster political democracy and freedom that cannot be achieved by diplomatic, political, or economic efforts alone. Some of the neocons refer to the situation they favor as one of "benign hegemony," an evangelical worldview that places the United States at the core of global peace and democracy through the imposition or threat of employing U.S. force when that vision is resisted. Regime change in Iraq was the prototype of the employment of this strategy, which is stated most forcefully in the so-called Bush Doctrine incorporated into the 2002 *National Security Strategy of the United States of America*. Although the cast of neocon advisors has changed somewhat in the second Bush administration (Wolfowitz became president of the World Bank, and Stephen Hadley became National Security Advisor), their influence on policy continues to be considerable and to send strong messages to the international environment.

The Homeland Security Emphasis. The changed environment induced by September 11 has also produced institutional change within the United States government. The trauma of the terrorist onslaught created an atmosphere ripe for proactive approaches to the apparently changed environment, and revelations that the government was not organized optimally to deal with the crisis only added to the clamor for change. The outgrowth of these factors was the institutionalization of homeland security.

The spotlighting of homeland security is, of course, much older than the function it purports to serve. Keeping the homeland secure from foreign enemies is a basic part of national security and has always been implicit in the problem of national security. For almost two centuries before September 11, however, the need to directly secure the homeland had not been an immediate, pressing matter because the United States was effectively immune (or invulnerable) to attack, a point elaborated in Chapter 3. Al Qaeda burst the myth of invulnerability and sent us scurrying for ways to protect ourselves from evidently capable violators of our safety.

The result has been an institutionalization of and emphasis on homeland security as a prominent aspect of American national security. It began within weeks of the disaster when, by executive order, President Bush created the Homeland Security

Council and appointed former Pennsylvania Governor Tom Ridge as its director. In 2002, the Homeland Security Act was passed, creating the Department of Homeland Security (DHS) as a Cabinet-level agency and attempting to bring a number of functions related to dealing with threats to security (notably terrorism) under one governmental roof. In 2005, legislation recommended by the 9/11 Commission was enacted to reorganize the intelligence community.

The homeland security emphasis remains a work in progress and one that serves as a useful bellwether to exactly how seriously the government takes the problem. While some functions dealing with the problem have indeed been transferred to DHS, many have not; Congressional oversight is a hopeless tangle of committees that overlap and contradict one another; and the reorganization of the intelligence community is still not completed nor the "turf wars" surmounted. In Chapter 7, we explore this evolution and ask whether homeland security word and deed match, and if not, what that says about the actual, as opposed to rhetorical, commitment to the problem.

GLOBALIZATION AND GEOPOLITICS

The other major theme of this volume is the competition between conceptualizations of the international system centered on the dynamics of globalization and geopolitics. Which of these basic dynamics has dominated across time? Which is the paradigm that most accurately depicts the national security situation?

Raising the distinction in this manner reflects the odyssey international politics has traveled over the last fifteen years. Geopolitics, the perspective that views military conflict (or its potential) in a hostile environment as the centerpiece of international concern, is the historically dominant perspective. That perspective, captured in some detail in Chapter 2 in the form of the realist paradigm, was clearly the central perspective during the Cold War, and it has returned to a position of central importance since September 11, 2001, with the GWOT and the rise of the neoconservatives. During the Cold War, this perspective emphasized "godless Communism" as the geopolitical enemy; now, it is international terrorism and the "axis of evil."

The 1990s represented an interlude between geopolitical ascendancies. Between the end of the Cold War and September 11, the forces of economic globalization—the spread of market democracies and a gradually expanding economic prosperity globally—took hold and spread as the major dynamic of international life. This period coincided with a receding threat environment for the major powers, and specifically for the United States. The implosion of Communism meant there was no major challenger to Western-style market democracy, ideologically or physically. The violence in the system was concentrated in the poorest parts of the developing world, and while it was often ghastly and gruesome, it did not threaten the integrity of the international system nor compel military action. In this environment, the so-called "American model" of development reigned supreme.

Casting a major thrust of our discussion in terms of these two forces helps us understand the direction of the present national security environment. It is not an either/or question, since both geopolitics and globalization coexisted before and continue to operate. The threat environment that is the central concern of geopolitics was present during the 1990s in the form of forces such as those led by bin Laden, but they were less prominent and compelling. Similarly, the machinations of globalization continue in the post–September 11 atmosphere but at a lower level of visibility. For example, the meetings of the Group of Eight (G-8) economic world leaders (which used to be the G-7 but admitted Russia in 2000 as a kind of honorary member) continue to be held and receive much public attention. The meetings of organizations like the Asia-Pacific Economic Cooperation (APEC), which President Clinton attended annually with much ado, have faded from center stage, however. President Bush's attendance at the November 2005 APEC summit in South Korea demonstrated that globalization has not left the agenda altogether.

The two dynamics also contradict one another, reflecting different worldviews on the parts of adherents of one force or the other. Globalization represents a highly internationalist approach to the world, placing global concerns and the reconciliation of international differences through international efforts at the center of national concerns. It raises idealist concerns with improving the human condition through international cooperation to a high priority and tends to view geopolitics through a more cooperative, multilateralist lens than does traditional geopolitics.

The geopolitical perspective is inherently more conservative and suspicious of the international environment. Reflecting its grounding in traditional realism and its skeptical view of human nature, the geopolitical perspective emphasizes *national* security as its central value (as opposed to international security) and thus is more inward looking and prone to unilateral as opposed to multilateral solutions to problems. The neocon philosophy represents the new thrust of geopolitics.

Which of these competing worldviews will dominate the early twenty-first century? In the immediate aftermath of the September 11, 2001, terrorist events, geopolitics enjoyed a renaissance as the United States responded to the activation of real threats that had been festering outside the spotlight of the 1990s. Support for globalization was eroding at the time as the world economy slowed and was further buffeted by revelations of corporate malfeasance in the United States and the subsequent downturn of the world's stock markets. The Bush administration's GWOT was a clear expression of a geopolitical direction from a president who had campaigned in 2000 as a free trade advocate (one of the central values of globalization). Whether there will be a resurgence of economic globalization in the near and midterm future is a possibility that we explore.

CONCLUSION: QUO VADIS?

This brief introduction featuring the two emphases of the nature of change and the conceptual competition between globalization and geopolitics helps frame the material that follows. Because this book is intended as a core text for national security courses that tend to emphasize the military, geopolitical side of national security, we do so as well. At the same time, it is clear that what makes the country safe is more than the clash or balance of arms, and the umbrella of globalization will facilitate exploring those other aspects of what makes us secure.

The text proceeds within the context of the two themes. Chapter 1 elaborates on some of the themes introduced here and adds other organizing concepts, notably the notion of fault lines and some preliminary assessment of how the United States fits into the system. As the Part I heading suggests, the next four chapters deal with the context in which the current debate over themes exists. Chapter 2 explores the roots and content of the realist paradigm that is the conceptual base of geopolitics. Chapter 3 views the basic underlying forces that have colored the American world-view on national security matters, and Chapter 4 concentrates on that part of the geopolitical past represented by the Cold War. Part I ends with a discussion of the rise and characteristics of globalization in Chapter 5.

Part II deals more directly with the issue of change. Chapter 6 explores the basic underlying concepts—notably the idea of instruments of power—with which national security must deal and how they have changed across time. In Chapter 7, we look at the American political system and how it responds to specific environmental challenges. Part II concludes, in Chapter 8, with an assessment of how so-called "traditional" defense problems—the stuff of symmetrical approaches to war—have survived the end of the Cold War and into the future.

Part III looks at contemporary challenges to national security, emphasizing both the dynamic of change and the competition between geopolitics and globalization. Chapters 9 and 10 deal primarily with assertions of change discussed in this introduction that represent changes in traditional geopolitical perspectives. Chapter 9 extends the discussion of whether there is a "new" kind of war, and Chapter 10 examines the most prominently emphasized form of asymmetrical warfare, terrorism. Chapter 11 begins with an examination of the dilemma posed by seemingly unresolvable regional conflicts and reintroduces the emphasis on global conflict resolution through the ideas of peacekeeping and state building, the latter being a bridge concept between globalization and geopolitics by injecting nonmilitary elements into geopolitical situations. Chapter 12 explicitly probes the relationship between the two core concepts and their relationship to change in a dynamic environment. This relationship is further projected into the future in the single chapter of Part IV, which also suggests some ways in which the two concepts may be compatible and reconcilable.

SELECTED BIBLIOGRAPHY

Allison, Graham T., Jr. "Testing Gorbachev." *Foreign Affairs* 67, 1 (Fall 1988), 18–32.

Byford, Grenville. "The Wrong War." *Foreign Affairs* 81, 4 (July/August 2002), 34–43.

Campbell, Kurt M. "Globalization's First War?" *Washington Quarterly* 25, 1 (Winter 2002), 7–14.

Delpech, Therese. "The Imbalance of Terror." *Washington Quarterly* 25, 1 (Winter 2002), 31–41.

Doran, Michael Scott. "Somebody Else's Civil War." *Foreign Affairs* 81, 1 (January/February 2002), 22–42.

Hoffmann, Stanley. "Clash of Globalizations." *Foreign Affairs* 81, 4 (July/August 2002), 104–115.

Howard, Michael. "What's in a Name?" *Foreign Affairs* 81, 1 (January/February 2002), 8–13.

Kagan, Robert, and William Kristol (Eds.). *Present Dangers: Crisis and Opportunities in American Foreign and Defense Policy.* San Francisco: Encounter Books, 2000.

Miller, Steven E. "The End of Unilateralism or Unilateralism Redux?" *Washington Quarterly* 25, 1 (Winter 2002), 15–30.

O'Hanlon, Michael. "A Flawed Masterpiece." *Foreign Affairs* 81, 3 (May/June 2002), 47–63.

Rotberg, Robert I. "The New Nature of Nation-State Failure." *Washington Quarterly* 25, 3 (Summer 2002), 85–96.

Shambaugh, David. "The New Strategic Triangle: U.S. and European Reaction to China's Rise." *Washington Quarterly* 28, 3 (Summer 2005), 7–26.

Snow, Donald M. *September 11, 2001: The New Face of War?* New York: Longman, 2002.

The National Security Strategy of the United States of America. Washington, DC: The White House, September 2002.

Tucker, Robert W., and David C. Hendrickson. "The Sources of American Legitimacy." *Foreign Affairs* 83, 6 (November/December 2004), 18–32.

Wallerstein, Immanuel. "The Eagle Has Crash Landed." *Foreign Policy* (July/August 2002), 60–69.

Watanabe, Akio. "A Continuum of Change." *Washington Quarterly* 27, 4 (Autumn 2004), 137 146.

PART

I

THE CONTEXT

Part I consists of five chapters, each of which provides some perspective, or context, for understanding the national security situation in the 2000s. In Chapter 1, we look at some basic dynamics of the system, including the idea of fault lines and their impact on change, the different perspectives people bring to the subject of national security, and the American role in the national security system. We then turn to the operating rules of international politics since the peace of Westphalia, the so-called realist paradigm that defines the geopolitical approach, in Chapter 2. That paradigm was under fire during the 1990s as an adequate description of a globalizing world; it has been revived with the campaign against terrorism and therefore must be assessed as the primary tool for a new reality. The United States has had a unique historical experience in matters of national security, and the evolution of that experience is the chief topic of Chapter 3. Among the elements of that experience has been a feeling of security based in the impregnability of the country—a feeling that has now been effectively deflated.

The Cold War was the major element in the environment in which much of current American national security policy was developed. Because of the holdover effect that Cold War thinking has on the present, Chapter 4 looks at the dynamics of how the Cold War worked and how it ended. The Cold War's end shares characteristics with September 11 in that both were almost entirely unanticipated and created the need for adjustment. The other thread in the ongoing debate about the nature of national security is globalization, the dominant theme of the 1990s. Because its relevance remains, Chapter 5 is devoted to the other important approach to the evolution of the post–World War II, contemporary international economic globalization.

CHAPTER 1

Fault Lines: World Politics in a New Millennium

PREVIEW

This chapter elaborates on themes laid out in the introduction. First, it examines the impact of two traumatic events, or fault lines, on American security. These events have accentuated and defined deep divisions among Americans about politics in general and national security in particular. We look at factors that contribute to that debate, including the relative role of geopolitics and globalization in the evolving nature of the world environment, the central role of the United States in the evolving international system, and the factors that divide Americans on these matters. The chapter concludes with some initial speculation about the continuing role of force in the national security system of the early twenty-first century.

The American public is deeply divided politically, as witnessed by the highly polarized presidential elections of 2000 and 2004 and the strongly partisan wrangling within Congress and elsewhere over a broad range of issues. This disagreement extends to the American role in the world and, more specifically, to American national security policy. To help you understand this disagreement and resolve personally how you feel about it, this chapter examines the debate from two angles. The first is the impact of the fundamental change events (the fault lines) on the operation of world politics. The second is through contrasting views of how the United States should deal with these changes based on differing political and philosophical orientations held by different individuals and groups.

Our interest in and concentration on matters of national security has varied across time, driven largely by the ebb and flow of events in the world and our reactions to them. In relatively tranquil times, when the United States feels unthreatened by forces that might do us harm, our level of interest and concern tends to be low. Most of American history between the end of the American Revolution and

World War II was of this nature; only the self-infliction of the Civil War seriously interrupted our national tranquility and made a concern about and commitment to the most obvious form of national security, military force, seem particularly important. We languidly reestablished the "normalcy" of nonconcern between the world wars. We will almost certainly look back on the period between the end of the Cold War and the terrorist attacks of 2001 as a time of similar tranquility.

Times have not always been so tranquil, of course, and when they have not been, our level of concern with national security matters—with geopolitics—has been heightened. The Japanese surprise attack on Pearl Harbor—delivered an hour before the Japanese ambassador to Washington presented the American government with an ultimatum tantamount to a declaration of war (which was part of the plan)—rocked the American psyche, ended the appeal of isolationism, and propelled us into a patriotic war to crush fascism. In the words of Japanese Admiral Isoroku Yamamato after learning of the failure to deliver the ultimatum before the attack began, "We have awakened a sleeping giant and filled him with a terrible resolve." That resolve carried over to the Cold War that followed World War II. The terrorist attacks of September 11, 2001, were similar in form and effect to Pearl Harbor; once again, our attention is focused on matters of geopolitics and national security.

We have undergone two profound events in the past decade and a half. The distinguished Harvard political scientist Graham T. Allison Jr. analogized the first event, the end of the Cold War, to an earthquake, a "tectonic shift" in the structure of international relations and our place in them; the effect of September 11 was similar. Put another way, 1989 and 2001 revealed major fault lines in the evolution of the international environment. Before the fault lines were revealed, the world looked one way; afterward, it looked very different.

The largest scale manifestation of this change is suggested in the subtitle of this book: *Globalization and Geopolitics.* Before the end of the Cold War, geopolitics was the large concern in a hostile world environment, and that emphasis and perception returned after New York and Washington were victims of commercial airliners turned into lethal missiles. The period between the two major events witnessed a major ascendancy of the emphasis on economic globalization and interdependence.

These alternate emphases are not mutually exclusive, of course. The seeds of the globalization of the 1990s were sown in the last decades of the Cold War, and the contemporary system is struggling with how globalization is affected by and must adapt to an environment in which dealing with the geopolitical reality of international terrorism occupies center stage. Similarly, our concern with geopolitics did not disappear in the geopolitical tranquility of the 1990s; it was just not as pronounced a concern as before and after the globalization decade.

The first fault line was revealed between 1989 and 1991 when the Cold War ended. Whether the beginning of that change is attributed to Poland's defiant election of a non-Communist president in 1989, to the breaching of the Berlin Wall on November 9, 1989, or to the official demise of the Soviet Union at the last tick of the clock in 1991 in Moscow's Red Square, the Cold War structure that dominated international politics for forty-plus years after the end of World War II has crumbled.

We were still adjusting to those changes when the airplanes slammed into the World Trade Center and the Pentagon.

The end of the Cold War traumatized policymakers mostly because it was so unanticipated. Certainly a few observers saw it coming: George F. Kennan prophesied in 1948 that vigilant containment could cause Communism's implosion, and New York Senator Daniel Patrick Moynihan consistently suggested its demise—but they were beacons whose message was largely ignored. The Soviet Union crumbled as Soviet republics declared their withdrawal from the union throughout 1991, but the policy of the American administration of George H. W. Bush tried to keep our mortal enemy of forty years intact nearly to the end, fearful and suspicious of the alternatives to a known enemy.

Had we anticipated what was going to happen, we might have been better prepared for it. World War II had hardly begun, for instance, when planning for the postwar world after the Axis defeat was instituted. As a result, the institution of a new structure for the international system could be implemented quickly after the guns were stilled. Unfortunately, so few believed in the end of the Cold War—and those who did were ridiculed for their "naïveté"—that no real planning was done to accommodate the possibility. We were caught nearly entirely off guard.

The result was to leave the large contours of foreign policy adrift, and there is no place where that drift was more apparent than in thinking about and planning for national security. In some ways, the trauma is natural because of the nature and impact of change. The Cold War was, after all, a quintessentially geopolitical competition, and the centerpiece of that confrontation was the military might that both sides possessed and projected against one another. Two great land masses were locked into a deadly dance, and keeping the competition below the level of mutual incineration was a time-consuming and energy-draining enterprise. With the stakes so great and the possibilities so grim, it is not surprising that those committed to the process would find the peaceful alternatives to Cold War the stuff of mere dreams.

But the Cold War ended, and we struggled for a decade conceptually and practically to describe and understand how the world was different. During the 1990s, the forces of economic globalization slowly overshadowed the forces of geopolitics within the American administration and raised questions about something like a paradigm shift from geopolitics to globalization. When George W. Bush entered the White House in 2001, he brought with him a foreign and national security team of Cold Warriors (people who had gained much of their knowledge and expertise in global affairs during the Cold War). Like the Clinton administration that preceded them, they struggled during their early months in office for a basis upon which to reorient national security policy. That Bush was an avowed free trader (the heart of globalization) added to the indeterminacy about the appropriate paradigm. Response to the terrorist attacks provided that focus and largely defines the administration to this day.

We are still struggling to describe the new international system and appropriate policies and strategies with which to cope with it. This book examines the ensuing debate and its impact on national security policy. The two perspectives through which we view the question, as already suggested, are those of traditional geopolitics and more contemporary globalization, including permutations and combinations of the two, along with the theme of change. The first lens through which we conduct that examination is focused on the fault lines and their impacts.

THE FIRST FAULT LINE: THE WORLD A DECADE AFTER THE COLD WAR

We entered the new century in a very different atmosphere and with very different perspectives and expectations than we did the 1990s. In 1990 and 1991, breathtaking political change was virtually the norm; the central feature of that change, of course, was the death of Communism, as country after country peacefully (except in isolated cases like Romania) eschewed Marxism-Leninism, and the Soviet Union, the leader and enforcer of Communist orthodoxy worldwide, stood idly by. As noted, in 1991 constituent parts of the Soviet Union itself began the process of secession from the Union of Soviet Socialist Republics; ultimately the Soviet empire (and it was, in many important respects, the last European empire, since much of the territory had been acquired by force by Russia) broke into fifteen independent states, all of which officially disavowed Communism. By the end of the decade, when the dust had settled on the Marxist experiment, only four states in the world remained nominally Communist. Two of those states, Cuba and North Korea, entered the twenty-first century professing a continued dedication to the principles of Communism, although most observers expect that façade to disappear when Fidel Castro leaves power in Cuba and North Korea reaches an accommodation with the South—both of which are events that could occur in the foreseeable future. The other Communist states, China and Vietnam, retain the dictatorship of the Communist Party politically but openly reject Marxist economics and are enthusiastic participants in the globalizing economy. As a competitive political ideology, the belief system articulated by Karl Marx and Friedrich Engels has essentially been consigned to the dust pile of history.

The implosion of Communism was the most obvious, dramatic, and important change of the last decade of the twentieth century and was arguably the most important international event since World War II. It was a unique series of events in the sense that a major global power source simply vacated the playing field without a shot being fired. The same Soviet Union that had, for the most part, brutally imposed Communist systems on most of what was known as the Second (or Socialist) World, simply watched those systems being toppled with scarcely a shrug of its national shoulders. The virtually peaceful implosion of the Soviet Union itself was an act of nonviolence without precedent; large states and empires had, of course, disappeared before, but virtually all the other dismemberments were the direct result of major hot wars. The Cold War ended with a whimper, not a bang, to borrow an old phrase.

The end of "operational Communism" (Communism as the official political organizing system for a country) has had major systemic impacts to which the world is still adjusting. The Cold War international system was what is called by political scientists a *bipolar system*, which means a system dominated by two opposing states (the United States and the Soviet Union) around which other states congregated and sought or imposed differing degrees of association. The nature of bipolarity had evolved during the Cold War period. In the first decade or so of the Cold War, the system was described as one of *tight* bipolarity, which meant the two dominant parties could influence or control the actions of their "client" states to a large degree. For a variety of reasons, this control was gradually relaxed, and the system evolved into one of *loose* bipolarity. The ultimate manifestation of loosening of control, of course, was the inability of the Soviet Union to keep the members of its bloc adherent to the political principle of Communism that was the source of their sameness.

The result has been a power vacuum. With one pole nonexistent, the system can no longer be described as bipolar. There is only one pole left because Russia, the successor to the Soviet Union, lacks the stature and resources to be a "superpower" in the Cold War sense beyond its continued possession of a large but, thanks to arms control agreements, shrinking arsenal of nuclear weapons (which was the major criterion for superpower status during the Cold War). No one is willing to designate the resulting system *unipolar* because that would imply a level of American control that does not exist and which most other states would (and do) oppose. The United States remains the central power, but defining what that centrality means has been a critical part of defining the new system. It is probably of some symbolic importance that we never formed a consensus on what to call the new system and that the most common name describes what it is not—the post–Cold War world.

As it evolved over time, the Cold War had the major physical and intellectual advantage of developing a very orderly set of rules of interaction. The competition for global power and influence between the Communist and non-Communist worlds was well defined, as were the rules by which that competition was carried out. It was conceptually a *zero-sum game* in which the gains of one side were assumed to be the losses of the other and the possibility of *positive-sum* outcomes to situations (in which both sides gained) were infrequent and considered unlikely in any particular situation. The lingua franca of this competition ultimately was the enormous military machines each side maintained, capped by the possession of enormous arsenals of thermonuclear weapons that, if ever employed against one another, would probably have ended civilization as we know it.

Yet the system produced an orderliness around which the Cold Warriors could think about world problems and dynamics based in the competition and its management short of war. The end of the Cold War shattered that order. As Georgi Arbatov, director of the Soviet USA and Canada Institute and a member of the Central Committee of the Communist Party of the Soviet Union, put it to the Americans in mid-1991, "We have done a terrible thing. We have deprived you of an enemy." Conceptually, it was indeed a terrible thing in the sense that national security thinking clearly grounded in the Soviet threat and deflecting and managing that threat suddenly lost most, if not all, of its relevance. The result was both physical and intellectual disorder in how to think about the world—a disorder that has not yet been resolved. While the process was going on in 1990, University of Chicago political scientist John Mearsheimer even lamented in the title of an *Atlantic Monthly* article, "Why we shall soon miss the Cold War." What we would miss, he contended, was the order and predictability of events and the ability to act appropriately within the bounds of that order.

The debate over what should replace the bipolar international political system raged inconclusively until the debate was suspended by the events of 2001. Deriving from the changes, however, are clear benefits that hardly anyone could or would try to deny. At the same time, there are evolving systemic dynamics about which there is a considerable amount of disagreement within the academic and policy communities that continue to enliven debates within both of those communities.

Undeniable Benefits

The most obvious and most dangerous manifestation of the Cold War was the military confrontation between the competing blocs led by the United States and the Soviet Union. Managing that confrontation—"preparing for and fighting the country's wars," in the military's parlance—was a serious consequence of the nature of international politics and one which, given the possible consequences of a misstep, had to be taken very seriously. The prospect of general war employing nuclear weapons even produced a fatalistic political culture about the future and resulted in the expenditure of large amounts of resources in its name. Keeping the Cold War cold was the preeminent international responsibility beside which other priorities paled by comparison.

The post–Cold War world produced no equivalent of the East–West, Communist–anti-Communist military confrontation, and this fact had two obvious and overwhelming benefits for the citizenry of the 1990s that were not enjoyed by people in the 1980s and before. Both benefits condition how we thought and still think about the problem of national security in the contemporary world, even after the second fault line was revealed.

The first positive change, and the one most relieving for those who participated in the Cold War period, is the absence of any real concern about the possibility of a general systemic war that could threaten national and international survival. Within the context of the Cold War, the possibility—thought by some to be a probability—of a global World War III in which nuclear weapons would be used massively was an ever-present prospect, a problem that never went away. The two sides were certainly politically opposed enough to find adequate cause for war between them, and managing the competition in such a way to reduce the likelihood that such a war would begin was a major task.

Since then, the situation is both radically different and the same. Physically, Russia and the United States have reduced the size of their nuclear arsenals and conventional forces sizably, but they retain large enough nuclear forces to be able to do great damage to one another on a scale only slightly smaller than during the Cold War. The demise of Soviet Communism, however, has removed the political differences that could provide the rationale for war. Today, we retain most of the means for fighting World War III, but we lack the motives. The world is still deadly but less dangerous.

This changed dynamic enormously relaxed the security environment because it removed the "worst case" planning problem. The United States and other countries still may face the possibility of going to war, as we did over Kuwait in the Persian Gulf area at the beginning of the 1990s, and in modified form, in Afghanistan and Iraq a decade later. All of the realistic contingencies for the present and foreseeable future are more limited in conduct and potential for expansion to general war. It is virtually impossible to conjure a realistic scenario that would lead the world to a general war that would cause the nuclear bombs to start being hurled in a general, systemic way.

We had become basically blasé to this new reality before the terrorist attacks reminded us the world could still be a dangerous place. During one of the televised debates of the 1992 presidential campaign, for instance, incumbent President George H. W. Bush proudly proclaimed that Americans no longer went to bed worrying about the possibility of awakening to nuclear war. Some older Americans could remember having such thoughts, but most younger Americans had *never* known the fear and wondered what the president was talking about.

The result was to take some of the urgency and fervor out of the national security debate. To borrow a distinction from one of my other books (*When America Fights*), the United States faced very few potential situations in which it would *have* to fight and especially to use its total military might (employments of necessity); rather, Americans debated in which kinds of places we *might* use our forces, knowing the decision would not likely compromise American interests greatly one way or the other (employments of choice).

The second change flows from the first. During the Cold War confrontation, both potential adversaries and their major allies maintained large and expensive military machines that could be quickly inserted into the fray should war somehow break out. Given the destructiveness such a war could rapidly produce, it was assumed that it would be fought and completed with the forces on hand when it began—what was called the "force in being"—and both sides maintained large forces for that possibility.

It was a very expensive proposition. During the 1950s, the United States dedicated as much as half the federal budget to defense. After the spate of entitlement legislation was passed during the 1960s, that proportion fell to about 25 percent of the budget and into second place among categories of federal expenditures. Although reliable budget figures for the Soviet Union were always elusive, the estimates were that they spent between 15 and 25 percent of gross national product (GNP) on the military (with a much larger economic base, the spending equivalent for the United States never exceeded 6 percent of GNP).

The end of the Cold War was accompanied by a sizable demilitarization among the major players, and especially the leaders of the Cold War coalitions. Troop strength for the United States went from 2.15 million active duty troops in 1988 to 1.4 million in 1998. The Russians have cut their forces down even more, although the ten-year comparison is distorted in that 1988 figures reflect the entire Soviet Union, whereas 1998 figures (which show an active force of 1.16 million) are all Russian. In any case, force sizes and expenditure levels are down substantially for all the major powers.

The cutbacks have been highly differential on a worldwide base, with the United States having reduced spending comparatively little compared to other countries. Using International Institute for Strategic Studies (London) figures for spending in 1998, the United States spent $265.9 billion on defense. By contrast, the next *seven* countries in descending order of defense spending (Russia, France, Japan, China, the United Kingdom, Germany, and Italy) cumulatively spent $259.2 billion, and only when the ninth-place spender (Brazil) is added does the total surpass that of the United States at $277.3 billion. At that, the American total was only slightly larger in actual dollars than the 1988 total, and as a proportion of the budget, it slipped to below 20 percent and to third place (behind entitlements and service on the debt) among categories of expenditure. What the comparisons reveal is that other countries have cut their military spending more in real terms (smaller amounts for defense) rather than slowing growth that would likely have been greater had the Cold War not ended, as has happened in the United States. That trend toward decline was reversed after 2001, as we noted in the introduction and shall see in the next section.

Debatable Changes

While the danger of global war and the need to prepare for it undeniably receded during the 1989 to 2001 period, the effects of other changes in the environment caused some level of disagreement. While making no pretense of inclusiveness or exhaustiveness, three interrelated changes with some impact on the security equation and the relevance of geopolitics and globalization are worth raising in this context.

One change, from which the others to an extent follow, is a greater emphasis on the developing world. In one sense, this emphasis did not represent much of a change at all in national security terms. While the focus of national security during the Cold War was on the major power competition, virtually all the actual fighting involving American forces occurred in the developing world. The United States, for instance, *deployed* forces worldwide, including in the developed world (Europe, Japan); it *employed* force exclusively in the developing world (Korea, Vietnam, Grenada, for example). The reasons for this state of affairs are complex, of course, but the fact that most of the violence and instability were in the developing world had something to do with this pattern of employment. As well, in most instances violent confrontations between clients of the two sides could be waged without a real danger of escalation to direct superpower confrontation. Since many of the conflicts that occurred had Communists battling anti-Communists, the use of force could be argued to have been necessary to avoid shifting the geopolitical balance between the East and the West.

The situation after the Cold War was both similar and different. Virtually all violent conflicts still take place in the developing states, and most of it is still internal in nature (a point elaborated on in the next section). This phenomenon has continued since 2001, because the developing world is also the seedbed for most international terrorism, the combating of which has become the fulcrum of national security concern. Thus, most of the opportunities to employ force are where they always were.

What is utterly different, of course, is that developing world violence no longer has a Cold War overlay. That is both good and bad. It is beneficial in that internal grievances are no longer distorted by what were largely irrelevant Cold War concerns. It is detrimental in that old Cold War sponsors are no longer around to insist upon restraint in the conduct of these affairs, which are often particularly bloody and gruesome. At the same time, the absence of the Cold War patina does not provide ideological guidance about which of these to engage in and which to ignore, meaning that participation is almost exclusively in the form of employments of choice. As we shall see, the criteria for involvement in the post–Cold War world tended toward humanitarian grounds, and these have shifted to the campaign against terrorism.

The result of tranquility among the major powers is that much more of our attention can be directed at the developing world than it could before. In a direct national security sense, this fact is reflected in an ongoing debate over the nature and appropriate uses of force in the developing world. It is also reflected in disagreement about the extent to which the forces of globalization are having an impact on this part of the globe.

The point of contrast and continuity cannot be overstated, because it is so often erroneously suggested that potential involvement in things like peacekeeping operations in the developing world marks a radical departure for the United States and other major powers. To repeat, using military forces to influence internal wars in the developing world is nothing unique to the post–Cold War world at all. What is different is the rationale for putting American or other troops potentially in harm's way and the ways in which they are employed.

During the Cold War, the developing world uses of American armed forces were conventional in terms of purpose and methods of employment: the reason to use American military might was to thwart Communist takeovers that might occur in the absence of American assistance, a direct extension of the central geopolitical competition. Whether that force was warranted or wise in particular places such as Vietnam was a matter of debate, but the central purpose was not. In those circumstances, the way forces were used—strategically if not always tactically—was conventional: the idea was military victory over a well-defined enemy. That enemy might fight unconventionally (what we now call asymmetrically) and thus create the need for tactical adjustment to bring about enemy defeat, as was the case in Vietnam, but the goal was traditional—fighting to support traditional governments.

Opportunities to employ force between the fault lines were different on both counts. The disappearance of Communism meant that involvement in an internal conflict could no longer be justified in terms of the kinds of geopolitics that underlay Cold War actions. More typically, justifications became "softer," framed in terms of arresting and reversing humanitarian disasters in situations where clearly military conflict between defined military forces was not present. The purpose was more often framed in terms of reinstituting peace and protecting civilian populations from the return of atrocity. As a result, military victory in a traditional sense gave way to an open-ended commitment to imposing, enforcing, and keeping a fragile peace. That reorientation runs counter to traditional military ways of thinking about the use of force in the American experience, as we shall see in Chapter 3.

When the new Bush administration entered office in 2001, it clearly demonstrated the ambivalence created by this debate over how and when to use force. During the 2000 campaign, Bush had come out strongly in opposition to future uses of American force for peacekeeping when American interests were not clearly engaged. Dr. Condoleeza Rice, who became national security advisor in the first Bush term and Secretary of State in the second, was the point spokesperson for this position, arguing that the United States should not act as the "world's 911," that it was an improper role for elite American troops like the 82nd Airborne to be used to escort children to kindergarten in places like Kosovo, and that endless deployments were eroding troop morale. The Bush team even suggested the desirability of terminating American involvement in Kosovo and Bosnia.

These positions did not long survive the oath of office. American European allies quickly informed the new administration of the necessity of maintaining the missions in the Balkans and of the vitality of American presence in those missions. The rhetoric of noninvolvement was quietly cooled, and Secretary of Defense Donald Rumsfeld quickly announced a comprehensive review of American military strategy and missions, which presumably included involvement in peacekeeping operations. The events of September 11, 2001, and the subsequent reorientation of policy left this debate moot for the time being.

Globalization is the other trend with a significant developing world element, and disagreement exists about what it does and how or whether it should be promoted. Bursting upon the scene and coinciding with or stimulating (there is disagreement about which) the worldwide economic expansion and prosperity of the global economy in the most developed states, globalization spread to selected parts of the developing world during the 1990s as well. During the first half of the decade and beyond, the results appeared overwhelmingly positive and formed the core of the Clinton administration foreign policy of engagement and enlargement (engaging those countries most capable of joining the global economy and thereby enlarging what he called the circle of market democracies). In its purest form, the expansion of the globalizing economy would be accompanied by political democratization and contribute to a spreading *democratic peace* around the globe. In this scenario, as democracies increasingly came into power, peace would follow, since it is well established (or at least well asserted) that political democracies do not fight one another. Moreover, as the global economy reached out and encompassed more and more countries, the motivation to fight would give way to economic interdependence.

In this happy scenario, a geopolitical perspective that seeks to minimize violence and instability in the world appeared to coincide with and reinforce globalization, since they are both aimed at the same ends. Unfortunately, the rosy outlook of the

1990s began to fade as the twentieth century wound to an end. As the international system faced the new century, the desirability and contribution of globalization became more debatable.

At least three things contributed to the ambivalence about globalization. First, its proponents were too optimistic in their advocacies, and events proved their most expansive projections to be at least partially wrong, thereby casting doubt on the process of globalization. During the height of the "go-go" 1990s economy, some analysts predicted that globalization had fundamentally altered the nature of traditional economics; modern technology could make adjustments heretofore impossible in areas like product mix and inventory control, meaning the business cycle of boom and bust could effectively be surmounted, even eliminated.

These predictions proved overly optimistic, even wrong in some cases. Knowing they were producing too many automobiles did not keep the world's automakers from producing 80 million cars a year for a market that could absorb only 60 million in the late 1990s, and the result was large excess inventories as the century changed that resulted in layoffs, unprofitable discounting, and other phenomena familiar in the old economy. In 1997, a currency crisis broke out first in Thailand and spread rapidly to other East Asian states that were considered pillars of globalization (discussed more fully in Chapter 5). When the signs of economic weakness became evident even in Japan, the "economic miracle" that accompanied globalization seemed suspect.

The geopolitical consequences of globalization provided a second source of controversy. The argument to use economic globalization as a way to entangle and drag countries into the web of market democracies was no more vigorously pursued anywhere than it was in China. The prevailing idea was that by tying the Chinese to the global economy through mechanisms like most favored nation (MFN) status and membership in the World Trade Organization (WTO), pressure could be brought to bear that would force the Chinese to improve their human rights record and to allow for increased political democracy in the country. The Communist regime's obdurate resistance to loosening its political monopoly or allowing greater political (as opposed to individual) freedoms has made that strategy suspect and has kindled a renewed debate on how to treat China, which has continued as China proceeds through the transition to the fourth generation of Communist leaders beginning in late 2002.

The failure of globalization to produce all of its most optimistic (and probably unrealistic) outcomes has created a third problem, which is a backlash against the phenomenon of globalization—and especially its most prominent institutional manifestations. The first overt demonstration of strident, organized opposition to globalization came in late November 1999 at the Seattle annual meeting of the WTO, where an estimated twenty thousand demonstrators voiced their objections to the consequences of globalization (and engaged in considerable destructive vandalism in the "Emerald City"). Prominent participants included labor unions fearful of the movement of jobs to cheap labor markets and environmentalists fearful that multinational corporations and other private firms would ignore environmental protection. Other groups with parallel concerns, such as those fearful of U.S. global domination and groups seeing globalization as an assault on sovereignty, added their voices to the dissent.

This backlash became a regular part of the institutionalization of globalization in its various aspects and of the dialog on globalization. Attempts to disrupt organizations meeting to promote global values like free trade have become an apparently inevitable part of such meetings. The 2000 meeting of the International Bank for Reconstruction and Development (IBRD) in Washington, D.C., was interrupted by roughly the same coalition of rejectionists as those who had appeared in Seattle. In April, 2001, this phenomenon was internationalized amid great worldwide television coverage as demonstrators at the third Summit of the Americas in Quebec City, Canada, battled teargas-wielding police to oppose progress toward forming a Free Trade Area of the Americas (FTAA) between the thirty-four democratically elected governments of the Western Hemisphere (all countries except Cuba) by 2005, opposition that was repeated during demonstrations at the 2005 meeting in Argentina. The groups that have attracted demonstrators are diverse. The WTO has been in existence for just over a decade with the purpose of promoting and monitoring the removal of trade barriers among its members (currently about 140 states); the World Bank is one of the original Bretton Woods institutions that came out of World War II to reorder the world economy principally by making loans to creditworthy countries; and the FTAA is an unratified proposal originally announced at the first Summit in Miami in 1994. The common thread among all three, however, is that they are a general part of the process of globalization.

THE SECOND FAULT LINE:
THE WORLD AFTER SEPTEMBER 11

It is difficult to specify the characteristics of the contemporary international environment. Like the post–Cold War world it supercedes, it does not have a universally accepted name: the closest we have come in the immediate wake of the traumatic events is to proclaim it as the GWOT, but that sobriquet is unlikely to endure as a description of the era. Indeed, Bush administration figures began in summer 2005, to use GSAVE (Global Struggle against Violent Extemists) as an alternative acronym. For one thing, the response to the terrorist acts is not a war in any traditional, recognizable way (a point argued at length in Chapter 10); and for another, it is not yet certain that we have witnessed a profound and *lasting* change in the way the system works. It is possible that international terrorism will be reduced to the status it had before the attacks (a peripheral place in the scheme of things) or eliminated, in which case we may view this period as an interlude in the post–Cold War world. Alternately, terrorism may be an enduring problem with which we have to contend concertedly for some time. It is simply too early to tell.

Our perspective is further clouded by subjective factors. Because the traumatic events were so recent, we have minimal perspective on the events or their long-term impacts. Powerful symbols of the United States were attacked, which make the events of September 11 more personal and emotional than they might otherwise have been. The obvious equation of the attacks with the Japanese attack at

Pearl Harbor creates a sense of "infamy" around the events, seeming to dictate a swift and decisive retribution that continues to remain elusive and adds to our frustration. The amorphous nature of a terrorist opponent that operates in the shadows makes it difficult to fashion effective ways to eradicate the "evil" that terrorism represents.

If it is difficult to specify the new environment in any detail, it is possible to discern differences on the post–September 11 side of the second fault line. Among other things, the balance between geopolitical and globalization concerns has clearly shifted from the latter to the former. Geopolitics has had a rebirth that is clear and undeniable if we still are searching for adequate ways to describe the new geopolitical reality. One of the new forces that has clearly entered the public international calculus is the emergence of so-called nonstate actors in the form of international terrorists whose base and loyalties do not coincide with any country. The debate between internationalism and unilateralism has also been affected, if in contradictory ways as events and reactions unfold. If globalization has receded, we are still trying to see exactly how far and in what direction.

The revealed vulnerability of American soil to attack has quickly revived an interest in the tool of geopolitics—military forces—in the American debate after a decade or more when they received much less attention. One of the most obvious beneficiaries has been military spending. In the patriotic outpouring following the terrorist attacks, this shift to an almost obsessive sense of national security emphasis went virtually unchallenged. In the area of defense spending, for instance, the expected tough debate over modernization—which new systems to buy—turned into a frenzy of trying to procure everything on the menu despite the tenuousness of the arguments of how different capabilities would contribute to the central thrust on combating terrorism. President Bush's suggestion during the 2000 campaign that the United States might simply leapfrog a generation of new weapons fell rapidly off the table in the process.

The ascendancy of geopolitics has been accompanied by the assertion that we are locked in a new kind of war, a theme raised shortly after September 11 by the Bush administration and picked up by the media, as already noted. While it was never quite clear what was new about combating terrorism, it was widely advertised that the new and amorphous enemy engaged in what has been called *asymmetrical warfare*, a concept raised in the introduction and discussed in detail in Chapter 9.

Calling such approaches "new" strains credulity to the breaking point. As noted in the introduction, the adoption of methods to negate the advantages of a larger and superior force are as old as the first time a weaker foe outdid a superior enemy, and the United States confronted—unsuccessfully—what we now call an asymmetrical enemy in Vietnam a third of a century ago. There is certainly nothing new about the use of terrorism—only the instruments have changed. What *is* new in the contemporary context is the relative emphasis we are now placing on combating unconventional opponents. During the Cold War, for instance, most of our emphasis was on strategic nuclear and large-scale conventional war with the Soviet Union in Europe—a sort of grand-scale reprise of World War II. Some emphasis on asymmetrical warfare—in forms such as antiterrorism or guerrilla warfare—was part of planning, but it was relegated to a lower order of priority. Special Operations Forces (SOFs) was the large repository of such concern, and because those missions were considered less important than the central conflict, the result was to help trivialize the importance of the SOFs. In a contemporary environment where there are few dangers of large-scale conventional warfare, priorities have been essentially inverted—witness the importance now attached to Special Forces as the United States confronts Bush's "axis of evil."

A more prominent characteristic of the new geopolitical order is its increased emphasis on nonstate actors, organizations that have neither a permanent territorial base nor loyalty to any particular country but that engage in activities that cross state borders. In a generic sense, such actors are also nothing new; the most prominent examples of nonstate actors are nongovernmental organizations (NGOs)—nonstate-based international organizations that perform a variety of useful functions within the system from provision of humanitarian assistance (CARE, Doctors without Borders) to monitoring of human rights violations (Amnesty International, Human Rights Watch), for example.

The terrorist attacks riveted our attention to a subcategory of nonstate actors who are violent in their actions. Once again, violent transnational groups are not a novel feature of the post–Cold War world and beyond. In contemporary terms, the international drug cartels have been a prototype of sorts, and international terrorist organizations have operated for years. What is different is that organizations such as Al Qaeda occupy a central position in our attention.

Dealing with nonstate actors in the form of international terrorist organizations poses some unique problems for national security policymakers (beyond the fact that they were not given high priority in the past). Our conventional and historical experience has been combating the agents of state-based governments who represented a conventional (or symmetrical) threat. Our armed forces, our doctrines for warfare, and the whole legal and ethical framework for warfare are geared to fighting such foes. International terrorism stands these concepts and rules on their heads in several ways.

One problem is how to depict efforts to combat international terrorists. The analogy of "war," which has its roots and designations in conventional interstate war and classic internal war over control of governments, does not clearly fit an opponent that has no territorial base or loyalty and is apparently uninterested in gaining and exercising authority over territory. Whom does one attack in this war? Historically, acts of war are committed against states and their agencies. In the case of international terrorists, such distinctions are at best indirect—for example, the designation of the Taliban regime as an opponent because of its shielding of Al Qaeda. It is relatively easy to assign blame when actions can clearly be identified with a particular state (and especially when that state acts overtly); it is more difficult when dealing with a nonstate-based opponent.

This difficulty became particularly clear in the case of Taliban and Al Qaeda prisoners sent to Guantanamo Bay (nicknamed "Gitmo") in Cuba in 2002 after the campaign to overthrow the Taliban in Afghanistan succeeded. Were these individuals prisoners of war (POWs), in which case they were subject to treatment as such under the Geneva codes of war (see Amplification 1.1)? Or were they "detainees,"

THE RULES OF WAR: WHO IS A POW?

One of the fallouts of American participation in the campaign to overthrow the Taliban government of Afghanistan was the question of the status of hostile prisoners captured by American and Afghan forces. It was a complicated problem in two ways. The first complication revolved around whether a state of war existed, since war was never declared formally either by the government, the coalition of forces seeking to overthrow the government, or the intervening United States. The other complication was that the prisoners included both soldiers supporting the Taliban regime and Al Qaeda terrorist members fighting alongside the Taliban. The first objection did not apply to international standards on treatment of prisoners; the second did.

The question of prisoner status was first raised when a number of captured Afghans were transported to detention at the U.S. naval base at Guantanamo Bay, Cuba. The explanation for the transfer was that the "detainees," as the Bush administration labeled them, were dangerous individuals who might escape if left in Afghanistan and cause havoc there. In addition, the United States wanted to isolate and interrogate suspected Al Qaeda members to aid in the campaign against terrorism.

The question became critical at this point. The Bush administration maintained that the detainees did not qualify for prisoner-of-war status under the Geneva Conventions of War (more specifically, Convention III: Relative to the Treatment of Prisoners of War, Geneva, August 1949), to which the United States is a signatory. After some discussion, it was conceded that the Taliban, as representatives of the government of Afghanistan, qualified under Article 4 of the convention, but that the Al Qaeda detainees did not. The administration, anxious to get as much information as possible from the detainees, initially resisted differentiating between members of the two groups. Article 5 of the convention, however, is quite clear on this matter: "Should any doubt arise as to whether persons, having committed a belligerent act and having fallen into the hands of the enemy, belong to any of the categories enumerated in Article 4, such persons *shall enjoy the protection of the present convention until such time as their status has been determined by a competent tribunal*" (emphasis added). Four years after their arrival, no tribunals had been convened for that purpose.

Why was the administration so reluctant to afford prisoner-of-war status to the Afghans? The answer was straightforward: if the detainees were legal POWs, there were sharp limits on the American right to extract information from them. Part III, Section 1, Article 17, defines the problem: "Every prisoner of war, when questioned on the subject, is bound to give his surname, first names and rank, date of birth, and army, regimental, personal or serial number, or failing this, equivalent information." Since that is *all* the information a POW is required to provide, granting that status would clearly have hamstrung the antiterrorist effort. The question is whether the additional information was worth the price of the United States apparently violating a basic treaty obligation.

Source: Convention III: Relative to the Treatment of Prisoners of War. Geneva, Switzerland, August 1949. (Text available from the Society of Professional Journalists at http://www. thespa.com/genevaconventions/convention3.html).

as the administration maintained? Had there been a literal, legal state of war, there would have been no question about POW status. Since there was not, their status was debatable and controversial. The compromise solution of treating Taliban prisoners as POWs because they were soldiers of the Taliban regime and treating Al Qaeda prisoners as something else was not legally or politically pleasing. The situation at Gitmo remains uncomfortable and highly controversial.

Nonstate actors such as international terrorists are difficult to combat in conventional military terms, as the U.S. military has learned. These groups do indeed engage in asymmetrical forms of combat, in the process not honoring traditional rules of engagement or conventional laws of states. As we discuss in Chapter 10, terrorist acts invariably break laws and are considered criminal by the targets, just as they are considered acts of war by the terrorists.

A further characteristic of the changed environment is how the American role in the world is viewed. In particular, the question that has been raised particularly frequently is whether dealing with terrorism has predisposed the United States to act in concert with its allies and the international community (a position known as multilateralism), or on its own with little regard for others in what it believes to be its individual self-interest (unilateralism). This distinction is developed more fully later in the chapter.

In the immediate aftermath of September 11, 2001, there was great agreement on the perfidy of the attacks and on the need to combat them through concerted, broadly international action, and the Bush administration responded by calling for such action. The rationale was that since international terrorism represented a threat that did not honor borders, the response to it must be international as well in areas such as intelligence gathering and sharing, detention of suspected terrorists, and the like. The internationalist instinct seemed to prevail.

By the beginning of 2002, however, that consensus had begun to erode as the campaign to capture and destroy Usama bin Laden and his associates proved more difficult than imagined. In that atmosphere, the United States government began proposing more militarily oriented actions that met with cool receptions almost everywhere else. The first lightning rod of international concern was directed at the detainees at Guantanamo and the stern refusal of the United States to listen to international entreaties about their treatment. When President Bush announced the axis of evil designation of Iraq, Iran, and North Korea in his 2002 State of the Union address and threatened vaguely about the likelihood of military action to deal with their alleged transgressions without consulting American allies in advance, many in the international community saw a return to the unilateralism they had suspected before the attacks.

Finally, September 11 dampened discussions and emphases on globalization. Some of the optimism about spreading globalization had already been dampened by economic events of the end of the 1990s, as already noted. The shock of the terrorist events further removed the luster that had surrounded globalization, as the system reoriented its focus toward the problem of international terrorism. The more profound effects of the changed environment on globalization are examined throughout the book. For present purposes, it is sufficient simply to suggest the contours of short- and long-term prospects.

In the immediate wake of the attacks, negative impacts tended to be emphasized. For example, one of the reasons the Al Qaeda terrorists were able to enter the United States is the relative ease that people and products have in entering and leaving the country. That penetrability is a distinct asset for increasing international economic activity such as trade, but it also makes monitoring and interception of terrorists more difficult than would be the case with greater restrictions on movement. As discussions turned to the prospects of terrorists moving weapons of mass destruction into the country (especially after the anthrax scare of November 2001), there were quite understandable calls for increased security on America's borders. The question was how this could be accomplished without unduly strangling trade, effectively undoing globalization, and threatening freedoms integral to the American way of life.

In the longer term, it is possible to think of the emphases on geopolitics and globalization as being potentially reinforcing, part of a comprehensive policy toward the world. A reasonable consensus has emerged that a basic reason for terrorism is abysmal living conditions in parts of the world that are breeding grounds for the hopelessness that makes terrorism an attractive option. Economic development— draining the "swamps" in which terrorism thrives—thus becomes part of a longer term means of eliminating the terrorist threat. Since a major component of alleviating human misery is improving living conditions through economic prosperity, the spread of the globalizing economy to places that have hitherto been those swamps can become part of overall geopolitical strategy.

DYNAMICS OF THE NEW INTERNATIONAL SYSTEM

The emergence of the fault lines has had major impacts on both the nature of the international system and how we think about our place in that system. In this section, we introduce and briefly explore three aspects of these changes. First, we look at the system's dynamics in terms of the relative ascendancy of geopolitics or globalization since the end of the Cold War and possible future relative emphases. Second, one of the obvious changes in the international system is the enhanced primacy of the United States in the international order, and we look at the nature and some of the implications of the United States being the sole remaining superpower. Third, this changing status has stimulated and coincided with a general political debate in the country about what the American approach and role *should* be, and we explore some of the major facets of that debate.

Globalization and/or Geopolitics

As the discussion of the fault lines clearly suggests, the relationship between geopolitics and globalization is an intertwined, intimate, and evolving proposition, not an either-or matter. During the Cold War, geopolitical concerns were clearly and appropriately dominant given the nature of the international situation. Yet, while the geopolitics of East–West confrontation dominated the international agenda, the forces that would propel globalization were being set in place, ready to enter the calculus.

During the 1990s, two quite opposite forces were at play that changed the relative importance of globalization and geopolitics and ended up creating an exaggerated view of the post–Cold War world. One of these forces was the apparently receding importance of the most visible manifestation of geopolitics: military force. The demise of the military confrontation clearly devalued standard, traditional military force within the First Tier conglomerate of important countries, and this devaluation led many states sharply to reduce their forces. Following the apparent last hurrah of twentieth-century-style warfare in the Persian Gulf War, military concerns shrunk to smaller tasks, such as peacekeeping.

At the same time, the impact of globalization was making enormous headway as the leading edge of the great and spreading prosperity of the 1990s. During the first seven or so years of the decade, economic growth and prosperity seemed inexorable at the very same time that major systemic instability and violence faded from the world stage. The result was a euphoria that would prove to be partially false with time. But to enthusiasts like *New York Times* correspondent Thomas L. Friedman, we were entering the "age of globalization," a systematic transition from the old to the new.

At one level, the rise of globalization is nothing more than the latest conceptual and physical reaction to the realism represented by the geopolitically dominated Cold War period. Because it is discussed in detail in Chapter 2, this is not the place either to describe or critique realism. Suffice it to say that realism and geopolitics represent the conflictual side of international relations, the dark side or yin in politics. Globalization, on the other hand, emphasizes the cooperative side of the international equation, the idealist assault on the worst outcomes of a realist-dominated world—war. This assault has known many names, from interwar idealism and its attachment to international organization, to the functionalism of the early post–World War II emphasis on the U.N. system to make war functionally impossible. The more direct lineage attaches to the idea of complex interdependence popularized by Robert Keohane and Joseph S. Nye Jr. in the 1970s. Globalization emerges as the yang to the geopolitical yin.

The result is a fast-moving and changing international dynamic. The seemingly inexorable ascent of globalization was delivered a sobering blow by the East Asian crisis that swept through the global economy in 1997 and 1998 and reminded us that the growing prosperity was neither automatic nor nonreversible. In turn, the ensuing turmoil brought geopolitical elements back to the fore in diverse places. In Indonesia, for example, the crash laid bare the last vestiges of corruption in the Suharto dictatorship, hastening his resignation from a presidency to which he had had himself appointed for life and setting in motion centrifugal forces in the archipelago that continue into the new century. In order to straighten out the economic mess revealed by the crisis, the old-fashioned economic instrument of power

Amplification 1.2

SYSTEM CHANGES AND CONTINUITY: 1900 AND 2000

It was the turn of the century, and there was great anticipation in the air. There had not been a major war in thirty years to interrupt the basic peace, and there was great physical prosperity that reached nearly everywhere in the developed world. The result was an atmosphere of almost unbridled optimism for the new century. In the minds of most pundits, the major cause for joy came from an economic system that was spreading itself globally and entwining all members in a web of economic interdependence that made war between them unthinkable and possibly even physically impossible. Those who grumbled about overly euphoric projections of this situation into the future were deemed grouchy doomsayers out of touch with the times.

The year, of course, was 1900, not 2000, and the pundits proved tragically wrong. The first round of globalization did not produce the general peace its enthusiasts projected; rather, it was the presage of the bloodiest, most war-torn century in recorded history. What does that say for the twenty-first century?

Mostly, it counsels restraint and modesty in our projections into the future. The simple fact is that we lack the scientific knowledge to make confident predictions about something as complex as the workings of the international system for anything but the shortest time periods. As we look at the kinds of forces in the contemporary environment, it is worthwhile to remember that almost all of them have been present before, but with very different outcomes. So, as we raise and try to answer questions about forces like globalization and geopolitics, we must consider that our projections are no more than well-informed speculation. No one, after all, predicted the attacks of September 11, 2001. We could be right, we could be wrong—more likely, we will end up somewhere in between.

(although not called that) was invoked in the form of International Monetary Fund sanctions in offending countries. At the same time, the carrot and stick of WTO membership and MFN status was dangled in front of the Chinese in order to secure their adherence to other quite different standards such as human rights. The dark side of geopolitics reasserted itself decisively as the commercial airliners slammed into the icons of geopolitics (the Pentagon) and globalization (the World Trade Center).

What this reveals is that globalization and geopolitics have become intertwined in complicated ways, which we explore in the pages that follow. In some ways, the economic aspects of globalization supplanted—at least part of the time and in some instances—the military aspects of geopolitics during the 1990s. Certainly this was true in relations within the First Tier, as already noted, and doubtless there are other instances. At the same time, globalization may be the servant of geopolitics, as in the complex motivations and debates about the use of economic incentives toward

China to entangle that country in a spiderlike web that will draw them toward the economic and political values of the First Tier–dominated system.

Globalization and geopolitics may thus be the yin and yang of modern international relations, sometimes competing with one another and other times complementing one another. Before beginning the journey to try to decide the direction, nature, and velocity of that relationship, it is necessary to introduce one other major characteristic of the contemporary environment: the central role of the United States.

The American Role in the New World System

As already suggested, one of the ways the new international order is different from the Cold War era is in the distribution of power and influence among states, and we continue to struggle for appropriate language to describe the new arrangement. The language of bipolarity and multipolarity is clearly no longer descriptively accurate, and the use of the term unipolarity has connotations of a level of control, even hegemony, that the United States does not possess and that most Americans, including their leaders, do not aspire to.

It has become fashionable, however, to describe the United States as the remaining superpower, but a new term has also entered the lexicon to describe how much more influential the United States is than other states in the system. That term is *hyperpower*, and it connotes the great qualitative advantage of the United States in addition to quantitative advantages such as having the world's largest economy and most lethal military. It is a term sometimes used out of awe and respect, but it is also attached to what the late Arkansas senator J. William Fulbright called in a book title "the arrogance of power."

What are the bases of American preeminence in the world? It is possible to use the traditional categories of measures of national power to compose that advantage: the political, economic, and military instruments of power. (As we shall see in subsequent discussions, notably in Chapter 7, many add elements such as information possession to this list.) During the Cold War, the United States had the advantage in power employing each of these measures, but its advantage was challenged by different powers in each category. Marxism-Leninism posed a challenge (that turned out to be overestimated) to the political appeal of western democracy, the economies of Japan and the European Common Market (now Union) posed an economic challenge, and Soviet nuclear and massive conventional forces challenged American dominance on the military dimension as well.

During the 1990s, the United States clearly established its preeminence on all three measures of power. Part of the reason was that the United States outperformed its rivals, especially in the economic realm. At the same time, the demise of the Soviet Union meant the source of both the political and military dimensions of power quit the field, leaving the United States alone as the sole possessor of significant amounts of all the instruments of power.

Politically, the United States emerged as "the indispensable nation," to use former Secretary of State Madeleine Albright's phrase. The basis of American political advantage was at least twofold. The power and appeal of the American system and political ideals (Nye's "soft power") have made the United States the model that many states and peoples worldwide seek to emulate. At the same time, the United States is the only country that has truly global interests. This means that whenever situations arise almost anywhere, the United States is affected and has an interest in influencing the outcome, a situation highlighted when the United States became the direct victim of international terrorism. Because of American power on the other dimensions, American preferences are consequential and sought out regardless of the location.

The economic dimension is similar. After nearly two decades of economic doldrums during the 1970s and 1980s when it became popular in this country and abroad to talk about American decline, the American economy revived and led the expansion of the globalizing economy during the 1990s and into the 2000s. The United States had remained the world's largest economy even during the down years, but as expansion occurred and the globalization system became penultimately a trading system, the United States also blossomed as the world's great market, which everyone sought to enter. At the same time, America's economic rivals relatively declined. The German economic "miracle" was slowed by the greater than anticipated burden of absorbing the former German Democratic Republic (East Germany) into the Federal Republic in the early 1990s. By the end of the 1990s, the Japanese economy was faced with a serious downturn; Joining the American-inspired and American-led "circle of market democracies" added to the luster of its soft power.

American military advantage increased the most. The most obvious reason for this was the decline of America's military rivals. Russian forces are far inferior in size and quality to the old Soviet military machine, and the burdensome retention of a nuclear arsenal comparable to that of the United States that the Russians cannot afford to maintain adequately is about the only way in which America's past rival poses any threat. Similarly, the People's Republic of China retains the world's largest army but has no way to project it far from its borders and spends about one-tenth the amount on defense that the United States does despite a major commitment to defense in recent years. As the adversaries have melted away, America's allies have also cut back their forces at a more rapid rate than has the United States, contributing to the substantial gap in military capability between the United States and everybody else.

The gap is qualitative as well as quantitative. As was first demonstrated convincingly in the Persian Gulf War, the results of the *revolution in military affairs* (RMA) in adapting technologies like electronics to the battlefield have given the United States (and its close allies) an enormous qualitative advantage militarily. The only other states that have undergone aspects of the RMA are First Tier allies like France and Great Britain. Second Tier states (like Iraq in 1991) simply stand no realistic chance when confronted by a military machine such as that which can be fielded by the United States and its NATO allies.

The result of these military advantages is that the United States has the military reach to match its global interests, and it is the only country that can project military power globally. At the operational level, the United States is the only remaining power with a global blue water (major oceangoing) Navy, and it is the only country that has global air power projection capabilities. This means not only that the United States has great advantage in projecting its own forces into faraway places but also that others must rely on American capabilities to get their own forces to distant battlefields or to deployments in the name of peacekeeping or emergency humanitarian relief, for instance.

This position of preeminence is not always or universally appreciated, and it is commonplace to hear objections to American global leadership on grounds such as American "arrogance" or some similar charge. At the same time, one of history's lessons would seem to be that nature abhors vacuums in all guises, including balances of power. Some argue that American singularity of power will create rivals to fill the vacuum left by the Soviets, and occasionally there is some mention of the possible formation of rival coalitions (such as Russia and China). These never seem to come to fruition, and American preeminence has remained unchallenged for well over a decade. In fact, following the Afghan campaign and American threats to bring down the government of Saddam Hussein unilaterally in the face of international opposition, there was speculation that American military prowess may have gotten too great—to the point the United States no longer needs its allies to accomplish military goals and thus can ignore their advice. Acceptance of American leadership, in other words, remains controversial.

What *Should* the United States Do?

There is a major cleavage within the American populace about the proper and appropriate American role in the world. Like much of the broader political debate within the country, much of this debate has been given simplistic, misleading labels to "describe" the positions people take—such as liberal, conservative, and neoconservative. These labels generally obscure rather than clarify the dynamics of the more subtle orientations toward national security concerns. These positions are generally nuanced combinations of a variety of views about the world. In this section, we look at views toward U.S. national security from five different perspectives that, individually and collectively, help clarify and elaborate the real positions people hold.

Our review encompasses five aspects of the values people combine to produce their view of what the United States should do in the world. The categories are not mutually exclusive, but holding one view on a particular dimension does not automatically entail a particular position on other dimensions. The dimensions are arranged in roughly descending order, although readers may quibble with the ordering or even the composition of the list itself. The five dimensions are basic worldview, political orientation, approaches to involvement in the world, participation preferences, and judgments on the generalized efficacy of force in international dealings generally and in particular situations. Each is discussed individually but briefly, recognizing that the discussions cannot exhaust all facets of the distinction.

Basic Worldview. This dimension refers to the generalized view that a person has about the nature of the international system; the acceptability, desirability, and immutability of the way the system works; and how or whether one should act to change the arrangements that do exist. The basic orientations that dominate discussions in national security debates are between *realism* and *idealism*.

Realism is the historically dominant philosophy and is the underlying belief system for the realist paradigm, which is the subject of the next chapter. Roughly speaking, realism (as the name implies) seeks to describe the world the way it is. Its central tenets are that world politics is a geopolitical struggle among sovereign states in an international system of anarchy (the absence of government), in which states are the central units that compete among themselves to maximize their most important values, known as national interests. Inherent in the description that realism portrays is that the maintenance of and occasional resort to organized armed force is one way that states achieve their values.

The realist world is a quintessentially Hobbesian construct intended both to describe the world and to provide a set of methods to survive and succeed in the world. The code of behavior associated with realism is the realist paradigm. Realism does not purport to place a value on the "goodness" of the conditions it says orders the world; rather, it suggests that the sensible approach of policymakers is to determine how to adapt to and make the best of the world as it is. Because part of the paradigm is the locus of power in the most prominent states of the world, realism is *state-centric* and generally opposes attempts to undercut the power and centrality of the state through efforts such as limitations on state sovereignty.

Idealism views the world differently. Most idealists accept the realist description of the world as basically accurate (if somewhat overdrawn). Where they differ is on the question of the immutability of the present condition and whether one should work to change the current arrangements. Idealists, in a general sense, believe that realism produces an imperfect world that is in need of reform and, in a more Lockean manner, that change is possible. For many idealists, the major imperfection of current international politics is its normalization of force as an acceptable method for bringing about change. The basic question idealists ask is, how can the world order be transformed to make the world a better (generally more peaceful) place?

Both realism and idealism are part of the American tradition. Realism tends to predominate among policymakers because it does offer a description of the structure and workings of the system and how to manipulate that system. For many people, attachment to realism also has a deceiving rhetorical quality—it is somehow more virile and worldly to be "realistic" about the world than to somehow be a dreamy idealist. As a result, many individuals describe themselves as realists without any particular philosophical underpinning behind the claim.

Idealism, however, also has its place, especially in the United States. As is argued in Chapter 3, Americans have always possessed a feeling of moral and other superiority (Ronald Reagan's depiction of the United States as the "shining house on the hill") that is accompanied by an evangelical desire to share that vision with the rest of the world. Thus, Woodrow Wilson sought to "make the world safe for democracy," and Wilsonian idealism, as it is known, had as its goal the restructuring of the international system along more democratic lines. Idealists often disagree on the method of achieving change. The Clinton and George W. Bush administrations, for instance, both had the idealistic goal of spreading democracy to places where it does not exist. They differed on how to go about the promotion: Clinton's goal was spreading American soft power through globalization, as opposed to the neoconservative credo of "regime change" (including the resort to force) of the Bush terms.

There is a political trick here as politicians align themselves on the realist–idealist axis. Politically, it is virtually suicidal to be viewed as an idealist because so many Americans view that orientation as "soft" or "unrealistic." As a result, an orientation that is indeed idealist must somehow be portrayed to the public as instead being realistic—that advocating basic change is the wisest geopolitical path. The prime current example of this attempted legerdemain is the neoconservative's open embrace of the Wilsonian ideal of advocating the spread of democracy (although through the use of force) as the proper—and thus realistic—course for the country.

Political Orientation. In the contemporary political debate, this is the most emotional and, in large measure, misleading dimension. It is most often manifested in the dichotomy between *liberalism* and *conservatism*, but these terms have become so emotionally laden that it is hard to determine their meaning out of context. Both terms can be used to convey either praise or condemnation.

It is helpful both to extend the categories and to define them. The basic liberal–conservative dichotomy omits too many other possibilities or requires placing people and their ideas into categories that do not truly fit them and whose inclusion unnecessarily broadens and distorts the meanings of the descriptive categories.

General political orientation can more usefully be divided into five orientations that form something of a continuum. Starting at the far "left" is *radicalism*. Radicals generally support substantial, even fundamental, change in political relationships, normally toward some currently nonexistent condition. Often, radicals display a willingness to resort to violence. Next comes *liberalism*. Classic liberalism has two major characteristics. First, it emphasizes tolerance of the views and opinions of others (indeed, one classic meaning of being liberal is that one is tolerant of others). Second, liberals are positively oriented toward political change and have a generally positive view of the role of government in promoting that change. Many liberals are also egalitarian and seek to level the conditions of citizens, although this is not a necessary part of being liberal (it *is*, however, the most controversial and criticized characteristic).

In the middle of the spectrum is *pragmatism*. Pragmatists do not espouse a predisposition one way or the other on the question of political change and the positive or negative role of government. Rather, they tend to be moderate on issues and to take positions on particular questions based on their assessment of the individual merits in particular situations. Pragmatism and moderation have historically been highly revered characteristics, but in an ideologically charged era, pragmatism has a bland image that seems to pale in the face of stronger positions across the board.

To the right of center are *conservatism* and *reactionism*. Conservatism, in its literal sense, means support for the status quo: conservatives seek to "conserve" relationships as they exist. Thus, conservatives are generally opposed to or suspicious of change, and since most change is associated with government activity, they generally favor a small and restricted role for the government. The major operational difference between liberals and conservatives indeed comes down to the question of how active government should be in promoting change or regulating behavior. Reactionism, on the other hand, is the advocacy of change to some past state of political affairs. Because such change generally includes a reduction of governmental activity and thus a reversion to some past set of relationships, reactionaries are more extreme than real conservatives.

Placing someone (including oneself) on this continuum is difficult. The boundaries between the categories, especially when presented as compactly as they are here, are not sharp and clear. At the same time, people do not always (even usually) consistently act from the premises of one position or another. An advocacy of tax cuts is, for instance, essentially a reactionary position, whereas setting up mandatory, federally regulated educational standards is a decidedly liberal act. Also, many people hold different philosophies when it comes to international and domestic issues. So-called Kennedy Democrats (supporters of the late president John F. Kennedy) were generally liberal on domestic issues but fairly sharply conservative on foreign policy matters.

Approaches to Involvement. The third dimension refers to how active the United States should be in world affairs. In more tranquil times when the United States was not so prominent an international actor, this distinction was more important than it is now, but it still retains some salience.

The two major positions on American involvement are *internationalism* and *neo-isolationism*. Internationalists generally feel that the United States should take a prominent, activist position in the world and that acting as a world leader best serves the national interest. Neo-isolationists, on the other hand, are less inclined toward such activism. Instead, neo-isolationists believe that the United States should limit its participation in world affairs whenever and to the extent possible and concentrate instead on domestic American concerns.

This historically was a much livelier debate than it is now. Isolationism as a pure force seeking to insulate the United States as completely as possible from world affairs was a powerful force until World War II, when the Pearl Harbor attack rendered "splendid isolationism" anachronistic. Its more moderate form, neo-isolationism, resides at the fringes of the debate over security in the face of people like Patrick Buchanan and tends to associate with opposition to globalization (arguing it hurts Americans more than it helps them). Most Americans consider themselves to be internationalists generally speaking, although the degree of international involvement that they advocate varies.

Participation Preferences. Regardless of how one feels about the extent to which the United States should involve itself in world affairs, a further question is the quality and nature of participation in those affairs. This concern centers around whether the United States should prefer to act in concert with as much of the international community as possible when it interacts with the world or instead should be willing to act on its own, even with the opposition of a substantial part of the international community, when it feels its interests are served by going it alone.

The two positions on this dimension are *multilateralism* and *unilateralism*. Multilateralism, which has been the dominant position for most of the period since World War II, asserts the belief that American policy and actions should generally be developed and coordinated with the policies of others in the international community, and especially American friends and allies. The underlying assumption is that American interests include keeping friends and that the wisest policies often reflect the development of international consensus on issues. Unilateralism, on the other hand, starts from the premise that U.S. interests should override international concerns and that the United States must be willing to go against international consensus when international views would harm American interests. This position has been most prominently associated with the neoconservatives within the George W. Bush administration.

Multilateralism and unilateralism are not entirely mutually exclusive. Multilateralists would, for instance, agree that there are occasions when the United States must ignore international views and act alone, and unilateralists would agree that developing an international consensus is preferable if possible. This latter position is the heart of President Bush's "distinctly American internationalism" imbedded in the 2002 *National Security Strategy of the United States*. Rather, the two positions can be thought of more accurately as predilections or strong preferences for ways to proceed in the world.

Efficacy of Force. The final distinction regards preference for *how* to attempt to promote American interests, and it hinges on the question of the broad range of situations in which the use of military force is appropriate and where in the hierarchy of "instruments of national power" one should place military power.

One way to state this distinction is between the *hawks* and the *doves*. The names, of course, are descriptive. Hawks are those individuals who have a generally positive view of the utility of force over a range of situations and thus believe that the possible recourse to "hard power" should be considered in a variety of cases. Doves, on the other hand, generally oppose the use of military force except in clear cases of employments of necessity and prefer to use "soft power" (economic and political instruments of power) to achieve national goals. One way to view the distinction is to ask whether military force should be used only as a last resort (doves) or whether it should be considered in less dire circumstances (hawk).

Historically, the hawk position has been associated with traditional realism. Traditional realism, however, has as one of its tenets the belief that military force should be used only in defense of vital American interests, or, in other words, in employments of necessity. This contrasts with the neoconservative version of the hawk preference, which is willing to employ force more broadly, including in pursuit of interests not unambiguously vital in their nature. This distinction helps explain, for instance, why a number of retired general officers opposed the neoconservative-inspired American invasion of Iraq. The retired officers were traditional realists who did not believe the outcome in Iraq affected vital American interests, and thus they opposed the deployment.

Compiling Profiles. The five dimensions can be combined to create profiles that are useful in distinguishing individuals and groups on grounds other than crude and generally ambiguous labels. Moreover, developing one's own personal inventory and comparing it to that of others (political candidates, for instance) can also provide a way to see if one agrees more with the position of one individual or side or another.

The profiles of the candidates for president in the 2004 election offer an interesting point of contrast. Senator John Kerry, the Democratic candidate, represented the traditional Eastern liberal position, which I call "the man of the world." Kerry considered himself a traditional realist in terms of overall worldview. His political orientation was much like the Kennedy Democrats discussed above: liberal on most domestic issues and moderate to conservative on international issues. He was strongly internationalist in his approach to foreign affairs and suggested a strongly multilateralist preference. Although showing a willingness to use force as a last resort, his views on the efficacy of force were moderately dovish.

Challenge!

YOUR OWN PERSONAL INVENTORY

To clarify how you feel about national security affairs, develop a personal inventory on the five dimensions. The central question about each dimension may help you categorize yourself.

Basic Worldview: Should the basic mission of policymakers be to adapt to and make the best of the world situation as it is (realist) or should they try to change world conditions (idealism)?

Political Orientation: Should government seek to induce change through any means available (radicalism); promote change through moderate, tolerant action (liberalism); view situations on their own merits alone (pragmatism); seek to preserve existing relationships within a limited view of government (conservatism); or seek to remove or roll back existing conditions (reactionism)?

Approaches to Involvement: Should the United States play a generally activist, leadership role in the world (internationalism) or avoid international involvement wherever possible (neo-isolationism)?

Participation Preference: Should the United States generally try to build international consensus before acting (multilateralism) or look at its own interests first without regard to international preferences (unilateralism)?

Efficacy of Force: Is force useful in a broad range of situations (hawk) or as a last resort (dove)?

President Bush offered a very different profile, one I call "the tough guy." Although calling himself a realist for political reasons, his actions (reinforced in his 2005 State of the Union address by an emphasis on promoting democracy) were fairly clearly idealist. This includes a belief in the use of force to induce change to democracy, an international orientation that can only be called radical. Domestically, he describes himself as conservative. He is also clearly an internationalist, but his orientation toward acting alone or in concert with others leaves him a rather clear unilateralist. He is also a hawk, but of the neoconservative rather than traditional variety.

Depicted in this manner, the choice between candidates was clear and distinct. The only dimension on which the two unambiguously agreed was approaches to involvement; on all others, they were at odds. Using the distinctions in the profile thus provides a way to compare and contrast different views on national security affairs.

Conclusion: The Continuing Role of Force

There are two broad interpretations about the extent to which the recourse to force has changed in the post–Cold War world. If one begins from an emphasis on the potential applications of force, then change has been dramatic, since the most notable potential use was the ultimate employment of necessity, a military confrontation with the Soviet Union. That contingency has obviously disappeared, and much of the potential use of force in conventional interstate warfare has faded in the general tranquility among those countries with conventional forces, notably the most developed countries. It is still possible to conjure interstate wars on the peripheries (the identification of the "axis of evil" states of Iraq, Iran, and North Korea as possible targets for American military wrath, for instance), but none of these has the immediacy and importance of the Cold War confrontation. Combating terrorism has replaced large-scale warfare at the pinnacle of national security priorities. This assessment, of course, has major implications for the kinds of forces the United States develops and the missions for which they are prepared.

The other way to look at the problem is how and where force is actually employed in the past and how it is employed in the present or future. From this vantage point, change is not very dramatic at all. As noted, the United States employed force exclusively in the old Third World during the Cold War, and the current pattern emphasizes deployments in the less developed countries of the world. In both periods, the conflicts were generally internal affairs, civil wars of one kind or another. The difference is in the motivation underlying involvement: during the Cold War, we were primarily motivated by ideological, Cold War reasons, whereas now we are tempted to intervene either to relieve human-induced chaos and suffering, in effect to save countries from themselves, or to root out sources of international terrorism.

This distinction is not insignificant for at least three reasons. One is the relative importance we attach to potential involvement. In the Cold War context, one could make the argument—admittedly sometimes a stretch—that we were impelled to act in the developing world because of the geopolitical implications of the outcome. Should our side lose, it would be yet one more instance of the "victory" of Communism in the global struggle. Thus, intervention could be arguably a matter of necessity. Such geopolitical motivations are generally missing in many contemporary situations, where the goal often is to restore order after some humanitarian disaster, promote democracy, eradicate terrorism, or some combination of those reasons. In any geopolitical sense, these are clearly employments of choice. The employments of necessity deal with terrorism; the elusive, secretive nature of the terrorist opponents, however, makes specification of where and how engagement might occur difficult.

What we do in internal wars has changed as well. During the Cold War, conflicts were usually clearly drawn competitions between a government and an insurgent group, each of which fielded an organized armed force and sought militarily to defeat the other. In these circumstances, the purpose of inserting American armed forces was to assist "our" side in defeating the enemy. American forces were sent "to fight and win" in familiar military terms. In the contemporary environment, this is not the case. Normally, the situation is one of more or less great chaos, where the contending parties are shadowy organizations with inarticulate political goals and supported by armed bands that are barely military in composition. The purpose for using force in these situations is to suspend the fighting and in effect to impose peace on the area. This is best done by simply intimidating the warring parties with a show of force and then keeping them physically apart. Ideally, the soldiers do no fighting at all because their simple presence accomplishes the goal. Force used in this manner is more difficult to understand than more traditional employment. The first phase of the Afghan campaign, where American force was used to help topple a regime, returned us to a more traditional reason for fighting, at least for a limited period of time.

Finally, the two different contexts require a rethinking of how we look at the international system and our place in it. During the Cold War, our thinking was dominated by geopolitics in the form of something called the *realist paradigm*, a construct that tied the use of force to the most important American interests and counseled that force not be used in less weighty circumstances. When the global balance between Communism and non-Communism was at stake, the paradigm provided guidance about when to use and when not to use force. Applying the same standards to the humanitarian disasters of the 1990s and 2000s could paralyze the use of force in ways that might be undesirable. Whether the realist paradigm is an adequate device for dealing with the use of force is one of the most fundamental questions facing contemporary thinking about national security. For that reason, Chapter 2 begins with a description and critique of the concept.

SELECTED BIBLIOGRAPHY

Allison, Graham T., Jr., and Robert Blackwill. "America's Stake in the Soviet Future." *Foreign Affairs* 70, 3 (Summer 1991), 77–97.

Friedman, Thomas L. *The Lexus and the Olive Tree: Understanding Globalization*. New York: Farrar, Straus, Giroux, 1999.

Fulbright, J. William. *The Arrogance of Power*. New York: Random House, 1966.

Fukuyama, Francis. *The End of History and the Last Man*. New York: Free Press, 1992.

Gaddis, John Lewis. "Setting Right a Dangerous World." *Chronicle of Higher Education: The Chronicle Review* 48, 18 (January 11, 2002), B7–B10.

————. "Grand Strategy for the Second Term." *Foreign Affairs* 84, 1 (January/February 2005), 2–15.

Keohane, Robert O., and Joseph S. Nye, Jr. *Power and Interdependence* (2nd ed.). Glenview, IL: Scott Foresman/Little Brown, 1989.

Mearsheimer, John J. "Why We Shall Soon Miss the Cold War." *Atlantic Monthly* 266, 2 (August 1990), 35–50.

Nye, Joseph S., Jr. *Bound to Lead: The Changing Nature of American Power*. New York: Basic Books, 1990.

Project Ploughshares. *Armed Conflicts Report, 1999: Sixth Annual*. Waterloo, Ontario: Center for Peace and Conflict Studies, 1999.

Singer, Max, and the Estate of the Late Aaron Wildawsky. *The Real World Order: Zones of Peace, Zones of Turmoil* (rev. ed.). Chatham, NJ: Chatham House, 1996.

Snow, Donald M., and Eugene Brown. *International Relations: The Changing Contours of Power*. New York: Longman, 2000.

————, *When America Fights: The Uses of U.S. Military Force*. Washington, DC: CQ Press, 2000.

CHAPTER 2

Geopolitics: America and the Realist Paradigm

PREVIEW

Realism and the realist paradigm have been central to the operation of the international system and American attitudes toward the world. Moreover, geopolitics, one of the two competing themes around which this book is organized, finds its philosophical and operational basis in realism and the realist paradigm. Because of these factors, the chapter lays out the realist argument, its implications in a geopolitical world, and the controversy over its continuing relevance to help in understanding the contemporary national security environment. Many opponents of realism, including some advocates of globalization, question the validity of the paradigm and its consequences, and their objections are discussed. The chapter concludes with a discussion of the future applicability of the realist paradigm.

The United States has been a leading member of the international system at least since the end of World War II, meaning it has occupied a position as a major international force for the entire lifetime of most present Americans. Most of us have never known a time when the United States was not a major player on the world scene, regardless of whether we were born here or immigrated to this land. This fact has the potential to distort our perceptions about global geopolitics and our role within the national security arena in which geopolitics is acted out. As Americans look forward into the new millennium, we are wise to place our experience in perspective, which is the purpose of this chapter and Chapter 3.

This American preeminence has not always been the case. The simple fact is that geopolitical participation and especially leadership has been the exception rather than the rule for the United States. For most of our history, Americans sought to be above what was viewed as the corrupting influence of power politics, and the result has been a historical ambivalence about our role in international politics, including its more openly geopolitical aspects. As a result, we wonder where we fit in the system and what role we want to take in structuring and participating in the geopolitical game. It also means that we are relative amateurs at geopolitics when our experience is compared with that of the traditional powers.

There are several reasons for this scenario, and while any list will be subject to criticism both for what it includes and what it omits, we can identify at least three factors from what might be called the American strategic culture that capture the essence of typical American attitudes toward the world of geopolitics.

The first factor is what some analysts have called *American exceptionalism*. Rightly or wrongly, Americans have always thought of this country as a special place, one that is qualitatively better than other places. The United States was, after all, the first country in the world to adopt political democracy, and it has long provided a refuge from the tyranny of political ideologies (fascism, Communism) and practices (e.g., involuntary military service) elsewhere in the world: Europe in the eighteenth and nineteenth centuries and much of the rest of the world since. As a result, Americans think of themselves as a kind of chosen people and view intrusions from the outside as a potential source of taint. The fact of steady immigration into the country (contrasted by essentially no emigration) reinforces this preference captured in the Statue of Liberty's invitation to bring us "your huddled masses" seeking freedom and Ronald Reagan's image of the "shining house on the hill."

The perception of being exceptional leads to a second strain in America's historical view of itself: *isolationism*. Because contact with and participation in the international system is potentially tainting, there is a residual sentiment to limit the degree of American participation in an essentially corrupt and potentially corrupting enterprise. In its most extreme form between the world wars, this sentiment manifested itself in a virtual withdrawal from international politics (although not international economics) under the banner of "splendid isolation," as noted earlier. In a more contemporary sense, *neo*-isolationism argues for sharp limits on the degree of American interaction with and leadership in the world. This sentiment finds substantive voice in policy areas as disparate as American misgivings about participation in United Nations–sponsored peacekeeping missions and opposition to economic globalization. There is, quite simply, a strand in the American political experience that, like the late Swedish actress Greta Garbo, simply wants to be left alone. To many foreign and domestic critics of American policy, this tendency manifests itself as American *unilateralism*, the tendency to ignore the sentiments and advice of others and to act alone in international affairs.

There is another factor, which is what we might call American *ambivalence* about the effects of geopolitical participation. Very few Americans would describe themselves as isolationists or maintain that the United States has no leadership role in the world. Pure isolationism ended effectively with the Japanese attack on Pearl Harbor, and neo-isolationism was badly crippled by September 11, 2001. Nonetheless, ambivalence remains. The consequence of involvement often is to ensnare the country in a web of international rules and regulations (what are sometimes called regimes) that limit American independence in ways about which many have second thoughts, because such involvement can preclude some actions the country might prefer to take. Traditional European geopolitics is one of those traps that Americans in their idealism have sought to avoid.

American attitudes toward its sovereignty stand out as examples of our ambivalence. Sovereignty, which means supreme authority, is central to the realist paradigm and is discussed more fully in the next section of this chapter. For present purposes, suffice it to say that the United States is among the strongest defenders of state sovereignty (along with China) because strict sovereignty minimizes the extent to which the judgments or standards of outsiders can be imposed on the country or individual Americans. Thus, for instance, the United States is one of only a handful of states that has refused to ratify the statute of the International Criminal Court (ICC), which has the jurisdiction to try people accused of committing war crimes. The reason for the American government's refusal to accede to the statute is our reluctance to permit Americans to be tried by foreign judges if they are accused of committing war crimes. As an example, when an American soldier was accused of raping and killing a young girl in Kosovo shortly after the United States joined the Kosovo Force (KFOR) peacekeeping mission in 2000—an act deemed a crime against humanity and thus a war crime—he was whisked off to an American base in Germany and tried there by an American military tribunal rather than facing the ICC. (He was sentenced to life in prison, which is the most severe penalty he would have faced if he had been tried and convicted by the ICC.)

This reluctance to dilute authority puts the United States at odds with much of the international community on a number of matters, and our ambivalence toward participation results in anomalies and inconsistencies in our relations with the world. For instance, while American insistence on maintaining our sovereignty is not something to be challenged or violated, there are situations in which the United States has felt perfectly within its rights to violate other countries' sovereignty. American relations with Cuba illustrates this ambivalence and occasional incongruity.

Since 1960, the United States has imposed an economic boycott on dealings with the Communist government of Fidel Castro. This boycott is viewed by virtually the entire international community as anachronistic (a recent vote in the U.N. General Assembly condemned it by a tally of 143 to 3), and U.S. legislation to enforce it brings cries of violations of sovereignty from friends and allies alike. For instance, provisions of the Cuban Democracy Act of 1992 and the Helms-Burton Act of 1995 impose sanctions against foreign governments and corporations for doing business with Cuba, in effect making it illegal in the United States for a British company to sell its products in Cuba. This is accomplished by imposing sanctions on doing business with the United States if one violates the provisions of the acts. These are clear and obvious violations of the sovereignty of foreign governments and corporations that, if imposed on the United States, would be roundly condemned in this country, according to critics of U.S. policy toward Cuba and foreign companies and governments.

These examples are simply illustrative of the tension, ambivalence, and complexity with which the United States fits itself into the geopolitics of the contemporary system, and these problems are likely to be accentuated as the United States adjusts its policies in light of the response to international terrorism. Moreover, these issues broadly define the differences between an internationalist emphasis on globalization and a narrower emphasis on geopolitics. To understand the geopolitical position more fully, we first look at the geopolitical system we inherited from the Cold War—the realist paradigm—and objections to it as the operating principle of international politics.

REALISM AND THE REALIST PARADIGM

Realism has been both a leading theoretical approach to the study of international relations and a useful way to organize our understanding of the world. In addition, realism has served as a practical guide for political leaders as they conduct foreign policy. Realism thus served as an intellectual tool and a set of guidelines for policy-makers. Whether it can continue to serve that purpose as well in the future as it has in the past is part of the contemporary critique of realism.

These dual functions are not coincidental. The academic basis of realism came from the study of international relations by scholars whose first interest was in physical observation of how world leaders, diplomats, soldiers, and the like actually carried on their relations. Developed and ordered into a coherent explanation of international relations during and after World War II, the content of theoretical realism roughly coincided with the actual conduct of international affairs at least through the Cold War. One of the reasons the approach is called realism is that it is said to reflect reality.

Realism is controversial, largely because many people—and especially a number of international relations scholars—dispute the reality the realists portray and seek more or less actively to reform or reverse some of the basic dynamics that the realists portray. Among the phenomena that realists describe and reformers wish to change is the "normalization" of the recourse to force—in other words, war.

As a basic approach, realism is as old as observation about the relations between independent political units. Many believe that Thucydides' *History of the Peloponnesian Wars*, written in the fifth century B.C., is the original statement of the philosophy of realism and would add the sixteenth-century Italian diplomat and advisor Niccolò Machiavelli's *The Prince* to the roster of realist classics.

Realism became a dominant approach to understanding international relations in the period surrounding World War II. At the end of World War I, a group of scholars known as "idealists" came to dominate the study of the international system. Given the enormous carnage of the Great War, there was considerable sentiment to reform a system whose rules—based in realism—had allowed the first great conflagration of the twentieth century to occur. They based their reform on the institutionalization of peace around the League of Nations and grounded their scholarship in ways to improve the peace system by improving the effectiveness of the League in reinforcing and preserving the peace.

Unfortunately, their advocacy (what they sought to accomplish) colored their observation of the actual international politics of the interwar period (what was actually occurring). The idealists either did not see World War II coming or felt it could be avoided, but the League-based institutional framework they had built to avoid war proved entirely inadequate to slow the rush to war in the 1930s. This failure was most dramatically stated by the English scholar E. H. Carr in his critique of idealism published in 1939, *The Twenty Years' Crisis, 1919–1939*.

Realism emerged from World War II as the dominant explanation and approach to international politics. In 1947, Hans Morgenthau published the first edition of his landmark exposition, *Politics Among Nations*, in which he laid out in detail the realist position. Emphasizing the roles of things like power, conflict, and war, the resulting realist paradigm seemed particularly well suited for describing (in a scholarly sense) and organizing the policy response to the emerging Cold War competition between the Communist and non-Communist worlds.

Even at the height of the Cold War confrontation, realism never lacked for critics. Part of that criticism comes from the conjunction of the academic and practical aspects of realism: it is not only an academic "theory" for understanding the world, it is also a set of rules of the road for conducting international affairs that includes at least a partial, implicit endorsement of its principles. The alternative to thinking about or acting outside the bounds of realism became thought of as unrealistic. Those who do not like the implications of a realist-run world generally do not like the academic approach either. In some cases, this intellectual objection is stated in terms of questioning the conceptual adequacy of the realist paradigm for describing and explaining international relations; in others, the objections are rooted in opposition to the effects of conceptualizing the world through the prism of the realist paradigm.

Resolving the theoretical debate about whether realism or some other theoretical framework produces better knowledge about international relations goes beyond our purpose here. As it relates to questions about the actual conduct of foreign and national security affairs, the basic concepts of realism have formed the framework within which national security decisions have been made at least since the 1940s. As a result, the pattern of historic and contemporary national security concerns cannot adequately be understood without understanding (but not necessarily embracing) the realist paradigm. If the post–September 11 environment indeed represents a return to the ascendancy of geopolitics, then the contemporary world can only be fully appreciated by understanding realism. Similarly, criticisms of realism are important to us because their implementation would alter those rules within which we think about national security in ways the critics feel more fully reflect reality and reflect the rationale for the globalizing 1990s.

BASIC CONCEPTS AND RELATIONSHIPS

Although it runs some risk of oversimplification, the realist paradigm can be reduced to a series of six propositions about the international system that can be arranged deductively in syllogistic order. Each individual statement contains one or more of the key concepts, and collectively they define the realist perspective. Numerous observers object to the implications of some of the observations that make up the paradigm and contest their implications. Because the paradigm has been such an important part of international reality, its content is important.

The six propositions composing the realist paradigm are as follows:

1. The international system is composed of sovereign states as the primary units in both a political and legal sense.
2. Sovereign states possess vital interests and are the only units in the system entitled to vital interests.
3. Vital interests become matters of international concern when conditions of scarcity exist and are pressed by competing state actors.
4. When issues involving scarce resources are present in the relations between sovereign states, then power must be used to resolve the difference.
5. The exercise of power is the political means of conflict resolution in international relations.
6. One political instrument of power is military force, which is one option for resolving differences between states.

Following the syllogism from the first to the sixth proposition, the conclusion must be reached that in a system of sovereign states, states must possess, and from time to time use, military force to resolve problems that arise for them in the system. The realist paradigm therefore justifies a concern with national security defined, at least in part, in terms of military force. It is not surprising, then, that the realist paradigm finds considerably more intellectual favor among most students and practitioners of military affairs and varying levels of disregard and disdain among people opposed to the use of military force as a "legitimate" tool for resolving differences among states. (Some military thinkers, of course, share the critique of various parts of realism.)

As stated in terms of these propositions, the realist paradigm is only a skeleton of concepts and relationships. It gains meaning when the basic concepts that compose it are examined and put together in the logical sequence of their presentation as depicted in that set of propositions.

Sovereignty

The most basic and critical principle of international relations is that of *state sovereignty*. The idea was originally articulated by a sixteenth-century Frenchman named Jean Bodin as a way to justify concentrating the authority of the French monarch by asserting his supreme authority over lesser French nobles. Sovereignty was enshrined as the basic operating principle of international relations through the series of agreements ending the Thirty Years War (1618–1648) known as the *Peace of Westphalia*. The Thirty Years War had, in large measure, been about whether the church or the state would be the principal holder of political authority in the future. Those supporting the notion of state authority prevailed, and they seized upon state sovereignty as the institutional and legal basis for institutionalizing their secular triumph over sectarian authority.

Sovereignty means *supreme authority*. Within a system in which sovereignty is the basic value, no entity can have authority superior to that of the sovereign. When Bodin coined the term and it was adopted by others, such as the English philosopher Thomas Hobbes, sovereignty was thought to be a quality that primarily applied to the domestic relations among individuals and groups within states rather than the relations between states. In fact, Bodin never considered the effects on the relations between sovereign entities. In the early days of the modern state system, that domestic sovereignty was considered to rest with the monarch. The extension of the principle to the international arena occurred over the next century and has been the principal operating rule underlying international politics ever since.

Both the domestic and international ramifications of sovereignty remain largely in force, although with quite opposite effects. Domestic sovereignty remains the basis of the authority of the state over its territory, although we now think of sovereignty as residing with the people (who confer part of their sovereignty on the government) rather than with a person—the monarch. The result of sovereignty applied domestically is to create the legal and philosophical basis for political *order*, since authority to act rests with the state.

The effect of sovereignty on international politics is to create *anarchy* (absence of government) as the basis of the relations between states. In the international arena, state sovereignty means no state can have any jurisdiction over what goes on within another state. Thus, all relations among states are among equals wherein no state has the authority to compel any other state to do anything, at least in a legal sense that does not always conform to actual practice. There is no authority above those with supreme authority, meaning there is no basis for governance in international relations; a formal state of anarchy therefore exists in the international realm. Jurisdiction over disputes resides with the parties to the dispute, who must figure out how to decide their differences on their own, usually without recourse to an outside authority. While the inviolability of state sovereignty has never been as absolute as the definition implies (states violate other states' sovereignty routinely), it remains the major organizational tool for defining relationships within the international system.

On the face of it, this seems like an odd way for the international system to conduct its business because the practical outcome is that there is no equivalent of the judicial branch of government to settle disputes, and the parties are left to fend for themselves when differences among them arise. The reason for this state of affairs, however, lies in the fact that states have matters of such importance to them that they are unwilling to have those matters left to the judgment of outsiders. As a consequence, states demand as total control over those matters as they can enforce. This leads us to the second major concept of the realist paradigm.

Vital Interests

The main reason states are generally unwilling to compromise on matters affecting their sovereignty is because states, unlike other entities in the Westphalian system, have what are called vital interests. Defined as properties and conditions on which states will not willingly compromise, vital interests are matters the outcomes of which are too important to be submitted to any superior authority. Such interests are to be guarded to the fullest extent the state is capable of. Some analysts would add that a vital interest is any interest that is sufficiently important that the state will use force to ensure its realization.

Generally, states formally or informally rank their interests in a hierarchical fashion that denotes how important a particular interest is and hence what measures it will undertake to realize the condition or property in question. Donald Neuchterlein provides a useful way to categorize these interests in the form of the national interest matrix (Figure 2.1):

Figure 2.1 National Interest Matrix

Basic Interest at Stake	Intensity of Interest			
	Survival	Vital	Major	Peripheral
Homeland Defense				
Economic Well-Being				
Favorable World Order				
Values Promotion				

Both dimensions of the matrix are hierarchical. Clearly, the most intense interest a state has is its physical survival, followed by those interests on which the state will not willingly compromise (vital interests). Major interests are matters that would inconvenience or harm the state but that can be tolerated, and peripheral interests are, as the label implies, matters more of inconvenience than basic interest. Similarly, the most important basic interest a state has is in defending itself, followed by promoting its economic well-being, its view of the world order, and its own values.

The critical point as it relates to questions of national security is the boundary between vital and major interests, because it is generally agreed that vital interests are ones over which the state will use force to guarantee, and major interests fall below that threshold. The location of that boundary is a matter of disagreement within the national security debate when it is applied to individual situations.

In the early and middle 1980s, for instance, there were different assessments of the implications of a Marxist government in the Central American republic of Nicaragua. The Sandinista-dominated government arguably threatened American interests in the area, notably protection of access to the Panama Canal, and the Sandinistas' existence had potential implications as a platform for the spread of Castroite Communism in the hemisphere. Some, notably the Republican administration of Ronald Reagan, found Sandinista rule intolerable, a threat to a vital American interest, and accordingly favored assisting an insurgent group, the Contras, to overthrow the regime by force. Democrats in Congress disagreed with this assessment, downplaying the significance of the Sandinistas. They passed legislation (the Bolland Amendment, named after the Massachusetts House Democrat who sponsored it) prohibiting assistance to the Contras. Violation of those prohibitions by members of the Reagan staff helped trigger the Iran-Contra scandal toward the end of the second Reagan term. The disagreement boiled down to different conclusions about the level of U.S. interest involved in the situation.

The boundary between vital and less-than-vital interests is and will always be an important point of contention within the domestic and international security debate, as illustrated in Amplification 2.1. Looking at the basic interests at stake, for instance, there is little disagreement that defending the homeland is vital to the state, and hence challenges to that interest will be met by force. Responding to the September 11 attacks clearly follows from this interest. As we go down the list of basic interests, the question of vitality becomes more debatable. In the Persian Gulf War, for instance, the American interests involved were clearly economic (access to

Amplification 2.1

FINDING THE BOUNDARY BETWEEN VITAL AND LESS-THAN-VITAL INTERESTS

One of the major alternatives to the definition we have used for vital interests is to say that vital interests are any interests worth fighting over. The danger of this definition is that, when reversed, it implies that any time a country is fighting, its vital interests must be engaged. This, of course, is a dubious proposition. But since people employ the distinction, it does mean the boundary between vital and less-than-vital interests is an important one in the study of national security.

Unfortunately, the boundary does not, in any literal sense, exist either in the abstract or regarding specific situations. The reason for this is psychological and subjective. What is an intolerable circumstance for some people may or may not be intolerable for others. One dictionary definition of security, for instance, is "safety or a feeling of safety." Beyond direct physical threats (e.g., a Russian missile or terrorist attack against the American homeland), most threats to security—or situations in which interests are at risk—fall within the psychological range of what makes people feel secure and hence feel that interests are imperiled. Because people can and do honestly disagree on these matters, the location of the boundary between vital and less-than-vital interests becomes the benchmark in the national security debate over when to use force.

If we apply this abstract notion to the contemporary trouble spots in the world identified by the Bush administration as constituting the axis of evil, the question to ask in each case is, How intolerable would the worst possible outcome be to American interests, and thus, would I be willing to use force to ensure that worst outcome does not occur? If you compare your assessments with others, you will likely find there are instances of large-scale consensus: most would endorse the use of force if Iraq invaded Kuwait again; there would probably be less support for military action against North Korea or Iran. How important are these countries—specifically, their alleged programs to gain weapons of mass destruction—to the United States? What actions are warranted against them?

petroleum energy that literally fuels the American economy). In contrast, promoting the American vision of the world, including our democratic and capitalistic values, is at a lower level of importance.

The activation of concern over vital interests occurs in situations of scarcity, where more than one claimant to a scarce resource asserts that claim as an interest. Scarcity, for our purpose, is the situation in which all claimants to a resource cannot simultaneously have all that they want (or feel they need). The definition, of course, is drawn from economics, and economic resources such as wealth are indeed one obvious arena where scarcity may occur. Scarcity may also be political (political power or office when more than one individual wants the position), social (everyone cannot, by definition, be part of the elite), or physical (possession of a piece of disputed territory or access to a natural resource like water). Conflicts over vital interests are activated when competing parties put forward incompatible claims to a scarce resource and insist on a quantity of the resource that does not allow the other party to have as much of the resource as they deem necessary.

A historical example may illustrate the point. In the 1850s, as the United States expanded west toward the Pacific Ocean, it came into direct conflict with Great Britain over where the northern boundary of the United States and the southern border of Canada should lie. The Americans claimed parts of what are now Canada (Vancouver Island, for instance), and the British claimed parts of what are now Washington and Oregon. Clearly both countries could not simultaneously possess the disputed territories, establishing their scarcity, and both sides deemed the outcome too important for compromise. At one point, there was even the threat of war by the American side under the slogan "Fifty-four Forty or Fight," the geographic latitude of the proposed American boundary.

Two final concepts about vital interests and sovereignty bear mention: Because vital interests are so important, the state is unwilling to accept contrary judgments about its interests when it can avoid them. As a result, the state is unwilling to submit disputes to a higher authority (a sovereign above the state) for fear such an authority might rule against the state in an unacceptable manner that would have to be disobeyed or ignored in order to ensure an acceptable outcome. Vital interests, in other words, are matters that are too important to relinquish control over the outcomes. Having said that, the word "willingly" is part of the definition of vital interests, because when vital interests come into conflict, somebody wins and somebody loses. Usually, it is the weaker party who must unwillingly accept an unacceptable outcome, with the upshot that the interplay of vital interests in a realist world is an exercise in power politics.

Power Politics

International relations is an inherently political enterprise in which the principal political actors are states seeking to maximize their advantage in an environment where all cannot be equally successful. Who gets what is the essence of the political process in this arena. For our purposes, we use a variation of David Easton's definition of politics: *politics is the ways in which conflicts of interest over scarce resources are resolved.*

Challenge!

JUSTIFYING THE U.S. INVASION OF IRAQ

Should the United States have invaded Iraq in 2003? What justifications were made in support of the decision? What does the realist paradigm tell us about whether or not the action was justified?

According to the arguments made by the U.S. government in 2003, the invasion was justified by the threat posed by the Saddam Hussein government to the United States and the rest of the world community. Stated that way, the criteria of the realist paradigm clearly can be applied to judging the decision. The assertion of a threat raises two questions by which the decision to invade can be judged. One is the truth of the threats asserted: Were the statements of threat accurate? Did the Iraqi government have the capability and intention to carry them out? The second is the adequacy of the threats to compel military action: Were the threats to vital or less-than-vital American interests?

At the time, the U.S. government made two interrelated claims about the Iraqi government of Saddam Hussein that it maintained constituted an adequate threat. The first was Iraq's possession of weapons of mass destruction (WMD): chemical and biological weapons and an alleged program to produce nuclear weapons. Given the instability of the Iraqi government and its hostility to the United States, these were asserted to pose a threat to American soil. The second was Iraq's purported ties to terrorism—and specifically to Al Qaeda—and thus an Iraqi link to the war on terrorism. The link between the two justifications was the possibility that the Iraqi government would supply its WMD to terrorist organizations like Al Qaeda.

When war was being contemplated, the truth of these assertions was unknown, and evidence for both their truth and falsity was and continues to be debated. Although both lines of argumentation have since been essentially discredited, policymakers were generally given the benefit of the doubt, and most Americans at least *believed* the assertions to be true (an assumption that has come to be widely questioned). In that case, did removing the threat rise to the level of a vital interest? Put another way, would Americans and their interests have been so compromised by the possession of WMD by Iraq and ties to terrorism to justify the recourse to force? What happens to the presumption of vitality of interest if one justification was true and the other false: Iraq had WMD but no ties to terrorism, or it had ties to terrorists but no WMD? What if both were false?

Were we justified in invading Iraq? What do you think?

This definition contains two related elements. The first is procedural: "the ways in which conflicts . . . are resolved." The second is substantive: what "scarce resources" have to be allocated and who gets those resources. The two dimensions are related both because the nature and importance of the resource may determine the procedures that are employed to decide the outcome, and because the procedures may influence or prejudice the substantive outcome. Generally, the less important the issue (in interest terms discussed earlier, major or peripheral interests), the more likely a state will be either to submit the matter to some outside authority to reach a judgment for an outcome or to accept a less than optimal outcome. When a matter is of the highest importance to the state (a survival or vital interest), then the state is likely to invoke its own sovereign authority to maintain as much control over the outcome as it can.

The unique possession by states of vital interests produces a political structure in which state sovereignty is the central feature in determining political outcomes. As already noted, sovereignty has opposite effects: within states it provides the basis for producing a political order; among states sovereignty precludes the formation of political processes that can authoritatively allocate values in areas deemed vital by the contending parties. The result is international anarchy—at least in dealing with matters of interests vital to the state. As long as states retain vital interests, this essential anarchy will remain the central procedural aspect of international politics.

In the situation of anarchical international relations, states achieve their interests to the extent they have the ability to do so—through a process sometimes known as *self-help*. Since the need to resolve important international political problems generally occurs when vital interests are involved and scarcity exists, the outcome is by definition likely to be that one or all parties must accept less of a condition or property than they previously deemed vital. Determining outcomes is thus an exercise in the application of power.

Power is an elusive and highly controversial concept, but it is a central characteristic of the realist paradigm. Its elusiveness comes from trying to operationalize and measure power in order to predict who will prevail when states clash in the international arena. This difficulty is discussed in Amplification 2.2. If the exercise of power is central to an understanding of international relations, then it clearly would be desirable to be able to observe the basis of power so that we could predict in individual situations which party to a dispute could apply power to the other and thus prevail. This has led to a good deal of effort being expended on trying to develop ways to measure the power of states, none of which has proven entirely satisfactory in predicting political outcomes.

Power is also a controversial concept because one of the most obvious and prominent forms that power takes in the international arena (and within some states) is military force. Those who oppose the use of military force thus find themselves in opposition to a system in which power, including military power, is a central, even normal, way to resolve differences. The key to a more tranquil, peaceful world lies in the abrogation of power as the basis of politics in this view.

Part of the controversy is definitional as well. Although some analysts would say our definition really describes influence rather than power, we can adopt a common and straightforward definition of power: *the ability to get someone to do something he or she would not otherwise do*. The definition skirts the controversy over measurement of power by not specifying what power *is* so much as describing the *effects* of the application of power.

The definition highlights two major characteristics of a power situation. First, it says that power is not an attribute possessed by parties so much as it is a relationship between an entity seeking to exercise power and another entity seeking to resist the

Amplification 2.2

MEASURING POWER

Although the concept of power is pervasive as a means to describe international relations, efforts to measure it have remained largely elusive. As noted in the main text, finding ways adequately to measure and thus to be able to compare the power that different states possess would be highly desirable because it would make the outcomes of interactions between states much more predictable than they are in fact.

There are two difficulties involved. The first is finding physical measures that adequately describe the abilities of states to influence one another. A concerted effort has been to try to find concrete, physical measures, such as the size or sophistication of countries' armed forces or the productivity of states' industrial bases, that should indicate which is the more powerful country in any head-to-head confrontation. The problem is that such measures work only part of the time. There is, for instance, no physical measurement to compare national capabilities that would lead to the conclusion that North Vietnam had any chance of defeating the United States in a war, but they certainly did.

The second problem is that measures have difficulty getting at the psychological dimension of will and commitment that people may possess. How can an outside observer determine, for instance, when a clash of interests is clearly more important to one party to a dispute than it is to the other (at least before the fact)? Once again, the Vietnam War is illustrative. The outcome of that war—unification of the country—was clearly more important to the North Vietnamese and their southern allies than its avoidance was to the United States and the population of South Vietnam. This is clear in retrospect; it was not at all clear before and even during the conduct of hostilities. Being able to see clearly after the fact is of very little comfort to the policymaker. Having measures that accurately predict the future is a far greater value.

application of that power. A power relationship is commonly applied through the issuance of a threat (a promise to do something harmful unless what is demanded is complied with) by one party against the other. The outcome depends on the action of the threatened party. If the threatened party believes the threatening party both can (has the capability) and will (has the credibility) to carry out the threat in the face of noncompliance, the threatened party may comply. If, however, the threatened party doubts either the will or ability of the threatening party to carry out the threat, it may conclude differently. At any rate, whether power is successfully applied is a mutual matter in the relationship between the parties, not something simple and concrete like a comparison of the sizes of military machines or industrial capacity (although these are clearly relevant when deciding if the threatening party has the wherewithal to carry out the threat).

The other characteristic of a power relationship is that it is situation-specific. What this means is that the application of power does not occur in an abstract sense but within very specific situations. It is important to recognize this fact because the vagaries and special circumstances surrounding any particular relationship may influence how a power relationship plays out, sometimes in unpredictable ways.

An example helps illustrate these characteristics. In the early 1970s, the African country of Uganda was ruled by a particularly harsh and objectionable ruler, Idi Amin Dada. Amin, a sergeant in the British colonial force who declared himself a general when Uganda achieved independence in 1962, had seized power from the postcolonial government in 1971. He had as many as three hundred thousand Ugandans of tribal origins other than his own killed, and in 1972 forty-five thousand Asian residents expelled, who had formed the backbone of the country's commercial system. As the country drifted toward chaos, the United States withdrew its diplomatic personnel from Uganda in 1973. Despite this, Amin continued to provide gratuitous advice to President Richard M. Nixon in a series of letters advising Nixon about how he should handle his Watergate difficulties.

The United States—as well as a number of other countries—wanted Amin removed from the Ugandan presidency. Since Amin was not amenable to leaving, this meant that power would have to be applied to get Amin to do something he clearly would not otherwise do. The problem was, what kind of power did the United States have over the dictator? By any objective measure, the United States was overwhelmingly more powerful than Uganda, but was that power relevant to the specific situation of overthrowing him? Was there some form of leverage the United States could apply to remove Amin? Was American power relevant in this case?

The answer turned out to be that it was not. To try to achieve its goal, the United States threatened and implemented an embargo on the importation of Ugandan coffee into the United States (a prohibition ignored by the American firms that bought Ugandan coffee until they were caught violating the sanctions), but the volume was not enough to cause Amin to step down. In the end, Ugandan rebels, assisted by the neighboring Tanzanian armed forces, which possessed far less absolute but much more relevant and believable power than the Americans, finally managed to drive Amin out of power and into exile in April 1979.

It is the combination of capability and will that makes power effective in individual situations. In the Ugandan example, for instance, the United States clearly had the military capability to overthrow the Ugandan regime (or for that matter, obliterate it with nuclear weapons). What it lacked was the credible will to apply that force in a situation that was at most annoying but clearly did not rise to the level of vital interests. There may be some parallel between this experience and the American effort to remove Iraq's Saddam Hussein from power, a prospect explored in Amplification 2.3 later in this chapter.

In order to exercise power, however, the state must be capable of carrying out threats. Doing this requires possessing the *instruments of power*. In conventional, traditional terms, these instruments are divided into three categories: diplomatic (or political), economic, and military power. Diplomatic power encompasses qualities such as the persuasiveness of a country's diplomatic corps, the attractiveness of the country's political profile, and the ability to use the other implements to back up political rhetoric. Economic power is the use of economic rewards and deprivations for compliance with a country's demands. Military power is the threat or actual use of military threats or applications to achieve the country's goals. As noted in Chapter 1, one of the reasons for designating the United States as the sole remaining superpower is that it is the only country with significant assets in each of these categories, although the characteristics of power noted here do not mean its power is unchallengeable in individual situations.

Some authors, as suggested earlier, believe the list of instruments should be extended in the contemporary environment. A leading candidate is informational power, the ability to control and manipulate the amount and quality of information an adversary has in a power situation. Elements of this power include information-gathering ability (intelligence) and manipulation (interrupting information sources and transmission or distorting that flow). An exotic form, *cyberwar*, attempts to disrupt and control computer systems and their ability to collect, analyze, disseminate, or even retain information.

In an anarchical system, power and politics are intimately related. Politics, after all, is about who gets what in terms of scarce resources, and by definition, scarcity means that some parties will have to do what they otherwise prefer not to do. In the absence of authorities who can decide on allocations, the parties must help themselves through the application of power, including the use of military force on occasion.

PARADIGM SUMMARY

With these basic concepts and relationships established, we can summarize the "rules of the road" that define the realist paradigm and how international relations are conducted in a system where its rules are paramount. While a growing number of people decry the paradigm and its implications, it remains the basis on which a great deal of international relations are conducted today. Moreover, the paradigm is especially applicable to thinking about matters of national security and remains dominant as an operational roadmap for those charged with the development and conduct of national security policy in most parts of the world.

The realist paradigm begins with state sovereignty as its basic value, meaning there can ultimately be no higher authority than the state in determining what happens to the state. The absence of a higher authority is not coincidental but is the direct result of the possession of vital interests by states (but not other political entities). These vital interests are matters of such importance to the state that it will not willingly compromise on them and will use all means available, up to and including military force, to ensure that they are honored. The two concepts, sovereignty and vital interests, require and reinforce one another. The prosecution of vital interests in an anarchical system precludes the possibility that a superior authority could—possibly capriciously—compromise a vital interest of the state. Sovereignty provides the conceptual bedrock to deny that possibility, and it is not coincidental at all that the governments of countries are among the strongest and most consistent champions of sovereignty.

The government of the United States has been and continues to be among the world's staunchest defenders of state sovereignty, and at the bottom of almost all its defenses of the concept is the insistence that no outside power should be allowed to create conditions to which Americans do not want to and should not be subjected. Although this insistence often puts the United States in awkward, even embarrassing, international situations, it is the fear that a dilution of sovereignty will permit the violation of American vital interests that provides the politically inviolable base for U.S. policy in this area.

In a world of plenty, the state of international anarchy would not be a particular problem because states would rarely come into direct conflict with one another over who gets what. In the real world, of course, scarcity, not abundance, is often the case, meaning that political processes to determine outcomes of disagreement are necessary. Sometimes those conflicts can be resolved peacefully and cooperatively, sometimes not. When these situations involve the vital interests of states, those states are generally unwilling to submit them to bodies that could exercise jurisdiction and instead rely on more informal means of conflict resolution to settle differences. Settlements in conditions of scarcity mean that some or all of the parties to a given dispute must accept less than they would have preferred—in other words, do something they would prefer not to do. Because of this, international politics inevitably are power politics.

In a world of sovereign states interacting through power politics, the state succeeds to the extent it can succeed—that is, through self-help. In order for one state to get others to do what it wants but the others do not, that state must possess the ability, in specific situations, to convince or compel other states to act in ways that serve its national interests. A state must, in other words, possess power to succeed.

Power comes in a variety of guises. The most common, but not only, forms are political or diplomatic power, economic power, and military power. While the applicability of any particular form of power will vary depending on the situation and both the ability and willingness of a state to use its power to gain compliance with its positions, generally speaking, the more power a state has, the more successful it will be in achieving its ends. In the anarchical situation of international politics, among the forms of power that must be available is military force. Thus, the international system ultimately is an environment in which the threat of or recourse to force is a "normal" activity some of the time and in which states that will succeed must possess armed forces "to prepare for and fight the country's wars."

CRITIQUES AND ANOMALIES
OF THE REALIST PARADIGM

Many analysts decry the sets of conditions produced by the realist paradigm, and point both to anomalies that it produces in the interactions among states and to questions about its continuing empirical adequacy in describing international reality. To the critics, there is simply too much that occurs in the world that cannot be explained by realism, and thus the day-to-day debate about national security policy must be expanded beyond realism.

An exhaustive criticism of the realist paradigm goes beyond present intent. For our purposes, the criticisms can be viewed from two perspectives. One of these argues that the principles underlying the realist paradigm, and especially state sovereignty, have never been as strictly adhered to in fact as they are in principle—in other words, the paradigm is only partially accurate in describing the operation of the world system. The other perspective maintains that adherence to the paradigm produces a flawed international system—in other words, the paradigm's effects are pernicious. In both cases, the conclusion drawn by the critics is that the international system should be reformed on principles other than those on which the paradigm is based.

Critiques

Because state sovereignty lies at the heart of the Westphalian system, it is the realist concept that draws the greatest negative attention. The principle of state sovereignty creates an international institutional setting of purposive anarchy that necessitates a world of power politics and guarantees that international relations will emphasize conflict rather than cooperation. The critics maintain that state sovereignty has never been as absolute as its extreme representation would suggest. However, the more closely one hews to the practice of absolute sovereignty, the more pernicious the effects are within the international realm. The basic underlying theme of this critique is that realism is *empirically* inadequate to describe the world, a position increasingly held in academic and policy circles.

Although early political theorists like Hobbes and Bodin favored something like the absolute sovereign powers of the state as a way to justify the power of monarchs. The suggestion that the principle of sovereignty creates an impenetrable state that is unaffected or unlimited by outside forces is not, and never has been, more than a fiction. States interfere in the political lives of other states all the time, and the behavior of states is limited by international regulations (usually ones that they have explicitly agreed to be limited by) on a regular basis. Moreover, contemporary forces such as economic globalization and the impact of the telecommunications revolution are making state boundaries increasingly porous and state control over everything that happens within its jurisdiction increasingly difficult to maintain. Critics of sovereignty argue it is empirically false to maintain otherwise. Moreover, important trends in international relations suggest that sovereignty will continue to erode in fact, if not in principle. The staunch defense of absolute sovereignty is, in other words, a losing battle.

As sovereignty erodes, so does the salience of some of the operating principles of the paradigm, and this is nowhere truer than in areas related to national security and the use of force. It is, for instance, not at all clear that some uses of military force to achieve national interests are as acceptable today as they were a century or even a decade ago. Wars between states have virtually ceased. All members of the United Nations renounced their right to declare war as part of their conditions for joining the world body, and although that does not mean that force has disappeared, no state has formally declared war on another state since World War II. As the international response to Iraq's 1990 invasion and conquest of Kuwait clearly demonstrated, the aggressive use of force across borders is no longer acceptable behavior. The issue of acceptability is, of course, not universal and is related to power. Iraq's action was deemed an unacceptable act of aggression against Kuwaiti sovereignty and was reversed. The failure of American efforts to influence the policies of Iraq after 1990 (see Amplification 2.3), which eventuated in the American invasion and conquest of Iraq in 2003, was never framed in terms of sovereignty.

Amplification 2.3

THE LIMITS OF POWER: DEALING WITH SADDAM

With the possible exception of Fidel Castro, there is no leader in recent memory who vexed American policy and policymakers more than Saddam Hussein of Iraq prior to his capture and incarceration. He became a major irritant when he invaded and annexed Kuwait in 1990, forcing the United States to take the leadership in forming the coalition that evicted the Iraqis from Kuwait in 1991. After the Persian Gulf War fighting ended, a series of demands were placed upon Hussein that, by and large, he refused to comply with. A review of the difficulty the United States had influencing Saddam Hussein helps illustrate the limits of power.

Under these circumstances, U.S. policy toward Iraq and Saddam Hussein had at least three goals, all of which the Iraqi leader refused to accept. The first and most obvious goal was his physical removal from power. The second was the abandonment of Iraq's program of developing weapons of mass destruction (WMD), including comprehensive inspection of suspected WMD production facilities. The third was to leave the Kurdish and Shiite minorities, who rose to overthrow Hussein with American encouragement in 1991, alone.

The problem was how to force Hussein to comply with these conditions, which was a question of having the appropriate instruments of power in this particular situation. To try to bring Hussein down before the ultimate invasion of Iraq, the United States attempted to employ the diplomatic/political instrument of power, sponsoring international condemnation of the Iraqi regime in international forums like the United Nations and supporting political alternatives to Hussein in Iraq (the Bush administration, for instance, proposed $92 million in aid to political alternatives in 2001). Economically, the United States was the mainstay behind economic sanctions designed to gain compliance with the WMD ban. Militarily, the United States and Britain (France previously participated but has dropped out) enforced the so-called no-fly zones over the Kurdish and Shiite regions of the country under the banner of Operations Northern and Southern Watch.

The difficulty was that, with the partial exception of the application of the military instrument of power in defense of the Kurds and Shiites, none of the attempts to apply power worked. International condemnations were ineffective, and there was growing opposition to continuing them. Hussein had most of his opponents killed or chased into exile, making the identification and nurturing of "moderate" alternatives difficult. The economic sanctions, as is often the case, caused well-publicized hardship to innocent women and children rather than to the leadership (the so-called "principle" of punishing the innocent), did not force compliance, and were increasingly opposed by the international community, which wanted them lifted. Moreover, the sanctions made smuggling into Iraq rampant. Operations Northern and Southern Watch kept the Kurds and Shiites reasonably safe, but they were open-ended commitments that, if abandoned, would almost certainly have resulted in swift, savage suppression of those they are designed to protect. Moreover, wider bombing campaigns such as Operation Desert Fox in 1999 failed to change Hussein's behavior.

The relationship between Saddam Hussein and the most powerful country in the world during the 1990s and up to 2003 demonstrated clearly the limits of power. By any measure, the United States was more powerful than Iraq, yet American power proved inappropriate in forcing the defiant Iraqi leader to do things he did not want to do but that the United States would have had him do. Ultimately, only the invasion and conquest of Iraq provided adequate power for the United States to impose its will on Hussein.

The other major manifestation of the realist paradigm that is under question is the use of vital interests as the benchmark against which to measure when force should and should not be employed. This assault is largely the result of changes in the international threat environment since the end of the Cold War, and particularly the result of what I call the *interest–threat mismatch*—the situation in which important interests and threats do not coincide.

During the Cold War, when the realist paradigm was clearly the dominant worldview of policymakers on both sides of the conflict, there was no mismatch: vital interests (national survival, for instance) were threatened, and thus the idea that force would be threatened or used in East–West confrontations provided clear guidance for the development, deployment, and potential employment of force. Interests, and threats to those interests, were clearly aligned and coincided with one another.

The situation changed radically after the implosion of the Communist half of the Cold War. The important interests of the United States remain what they were before: American homeland security and a free and democratic Western Europe and Japan with which the United States can engage in commerce and political relations, for instance. What changed was that those vital interests were essentially no longer threatened. There is no Communist menace hanging over Western Europe; the West Europeans move steadily to incorporate more and more of formerly Communist Europe into institutions such as the European Union. Thus, where there were American vital interests, there was no meaningful threat that would justify the use of force—important interests and threats were misaligned.

There were and are, however, situations in the world that are threatening to the United States or the international system more generally. For instance, a whole series of internal wars rage in parts of the developing world, notably in Africa and parts of Asia. Indonesia, the world's fourth most populous country, has several ongoing conflicts the basic purpose of which is secession from the Indonesian republic. In Africa, the HIV-AIDS pandemic has reached such enormous proportions that in 2000 then President Clinton declared it to be a national security concern, an emphasis that the Bush administration continued through the personal concern of former Secretary of State Colin Powell.

What these and other examples of world problems share is that essentially none of them reach to the level of being vital interests that would activate the American security system within the realist framework. In terms of interests at stake, they are mostly favorable world order or value questions at the intensity level of major or, in most cases, peripheral interests to the United States. Threats do not measure up to important interests.

The interest–threat mismatch takes form from this assessment of the post–Cold War environment: *the most important American interests in the world are hardly threatened, and the threats that do exist are largely tangential (are hardly interesting).* In these circumstances, if the realist paradigm is used as the sole (or main) criterion to determine when or if the United States will employ force in the world, the result will be paralytic because hardly any situations will meet the criterion of engaging vital interests and thus justifying force. During the Cold War, the realist paradigm was the hawk's standard because it counseled large and robust forces to deal with real threats to vital interests. In the post–Cold War world, that same paradigm turned the hawks into doves, since the paradigm directs noninvolvement with military force when vital interests are not threatened. The post–September 11 response to international terrorism, of course, realigns interests and threats in that area of concern. Whether this produces a Cold War–like coincidence of interests and threats across the board or a narrower coincidence in a more general environment of mismatch remains to be seen. Moreover, it is not clear to what extent military power is the appropriate instrument to deal with this threat.

An example may demonstrate how a part of the changing environment affects the relevance of the realist paradigm. One of the major sources of violence and instability in the world is the series of very bloody internal (civil) wars occurring in parts of the developing world. A number of these conflicts (e.g., Somalia, Bosnia, Sierra Leone, East Timor) have gone beyond the ability of the countries involved to resolve, resulting in great suffering to the affected civilian populations (casualty rates in these conflicts often approach 90 percent civilian). The gruesome nature of these conflicts has led to international pleas for involvement with military forces designed to stop the fighting and suffering under the guise of something like *humanitarian intervention.* These conflicts generally occur in places where important American interests are absent, and the application of the realist paradigm would suggest that the United States remain aloof. The only way to justify the employment of force is either to ignore or expand the paradigm or to try to rationalize that heretofore less-than-vital interests are now more important (e.g., "Macedonia is important to the United States because it is important to American allies").

The salience of the realist paradigm in describing reality is not the only source of opposition by critics. To a large number of interested observers, the paradigm is objectionable both because of the activities it legitimizes and the kinds of viewpoints it deemphasizes. The most obvious objectionable activity is the acceptance, even promotion, of military force as a normal form of state action; the most obvious example of what it does not emphasize is cooperative behavior among states.

The realist paradigm legitimizes the recourse to armed violence as a means to achieve state interests by acknowledging military force as one of the normal instruments of power. In addition, the approach's emphasis on observation of "reality" (actual behavior of states) notes that states (and groups within states) do in fact occasionally resort to the use of force to achieve their ends and that in some cases they succeed in achieving their ends by doing so—the ends justify the means. Many realists would contend, for instance, that the attempt by the idealists to downplay and even ignore the role of military forces between the world wars contributed to the destabilization of the 1930s that ended with World War II. Moreover, given the predatory nature of some states (Bush's "axis of evil" is an example), the absence of force is a virtual invitation for states to take advantage of the militarily disadvantaged.

Opponents of realism contend that it is the very structure of an international system based in the realist paradigm that creates—even promotes—an emphasis on military force and the recourse to war. The villain, of course, is sovereignty-induced anarchy that leaves international politics a Hobbesian "war of all against all." In this view, the solution to the "problem" of war is institutional reform of the international system that creates orderliness through institutions that can enforce the peace and remove the vigilantism of a realist order. In order to accomplish this, the conceptual victim must be state sovereignty, replaced with ultimate authority in the hands either of a superior entity (e.g., a world government or the like) or returned to the people—popular sovereignty. At any rate, the object is the sovereign state, which the opponents of war argue must be fundamentally reformed before peace can be instituted and enforced.

In addition to its alleged warlike implications, other critics point out, the principle of state sovereignty also tends to emphasize noncooperative rather than cooperative behavior in the relations among states more generally by erecting barriers to interaction across state boundaries. For instance, the sovereign independence of states, it is argued, runs counter to the growing globalization of the world's economy by erecting physical barriers to the movement of people and goods across sovereign boundaries. This argument has particular salience in an age of terrorism when the protection of boundaries is an important part of protecting citizens from attack, a proposition we will investigate in terms of its national security implications. Because examples of international cooperation are numerous and growing, the inability of strict realism to explain these exceptions to its anarchical, conflictual description of the world raises questions about its adequacy as an intellectual ordering device.

This line of objection can be put in a more general and theoretical form. Realism as an approach tends to emphasize the conflictual elements of international relations and to downplay evidence of international cooperation. While conflict is clearly an element of international relations, so too is international cooperation. There are certainly aspects of international interactions that are zero-sum (one party loses what the other party gains), but there are equally positive-sum situations (where both parties can gain). Those critical of realism argue that realists dismiss the cooperative aspects too often and that an approach placing great emphasis on cooperation not only results in a more accurate description of international relations but also leads to the promotion of a greater level of cooperation and thus enhanced international tranquility.

In some ways, this difference goes back to the disagreement in the philosophies of Thomas Hobbes and John Locke (among others) about the nature of man and society. The realists portray a more Hobbesian world (indeed, some of the early realists explicitly included their assessment of man's base nature as flawed as part of the philosophical underpinning of their theorizing), whereas those who emphasize cooperation are manifesting a more Lockean philosophy (wherein people enter into society out of a positive desire for association with their fellows). In more contemporary terms, the debate can be couched in terms of which is the dominant international reality, globalization (cooperation) or geopolitics (conflict), or some combination—which of course is the underlying theme of this book.

Anomalies

There are also anomalies in an international system built on the philosophical basis of realism but that in practice does not precisely conform in its operation to the realist mold. Two examples, one American and one Russian, illustrate both the paradigm and its inconsistencies and difficulties.

As noted earlier, the United States is one of the staunchest defenders of the principle of state sovereignty in the world (along with the People's Republic of China). The political and philosophical base of this strongly held position is the belief that Americans and the United States more generally should not be subject to imposition or control by foreigners and that, as a result, the United States should resist international attempts to place the United States under regimes that restrict the freedom of action of the country or its people.

Regardless of its merits, this position often forces the United States into a politically uncomfortable position in the world—often in opposition to the vast majority of states and in the company of states with which we do not particularly like to be associated. Invariably, these situations involve American resistance or refusal to join international agreements that limit the right of signatories to engage in certain behavior (and are most ominous when the treaty includes provisions for international enforcement—a direct abrogation of sovereignty). Ironically, the agreements to which the United States objects are often proposed by the U.S. government itself (either the permanent bureaucracy or a previous administration), indicating substantial disagreement within the United States itself on the sovereignty issue.

The Bush administration's withdrawal of support for the Kyoto treaty on global warming in 2001 is a contemporary example of this situation. The treaty was negotiated and supported by the Clinton administration, which had announced its intention to join the international regime created by the accord. When he entered office, President Bush announced his administration's withdrawal from the agreement. Bush did not cite sovereignty directly but instead argued against what he called unequal and unfair obligations the United States would be forced to bear under treaty provisions and its preference for voluntary rather than mandatory compliance enforced internationally. The United States stands virtually alone among developed countries in its position and has earned a good deal of international criticism for its unilateralist stance.

The anomaly extends to a number of other issues. During the latter 1940s, the United States helped sponsor two important treaties establishing universal standards of human rights, the Universal Declaration on Human Rights and the Convention on Genocide. The Universal Declaration, in particular, was based largely on the American Bill of Rights, but the U.S. Senate refused to provide advice and consent on either document until the 1990s on the ground that they infringed on the rights of the American government to behave in ways prohibited by the agreements. In more contemporary, national security–related areas, the United States is one of the few countries that refuses to sign the international treaty banning land mines (which was originally proposed by a private American citizen) and the statute establishing a permanent war crimes tribunal, the International Criminal Court (ICC). In the latter case, the United States joins a handful of generally rogue states such as Myanmar and Iraq as the only states that refuse to accept the jurisdiction of the ICC.

The United States is not alone in being party to anomalies in the current system. Russia, which has acceded to the ICC, is waging an arguably genocidal campaign in the renegade province of Chechnya, which has been actively attempting to secede from the Russian Federation since the middle 1990s. The Russians have brutally repressed this movement, and war crimes have clearly been committed under orders that possibly go all the way to the top of the Russian political leadership. Yet, there have been no serious calls for an investigation of the situation by the international war crimes apparatus. Why? One reason is that Russia maintains the situation in Chechnya is purely an internal matter within the sovereign jurisdiction of the Russian government (and thus beyond the purview of any other authority). For another, Russia maintains its Muslim Chechen opponents are terrorists, since many of the "freedom fighters" waging the war allegedly are associated with the training regime that produced Al Qaeda terrorists (thus giving the Russians status as participants in the war against terrorism). Finally, Russia is also a large and powerful country that no one wishes to antagonize unnecessarily, so the position goes officially unchallenged.

The staunch American defense of sovereignty and the ambivalence Americans display when anomalous issues arise from its defense often confuse and mystify other countries, including both American friends and foes. Defying international norms in the name of defending American freedom of action is often equated with American unilateralism—a kind of disregard for the rest of the world. This was clearly the case in the early George W. Bush administration. Beyond reaction to the Kyoto convention, this was evident in 2001 regarding the administration's obdurately defended intention to field a national missile defense in the face of essentially universal opposition from abroad, in addition to opposition to the ICC and the land mines convention.

Defense of sovereign prerogative is also a politically partisan position in the United States, adding to international confusion. Although there are exceptions, the strongest advocates of protecting American sovereignty have tended to be conservative and Republican, whereas a willingness to subject the United States to sovereignty-restricting provisions of international agreements has tended to be more liberal and Democratic. On other than trade matters, the Democratic Party has been more internationalist than the Republicans, meaning there is a likelihood that the transition in control between the parties will continue to have a real impact on attitudes toward international issues with ramifications for American state sovereignty across time.

CONCLUSION: THE REALIST PARADIGM TODAY

Despite its limitations and the mounting criticism of it, realism remains the dominant organizational device by which the governments of sovereign states organize their approach to dealing with the world. The criticisms are, without doubt, growing. During the Cold War, these criticisms tended to be isolated within groups outside national governments—academics, liberal commentators, and members and advocates of NGOs, for example. Given the gravity of the task of managing international affairs in a world where the Soviet opponent was thoroughly committed to realist power politics, advocacies of ideas such as reducing the influence of sovereignty fell on mostly deaf ears, particularly among political decision makers responsible for protecting national interests in a dangerous world where the Soviet opponents were the ultimate realists. Communism could only be opposed in kind, according to the prevailing wisdom.

A less threatening, apparently more globalizing environment in the 1990s saw critical, less realist views become more acceptable in practice and in principle. At one level, the series of interventions in peacekeeping roles by UN-deputized forces represented an indirect assault on the notion of total sovereign control of territory. International agreements like the ban on land mines and the establishment of the permanent war crimes tribunal are more direct assaults, as they subjugate the rights of states to act unilaterally in the face of international norms. Some see this trend as a healthy maturing of international relations. Others see grave dangers in these erosions of state sovereignty and assaults on the structure of the Westphalian order. The Clinton administration was more receptive to change; the Bush administration has proven less so, a predilection reinforced after the terrorist incident of 2001 and responses to it.

Does the realist paradigm fit the new, evolving international order? Any direct, categorical answer will, of course, oversimplify a more complicated world order in which yes-no answers exclude the middle ground between them and result in a distortion of ongoing reality. Cold War realism may not be the perfect paradigm for a post–Cold War and post–September 11 world, but its basic structure has not disappeared. The fault line that began to emerge in 1989 raised questions about the continuing relevance of the paradigm; such criticism has been much less evident since 2001.

A remarkable example may illustrate the evolution of the realist paradigm. On June 29, 2001, Slobadan Milosevic, the former president of Yugoslavia, was extradited from Belgrade to the Hague in the Netherlands, where he faced charges of crimes against humanity as specified in the statute of the ICC, which had issued the indictment under which his extradition was carried out (since the ICC statute had not been ratified by enough states to come into permanent being at the time, the indictment came from the tribunal established specifically for Yugoslavia).

The extradition was the remarkable aspect of the event. Milosevic had been indicted in 1999 for his alleged participation in crimes against humanity committed against Albanian Kosovars in Kosovo in 1999. Although Milosevic was defeated in 2000 in his bid for reelection, it was widely believed that the indictment was symbolic and that any trial of Milosevic would have to be carried out in his absence (*in absentia*) because the Yugoslav government, which was not a signatory of the ICC statute, would protect him on the grounds that any attempt to arrest and extradite him would be a violation of Yugoslav sovereignty. This obstinacy flew in the face of widespread world opinion which regarded Milosevic as a war criminal—or at least believed he should face the charges against him. International economic sanctions against the country were put in place in 2000 to pressure the government into honoring the indictment.

So what changed the minds of members of the successor Yugoslav government of Vojislav Kostunica and caused them to turn over the former dictator to international authorities? The answer is that several factors, two of which bear mention, were involved and demonstrate the continuity and change of the new order.

The first was domestic and had the effect of eroding resistance to international demands for his surrender to international authorities. While many ethnic Serbs had denied the early charges of atrocities against the Kosovars ordered by the Milosevic government, evidence emerged in 2001 clearly showing that mass murders had been committed that could only be linked to the government in power at the time. Defense of Milosevic became much harder to sustain, and the defense of his freedom based in national sovereignty gradually eroded. In the end, fully 60 percent of the Serbian population of Yugoslavia favored extradition.

The other factor was international, the effect of the sanctions imposed by the international community because of the Yugoslav campaign in Kosovo. The people of Yugoslavia became more intolerant of the physical deprivation they were enduring as a result of the sanctions than they were committed to their sovereign control and protection of the former leader. The NATO allies promised the Kostunica government that economic penalties would be lifted as soon as Milosevic was turned over to authorities; it was hardly a day after he reached the Hague that economic assistance began to flow to Belgrade.

So which principle prevailed? Geopolitics or the new order of globalization? The answer is clearly both. The international norm was strengthened by the fact that Yugoslavia relented and allowed the dilution of some of its sovereign jurisdiction over a distinguished citizen, hardly a vindication of the realist paradigm. At the same time, what caused the international norm to succeed was the application of the economic instrument of power in a way that would make the most hardened realist proud.

SELECTED BIBLIOGRAPHY

Art, Robert A., and Kenneth N. Waltz. *The Use of Force: Military Power and International Politics* (6th ed.). Lanham, MD: Rowman and Littlefield, 2004.

Bodin, Jean. *Six Books on the Commonwealth*. Oxford, UK: Basil Blackwell, 1955.

Brodie, Bernard. *War and Politics*. New York: Macmillan, 1973.

Carr, E. H. *The Twenty Years' Crisis, 1919–1939*. London: Macmillan, 1939.

Cusimano, Mary Ann (Ed.). *Beyond Sovereignty*. New York: Bedford St. Martin's, 1999.

Fromkin, David. *The Independence of Nations*. New York: Praeger Special Studies, 1981.

Kegley, Charles W., Jr., and Gregory A. Raymond. *Exorcising the Ghost of Westphalia: Building World Order in the New Millennium*. Upper Saddle River, NJ: Prentice Hall, 2002.

Machiavelli, Niccolò. *The Prince*. Irving, TX: University of Dallas Press, 1984.

Morgenthau, Hans. *Politics Among Nations* (6th ed., rev.: Kenneth W. Thompson). New York: Alfred A. Knopf, 1985.

Nuechterlein, Donald E. *America Recommitted: United States National Interests in a Reconstructed World*. Lexington: University of Kentucky Press, 1991.

Schelling, Thomas C. *Arms and Influence*. New Haven, CT: Yale University Press, 1966.

Snow, Donald M., and Eugene Brown. *International Relations: The Changing Contours of Power*. New York: Longman, 2000.

Snyder, Jack. "One World, Rival Theories." *Foreign Policy* (November/December 2004), 52–62.

Thucydides. *The History of the Peloponnesian Wars*. New York: Penguin Books, 1954.

Waltz, Kenneth. *Man, the State, and War: A Theoretical Analysis*. New York: Columbia University Press, 1959.

CHAPTER 3

The American Experience

PREVIEW

The extent to which a country embraces a purely geopolitical, realist orientation toward the world or some alternative is influenced by the generalized historical experience the country has had. For most of American history, that experience has been primarily positive, with low levels and qualities of threat that make the current high-threat environment all the more distinct. This chapter begins by identifying general influences on the American experience, then looks at the question historically, designating and describing three parts of the national security experience. The chapter concludes with suggestions of how the past may influence the present and future.

As it is in all countries, the American attitude toward its security is conditioned by its historical experience and the "lessons" that experience appears to have taught. For some countries, the experience has been harsh. It is, for instance, impossible for the citizens of any country on the northern European plain not to have some historically based fear of a possible invasion against its territory from one direction or another and to view matters of national security very seriously as a result. At the other end of the spectrum, a country like Japan that successfully isolated itself physically from the rest of the world for hundreds of years has an equally distinctive worldview and perception of what constitutes security.

The United States is no exception to this effect of history. Although the American experience is shorter than that of the traditional European and Asian powers, it has been conditioned by a series of factors that are both historic and physical. The result of American history has been a generally positive view of the world and the security of the American place in it that did not require a great deal of emphasis or continuing effort on matters of national security until World War II and its aftermath. Americans have felt secure for most of their history as a country. This general sense of tranquility has certainly accentuated the sense of insecurity most Americans have experienced since September 11, 2001.

We divide the American experience with national security concerns into three basic periods. Following a discussion of basic, underlying, conditioning factors that help shape the American worldview, we begin with the formative period, from the beginning of the republic in the eighteenth century through World War II, a period of relatively low, episodic American involvement in international affairs, including concerns over national security. The second period encompasses the Cold War, when the United States was thrown literally into the middle of the geopolitical fray as one of the two major actors in the international system and had to learn to act in that environment. We conclude the chapter with a discussion of the third period, the contemporary system, and the impact of the two major fault lines on the ongoing period. Our discussion includes consideration of how the current situation resembles aspects of the formative or the Cold War system.

CONDITIONING FACTORS
IN THE AMERICAN TRADITION

At least three factors stand out as important influences on the way Americans have come to view questions of defense and national security. Alternative lists could undoubtedly be constructed, but these influences are the essential American lack of a sense of history, particularly shared history; the unique American geographical endowment, which both isolated the United States from hostile others and provided the country with abundant resources that nurtured and permitted its isolation; and the country's Anglo-Saxon heritage, which affected Americans' earliest political attitudes.

American Ahistoricism

It is not unfair to typify the American people as basically ahistorical in their general attitude. This ahistoricism has several bases. One is that the American experience is fairly brief when compared to the historical experience of the major European and Asian counterparts. While the territory that occupies the United States was inhabited for thousands of years by native Americans, most of those Indians did not keep a systematic history, and most Americans do not share a sense of ethnicity or history with these natives. Rather, American history, as most Americans perceive it, is a little less than four hundred years old, and it is not even a history shared by most current Americans or their ancestors. The pattern of American population settlement has been in immigrant waves, and this means relatively few Americans can trace their own roots back to the beginnings of the American experience. It is, for instance, no coincidence that there are no Vietnamese Americans who are members of the Daughters of the American Revolution, and the same can be said for many other Americans whose ancestors had not immigrated to these shores when the "shot heard round the world" was fired in Massachusetts in April 1775.

This lack of historical experience has not been an altogether bad thing. Most Americans came to the United States either to escape some form of tyranny or calamity in their native lands or with the hope of becoming part of the greater prosperity that the United States appeared to offer. As a result, there has been a greater sense of optimism in this country than is present in many more established cultures where the historical record offers a greater balance of positive and negative legacies. More pointedly, with the exception of some aspects of the Civil War, the United States has no national tragedy that mars the national consciousness and tempers our optimism in the way, for instance, that the Battle of Kosovo in 1389 has tainted Serbian history (after losing the battle to the Ottoman Turks, Serbia fell under foreign control until the early twentieth century).

American ahistoricism contributes to the American sense of exceptionalism and thus to American attitudes toward national security in a couple of ways. When combined with the fact and perception of American physical isolation from the world, the result has been a positive self-image about the United States and its military experience. On a general level, this perception of success extends to the American attitude toward war and matters of national security. Americans have historically viewed themselves as winners both at war and at peace. The contemporary revival of interest in America's most successful—and cherished—military experience, World War II, is emblematic of this attitude. The general ahistoricism also allows Americans to ignore less glorious aspects of the military experience, such as our performance in the War of 1812 (in which the United States won decisively exactly one land battle, at New Orleans, fought two weeks after the peace treaty was signed). This general attitude of success has made acceptance of the outcome of the Vietnam conflict all the more difficult, just as the territorial attacks by the September 11 terrorists have assaulted our sense of isolation and invulnerability.

Americans have also liked to portray themselves as an essentially pacific people, slow to anger but capable of vanquishing any foe once aroused. The premise underlying this belief is the idea that peace is the normal and preferred condition and war is an abnormality that is thrust upon us and that we must dispatch. The Japanese sneak attack at Pearl Harbor that dragged a reluctant United States into World War II is symbolic of this conviction, as has been the introduction of terrorism to our shores. When we are victimized, we become Yamamoto's "sleeping giant," reference to which was made in Chapter 1.

Many outsiders, as well as Native Americans, would of course contest both the notion of American passivity and the need to be provoked into violence. It is hard, for instance, to argue that most of the wars against the Indians of the plains and American West were "thrust" upon the United States, and the Spanish, who had already agreed to all of our terms when we declared war on them in 1898, would certainly question the reactive nature of the Americans in that situation. During the course of American history, the United States has fought six major wars (the Revolution, the Civil War, World Wars I and II, the Korean War, and the Vietnam War) and four minor wars (the War of 1812, the Mexican War, the Spanish-American War, and the Persian Gulf War). When one adds more minor engagements that do not qualify as wars (it is hard to know how to classify the campaign against Iraq since 2003 in these terms), the number of times Americans have taken up arms in anger rises to around 200, hardly the clearest evidence of peacefulness unless one is prepared to argue each instance was a response to an injustice.

Accident of Geography

Geography blessed the United States in at least two distinctly benign ways. First, the physical location of the United States between two of the world's great oceans made it virtually an island, at least as far as potential foreign incursions from Europe or Asia were concerned. When combined with comparatively weak or friendly countries on the northern or southern borders of the country, the result has been a condition of effective physical invulnerability for much of American history. With the exception of Pancho Villa's raids into the Southwest in the second decade of the twentieth century and a few submarine incursions during World War II along the West Coast, the forty-eight contiguous states (the continental United States, or CONUS) were safe from the danger of physical harm from 1814, when the British left at the end of the War of 1812, until 1957, when the successful testing of a Soviet intercontinental ballistic missile (ICBM) made the United States vulnerable to nuclear missile attacks. The only other sources of American physical vulnerability have come when the United States has expanded beyond the continental mass (e.g., Hawaii) or added foreign colonies (e.g., the Philippines).

The other part of the geographic legacy is resource abundance. The American continental land mass was blessed in two ways. First, the farmland in the central United States—some of the best in the world—allowed the United States to produce enough food for itself (and surpluses for export) without any necessary recourse to foreign sources. Second, the United States also possessed adequate supplies both of mineral wealth (e.g., iron ore, copper) and energy (e.g., coal, petroleum, natural gas) to allow it to proceed through most of the industrialization process without the need to rely on foreign sources of natural resources.

The result of both these geographic factors was to produce, as part of the American worldview, an essential independence and sense of invulnerability that set the country apart from most other countries of the world, most of which were physically vulnerable, foreign resource dependent, or both. The United States thus had to spend little time or effort framing its basic needs in national security terms. Absent the need to defend American territory from invading enemies, most uses of American force have been expeditionary, sending forces overseas either to defend some American interest (e.g., U.S. colonies) or to aid a besieged country somewhere in the world. At the same time, there was no need to prepare to protect access to natural resources or food supplies from vulnerable foreign sources. Effectively, the result was that the United States had, for most of its history, no compelling need to form a national security strategy to protect it from the vagaries of a world that it could largely ignore if it chose to do so.

These unique geographic advantages began to diminish by the middle of the twentieth century. The Pearl Harbor attack and the Japanese conquest of the Philippines demonstrated that an extended United States was no longer physically invulnerable. Soviet missile capability made that vulnerability more dramatic, and advances in telecommunications and transportation have produced arguable American vulnerabilities to things such as terrorist attacks or cyberwar, a vulnerability dramatically brought home in 2001 and a continuing source of concern.

American resource independence has also been eroded. Increased demand for energy resources such as petroleum at low prices has made the United States dependent on foreign supplies, with strong and controversial national security consequences in places such as the Persian Gulf, as discussed in Amplification 3.1. At the same time, the development and use of more exotic materials that are unavailable in the United States, such as titanium for jet engines, has also reduced resource independence. The desire for exotic foodstuffs, such as year-round access to fresh fruits and vegetables, has made the United States an agricultural importer as well. The reversal of American long-time isolation has made exposure to vulnerabilities more traumatic than it might otherwise have been.

The Anglo-Saxon Heritage

Although the country has greatly diversified ethnically and nationally and much of the original American culture has changed as a result, the United States was, of course, originally a British colony. Most of the original settlers in the United States were of British extraction, and they brought with them many of the customs and predilections of the mother country.

The Anglo-Saxon heritage affected the early American experience in a couple of obvious and enduring ways. First, it created an aversion to and suspicion of the military, and more specifically, the army, in peacetime. This aversion is largely the result of the British experience during the seventeenth century. During the Cromwellian period in the 1640s and beyond, the Commonwealth's armies were used to suppress political opposition to the regime. When the monarchy was restored in 1688, one of the provisions of the settlement of the Glorious Revolution was to forbid a standing army on British soil during peacetime to avoid a recurrence of military intrusion into civilian life. The British insistence on stationing elements of the British army in the American colonies after the French and Indian Wars became a serious issue that helped produce the American Revolution. (Americans resented being subjected to a condition that citizens of the mother country would have found intolerable.) This aversion manifested itself throughout the formative period of the American national security experience (see the next section) in the tendency to essentially disarm after major wars and to rely disproportionately on part-time citizen-soldiers for the country's defense. The prohibition on the use of American forces in a law enforcement role on American soil (known as *posse comitatus*) further reflects the fear of military abuse that has been invoked when some officials proposed an expanded military role in GWOT.

The other Anglo-Saxon legacy is a strong commitment to constitutional rule, especially to the guarantee of individual rights and liberties. Since military service, especially when it is the result of conscription, is a clear intrusion on individual liberty, there has always been a political reluctance to compel Americans into service. The only exceptions to this have been American involvement in major conflicts requiring the raising of large forces, such as in the world wars, and during the Cold War, when it was accepted that a large "force in being" (standing active-duty armed force) was necessary to deter the menace of expansionist Communism. This aversion

Amplification 3.1

DEALING WITH DEPENDENCE ON PERSIAN GULF OIL

The Persian Gulf littoral, under which two-thirds of the world's known reserves of petroleum are located, has been a major concern and problem for the United States since 1979. Prior to 1979, American interests in the region—almost exclusively based in uninterrupted access to reasonably priced oil—were ensured by America's closest ally, and the strongest power in the region, Shah Reza Pahlevi's Iran. In 1979, the Shah was overthrown by a violently anti-American revolution that catapulted Ayotollah Ruhollah Khomeini into power and resulted in the capture of the American embassy in Teheran and the capture of its personnel for the duration of the Iran hostage crisis. It also removed the enforcer of American policy in the region from power and thus called into question the continuing security of American access to the region's oil.

The Persian Gulf has been a source of major foreign and national security concern ever since. In 1980, President Jimmy Carter issued the Carter Doctrine declaring access to Gulf oil to be a vital American interest. In 1990 and 1991, the United States led the coalition that evicted Iraq from Kuwait, followed by American leadership in trying to keep Iraq's Saddam Hussein from obtaining weapons of mass destruction. Usama bin Laden's ordered terrorist attack on the United States in 2001 was, by his own profession, carried out to help convince the United States to leave Saudi soil. The result is a continuing presence in Afghanistan. Most Persian Gulf states also oppose Israel in its struggle with the Palestinians, thereby complicating American policy in that part of the Middle East.

American policy in the Persian Gulf derives directly from U.S. dependence on petroleum from the region. There are alternative sources of oil, but they are either inadequate, inaccessible, or more expensive than Persian Gulf oil. In the case of Russian reserves, there is the ongoing question of political stability. Assuming the United States would prefer to be less dependent on oil from the region—and thus more independent in its policy options—what are the alternatives?

As framed in the partisan American debates on the subject, there are two alternatives. One, largely associated with Democrats, calls for an emphasis on conservation, thereby reducing the amount of Persian Gulf and other foreign oil needed by actions such as better fuel economy in transportation, movement to other sources of energy, and the like. The other alternative, favored by the Bush administration, features the development of alternate sources of petroleum and other energy sources plus some conservation, such as opening the Caspian Sea reserves or sources in places such as Alaska. Until one or both of these approaches is adopted, it seems inevitable that the United States will be inextricably bound to the politics of the region, including its violence.

reappeared when American opinion turned decisively against the war in Vietnam, which, in its latter stages, was fought mostly by draftees. The fact that no American has been involuntarily inducted into service since the end of 1972 partially reflects attitudes that go back to the formation of the republic; the involuntary extension of voluntary enlistments under the so-called "stop loss" provision of service in Iraq is a partial exception to this trend, arguably necessitated by the need for larger forces than could be recruited voluntarily.

EVOLUTION OF THE AMERICAN EXPERIENCE

What can be viewed as the American military tradition has evolved over time and with different experiences the country has endured. As noted earlier, that experience can be divided into three historical periods: a formative period from the beginning of the republic to the end of World War II, the Cold War experience, and the contemporary, ongoing period. The two earlier historical periods were distinct from one another in two clear ways. In terms of the levels of threats posed to the United States and the American role in the world, the longer, formative period was one of low threats and commitments, and the Cold War featured high threats and commitments. As we look at the contemporary environment, however, neither historic combination perfectly fits. On one hand, the level of American involvement in the world since 1989 has never been higher. At the same time, the degree of threat to the United States was greatly reduced during the period between the fault lines (1989–2001), but threats appeared to intensify greatly after September 11, 2001. A question that we address in the conclusion of the chapter is which of the historic parts of the past may best inform our grasp of the present and future.

THE FORMATIVE PERIOD, 1789–1945

The period following the birth of the American republic was obviously critical in developing what would become the American military tradition and how Americans would look at military force. The period was heavily influenced by the events surrounding the Revolution itself and why it had come about. In retrospect (and certainly in comparison to the nature of modern revolutions), the American Revolution was a rather low-key affair in terms of both its motivations and conduct. As Dennis Drew and I have argued elsewhere, it might not have occurred at all had the British government acceded to the American demands to be treated not as colonial subjects but as British citizens, including not stationing British forces on American territory. When the fighting began more or less accidentally at Lexington and Concord in April 1775, it took the colonials almost 15 months to declare they were in fact revolting by issuing the Declaration of Independence on July 4, 1776. The war itself was, by current standards, a fairly low-intensity conflict fought between relatively small armed forces mostly when the weather was good. Although the style of linear warfare fought at the time could produce sizable casualties in pitched, "set piece" battles, bloodshed was also modest by contemporary standards.

A series of "lessons" about military force arose from the revolutionary experience and were, by and large, reinforced during the next century and a half before the United States was thrust into World War II and could no longer remain aloof from the power politics of the world. Five elements of the American military tradition were born during this formative period. The first four—an antimilitary bias, the belief in the efficacy of the citizen-soldier, the preference for rapid mobilization and demobilization, and the myth of invincibility—can be directly attributed to the revolutionary experience. The fifth, a preference for total war, was more a product of the Civil War and the events that followed that conflict in the international system generally. All of these elements collectively reinforce a general sort of disdain for things military that manifested itself, until the Korean War, in an American military establishment that was, except during wartime, small, physically isolated, and generally held in low regard.

Antimilitary Bias

It may sound strange to assert today, when public opinion polls regularly rate military service as one of the more prestigious professions, but prior to the Cold War, military service was not universally held in high regard in the United States. The peacetime military was generally a small, skeletal body whose purpose was to be ready to train a civilian force for military duty when the need arose. For the most part, the professional military (especially the army) was consigned to military posts in remote areas of the country, where the general population's day-to-day exposure to it was fairly limited. Moreover, outside the ranks of the professional military itself, soldiering was not thought of as a particularly prestigious occupation. Bar signs can still occasionally be found in New England antique stores declaring "No dogs or soldiers allowed," capturing the sentiment held by many Americans. As is the case today, there were regional differences in the extent of this bias, with Southerners more generally supportive of the military than their Northern counterparts.

Much of this sentiment has its origins in the Anglo-Saxon tradition and the issue of British military presence in the colonies prior to the American Revolution. After the French and Indian Wars that coincided with the Seven Years' War in Europe between 1756 and 1763, the Redcoats were stationed on colonial soil to provide protection against frontier Indians. The colonists thought they could contain the Indians themselves. The presence of the Redcoats would not have been tolerated in England itself; moreover, the colonists were expected to subsidize this unwanted element by paying taxes, the levy of which was enacted without their permission. The soldiers were a potential menace politically, and when they were used to aid in tax collection, they became overtly political actors as well. This revulsion and suspicion were most highly developed in New England, where most of the soldiers were assigned and their negative consequences suffered.

In addition to creating a predilection toward keeping the military as small— and thus nonthreatening—as possible, this antimilitary bias also favored keeping the military apolitical, and hence politically nonthreatening, as well. The United States Military Academy at West Point, for instance, was designed essentially as an engineering school to teach the science of war but not the reasons for war (a precedent primarily followed in the other service academies). The leading work detailing the relationship between war and its political purposes, Carl von Clausewitz's *On War*, was originally published in 1832 but was not translated into English and entered into the West Point curriculum until 1876. Moreover, professional members of the military were effectively disenfranchised until 1944, when legislation permitting absentee balloting was enacted. Prior to that, military personnel could vote only if they happened to be physically in their hometowns on election day, which rarely happened. Keeping the military apolitical was thought to be important enough that disenfranchisement was not abrogated until the heat of World War II.

The Citizen-Soldier

How could a disdain and distrust for the military be reconciled with the occasional need for military forces to prosecute the wars foisted on the United States? Part of the answer, of course, was to keep the military as small and unthreatening as possible during peacetime. Because much of the distrust was based on the fear of military intrusion into politics, another part was to make the military as apolitical as possible. In addition, the other element was to develop a part-time military whose members were also integral parts of the civilian society from which they came. The result was to reinforce and glorify the militia tradition that was part of the colonial experience.

Militia members were part-time soldiers. As the lineal forefathers of the National Guard and Reserves, they served in the militia for fixed terms and with limited commitments as members. Just as contemporary Guard and Reserve units serve for limited periods each year (e.g., a weekend a month, two weeks in summer camp), militia units would drill periodically, often for short periods (some as little as a few days per year). The idea was that such limited commitment would not "infect" these citizen-soldiers with military values to the point they would lose their primary attachment to the civilian community. The citizen-soldiers would, in other words, remain more citizens than soldiers. The activation of Guard and Reserve units for extended (including involuntary extended) deployments in Iraq is a direct violation of this tradition that has effectively made members more soldiers than citizens, at least temporarily. This alteration of roles also helps explain the hemorrhage in reenlistment rates in the Guard and Reserves that became evident in 2005.

This arrangement was satisfactory if we could assume the militias were competent to carry out the country's military needs. From the revolutionary period, the myth was developed that this was indeed the case. To some measure, this belief was little more than wishful thinking, but militia units were involved in enough successful operations (Lexington and Concord, Breed's Hill, Saratoga, Cowpens) that their performance could be embellished and instances when militia units dissolved and ran when confronted with regular British Army opponents (Camden) could be ignored. When the country was not at war, the question was largely moot because militias were rarely called upon to demonstrate their strictly military competence.

The argument over the efficacy of the militia has never disappeared and remains an active part of the debate over current and future forces. Reserve and Guard units remain an integral part of the U.S. armed forces, although they are assigned generally noncombatant roles. Their virtues are that they are less expensive than active-duty soldiers, and their attachment to their communities makes them popular politically, especially with members of Congress in the districts where they are located. The regular armed forces have a generally lower opinion of these successors of the militia men, emphasizing that the citizen component makes them less effective soldiers and thus of lesser value in military operations than full-time, active-duty forces.

Myth of Invincibility

The myth of invincibility asserts the indomitable nature of the American military and is the product of a selective reading of American military history. Its core is the idea that regardless of the circumstances, when the United States is forced to fight, it prevails. The general truth value of this belief is, of course, questionable. While it is true that the United States has generally been successful in war, American triumphs are liberally interspersed with episodes in which the country was less than successful. A more precise statement of the myth would probably be that when the United States becomes involved in long, total wars in which superior American physical resources can be brought to bear to wear out an opponent, fighting according to prevailing rules and American preferences (in other words, symmetrically), it generally prevails. But even that generalization must be tempered; in Vietnam, the opponent refused to wear out or to fight according to established norms (it fought asymmetrically), and the result was certainly not victory. The same may be true in Iraq.

This generally positive assessment of the American military experience has two corollaries. The first is the "can do" syndrome, the idea that no military task is too difficult to overcome if Americans truly apply themselves to surmounting it. Conjuring the image of a John Wayne World War II movie, the syndrome can be a major impediment to objective assessment of potential missions for which American military forces might be employed. There is, for instance, little on the public record to suggest that any appropriate military officials considered in advance the prospects that the United States might not be able to prevail in Vietnam; no one in the appropriate position to do so effectively said "*can't do*," a more accurate assessment and one held by many mid-level professional military and civilian analysts at the time.

The other corollary is that Americans prevail because of the brilliance and skill with which they fight. The facts fly largely in the face of such an assertion. The United States has, for instance, produced no major strategist of land warfare, although it has produced exceptional battlefield generals like George S. Patton and strategists who have contributed in other media (sea and air). Moreover, although American fighting forces have acquitted themselves well, the United States entered all its wars prior to Vietnam almost absolutely unprepared to fight them, meaning that in the early stages of those wars, American forces did not excel.

Mobilization and Demobilization

Through most of American history, the pattern of mobilization and demobilization has dominated the American military experience: when war seemed imminent or was thrust upon us, we would raise and train a force to fight it, but as soon as the fighting ended, we would decommission that force and return it to the normalcy of civilian life. This preference reflected numerous elements of the American culture, from a belief in the abnormality of war to the fear of a standing military in peacetime. It also meant that after every major war until Korea, the United States returned its armed forces to the skeletal form that had existed before the war.

Amplification 3.2

READINESS AND PEARL HARBOR

The Japanese air attack on American naval and other military facilities at Pearl Harbor was one of the most traumatic events in American military history. Despite a variety of warning signs (e.g., intercepted intelligence reports, suspicious ship movements, growing strains in relations between the two countries), the United States was totally unprepared for the attack when it came early in the morning on Sunday, December 7, 1941. None of the bases on Oahu were on alert status—in fact, most of the personnel at Pearl Harbor had been out at social events the night before and had not yet reported for duty when the Japanese arrived. Virtually no one was even looking for evidence of an imminent attack, which added to the tragedy and destruction when it occurred.

It was partly the fault of the American military tradition that the attack came as such a complete surprise. To most Americans, nearly a century and a third of virtual invincibility had left them complacent, not mindful that such an attack could occur. Despite a war that had been raging for over two years in Europe and the growing expansion of the Japanese Empire into the South Pacific and East Asia, where it would inevitably collide with American interests, there had not yet been anything resembling a mobilization of the military by the United States. Prominent Americans like Charles Lindbergh and his fellow members of America First argued that the war was none of America's business and should be avoided at all costs. American isolationism, prominently a part of the tradition in the formative stage, was still in full bloom before Pearl Harbor.

The elements of the American tradition that allowed the country to be so unready at Pearl Harbor suffered a humiliating discrediting when the Japanese attacked and destroyed much of the American Pacific fleet that, ironically, had been moved from San Diego to the much more militarily vulnerable base at Pearl Harbor to be closer to the theater should war occur. But the lesson was partially lost in the war itself. When the Japanese surrendered aboard the USS *Missouri* (which is moored permanently at Pearl Harbor) to end hostilities, the United States promptly demobilized again, only to be shocked back to reality five years later by the North Korean invasion of South Korea.

The tradition was sustainable throughout the formative period because the United States was never confronted with an enemy that could pose a direct and imminent threat to American territory—the accident of American geography prevented that occurrence. The luxury of forming a force only when necessary was always available as a policy option. The experience in World War II and the Cold War that followed changed that conclusion. Following the attack on Pearl Harbor, American forces in the Pacific were nearly overrun and defeated to the extent that it would have been difficult to regain the initiative, and only the heroic efforts of Americans at places like the Battle of Midway and Guadalcanal allowed the United States to recover while it rapidly mobilized an adequate force to meet the emergency. The absence of preparedness was the problem then, and when a similar circumstance nearly prevailed in Korea (only the ability to rapidly call up World War II veterans in the reserves prevented the allies from being pushed off the Korean peninsula), the luxury of not having forces in existence was revealed as unacceptable.

Total War Preference

While the impact of the first four elements of the American tradition are largely negative in their influence on thinking about the use of military force, there developed during the formative period a preference for involvement in total wars that at first glance appears paradoxical in light of the rest of the tradition. At one level, this development reflected changes in the international environment between the eighteenth and the middle of the twentieth centuries regarding the purposes of war. At the same time, it also was the result of an American perception that if it were to go to war, it should be for grand, righteous purposes that made it worthwhile.

The period of time between the mid-nineteenth and mid-twentieth centuries witnessed an expansion in both the means by and the purposes for which war was conducted. The expansion of means was largely the result of the progressive application of the innovations of the Industrial Revolution to warfare. Gradually, it became possible to expand the extent of warfare by increasing the deadly effects of weapons and by increasing the media in which war could be fought. In 1789, warfare was largely limited to ground combat wherever armies could march and organize their linear formations (essentially large, open fields) and the surface of the ocean; by 1945, the only place war could not be conducted was in space (a deficiency since overcome). War became larger in terms of where and to what effect it could be fought.

This expansion in means coincided with and reinforced an expansion in the reasons for fighting. The triggering events in the expansion of purposes were the American and (especially) French revolutions, which reintroduced political ideology into the causes of war. In the period after the end of the Thirty Years War in 1648, the system had been dominated by more or less absolutist monarchies who did not disagree on political matters and generally limited their fighting to small purposes. The French Revolution's evangelical period, when it spread its ideas across Europe, changed that, and as the means to conduct war expanded, so too did the reasons for fighting.

The purpose of war became the overthrow of enemy governments, which is the definition of total war. Although it was scarcely realized as such at the time, the prototype was probably the latter stages of the American Civil War, when the destruction of the Confederate Army and the overthrow of the government of the Confederacy were accepted as the necessary preconditions for reunion. The overthrow of the German government became the ultimate goal in World War I, and the epitome of total war was reached in the commitment to the unconditional surrender of Germany and Japan in World War II.

Total war fit the American worldview. American exceptionalism has always had an evangelical component that suggests the virtue of sharing the American ideal with others, and that evangelism could be extended to provide an adequate moral justification to breach the normalcy of peace and go to war. The epitome of this zeal is captured in Woodrow Wilson's address to Congress proposing an American declaration of war in 1917: "The day has come when America is privileged to spend her blood and her might for the principles that gave her birth and happiness. God helping her, she can do no other."

For anyone whose experience is totally restricted to the period since the end of World War II, or even the end of the Cold War, the listing and discussion of these elements of the American tradition may seem odd, even anomalous, because they seem so far from our present experience. The antimilitary bias of the revolutionary period is behind us; we no longer rely heavily on citizen-soldiers for our mainline defense (although the Reserves have been more highly integrated with active-duty forces in Iraq than at any time since Korea); we recognize the limits of military power and accept the ongoing necessity of permanent standing forces. So what is the point of this historical excursion?

The answer is that these elements represent an experience accumulated over the majority of American history, and they are not entirely missing from the ongoing debate. They are largely the product of a different environment, when America's role in the world was much more restricted; nonetheless, they still pop up from time to time. As we complete the transition from the end of the Cold War to a consensus on the contemporary environment, more may reenter the debate.

THE COLD WAR, 1945–1989

The end of World War II radically changed America's place in the world and the way in which the United States had to consider matters of national security. As the wartime collaboration with the Soviet Union gradually deteriorated into the confrontation that would be the key reality in the Cold War, the question of national security moved from the peripheries to center stage in the political constellation. When North Korea invaded South Korea on June 25, 1950, and the United States responded (through the United Nations) by coming to the aid of the southerners, any doubt about the changed nature of international politics and the American role in it disappeared.

The Cold War made military affairs—national security defined in largely military terms—a central reality of American peacetime life. Geopolitics was clearly dominant for the first time in U.S. history. Realizing from the Korean experience that a demobilized United States could not compete with a heavily armed Soviet opponent, the traditional practices of the formative period could no longer be afforded.

The Cold War presented the United States an apparently permanent military enemy for the first time since the rivalry with Great Britain was resolved after the War of 1812. Since the Soviets posed primarily a military threat through the challenge of expansionist Communism, American policy had to respond militarily. The result was the emergence of a *national security state* in which matters of national defense took on a co-equal footing with other foreign policy considerations, and a large, permanent military establishment became a permanent part of the landscape.

The military culture changed because of several new conditioning factors in the environment, especially after the Korean conflict. Each factor represented a direct change and even, in some cases, contradiction with the previous American experience, yet the nature of the Cold War caused these changes to be accepted without fundamental challenges from most Americans.

First, the Korean war created the recognition that the Cold War would require the United States to maintain a large active-duty force all of the time. Part of the reason for this was the nearly disastrous Korean experience. At the same time, the Soviets did not demobilize after World War II, and they and their allies maintained large, offensive forces. Should the Soviets decide to invade western Europe, as was widely feared, there would be no time to mobilize, train, and transport a force to the war zone. Instead, what became known as the "force in being" would have to be available on the scene at all times.

Second, this prospect of large standing forces meant that the United States would be in a permanent state of mobilization. During peacetime, a force of this size could be sustained only by the existence of a national conscription system, the first time an involuntary draft system had actually been used in peacetime in American history. As well, this state of perpetual mobilization meant that defense budgets had to be greatly expanded to support the defense effort. During the middle 1950s (before the entitlement programs of Lyndon Johnson's Great Society inflated the overall government budget), the defense budget was fully half the overall federal budget; between the end of the Vietnam conflict and the end of the Cold War, defense spending hovered between 20 and 25 percent of government outlays.

Third, this expanded role and prominence of the military resulted in much greater prestige being bestowed on members of the military profession than before. With a constant threat against which to protect, the work of the military now seemed more vital than it had previously. The respect that Americans had bestowed on the World War II military was transferred to the Cold Warriors as well. Military service, and even a military career, now became attractive to growing numbers of Americans who would probably not have considered such a career before, a fortuitous phenomenon given the need for more military members.

Fourth, the growing lethality of the military balance created an urgency and vitality toward national security that had heretofore never been bestowed upon it. The major agent of this change was the advent and expansion of thermonuclear weapons and the development and deployment of intercontinental range missiles by both sides. At the height of the Cold War competition, the two sides faced one another with arsenals of between ten thousand and twelve thousand thermonuclear warheads capable of attacking targets in the other country and against which there were no defenses. An all-out nuclear war between the two would clearly destroy both as functioning societies and would have unknown but possibly catastrophic consequences for the rest of the world. In those circumstances, the successful management of the nuclear balance in such a way that nuclear war was avoided— nuclear deterrence—was the country's most crucial business (a literal survival interest). This life-and-death struggle added to the prestige and importance of the national security establishment that designed, deployed, and developed strategies for deterrence. The Cold War world was a potentially very deadly place.

Fifth, there was also general acceptance that the Cold War confrontation was a protracted competition from which no one could project a peaceful ending. In the minds of almost all analysts, the only alternatives were Cold War and hot war, and since the latter would probably be nuclear, it had to be avoided at virtually all costs. This added a sense of grim vigilance to the entire national security enterprise. It also contributed to the absolute surprise of nearly all observers when the Communist world began to disintegrate in 1989. The possibility that one side or the other would simply collapse and that the competition would end with a whimper rather than a bang had not even been considered by most students of the Cold War, nearly all of whom would have dismissed the possibility as fuzzy-headed idealism.

Two things are notable about all these factors. The first and most obvious is that they represent circumstances that directly contradicted the American experience to that point. The idea of permanent mobilization of large standing forces, for instance, would have absolutely appalled the Founding Fathers. A world of perpetual and potentially disastrous military conflict requiring constant vigilance and extensive preparation and spending was entirely foreign to a country whose broad oceans had provided a barrier that permitted the leisure and luxury of a general mobilization. The idea that a military career would bring great prestige would never have occurred to most of the champions of the militia tradition.

The second remarkable thing about these changed conditions is how readily they were accepted. Americans who had never been willing to (or had the need to) allow themselves to be taxed to support a large standing military and who would previously have been fundamentally opposed to the existence of a draft during peacetime accepted both with virtually no complaint. The main reason for this changed acceptance, of course, was a threat that was real and ominous enough to justify greater sacrifices than during the formative period of the American experience.

During the Cold War period, two additional elements of the American military tradition rose in prominence to become permanent parts of the military environment. Both the news media and democratic institutions had, of course, been present throughout American history. In the period surrounding the Vietnam conflict, however, their roles became more defined and influential.

The Role of the Media

The relationship between the media and the military has changed over time. At times, the media have championed acts of war (e.g., the Spanish-American War); at other times (e.g., Vietnam) they have opposed it. It has always been a complex and contentious relationship, with the two institutions eyeing one another with some distrust and occasionally disdain that was worsened by the very sour experience of the Vietnam conflict and coverage of it. The relationship has arguably become even worse since the end of the Cold War.

There have always been two major concerns about the relationship of the media to national security matters. The first has to do with what is reported, a concern that centers especially but not exclusively on combat operations. The positions are diametrically opposed. From the vantage point of the press, coverage should be as complete and unfettered as possible. The press should have access to combat operations (whether they have a right to protection in combat zones is another controversial matter) and should be allowed to report what they observe. The media's underlying value is the public's right to know what its government's representatives (in this case its military) are doing.

This viewpoint creates two problems for the military. The first is whether unfettered coverage will provide too much information, including material that, in the hands of the enemy, could compromise the integrity of military operations and even put soldiers at additional risk. Reporting the locations and outcomes of battles and the directions of troop or other movements are examples of how reportage could aid the enemy and jeopardize our own forces. The other concern is that reportage, particularly of less-than-successful military actions, can have a negative impact on public morale, in effect undercutting our own morale and giving solace to an enemy. As an example, pictures of American Marines raising the flag on Mount Surabachi at Iwo Jima during World War II were a morale booster that became an important symbol for the Marines. Photographs of the bodies of Americans floating in the surf where they were killed assaulting the beaches at Iwo Jima (which were not published at the time) would have had quite a different impact.

The solution to this dilemma historically has been military censorship. Reporters at the front could get their stories to their media outlets only by using military means of communications, thereby allowing the military to inspect outgoing material and remove anything it viewed as objectionable. The workability of this arrangement depended on two underlying dynamics. The first was a relative degree of trust between the soldier-censor and the reporter. The reporter had to believe the censor was acting out of legitimate security concerns and not trying to hide evidence of military ineptitude; the censor basically had to believe the reporter was acting out of good faith in the stories he or she filed. While that relationship always had some adversarial content, it worked adequately until the Vietnam conflict. The other dynamic was the dependence of the media on government means of transmission of their stories from the battleground to home. That dependence has been broken by the invention of the video camcorder and the telecommunications satellite. In combination, these two technologies allow the reporter to witness, record, and transmit material without any assistance (or interference) from military censors.

The interaction between the media and the military in Vietnam transformed the relationship to one of nearly total animosity. Early in the war, the relationship was tranquil because reportage was passive: the military would tell the press its version of what happened in the fighting, and the press would dutifully report that information.

The picture portrayed was uniformly positive and suggested not only that progress toward winning the war was occurring but that victory was imminent.

That tranquility was destroyed by the Tet offensive by the North Vietnamese and Viet Cong in January 1968. The enemy launched a general attack throughout the country, and especially against the cities, including the South Vietnamese capital of Saigon. The press was outraged and dismayed as they watched Viet Cong racing around the grounds of the American embassy. When the first footage of Tet reached New York, Walter Cronkite, the most revered and trusted figure in American journalism at the time, replied, "What the hell is going on here?" The basis of his question was that the adversary could not possibly have mounted such an extensive action if the numbers of enemy killed that had been reported to the media in the months and years before Tet were true. The conclusion was that the military had systematically lied about enemy casualties and that the media had been duped into accepting inflated figures that, if true, would have left the North Vietnamese Army and the Viet Cong with too few remaining effective forces for such an attack. Tet showed that the media had been lied to about progress and had been duped into reporting those distortions as facts. As a result, the media lost trust in the military and refused to report successes—even when they were quite genuine. The military, in turn, blamed the media for undermining morale by refusing to report success after Tet. The relationship had become more adversarial than ever before.

It was in that atmosphere that the ability of the media to bypass military censorship electronically became a major factor. The military's response to the inability to edit coverage before its release has been to restrict media access to military operations. The intended effect is to restrict what the media can report (or misreport). This approach, predictably condemned by the media, was demonstrated in the Persian Gulf War, when only a few press members were allowed to accompany military forays, and then only carefully selected actions. Although media criticism of the military was muted by patriotic concerns in the Afghan campaign, reporters rarely witnessed military operations in that theater either or in Iraq (see Amplification 3.3).

The other concern, especially since Vietnam, has been the supposed role of the media as agenda setters. Vietnam was the stimulus because many veterans who were in the military during Vietnam were convinced that adverse coverage of the war effort after the Tet offensive was decisive in forcing an unsuccessful termination of the American participation in the conflict. It is, of course, a matter of major disagreement whether the United States could have prevailed in the Vietnam conflict under any circumstances, and the argument that the media helped force the American withdrawal—thus preventing victory—has obscured that argument for many critics.

The perception was also affected by electronic technology that broadened both cable television and worldwide television. One of the outgrowths of the telecommunications revolution has been the development of 24-hour-a-day news networks, the prototypes of which are the Cable News Network (CNN) and the British Independent Television Network (ITN). These outlets, and others that followed the 1980 birth of CNN, have voracious news needs, and they have greatly internationalized news coverage, especially in combat zones.

Amplification 3.3

THE MEDIA AND THE IRAQ WAR

Coverage of the Iraq War illustrates vividly the ever-changing relationship between the media and the U.S. military. That relationship had become highly adversarial during the Vietnam conflict. After Vietnam, the media remained suspicious of anything the military told them that they had not witnessed themselves, and many in the military continued to believe the "liberal" media was out to get them.

The military's position combines legitimate concern over compromising security, which leads it to want to restrict media access, with a great—arguably exaggerated—sensitivity toward criticism over how it does its job, which reporters want to observe and report. Finding the proper balance between these concerns is contentious and is manifested in the pull-and-tug over how much access the media should have to combat zones. It is an ongoing debate to which Iraq has contributed.

The military's solution to this problem in Iraq was to "imbed" reporters with individual units. Under this arrangement, a few selected reporters were allowed to accompany military operations in Iraq, but they were highly restricted in what they were allowed to observe and report. The military argued the restrictions were necessary to avoid reporting things that might compromise military operations and for the physical safety of the reporters. The media generally accepted this arrangement because it allowed them to be part of the "action" more than had been the case in Desert Storm a long decade earlier, and many more reporters were allowed some access than were allowed twelve years earlier. The major criticism of the arrangement was that it fostered narrow, myopic reporting because it restricted reporters to observation only of narrow aspects of the war.

That the media accepted the restrictions placed upon it in Iraq has itself been the cause of additional controversy. Many have argued that the imposed myopia created by narrow access to isolated aspects of the war has produced bland, unanalytical coverage that has been generally uncritical as well. Moreover, many conservatives inside and outside the military have come to equate critical coverage with a lack of patriotism and have in some cases impugned the motives of critical reporters. The debate that centers on but ultimately transcends Iraq is whether timid, even cowed, reporting serves the national interest.

Two additional factors have influenced coverage. One is the existence of foreign media forms like Al Jazeera, whose coverage cannot be censored. The other is amateur recordings of events, such as videotapes of abuses at Abu Ghraib prison. Both limit the ability of the U.S. government to restrict information flow.

The result is something known as the "CNN effect" that is the core of the concern for those who argue that the media serves as agenda setter. Critics allege (and the media itself generally denies) that policymakers tend to emphasize those international events that CNN and the others publicize, and that the news items they bring to light are often those involving war and other forms of human suffering for which military force may be viewed as an appropriate response. Thus, the argument goes that emphasis of policy becomes the handmaiden of the media and the media's attention or inattention on different matters. General John Shalikashvili, chairman of the Joint Chiefs of Staff under Clinton, somewhat cynically captured the CNN effect on military operations: "We don't win until CNN says we win."

The public certainly first becomes aware of many events through television. The first public images of Somalia in 1992 were pictures of rail-thin Somali children with their distended stomachs, and Bosnia became public knowledge through the haunting pictures of prisoners of war that look disturbingly like pictures from the Nazi death camps that same year. Whether this sets the public agenda or reflects simple coverage of what is occurring in the world is a matter of disagreement between the military and the media. It is, however, aided by anecdotal evidence. Early in the Clinton presidency, the National Security Advisor, Anthony Lake, was asked by reporters as he headed into the White House what the day's agenda was. He replied, "I don't know. CNN hasn't told me yet."

The Impact of Democratic Institutions

Within a political democracy, popular will is, of course, always a matter of concern in the making of policy and especially in an area such as national security, where the ultimate expression of that policy can be war and the placing of citizens at physical risk. Having said that, the "democratization" of national security affairs is largely a post–World War II phenomenon that, like so many other influences on contemporary affairs, was accentuated by American participation in Vietnam. During most of the formative period of the American republic, national security affairs were either of lesser importance or were more consensual in nature. During peacetime, there was little concern with military affairs, and most wars were either highly popular (the World Wars, the Spanish-American War) or affected relatively few Americans directly by compelling them into service for unpopular causes (the Indian Wars). A partial exception to this depiction was selective northern resistance to the Union cause in the American Civil War, particularly by immigrant groups such as the Irish who could not avoid forced service.

The Cold War placed national security concerns into the spotlight. Suddenly, matters of national security quite literally became matters of potential life and death, and how well those matters were conducted became very serious and very personal business for the entire population, especially for those young Americans who might be involuntarily conscripted into military service. This first became a concern in 1950 when thousands of World War II veterans had to be recalled to active duty and an army of draftees was assembled to defend a Korea that many of them were unaware of before they were called into the service. It became particularly a concern as the Vietnam conflict dragged on and the American conscript force fought a war the public, including many of those inducted, opposed.

The sour taste left of the Vietnam experience for many Americans helped elevate the role of popular control over the democratic institutions making decisions about war and peace. In the wake of Vietnam, the military itself engaged in a good deal of self-examination of what went wrong, and a large part of its conclusion was that the war effort was undermined by public support and opinion that evaporated around them as the war dragged on (Vietnam was the longest war in American history). To the military, the war violated the Clausewitzian trinity, which posited that war can only be successfully waged when there is a bond between the people, the military, and the government. Reasoning that the political authority had never explicitly solicited popular support for the Vietnam conflict (for a discussion, see Snow and Drew, Chapter 7), the armed forces (especially the Army) vowed that this would not happen again.

The concern over popular support of military actions can be seen in a couple of ways in the contemporary environment. One of the victims of the Vietnam experience was the selective service system that has periodically conscripted young Americans into service. The draft was suspended at the end of 1972 and the whole question of conscription has disappeared effectively from the national agenda, as witnessed by the absence of serious consideration about the draft to man the force in Iraq. Another concern is with the placement of American forces at risk. This has resulted in a level of concern about casualties in American deployments in faraway places. As Iraq casualty figures have accumulated, they have become a part of this concern.

Conclusion: The Contemporary Period, 1989 to Present

The end of the Cold War represented a major change in the environment and thus in the ways Americans think about matters of national security. This change was not immediately recognized, nor was there a great initial effort to test the nature and implications of the collapse of the Soviet empire. The response to September 11, 2001, has further stimulated changed thinking.

The reasons for a slow intellectual adjustment during the 1990s are numerous, and they are discussed in some detail elsewhere (see Snow, *When America Fights*, Chapter 1). One reason was that the national security and foreign policy community was caught off guard by the sea change represented by the collapse of Communism. Planners had four years of combat to plan for the post–World War II international order and devoted considerable effort to the task. There was no equivalent adjustment period when Communism imploded.

Our thinking about and adjusting to change was also retarded by the fact that the national security bureaucracy was dominated by veteran observers of the Cold War who were both very conservative and suspicious of the changes they were observing. The tendency was either to disbelieve how fundamental the change was or to hedge against the possibility that the confrontation might soon reappear. Moreover, the Cold War mindset was a comfortable intellectual construct that, once mastered, made people reluctant to shed it for the greater uncertainty apparent in the unfolding post–Cold War environment. At the same time, this new environment was clearly less threatening than the Cold War had been, and even if it contained new and annoying problems such as terrorism, the urgency of adaptation was clearly not as great.

Figure 3.1: American Roles and Threats

Role	Threats	
	High	Low
Large	Cold War	?
Small	?	Formative

With over a decade and a half of the new environment behind us and the second fault line of terrorism revealed, how will the American tradition adapt to and be shaped by the contemporary situation? Key elements in the past two situations have included the role of the United States in the international system and the level of threat the environment provided, as noted earlier. The American past experience reveals a contrast on these two variables, as shown in Figure 3.1. As the figure reveals, the two historic periods show the United States has experienced both the "pure" combinations: high threat and a large international role during the Cold War and low threat and a small role during most of the formative period.

The contemporary period represents a hybrid of these circumstances. Clearly, the American role in the world is large, and with the collapse of the Cold War opposition, it is arguably relatively larger than it has ever been before. The question becomes, which part of the American tradition will dominate the contemporary view of the world? In some manner, the neo-isolationists, who would reduce America's aggressive presence and role, represented the legacy of the formative period's preference basically to be left alone. The cutback in active-duty troop strength and the disappearance of conscription as part of the potential political agenda suggested that all the elements from the formative period have not disappeared and may reassert themselves as the United States returns from the "abnormality" of the Cold War to a more comfortable past.

The role of the United States, however, did not recede to where it was in the formative period, but has remained at least as prominent as it was during the Cold War. Does this mean that the internationalism that dominated the Cold War approach of the United States toward the world has become such a permanent part of the landscape as to be inescapable? The Bush administration entered office in 2001 with the stated intention of trimming back America's commitments in areas such peacekeeping, but it was mere months before the terrorist attack caused it to quietly jettison that rhetoric and adopt an aggressive military posture favored by the neoconservatives to the international environment. In 2003, it reactivated the Middle East peace process between Palestine and Israel (discussed in Chapter 11) and invaded Iraq. The continuing struggle in Iraq and the ongoing GWOT suggest a commitment to a major role in the world for the United States, if a more military approach than in the 1990s.

The past is never, of course, a perfect roadmap for the present or future, but the past is the context within which the future comes to be. As suggested in the preceding pages, there have been two distinct historical influences on how the American military tradition has evolved and shaped the way Americans view the role of force

Challenge!

How Much Has Changed?

Did the terrorist attacks on New York and Washington and the subsequent worldwide campaign against international terrorism fundamentally change the threat and role of the United States in a security sense? Prior to the attacks, the United States was in the new situation of having a large role in an international milieu that posed few meaningful threats—a kind of hybrid of the formative and Cold War experiences. But what is the situation now?

The question requires an assessment of how fundamental the threat posed by international terrorism really is. In the immediate wake of the 2001 incidents, the initial response of both the administration and the public was to portray the problem as global, pervasive, and extremely highly threatening. The Bush administration's pronouncements and actions seemed to reinforce, even to inflame, this perception. Troops were sent to Afghanistan in 2001 and the Philippines in early 2002 to fight the "war" on terrorism, and deployments were contemplated in numerous other places. The President's labeling of Iran, Iraq, and North Korea as the "axis of evil" extended the problem beyond a contest with nonstate actors to an interstate basis. Domestically, the Office of Homeland Security was created and began periodically issuing terrorist alerts, while an alternative government went underground to insure governmental continuity in the event of a massive, crippling terrorist attack. The creation of the Cabinet-level Department of Homeland Security (see Chapter 7) capped this effort.

Is all this activity warranted by the actual scale of the threat? Al Qaeda certainly does not have the capabilities to wreak havoc that a nuclear-armed Soviet Union could, but it also has shown the ability to launch an operation that killed three thousand Americans. Where does that place us in the matrix presented in Figure 3.1? In a high-threat environment, a low-threat environment, or somewhere in between? What we conclude has, or should have, major implications for future national security considerations.

in the world. Whether one of those influences will dominate the future or whether that future orientation will be a polyglot of those influences is an interesting question to ponder and to observe.

Selected Bibliography

Applebaum, Anne. "In Search of Pro-Americanism." *Foreign Policy* (July/August 2005), 32–41.

Brodie, Bernard. *War and Politics*. New York: Macmillan, 1973.

Clausewitz, Carl von. *On War* (rev. ed.). Translated and edited by Michael Howard and Peter Paret. Princeton, NJ: Princeton University Press, 1984.

Dupuy, D. Ernest, and Trevor N. Dupuy. *The Encyclopedia of Military History*. New York: Harper and Row, 1972.

Gaddis, John Lewis. *Strategies of Containment: A Critical Appraisal of Postwar American National Security Policy*. Oxford, UK: Oxford University Press, 1982.

Hassler, Warren W., Jr. *With Shield and Sword: American Military Affairs, Colonial Times to the Present*. Ames: Iowa State University Press, 1984.

Leckie, Robert. *The Wars of America* (revised and updated edition). New York: Harper and Row, 1981.

Millett, Allan R., and Peter Maslowski. *For the Common Defense: A Military History of the United States of America*. New York: Free Press, 1984.

Snow, Donald M., and Dennis M. Drew. *From Lexington to Desert Storm and Beyond: War and Politics in the American Experience*. (2nd ed.). Armonk, NY: M. E. Sharpe, 2000.

Tucker, Robert W., and David C. Hendrickson. "The Sources of American Legitimacy." *Foreign Affairs* 83, 6 (November/December 2004), 18–32.

Weigley, Russell F. *The American Way of War*. New York: Macmillan, 1973.

Williams, T. Harry. *A History of American Wars: From Colonial Times to World War II*. New York: Alfred A. Knopf, 1981.

CHAPTER 4

The Nature and End of the Cold War

PREVIEW

Although the Cold War has been over for more than a decade and a half, the structures and attitudes it produced continue to have an impact on the contemporary world. A distinctly American form of geopolitics was one product of the forty-year confrontation, many of the national security leaders today had their intellectual grounding during the Cold War, and the American military structure still predominantly reflects preparation to fight World War III against a Soviet-style opponent. The Cold War is the dominating influence of the American experience as we face a changed environment. Understanding how the Cold War occurred and evolved—especially in a military sense—and what residues remain is therefore crucial to understanding how we are predisposed to respond to the future.

The contemporary international environment can only fully be understood in the context of the Cold War international system from which it evolved and which helped form the world in which we live. These impacts of the Cold War on the present and future include the enormous influence the Cold War had on reforming the American attitude toward the world and the United States' role in it; the influence the Cold War had on the worldview of the generations who presided over it, including much of the present leadership; and the traumatic effect of the Cold War collapse.

The Cold War was a national baptism for the United States into the world arena. In the formative period, the country had not been a consistent major player in international relations for reasons already discussed: the accident of geography, disdain for a corrupt international system, and a general preference to be left alone to realize American manifest destiny. These factors combined to keep the United States on the periphery of a European-centered international system. That system, in turn, had little need most of the time for American involvement in its affairs except during systemic traumas like the world wars.

The end of World War II left a return to isolation from the world impossible and thrust a reluctant, inexperienced United States onto the center stage of world events. When the last guns of the war were stilled, only two states, the United States and the Soviet Union, retained enough power to influence international events and to reorganize an international system laid prostrate by the war. The implications of this bipolar balance of power—and especially its adversarial content—were not clear immediately but took shape in the five-year period that was climaxed by the Korean conflict. As a result, the United States was propelled into the *realpolitik* of international relations for the first time.

Understanding and managing the Cold War became the central task for the next generations of American policymakers, strategists, and scholars who had to manage and explain change as the world slid toward the Cold War between 1945 and 1950 and then had to adapt to the Cold War system for another forty years. Lurking constantly over their shoulders was the shadow cast by the possibility the Cold War could go very hot in a totally ruinous nuclear war.

The major organizing construct they built and managed was, of course, the realist paradigm discussed in Chapter 2. It was a harsh, confrontational relationship for most of its existence, and it became a very *conservative* construct in the pure sense of that term: it sought to conserve the system below the level of general war that both sides quite rightly feared. In the end, that construct and fear helped contribute to the end of the Cold War. But while the Cold War lasted, it provided a virtually uncontested worldview, and those who challenged it were dismissed as dreamers and visionaries whose suggestions were too risky or foolhardy to be considered seriously.

It is important to emphasize the pervasive nature of the Cold War because it still permeates, especially in official circles, the way many people look at the world. The people who have flag rank (generals or admirals) in the services today were by and large educated in the 1960s and 1970s and had their first personal experiences in the world in the 1970s and 1980s, and the same is true of the majority of civilians in the foreign and national security community. Many have, with varying degrees of success, sought to shed some of the inapplicable aspects of the Cold War mentality, but they remain Cold Warriors nonetheless. The equation of the U.S. response to terrorism as a war between good and evil, for instance, has antecedents in the Cold War against "godless Communism." President Bush's "axis of evil" and President Reagan's "evil empire" come from the same intellectual cloth. Certainly, the Cold Warriors will eventually be replaced by a leadership cadre unencumbered by the Cold Warriors' worldview, but that group's ascendancy is somewhere in the future.

The way the Cold War ended influences us as well. It was neither a planned nor anticipated event. With the considerable benefit of hindsight, we find a whole series of signs of the impending doom for the Soviet Union that were nowhere nearly so obvious at the time. The key player in the drama was clearly Mikhail S. Gorbachev, who became the Soviet leader in 1985 at the end of a succession crisis following the death of long-time strongman Leonid Brezhnev.

Gorbachev realized there was a deadly malaise in the Soviet system and sought to reform it and make it stronger and once again competitive with a West (and especially United States) that was clearly surpassing the Soviet Union by all measures of comparison. A lifelong, dedicated Communist, Gorbachev sought to strengthen his country and the Communist Party of the Soviet Union (CPSU). The actions he ended up taking contributed to the demise of the dominance of the CPSU and eventually led to the breakup of the USSR itself. Had someone convincingly predicted for Gorbachev the effects his policies would have, he would almost certainly have resisted the changes he helped institute.

The Western leadership was equally at a loss to explain or understand events as the structures came falling down (literally, in the case of the most dramatic physical symbol of the competition, the Berlin Wall). Initial public and private reaction to the seismic changes ranged from disbelief to suspicion that it was all a ruse, some of the clever disinformation for which former Soviet leader Yuri Andropov (Gorbachev's mentor and the former head of the Committee for State Security, or KGB) had been famous. As late as the middle of 1991, with the Soviet state publicly disintegrating through the unopposed secession of its member states, the first Bush administration debated whether the United States preferred a strong or a weak Soviet Union at the end of the process.

The Cold War and its demise is history, but it is important history that is relevant to us now. As a result, we devote this chapter to the Cold War. We begin by looking briefly at the essence of the Cold War relationship as a distinct international system. We then turn to the distinctly military competition that was at the center of U.S.–Soviet conflict. That military confrontation, in the end, helped contribute to the end of the Cold War, for reasons we will examine. Finally, some residues of the Cold War remain part of our current reality. For instance, as the United States aligns itself with former Soviet states in the name of fighting terrorism, some of these concerns affect the content and effects of policy on our future.

THE COLD WAR SYSTEM

At the end of World War II, the international system was confronted with two fundamental questions, the consequences of which would evolve and dominate international relations for most of the rest of the twentieth century. One question centered on nuclear weapons. The use of atomic bombs against Hiroshima and Nagasaki, Japan, by the United States helped to break Japan's will to continue the war and meant these novel and enormously deadly weapons would be part of the calculation of future military affairs. Hence, a fundamental question facing planners was what difference these weapons would make.

The other question was about the wartime collaboration between the United States and the Soviet Union. Would friendship continue in the postwar world, or would the deep ideological differences between them result in a future of conflict and confrontation? In retrospect, the answer seems stunningly obvious, and most observers at the time suspected that the collaboration could not be sustained. But, if continued cooperation could be maintained, the result could be a much more tranquil international environment, and this hopeful possibility could not be dismissed out of hand.

Planning for dealing with these postwar contingencies had gone on throughout the war in the United States and especially in collaboration between the Americans and the British. Unlike the end of the Cold War, which caught everyone off guard, there was ample time to think about and plan for the postwar world. Uncertainty about what kind of relationship would exist among what became the superpowers of the Cold War system dominated the policy process. In the face of this uncertainty, the planners devised a structure to accommodate both outcomes—collaboration or confrontation.

The principal instrument for organizing the postwar world was the United Nations Charter. The primary purpose of the organization was to create a viable mechanism to organize the peace that would avoid a repetition of the slide to World War II. Critical to crafting a viable, working system was whether the major powers, the United States and the Soviet Union, could agree upon a form of the peace they were willing to enforce.

Since the two powers had very opposing worldviews, the task of finding a mutually acceptable peace to defend was not going to be easy. Clearly, the United States preferred a world of Western-style political democracies and capitalist-based economies like its own, and the Soviets equally fervently wanted to promote the expansion of Communism in the world. Both sides were evangelical, and the secular "religions" they were promoting were incompatible. Thus, the prospects of peace and cooperation were prejudiced from the beginning.

What the UN Charter drafters sought to do was create a mechanism that would allow enforcement of the peace if the major powers could cooperate on a common vision but that would be disengaged if they could not. Cooperation would be accomplished institutionally through the UN Security Council, which the Charter empowers (through Chapters VI and VII) to take effective actions to squelch threats to or breaches of the peace. Each of the permanent members of the Council (the major victorious allies in the war—the United States, the Soviet Union, Great Britain, France, and China) was given a veto over any action, thereby providing the disabling mechanism when the major powers disagreed in any given situation. In the event that disagreement became pervasive, the Charter, through Article 51, allowed the members the right to engage in "individual and collective self-defense," providing the basis for the opposing military alliances that institutionalized confrontation.

Collaboration was not sustainable, of course, because the two sides could not agree on the world they preferred. Thus, the mechanisms for organizing the peace through cooperation remained disabled and disengaged for the duration of the Cold War. The United Nations was able to act on Korea in 1950 because the Soviets were boycotting the organization in protest of the refusal to seat the new Communist government of China rather than the Nationalist government of Chiang kai-Shek in Taiwan and thus did not veto the action. After Korea, the mechanisms for enforcing the peace in essence went into a veto-induced hibernation for forty years. Then, a Russia that was no longer Communist did not have ideological grounds to veto UN potential actions, and the world body returned to life as promoter of the peace.

The North Korean invasion of 1950 removed any lingering doubt that confrontation rather than collaboration would be the central feature of the Soviet–American relationship. After the Soviets exploded their first atomic bomb in 1949, the question of the role of nuclear weapons was added to the calculus of what became the Cold War international system. This system had several prominent characteristics that are worth considering. It also had within it the sources of future change.

Characteristics

First, the Cold War *political and military competition dominated international politics*. Among the world's powers, only the United States and the Soviet Union emerged from World War II with enough residual power to organize and influence international events. The bases of American power were economic and military. The American industrial system was strengthened by the war and towered above everyone else (for a period in the 1940s, the American economy accounted for nearly 40 percent of world productivity, as opposed to about half that today). Military power was guaranteed through the sole possession of nuclear weapons. The much weaker Soviet economy had been virtually destroyed by the war, but the Soviets kept armed forces of close to 12 million under arms (the United States was demobilizing to around one million in 1946).

This distribution of power defined the international system as *bipolar* in nature: the United States and the Soviet Union stood as the two remaining powers (or poles) around which other states congregated and could be controlled or influenced. The American lever of power was economic; everyone in the West needed American money and goods for recovery. The Red Army occupation in Eastern Europe was able to impose friendly regimes in the occupied countries that became reluctant parts of its orbit; it could not then and was truly never able to compete economically.

The Cold War's pervasive nature took root first in a Europe divided by what British statesman Winston Churchill first called the Iron Curtain in a speech in Fulton, Missouri, in 1947. The relationship became formally militarized through the formation of the North Atlantic Treaty Organization (NATO) in 1949 and later its Communist counterpart, the Warsaw Treaty Organization (WTO or the Warsaw Pact) in 1955. The ideological struggle spread to the developing world as countries emerged from colonial rule principally in Asia and Africa during the 1950s and 1960s.

Nothing symbolized the fervor of the Cold War more dramatically than the superpower nuclear competition. At one level, the competition was incongruous as both sides built arsenals for potential use against one another so large and excessive that a war between them would almost certainly destroy both. It became popular to depict the relationship as two scorpions in a bottle: each scorpion was ready to kill the other and itself in a conflict both feared the other might be tempted to initiate if they showed weakness or vulnerability. Each came gradually to dread the prospect of that conflict enough that nuclear weapons contributed to defusing the Cold War. The ultimate lunacy of the relationship, however, did not prevent either side from spending lavishly to insure that the other did not gain what was sometimes described as an "exploitable advantage" in some measure of the weaponry.

Second, the conflict was viewed as *protracted*, a long-term competition for which only great patience would suffice and the management of which required great vigilance. The Cold War was a battle between two diametrically opposed systems of political belief that was enduring and that had an uncertain outcome. There was very little consideration of a peaceful end of the relationship. It was broadly assumed that the only means by which closure could come was through a massive military clash, World War III, that would likely become nuclear and could destroy both sides. In that circumstance, the logic of avoiding war meant maintaining huge conventional and nuclear forces in Europe to keep the war cold.

The protracted nature of the competition became both a prediction of the future and a prime value, given its extremely destructive alternative. There was always something curious in this assessment, however. It was a matter of firm belief in the West that the Communist philosophy was inherently inferior to its capitalist economic and democratic political ideals. Somehow this belief was hardly ever translated into the idea that Communism might collapse on its own as those flaws became manifest (which, of course, is exactly what happened). Indeed, for a time it was even argued in some circles that Communism had a competitive edge in the developing world where much of the competition played out, because Communist ideology laid out a concrete blueprint for development, whereas democracy offered only choices but little guidance. That the concrete blueprint was itself flawed and the choices it offered ultimately unpalatable never really entered the discussion.

The perceived basis of Communist strength was the totalitarian nature of Soviet rule. Soviet Communism, the argument went, could not fail because its coercive strength was so great that any opposition would be crushed mercilessly. Thus, even if the regime lacked broad popular support, as it did, its power could not be challenged effectively.

In retrospect, this was also a curious proposition. In the western tradition, democratic theory argues that the basis of political stability is popular support for the government, or legitimacy. Legitimacy was the source of strength in democracies. Arguments about the endurance of Communism implicitly maintained that legitimacy simply did not apply if a regime had enough guns and other forms of coercion to control the population. Coercion effectively trumped legitimacy. What this line of reasoning failed to consider was that the reason Communist governments needed to be totalitarian was because they were illegitimate. The monopoly on power was really an indirect indication of the weakness, not the strength, of regimes. When populations throughout the Communist world shucked the system with no remorse or regret starting in 1989, it demonstrated that coercion only artificially and temporarily substitutes for legitimacy.

These intellectual blinders meant that there was much less consideration about ending the Cold War than if participants began with the proposition that the competition was intellectually tilted in favor of the democracies. Over the years, a

Amplification 4.1

BETTER DEAD THAN RED?
BETTER RED THAN DEAD?

The 1950s was the decade when the Cold War was at its most intense and assessment of the future was most pessimistic. The Korean War, which had become intensely unpopular after it stalemated in 1951 but dragged on until 1953, was a recent memory of apparent failure. The liberation of North Korea had not been accomplished, and the Communist Viet Minh of Ho Chi Minh had prevailed in French Indochina, another victory for expanding Communism. When the Soviet Union beat the United States into space by launching *Sputnik* into the heavens first and Americans peered into the nighttime sky and saw it blink by overhead, there seemed reason to be suspicious of who was prevailing in the competition. Nuclear war drills in schools and public buildings only added to the growing hysteria. The flaws of operational Communism had not become obvious to anyone.

In this atmosphere, a kind of despair emerged about how the Cold War might end. One possibility was that the Soviet Union might actually prevail, in which case the debate was whether it would be preferable to accept Soviet domination or to go down fighting in a cataclysmic nuclear war: better Red than dead? The second possibility was that war between the two systems was inevitable. It was not a question of whether there would be war, but *when*. The debate was turned around to ask if perishing in such a conflict was preferable to Communist overlordship: better dead than Red? In that atmosphere, hardly anyone could imagine the outcome that eventually prevailed: *neither dead nor Red*.

few observers had seen this, but their prophecies were largely ignored. George F. Kennan, the American diplomat who was the intellectual father of the American foreign policy of containment, argued that a policy of diligence could contain Communism within the boundaries it had achieved. If containment was applied consistently, the inherent inferiority of the Communist system would eventually cause it to implode. He was, of course, proven correct.

A third characteristic of the Cold War system was that it became *global*. Originally, it was geographically limited to the boundary between western and eastern Europe and, after 1949, the area surrounding China. As independence movements produced new states in Asia and Africa during the 1950s, 1960s, and into the early 1970s (decolonization was effectively over in 1975 when Portugal granted independence to the last members of its empire), both sides scrambled to gain favor, even allegiance, from newly installed governments in new states.

Because the new countries gained their independence from European states, and most adopted nominally democratic systems based upon the colonialist's form of government, the West initially was thought to have the advantage in this competition. Most of these new states, however, were desperately poor and in need of developmental assistance that was generally not available in adequate supply. Their new governments often proved to be inept or corrupt (or both), leading to a spiral of instability and violence. Those circumstances presented the Soviets with an opportunity to attempt to spread their influence by arguing they advocated a superior alternative to the West.

This global spread of the competition universalized the Cold War, meaning Cold War concerns permeated even the most remote parts of the globe. The American policy of containment was extended all along the Sino–Soviet periphery (over the objections of Kennan) and was manifested in a whole series of bilateral and multilateral collective defense arrangements (alliances) that globalized U.S. commitments and both justified and demanded robust forces capable of global projection. While the competition generally remained below the level of direct military confrontation, American- and Soviet-supported forces did fight in areas where American interests consisted mainly of denying Soviet interests, and vice versa.

The Cold War competition changed over time. The presumption of an intractable, negative relationship in the 1950s softened with experience to the point that, at the time the Cold War ended, Soviet political leader Gorbachev was one of the most popular politicians in the West and adorned the cover of *Time* magazine as its Man of the Year.

Sources of Change

The Cold War dynamics led to change in two ways. The first occurred in the 1950s but was not widely recognized at the time—the two superpowers began to lose some control over their individual blocs. The early postwar system had been known as one of *tight* bipolarity, meaning the major powers could control events within their blocs fairly closely. The system evolved, however, to one of *loose* bipolarity, wherein the ability to order events slipped for both.

Two events in 1956 started the change from tight to loose bipolarity. First, Great Britain joined France and Israel in an attack on Egypt, the purpose of which was to occupy the Suez Canal Zone (which Egyptian President Gamal Abdul Nasser had nationalized the previous year). The action was taken without prior consultation with the U.S. government (which almost certainly would have opposed it). When the United States joined the Soviet Union in sponsoring a Security Council resolution condemning the invasion, the French concluded the United States could no longer be trusted and began the process of moving away from the United States to a more independent position in international affairs. The American ability to control its bloc suffered a major setback.

The second event that started this change in control was the brutal suppression of the Hungarian Rebellion by Soviet forces later in that same year. Initially seen as proof of Soviet ruthless control over its bloc, there was a longer-term and quite opposite effect. The United States took the lead in an anti-Soviet publicity campaign that included widely disseminating pictures throughout the developing world of Soviet tanks rumbling through Budapest. The Soviets suffered an enormous propaganda black eye, because they had portrayed themselves as the peace-loving champions of freedom and self-determination, and they were clearly lying. The result was that the

Soviets—and their client states—realized they needed to avoid another similar embarrassment. East European countries learned that as long as they did not threaten Soviet security, they could act more independently than before, a sign of decay in the Soviet control of their bloc.

The second great change was in the nature of the competition, and the symbolic event was the Cuban Missile Crisis of 1962. In that confrontation over the Soviet attempt to deploy nuclear-tipped missiles aimed at the United States from Cuba, there was a military standoff that almost all observers believed was the closest the two sides had come to nuclear war. That realization convinced both powers that their prior assessment—that they had nothing in common—was at least partly wrong. At a minimum, both sides realized a joint interest in avoiding destroying one another and possibly the world.

The Cuban crisis was the watershed in the confrontational nature of the Cold War. Prior to the crisis, the relationship was regularly marked by direct confrontations with at least some potential to spiral out of control—the Berlin blockade, Korea, and the Berlin Wall incident, to mention three. These crises shared an escalatory potential to direct confrontation. After the Cuban missile crisis, that changed, and direct Cold War confrontations with obvious escalatory potential essentially disappeared.

The Cuban watershed changed the nature of the relationship in two ways, both of which reduced the likelihood they would once again meet at the precipice of nuclear war. First, they began a process of nuclear arms control, signing a whole series of treaties aimed first at limiting where nuclear testing could occur and later at limiting the size and characteristics of the arsenals they aimed at one another (a process that has continued to the present). This process became a prominent forum for Soviet-American dialog for the rest of the Cold War. Although avoiding the proliferation of nuclear weapons to states that did not already have them was part of the motivation, the shared realization of an interest in avoiding mutual incineration provided the compelling rationale for the efforts. After the missile crisis, direct confrontations with escalatory possibilities simply vanished from the international scene.

There is one apparent exception to this observation that actually proves the rule. During the Yom Kippur War of 1973, the Israelis pinned an Egyptian Army in the Sinai Peninsula against the Suez Canal with no way to retreat to Egyptian soil and threatened to destroy that army "in detail." The Soviets reacted by threatening to airdrop Soviet paratroopers into the Egyptian lines to aid in their defense (a militarily ineffective act, since the lightly armed paratroops would have been facing Israeli tanks). The United States responded by putting its forces on worldwide alert, and in the next 24 hours, there was a growing fear of escalation—with unknown consequences.

Frantic shuttle diplomacy by American Secretary of State Henry Kissinger defused the crisis. Flying back and forth between Tel Aviv and Moscow, he convinced Israel to back down from its threat against the Egyptians and the Soviets to cancel plans to intervene. The rapidity with which both sides moved back from the brink demonstrated the understanding they had about the dynamics and their commitment to avoiding confrontation.

From a twenty-first-century perspective, much of this flavor of the Cold War may seem odd, even anachronistic and unreal. It was, however, very serious business to those who made and implemented policy, many of whom, to repeat, are still active in national security policy today. Nowhere is the furtiveness of the competition more evident than in the way the two sides prepared themselves for potential armed conflict.

FORMS OF MILITARY COMPETITION

The Cold War was both a military and a political competition, with emphasis on one aspect or another across time and in different places. Originally, it was both. The communization of the occupied Eastern European countries was accomplished almost exclusively by the Red Army rather than the political interplay of Communist and non-Communist elements. At the same time, Communist parties competed politically in several western European countries and even enjoyed some electoral success in France and Italy. By the end of the decade, however, the totalitarian nature of Communist regimes had been clearly demonstrated in countries like Czechoslovakia (where a democratically elected government was overthrown by the Soviets and their Czech surrogates). From 1950 until 1991, the Cold War in Europe was almost exclusively a military competition between NATO and the Warsaw Pact (after the WTO became operational in 1956).

The political dimension of the Cold War was limited to the peripheries—Africa, Asia, and to a lesser extent, Latin America. The process of decolonization and the subsequent emergence of inexperienced postindependence governments created considerable political ferment into which both sides plunged hoping either to gain influence or, more modestly, deny influence to the other side. One of the means of currying favor was providing military aid to various governments (or factions within countries). Occasionally, involvement would devolve into military intervention, as it did for the United States in 1965 in the Dominican Republic and Vietnam and for the Soviets in Afghanistan a decade and a half later. Nonetheless, the competition in the developing world had both a political and a military dimension.

The heart of the Cold War, however, was played out in Europe along the Central Front in Germany, the presumed focus of a Soviet invasion of western Europe. That possibility formed the worst-case scenario against which NATO planners prepared. The rarely questioned presumption within NATO was whether the Soviet Union had serious designs on controlling western Europe and whether it might unleash the vast Red Army into NATO territory unless NATO demonstrated sufficient military strength and resolve to convince them of the futility of such an attack.

How serious a threat the Soviets indeed posed to western Europe is not the point here. Certainly the Soviets maintained military forces far in excess of those needed for a purely defensive stance in Europe (as did NATO), and there was ample ideological antagonism between the two sides to place the worst possible interpretations on the intentions of the adversaries. Thus, it was not at all difficult for members of the alliance to project a real and lively threat against which vigilant defensive preparation was the only prudent recourse. The underlying point is thus that planners *believed* in the existence of the military threat and acted militarily on those beliefs.

The perceived nature of the military threat was colored by the time and place in which it occurred. The fact that the competition emerged in Europe on the heels of history's largest conventional war affected the shape and purposes of military forces to this day, when the military situation is quite different. Militarily, the Cold War began as an extension of the global conflict featuring conventional armed forces preparing to fight symmetrically. The military dimension of the Cold War mirrored this inherited reality both in terms of how it would be fought and with what kinds of forces. Even though the weapons became more sophisticated and deadly across time and would have produced a much bloodier result, a war in Europe where the United States and the Soviet Union were the principal adversaries would have been very much like World War II. Since the military and political leaders on both sides were, by and large, veterans of World War II, this was not an uncomfortable projection and basis for preparation for them. Hidden within the assumptions about preparing for World War III was the notion that the forces and doctrines would also be effective against smaller, unconventional (asymmetrical) foes. That assumption has proven dubious.

The wild card, of course, was nuclear weapons. The Cold War provided the first occasion when a war could be fought by two opponents both armed with these remarkably destructive weapons. Whether a war in Europe could be fought without releasing the nuclear genie was a hotly debated issue in military, political, and academic circles around which no real consensus ever emerged. A second lively question was whether their employment could be restricted to the immediate theater of operations (a possibility about which the Europeans who would experience a nuclear defense understandably had little enthusiasm) or whether their use would somehow inexorably spread more widely beyond the battlefield. Whether conventional war in Europe would escalate into a general nuclear exchange engulfing the homelands of the superpowers was the ultimate concern for American, and presumably Soviet, planners.

These concerns have not entirely disappeared. The nuclear balance remains intact, if at reduced levels, even if Russia and the United States lack the realistic motivation to attack one another. American conventional armed forces are still largely structured basically the same way they were during the Cold War. Despite the efforts of Secretary of Defense Donald Rumsfeld and others before him to reshape that force, such efforts continue to be resisted by military and civilian leaderships at least implicitly clinging to Cold War roles and missions. Understanding those forces and why they are constructed the way they are is a necessary preface to dealing with contemporary forces for contemporary problems.

Conventional Forces

Militarily, the heart of the Cold War was a confrontation between conventional (nonnuclear) forces facing one another across the no-man's-land that comprised the Iron Curtain, and most especially the so-called inter-German border that divided

East and West Germany and was widely expected to be the initial battleground in a NATO–Warsaw Pact war. For NATO planning purposes, a heavily armored Soviet breakout at the Fulda Gap in Germany seemed the most likely way that war would begin.

World War II and the military predilections of the leaders of the two coalitions heavily colored the way they conceptualized the problem. Everyone envisioned the battlefield would be somewhere on the northern European plain, relatively flat terrain that gave the advantage to mobile yet heavily armed forces, such as the tank armies that leaders like General George S. Patton had popularized in World War II.

Both the Americans and the Soviets were oriented to this style of warfare in which huge forces slugged it out in an orgy of incredible violence until one side collapsed. For the Americans, this had historically meant committing the superior American productive system to building so much sophisticated equipment that the enemy eventually was beaten down by the sheer weight of arms. The Soviet experience on the Eastern Front had taught them that overwhelming numbers of troops could eventually carry the day, if at terrible human costs. The scenario of these two behemoths colliding on the battlefield produced a prospect of unprecedented carnage and destruction that, among other things, would leave the European landscape on which it was fought largely devastated. It was a plan for the ultimate expression of European-style symmetrical warfare.

The way the war would likely be fought affected the politics of war preparation. The focus of NATO preparation was to provide a sufficiently daunting prospect to the Soviets that they would be deterred from starting a war. But politics got in the way. Since the Soviets always had a quantitatively much larger force than NATO and would have the advantage of choosing when and where to attack, how was NATO to provide such an inhibiting presence? The domestic politics of the NATO democracies made it politically suicidal to suggest conscripting a force that could match the Soviets soldier for soldier. Moreover, the longer that war was avoided, the less belief in the need for the sacrifice of military service existed.

This left two major politico-military problems: where to fight, and with what? In order to blunt a Soviet attack, NATO had three options, each of varying military and obverse political appeals. From a purely political viewpoint, the most desirable outcome would be to stop any Soviet assault dead in its tracks—before it penetrated western Europe—and throw back the attackers. The problem was this solution was not militarily feasible because the boundary separating the Germanies was basically unfortified. The solution—erecting a Maginot Line–like structure to provide a barrier to invasion—would have required tearing up of the richest farmland in West Germany, a political impossibility in Germany.

A second alternative was to allow the invasion to occur but gradually to slow it down and bring it to a halt before it could achieve its presumed objective—conquering West Germany at least to the Rhine River. This defense in depth, as it is known, would have to have been carried out in West Germany where, for instance, one means of slowing the Soviet advance would have been at choke points in German villages that almost certainly would have been leveled in the process. That solution was absolutely politically unacceptable in the German Federal Republic (West Germany).

That left carrying the war eastward in the direction of the Soviet Union as the only other alternative. If physically possible, such a solution would avoid the military devastation in West Germany associated with the other approaches. The problem was that NATO explicitly fashioned itself as a defensive alliance, and thus it could not publicly endorse aggression into Eastern Europe.

The other concern was with what NATO fought, and this concern was colored by perceptions of the conventional military balance that heavily favored the Communists. In 1985, for instance, the Red Army was nearly two-and-a-half times the size of its American counterpart and had four times the number of tanks and armored vehicles and half again the number of combat aircraft. The United States had the advantage in helicopters and naval vessels, but their direct applicability to the central front in Germany was questionable. Numbers favored the Soviets.

Regardless of how the relative quality of the two forces was rated, these comparisons left the very real prospect that a Soviet-led assault in Germany might succeed *if the war remained strictly conventional.* What the NATO allies needed was so-called force multipliers, ways in which to enhance the comparative capability of those NATO forces (multiply their effectiveness). The most obvious candidates for this enhancement were battlefield and theater nuclear weapons, and analysts wondered out loud whether it would be better to accept conventional defeat on the battlefield or to escalate to nuclear exchange, with all the uncertainties that such a change would create for possible escalation to a general homeland exchange between the two superpowers.

How did the United States respond to these challenges? The question is germane because the blueprint for defending Europe is still largely in place as the rationale for current forces (despite efforts at change by Rumsfeld and others) and was the basis for the plan that defeated Saddam Hussein in 1991.

The plan for the defense of the central front represented a political and military compromise on the question of where to fight in the guise of something known as *Air-Land Battle.* The basic idea was to allow Army corps commanders on the ground in Germany considerable latitude in how and where they would engage the invading Soviets. Armed with highly mobile armored assault weapons and supported by Air Force close air support, the Army would engage in highly mobile warfare similar to the final campaigns of World War II.

It was implicit that one of the places such maneuver warfare would take place was behind the enemy's front lines—in other words, in eastern Europe. At the same time, the highly sophisticated NATO air forces would attack Soviet and Warsaw Pact relief columns, supplies, and the like, in eastern Europe in what were called *Follow-On-Forces Attacks (FOFA).* The idea was that the advanced thrust of the Soviet attack would be isolated, cut off from its supply and logistical base. So entrapped and isolated, it could be surrounded and forced to surrender.

These strategies were never implemented in Europe, of course, but they did produce a distinctive force structure and mindset for fighting that continues to this day. To many military planners, the plans were vindicated in the Persian Gulf War, where the basic blueprint for engaging and defeating the Iraqis was the highly mobile air-land battle concept (a plan made easier to implement because there were no natural or man-made obstacles to rapid mobility in the Kuwaiti desert). That very success reinforced the continuing adherence in the Army to a heavily armored concept and in the Navy to forces based on aircraft carriers (which carried out a large part of the air mission in Desert Storm), despite that some maintain both tanks and carriers are vulnerable and obsolete in an era dominated by missiles.

Nuclear Forces

We should, of course, be grateful that the concepts adopted by the United States to fight the Soviet Union were never tested, because, as already noted, there was considerable question both about whether they would have been effective and what their larger consequences might have been. Indeed, in some circles it was privately maintained that NATO's conventional role was simply to slow a Soviet invasion down enough so that one of two things could occur: either the diplomats could arrange a truce wherein the Soviets could be convinced to settle for less than their total goals, or there would be time to make a rational decision between escalation to nuclear weapons use or capitulation.

Nuclear weapons were the other legacy of World War II. A number of countries were studying nuclear physics on the eve of the war, and Albert Einstein convinced President Franklin D. Roosevelt of the need to engage in research on the weapons potential of nuclear power to hedge against the success of the German research program (which never reached fruition in large part because a number of the critical German scientists were Jewish and fled the country). The American Manhattan Project succeeded in producing a bomb in early 1945, and the United States emerged from the war as the only nuclear power.

The U.S. nuclear monopoly did not last long. The Soviet Union exploded its first atomic (fission) device in 1949, and both countries successfully developed far deadlier nuclear explosives in the early 1950s. These thermonuclear (fission-fusion) devices replicate the energy production methods of the sun and produce explosions measurable in the equivalents of *millions of tons (megatons) of TNT*; by contrast, the atomic bombs of the 1940s produced explosions the equivalent of thousands of tons, or kilotons, of TNT. For some real world comparison, the explosion of Mount St. Helens in Oregon in the 1980s was estimated at 40 megatons.

Parallel research was going on in the area of delivering nuclear and other weapons to their targets. Advances in rocketry produced the first successful Soviet intercontinental ballistic missile (ICBM) in 1957, a feat rapidly duplicated by the United States. Combined with similar work on shorter range missiles, both sides had missile-borne nuclear bombs aimed at one another by the time of the Cuban crisis, and the weapons could be delivered against their targets with no reasonable expectation they could be intercepted or neutralized. During the 1960s and 1970s, the arsenals grew enormously on both sides, with strategic inventories (those aimed at one another's homelands) numbering over ten thousand apiece and shorter range missiles dedicated to support of military forces in the European or other theaters numbering in the tens of thousands. Nuclear weapons thus served two distinct functions. The most dramatic and best publicized function was that assigned to the strategic nuclear forces (SNF), developed for potential use against the adversary's territory.

As the arsenal sizes grew and became impossible to defend against, the thrust in nuclear weapons thinking and planning shifted to *deterrence*, the development and maintenance of weaponry to convince the opponent not to use its weapons against you. Since neither side could defend itself against an attack that was launched against it by nuclear-tipped missiles, the threat had to be based in retaliation and punishment of a nuclear transgressor. The idea was that a potential aggressor would realize that the victim of the attack would retain such a large surviving force as to be able to launch a devastating retaliatory strike, making the initial attack in effect suicidal. One concept used to describe this dynamic and the strategy to implement it in the 1960s was *assured destruction*, to which a detractor added the prefix "mutual," thereby creating an acronym reflecting his assessment of the idea: MAD.

It required the mindset of the Cold War for this nuclear balance to make sense, especially as the arsenals grew to the point that an all-out attack possessed enough destructive capacity to effectively immolate the enemy several times over—"make the rubble bounce," in Winston Churchill's phrase. Both sides continued aggressively to research and deploy yet more deadly weapons out of the fear that failing to do so would create some advantage the other might feel it could exploit in a nuclear attack. Lamenting this aspect of the nuclear arms race, President Jimmy Carter's Secretary of Defense Harold Brown summarized it: "We build, they build; we stop, they build." That the result was a policy and effective strategy of genocide and countergenocide (the effect if the arsenals were used) bothered mostly the nuclear disarmers.

The other role for nuclear weapons was in support of conventional operations, primarily in Europe. The purpose of these "battlefield" or "theater" nuclear weapons (TNFs) was as a force multiplier. In American planning, for instance, a major mission for TNFs was to help blunt the massive Soviet tank offensive that was presumed would be the opening foray of World War III. When masses of Soviet tanks approached the border, they would be attacked with nuclear warheads, thereby breaking up the assault. A special form of nuclear explosive, the enhanced radiation warhead, or neutron bomb, was applied specifically to this purpose (see Amplification 4.2).

Theater nuclear weapons were always more controversial than their strategic counterparts, especially among the European allies who would be "defended" by them. There was deep suspicion in Europe that their use could not be controlled: once the first nuclear weapons were used on the battlefield, the result would be escalation to broader use. Whether expansion would be limited to the theater or would expand to homeland exchanges between the superpowers could not be demonstrated. Since nuclear weapons had never been used in anger when both sides possessed them, there was absolutely no evidence to support or refute claims about whether or how escalation might occur.

Regardless of escalatory potential, most Europeans agreed that anyplace nuclear weapons were used would be a loser, an irradiated wasteland that would be uninhabitable until the radiation dissipated. Some Europeans even suspected that after decimating parts of Europe, the superpowers would pause, conclude that any further

Amplification 4.2

THE CAPITALIST BOMB

A major objection to the contemplated use of nuclear weapons in Europe was the enormous devastation their use would create for the very territory they were designed to defend. Europe—and especially Germany, where the bulk of the initial fighting would take place—would be a scarred and cratered radioactive moonscape unlikely to sustain life for years to come. On the other hand, nuclear weapons seemed militarily an effective way to destroy the concentrated armored tank assault that would spearhead the Soviet attack and against which there were inadequate alternatives.

These two diametrically opposed priorities were partially reconciled by a new form of nuclear explosive first tested in the early 1970s and proposed for deployment by the Carter administration during the latter 1970s. The new technology was something called the enhanced radiation warhead (ERW), which quickly earned the popular name the neutron bomb. Its innovation was to rearrange the relative effects of nuclear explosives. Any nuclear explosive produces four effects: a fireball of heat, extremely high winds known as blast overpressure, initial or prompt (beta and gamma ray) radiation, and residual radiation, also known as fallout. The chief culprits in a conventional nuclear explosion were blast overpressure, which knocks down structures and craters the landscape; the fireball, which causes fires; and fallout, which lingers in the physical environment for years to come. The fourth effect, prompt radiation, sends out deadly rays during the explosion itself, but once the explosion ends, it becomes relatively benign.

The neutron bomb rearranged nuclear effects so that 75 to 80 percent of the nuclear explosion involved the release of prompt radiation. This had two advantages given the problem it sought to overcome. First, the other effects of the weapon were reduced greatly, thereby doing less environmental damage—the concern of the local citizenry. Second, it seemed ideal against the Soviet tank threat. If the weapons were detonated over advancing Soviet tank columns, the deadly gamma and beta rays would penetrate Soviet armor and incapacitate and eventually kill the crews without destroying the tanks. The attacks would thus be halted, and one grisly plan was to have NATO troops remove the bodies and turn the tanks on the aggressors with NATO crews.

The Soviets howled at the proposal. They labeled it "the capitalist bomb," a weapon that killed people in a grotesquely cruel manner but did not destroy the productive system it sought to protect. They threatened to produce their own neutron bombs, and the Europeans could never quite bring themselves to support any nuclear defense of Europe. Deployment was delayed, and eventually the plan to deploy the capitalist bomb in Europe was scrapped with the signing of the Intermediate Nuclear Forces (INF) Treaty in 1988, which removed most nuclear weapons from Europe.

escalation placed their own territory at risk, and stop, arguing that they had done their duty to defend their allies.

The French took this argument a step further. They argued that no ally (in this case, the United States) would in the future honor an alliance commitment if doing so potentially threatened its physical existence. Since any defense of Europe could escalate to disastrous homeland nuclear exchange, the French concluded that ultimately the United States would not risk defending Europe. The United States, of course, vigorously denied these allegations but, once again, could offer no hard evidence to refute them. As a result, the French concluded they needed their own independent nuclear strike force with which to threaten the Soviets.

In retrospect, the logic and implications of the nuclear competition may seem bizarre. How could serious people embrace a policy and strategy that, if carried out, would amount to nothing less than genocide? Once arsenals grew to the point that they exceeded any rational purpose other than genocide, why did both sides continue to build more and more deadly weapons?

The answer lies in the enormous distrust and suspicion that engulfed the participants in the competition. It is hard to imagine a country would engage in the hideous calculations that underpinned operational nuclear policy unless it assumed its counterparts were planning for and willing to do the same thing. The American planning process, for instance, produced something called the Single Integrated Operational Plan (SIOP), a series of options for attacking various sets of targets in the Soviet Union, graded in terms of their importance. Their implementation would have resulted in the deaths of countless millions of Soviets. How could such an inhuman enterprise be justified? The answer: by assuming the other side was doing the same thing. If the pilots who would drop the nuclear bombs or the missileers who would release the nuclear rockets were asked if they would hesitate to carry out their missions, the answer would uniformly be that they would not hesitate, because they would assume they were retaliating on behalf of and avenging lost loved ones.

DEADLOCK OF THE COMPETITION

Even when the Cold War competition was proceeding in its most vigorous manner, the seeds of its demise were being sown. By the 1970s, two trends, unrecognized at the time, were beginning to congeal that would militate toward the end of the Cold War. One trend was the weakening of the Soviet economy both absolutely and in comparison to that of the United States. The other was a growing recognition of a deadlock in the military competition between the superpower blocs. By the 1980s, they coalesced to create the conditions that led to the end of the Cold War.

The Economic Dimension

The economic implosion that eventually engulfed the Soviet state had its roots in the 1970s. At that time, economic growth began to slow, and by the end of the decade, the Soviet economy had stopped growing altogether, what Soviet economists would later call the "era of stagnation." By the early 1980s, the only economic growth in the Soviet Union was apparently in the production of vodka, and if vodka production was removed from measures of productivity, the Soviet economy was in absolute decline. Indeed, when Gorbachev mandated limits in vodka production in the mid-1980s, the economy was adversely affected.

This problem was known to some Soviet academic economists, but they lacked access to the leadership cadre associated with Soviet leader Leonid Brezhnev (known as the *nomenklatua*), who benefited from the system and were uninterested in seeing change that might adversely affect their privilege. Instead, the academic economists allied themselves with a rising star within the Communist Party, Mikhail S. Gorbachev, whose wife, Raisa, was their colleague at Moscow State University. When Gorbachev achieved power in 1985, this cadre was ready to roll out the mechanisms of reform. Unfortunately for them, their efforts were too little and too late.

A good bit of the Soviet decline was due to lagging behind in science and technology. The Soviets were largely excluded from the high-technology revolution in the West that underlay the economic expansion of the 1980s and 1990s and the process of globalization of the world economy. Part of this exclusion was purposive—to shield a shaky economy from outside competition. This progressive technological backwardness was an unintended result of a conscious decision in the 1960s to concentrate Soviet scientific effort on weapons development rather than basic science. Soviet scientists such as Andrei Sakharov had warned this emphasis was shortsighted and would place Soviet science at a disadvantage in the future. Sakharov was correct.

Two additional dynamics exacerbated this technological gap. First, the problem was progressive. The motor of technological growth was the development of more sophisticated generations of computers. This is a progressive process, because the major tool for designing the next generation of computers is the current generation. Thus, the computer's future health depends on its current competitiveness. Moreover, the developmental time between generations has grown shorter because of the greater power of newer machines. Translated, that means the farther a country is behind (the more generations removed from the cutting edge), the farther it gets behind in the future. By the early 1980s, the Soviet Union was approximately three generations behind the United States, and the gap was widening.

The Soviets could not close the gap. The decision to concentrate on military development had been at the expense of the computer research section of the Soviet Academy of Scientists in the 1960s, and its personnel were distributed to military research. The Soviets even stole computers, tore them down, and put them back together again so they could replicate the system (a process known as reverse engineering). It did not help. The systems they stole represented current technology becoming obsolete, and reverse engineering took longer than the development of new generations.

The second dynamic was that the Soviets were not allowed to collaborate with the West in technology. Almost all the technologies in which the Soviets were behind were *dual use*, meaning they had both military and civilian applications. For instance, a computer designed for research in theoretical physics could be converted to applying physical principles to weapons design. As long as the Soviet Union was the avowed enemy, the United States and the rest of the West was not going to provide the Soviets with capabilities that might produce weapons with which to menace them.

Most of these dynamics went largely unnoticed in the West. Soviet economists were rarely allowed to communicate with their western counterparts, the Soviet government doctored economic statistics that were notoriously inaccurate anyway (and thus disbelieved), and the military production system, on which attention was concentrated, seemed to be working well. In fact, when the Central Intelligence Agency produced an analysis of the Soviet economy in the middle 1970s suggesting the possibility of its decline, the report was condemned and an alternate panel was assembled to reassess the material. That group produced a more ominous analysis, which was largely wrong. Since its conclusions reinforced what officials believed to be the case, it was accepted.

The Military Dimension

The military competition was, by the end of the 1970s, also undergoing change to the ultimate disadvantage of the Soviet Union. The competition had essentially deadlocked into a very deadly but ritual confrontation in which neither side seemed to be able to obtain meaningful advantage. This competition was enormously burdensome to a Soviet economy that was much smaller than that of the United States and that needed to divert the resources devoted to the military for economic purposes if the Soviets hoped to compete economically. The military competition, in a word, had become a millstone around the neck of the Soviet future. The weight became unbearable in the late 1980s, when their ill-fated, expensive, and unpopular intervention in Afghanistan contributed to the demise of the Soviet state.

The seeds for military deadlock can be traced back to the Cuban crisis, when both sides confronted the potential reality of nuclear war and did not like what they saw. Despite the recognition of a mutual interest in avoiding nuclear war that was the major outgrowth of that crisis, the military competition, if anything, expanded and intensified in the following years. Many in the American national security community remained deeply suspicious of anything the Soviets did (and vice versa) and continued to build up stocks of arms, especially in the area of strategic nuclear forces, as if the Cuban experience had not changed anything.

While the potential deadliness of the nuclear balance expanded, the danger of nuclear war was actually declining, even if this decline was mostly unrealized. The prospect of nuclear war with the levels of arms available in 1962 was sobering, but the prospect of such a war fought with the arsenals of 1980 was positively catastrophic. Leaders on both sides going back as far as President Dwight D. Eisenhower in the 1950s and Soviet Premier Nikita Khrushchev in the early 1960s had publicly proclaimed the unacceptability of nuclear war as a means to resolve East–West differences. These original pronouncements were made when arsenal sizes numbered in the hundreds; when both sides recognized what could happen if the ten thousand or more weapons both possessed were unleashed, avoiding such a war became imperative.

The necessary step to reduce the danger—or likelihood—of war between the two sides was to add the unacceptability of conventional war to the relationship. The key element in accomplishing this was the uncertainty of the escalatory process. A conventional war would become a nuclear war if escalation occurred, and there was no empirical basis on which to predict confidently whether that escalation would occur. In that circumstance, the only certain way to avoid nuclear war between the superpowers was to avoid *any* war between them.

This "necessary peace," as I described it in a 1986 book with that title, reduced the Cold War military competition to ritual status. Both sides developed and deployed weapons and conducted war games with them for the precise reason of avoiding their use in war. The old military axiom of "preparing for and fighting the country's wars" became twisted to "preparing to avoid fighting the country's wars."

The recognition of military deadlock came at a time when the burden of the arms race was clearly contributing to the crisis of the Soviet economy. The Soviets were plowing upward of one-quarter of a gross national product (GNP) into defense spending from an economy probably only about one-third the size of the American economy. When support for foreign adventures in places like Cuba and Mozambique and the direct expense of their war in Afghanistan were added to the Cold War "bill" for the Soviets, the burden was becoming overwhelming. In 1981, the administration of Ronald W. Reagan announced the largest arms buildup in peacetime American history, and one of the explicit purposes of the increase in arms was to force the Soviets into an economically ruinous arms race by trying to keep up with the American expansion.

Convergence

These two dimensions had converged as Gorbachev succeeded Konstantin Chernenko as the Soviet leader in 1985. Gorbachev seemed a new kind of Soviet leader. He was the first leader of the Soviet Union with a college degree, was a lawyer by training, and was clearly more urbane and sophisticated than his predecessors, preferring well-tailored Italian silk suits to the baggy gray gabardine associated with older Soviet leaders. His professor wife Raisa was also a handsome, urbane, and very public figure—in contrast to the dowager images of Gorbachev's predecessors' wives (some of whom were never seen in public). When Gorbachev went to London as one of his first acts and clearly charmed British Prime Minister Margaret Thatcher, it was clear that he was a different character than those he succeeded.

Gorbachev faced a daunting set of problems. He knew about the economic problems from the Soviet professors, and he sought to reform the economic system. As a believing Marxist, his approach was to fine-tune the existing system, but the system itself was beyond repair, and he was slow in recognizing that the system and the assumptions on which it rested was the problem.

He also realized that much of the economic problem was the result of the isolation of the Soviet economy. Gorbachev ultimately recognized that the only chance for economic redemption was to open their country to the West. Western technology was absolutely critical to any attempts at economic modernization and hence competitiveness, and an influx of Western capital was clearly necessary to fund improved economic performance. But how could the Soviets convince a suspicious West to engage itself with the Soviet economic system? How could they convince an even more suspicious American national security establishment that shared technology would not be turned into hostile tools of war?

The military problem was much the same. When Gorbachev entered office, the Soviets were engaged in their fifth year of a frustrating, unsuccessful war in Afghanistan that was draining the treasury and corroding the society in ways not dissimilar to the effects of the Vietnam War on the United States. Eventually, Soviet forces would have to withdraw from Afghanistan in disgrace, which became a factor in the ultimate demise of the Soviet Union. The effects of trying to match the Reagan buildup were adding to the strains, and pitiful client states like Cuba looked increasingly like unaffordable luxuries.

What was Gorbachev to do? The choices were not attractive. The status quo certainly could not be sustained, and trying to tinker with the system through the economic and political reforms known as *perestroika* was not working. The Soviet Union was sinking fast as a state and as a power. A radical solution was needed.

The answer was to sacrifice the Cold War competition. The logic of the Soviet situation dictated the decision. Economic stagnation was eroding the standing of the Soviet Union in the world and was progressively reducing the standard of living of Soviet citizens. The Soviet Union was becoming, as many critics described it, "a third-world country with nuclear weapons." To change that situation, they needed access to Western technology and capital, and their only hope was to cease being the enemy and to join the community of states as a normal, rather than a rogue, member. The same logic held for the military dimension. Competing with the Reagan buildup, continuing the frustrating burden of the Afghanistan war, and supporting losers like Castro were becoming unbearable and unsustainable. Canceling the losing game the Cold War had become was an increasingly attractive option.

The world stood by in stunned silence as the Soviet leader began to unravel the forty-year-long confrontation. Gorbachev published a blueprint of the changes he proposed in a 1986 book, *Perestroika: New Thinking for Our Country and the World*. In it, he proposed a detailed internal reform plan. In the international realm, he detailed the transformation of the Soviet Union into a "normal" state by policy changes such as noninterference in the affairs of other states and renunciation of the so-called Brezhnev Doctrine that had justified Soviet intervention in Socialist states and had been used as the rationale for Soviet invasions of Hungary, Czechoslovakia, and Afghanistan.

Perestroika was initially greeted with skepticism in the West. Many analysts presumed that the book was nothing more than an elaborate web of lies to lower the West's guard. But then Gorbachev began to act in accordance with the book's proposals. In 1989, the Soviet Union completed its military withdrawal from Afghanistan, despite having accomplished none of its goals. Also in 1989, it stood idly by when the Polish parliament seated a non-Communist government, an act that opened the floodgates for the rapid de-Communization of Eastern Europe and, in 1991, the formal dissolution of the Warsaw Pact. These inactions seemed to implement renunciation of the Brezhnev Doctrine and the principle of noninterference in the affairs of other states.

Domestic reform was not dramatic or attractive enough to avoid the breakup of the Soviet Union itself. Led by the Baltic states (Lithuania, Latvia, and Estonia), the constituent republics of the Soviet Union announced their intention to withdraw from the union and establish themselves as independent states. On the last tick of the clock of 1991, the red Soviet flag came down from the Kremlin for the last time, replaced the next day by the Russian tricolor of red, white, and blue.

The peaceful implosion of the Soviet state was—and is—an unprecedented political act in world history. States, including major powers, have from time to time ceased to exist through Carthaginian peaces or partition at the ends of wars, but for one of the world's two most powerful countries simply to vote itself out of existence was something that had not happened before and that was entirely unanticipated both within and outside Russia. Ultimately, the reason we did not consider adequately the excluded possibility of a peaceful end of the Cold War was because nothing like what happened ever had occurred before.

So why did Gorbachev end the Cold War? The short answer is that he had no choice. The old system was broken, if not exactly the way he and his advisors thought at the time. Knowing the system could not be revived without considerable outside assistance, Gorbachev also understood that the *sine qua non* for assistance was to end the Cold War and to remove its most obviously annoying symbols: the Iron Curtain, the Berlin Wall, and most important, the structure of military confrontation. They did not foresee that the cost would be the destruction of the edifice they had sought to strengthen.

Fascinating questions remain. Could the Cold War have been ended without the destruction of the Soviet Union? If so, what would world politics look like today? If Gorbachev had anticipated the real price of ending the Cold War, would he have gone through with it? In another vein, was the outcome foreordained regardless of who was in the Kremlin in the middle 1980s, or was it the unique contribution of Gorbachev to stimulate the destruction of the internal barriers to change and the Soviet state itself? What problems did the end of the Cold War leave behind?

COLD WAR RESIDUES

The end of the Cold War left a geopolitical void in the international system. Most of the gaping hole was in Europe and centered around two axes. The first, and potentially most traumatic, was what succeeded a former Soviet Union now divided into fifteen independent states, of which the Russian Federation is the pivot. The second was the collapse of the Communist order in Eastern Europe, and what governmental forms and new international associations would replace the dark days of Communism.

Russia and the Successor States

When the Soviet Union dissolved, Russia was the largest single state that emerged from the breakup, containing roughly half the population and three-quarters of the land mass of the old Soviet Union. Russia also has maintained most of the military power of the old Soviet Union, notably the thermonuclear arsenal. Although beset by enormous and debilitating political and economic problems that have unquestionably diminished its place in the world, Russia and its future remain an important international concern.

The Russian situation can be divided into political, economic, and military questions. The political and economic aspects focus on the transformation of the Russian system away from its totalitarian, Socialist past under Communism to some more Western democratic and capitalist future. Its progress in these areas has been mixed. Militarily, Russia has been in a process of decline that began before the fall of Communism, but it remains a nuclear superpower.

The political and economic transformation of Russia has moved forward in interrelated fits and starts. The political system has had to develop democratic support in a system where economic chaos and even free fall have become virtually institutional features. Economically, an attempt to institute market practices is being grafted onto an inherited institutional framework woefully inappropriate and inadequate for the market to take hold and prosper. When the Soviet Union became Russia, for instance, the country had essentially no banking or other financial laws or institutions, making it virtually impossible to regulate financial dealings. It lacked mechanisms to collect taxes to run the government. The breakdown of the Communist levers of state coercion left the country with inadequate policing capacity that has resulted in the violent actions of the *Mafioso* and other forms of lawlessness. Pensioners who believed the Communist state would support their old age have found themselves holding the bag, as the "social net" promised by the Communist state has been withdrawn from them.

Politically, the record is also mixed. Russia has held four relatively free elections for president, and in the third one in 2000, power was peacefully passed from Boris Yeltsin to Vladimir Putin, a momentous occasion in Russian history. Since the reelection of Putin in 2004, some international concern has been raised (especially by the United States) about the Russian president's commitment to Western democracy as a result of actions that have had the effect of greatly centralizing power in his hands. Putin dismisses these criticisms as manifestations of a distinctly Russian form and evolution of democracy, a stance that continues to raise concerns.

Russia also has serious military and security problems. One of the major themes of Russian history has been a concern—some argue paranoia—with military security that has been reinforced by invaders as diverse as the Mongol hordes, Napoleon Bonaparte, and Adolf Hitler. A major reason for constructing the Communist empire in Eastern Europe after World War II, after all, was to provide a *cordon sanitaire* (buffer zone) between Russia and future invaders. That buffer zone is gone.

The relative assurance of Russian physical security was a victim of both the end of the Cold War and the breakup of the Soviet Union. The demise of the Cold War meant Russia lost its Warsaw Pact allies; the breakup of the Soviet Union meant Ukrainians, Moldavians, and others were no longer part of the Russian security scheme and might even become part of the new security problem.

Russia has other military problems. Partly because of budgetary problems, the military itself has deteriorated markedly. Because they are unable to subsist on wages that often are not paid, it is not unusual to see Russian soldiers in uniform working second jobs or panhandling on the streets of Moscow. The backbone of the Russian army is first-term conscripts, many of whom desert at the first possible opportunity with the implicit approval of the society. Even the prestigious Strategic Rocket Forces that control the Russian nuclear forces are leading advocates of arms control–dictated deep cuts in arsenal size, since they cannot maintain the current arsenal at any acceptable level of readiness and security. The Army's efficiency has been reduced to the point that it was unable to put down a ragtag Muslim rebellion in Chechnya and resorted to atrocities and the virtual leveling of the province to maintain control. The importance of Chechnya to Russia is explored in Amplification 4.3.

The solution to the Russian security problem centers on its evolving relationship with NATO. Originally, of course, NATO was formed largely to deter Soviet aggression; today, security is served by courting and embracing Russia. The problem is, how? Full NATO membership for Russia is one possibility, but it faces opposition that has to this point proven insurmountable. The chief obstacle is the status of Russia if it is a member—would it be a regular member like France or Germany, or a "special" member like the United States? Currently, the solution is Russian participation through the NATO-Russian Council, a consultative relationship and arrangement that allows Russian access to NATO short of being a member.

The ideal outcome to the Russian situation is the gradual emergence of Russia as a fully westernized political democracy with a growing and prosperous market-based economy that is a full participant in the international system. Some semblance of such an outcome is provided by the "honorary" membership of Russia in the G-8 deliberations of the world's most powerful economies and increasing inclusion in NATO.

The direction and future of the poorer and more remote successor states, and especially those in central Asia, have also become a source of concern. Most of these new countries are very poor, have few prospects for economic development or the emergence of democracy (generally lacking any democratic traditions), and have Muslim majorities or minorities that threaten to drag them into the instability of Muslim fundamentalism. In 2002, a number of these states were drawn into the campaign against international terrorism by the United States, with uncertain effects (discussed in the *Challenge!* box).

The European Security Problem

The end of the Cold War also destroyed the Eastern European security system. There was some initial concern that NATO might atrophy and collapse without the military opposition that had provided its *raison d'être* for over four decades, but those concerns have faded. NATO has retained a vitality born of new roles, including extending

Amplification 4.3

CHECHNYA AND THE PIPELINE

Russian security concerns and adaptation to a post–Cold War world have, in important ways, coalesced over the issue of Chechnya, a renegade republic in the Caucasus region of Russia that declared its independence from the Russian Federation in 1994 and has been fighting the Russians ever since to become an independent Muslim state. Like many other areas of the southern part of Russia, the citizens are not ethnic Russians and live in areas forcefully annexed to Russia.

Chechnya represents the Soviet dilemma of dealing with the post–Cold War period in at least three ways. One is clearly the precedent that would be set if Chechnya were allowed to secede from a Russia already diminished by the dissolution of the Soviet Union. Second, the ferocity—even barbarism—of the fighting created a public relations nightmare for the Russian government. The once proud Russian army has largely been ineffective in putting down the rebellion and has been reduced to leveling Chechen cities like Grozny to the ground, with pictorial documentation widely available worldwide. In the process, widespread accusations by human rights groups of atrocities committed by the Russians have caused embarrassment to the Russians and slowed the flow of developmental assistance to Russia. Since September 11, 2001, the Russians have sought to portray the Chechens as part of the web of international terrorism operating out of Afghanistan and Pakistan. Some of the Chechen "freedom fighters" have been shown to have common roots with Al Qaeda and other terrorist groups, and this depiction by the Russians has stilled much of the criticism of their brutality toward Chechnya.

The real heart of the Russian problem in Chechnya, however, revolves around getting Caspian Sea oil from Azerbaijan to markets in the west. Because the pipelines that will carry the oil can be taxed, there is great potential wealth that can be accrued to whatever country wins the competition to have the pipeline built across its territory. The possible routes are across Iran (not much of an alternative, since much of the reason for exploiting Caspian oil is to reduce dependence on the Persian Gulf), Turkey, and Russia. The Russians argue the revenue is absolutely vital to Russian economic development because it would greatly augment the central government's tax revenues. The problem, however, is that by far the most direct and economically viable way to build a pipeline across Russia is to build it through Chechnya. As long as there is an embarrassing armed rebellion in that republic, Russia's chances are visibly diminished (the pipeline problem is discussed in some detail in *Cases in International Relations*, Chapter 14).

membership to the formerly Communist world. The European security problem thus comes down to providing security to eastern Europe and the former Soviet Union so that those countries do not threaten the security of the West. It is well under way.

In 1991, there was an initial fear that the toppling of Communist regimes would result in political instability in some of the poorer eastern European countries (e.g.,

Challenge!

THE FORMER SOVIET UNION AND THE WAR ON TERRORISM

War, it is sometimes said, makes strange bedfellows, and the attempt by the U.S. government to internationalize its warlike campaign against terrorism seems to provide some evidence for the truth of that proposition. Nowhere is that relationship more clearly demonstrated than in the extension of partnership in the "war on terrorism" to central Asian states and Russia itself.

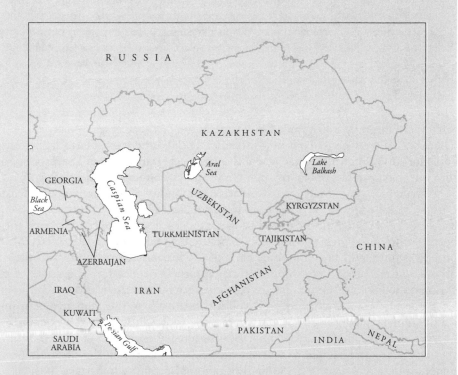

One of chief problems the Bush administration encountered early in trying to mount military, and especially ground, operations to clear out Al Qaeda and Taliban residues in Afghanistan was staging grounds for such efforts. For a variety of reasons, the territory of some American associates was either unavailable politically for such actions (Saudi Arabia, Pakistan, for instance) or was too remote for efficient use (Turkey). In those circumstances, the United States turned to contiguous states, former Soviet central Asian republics that had gained their independence with the breakup of the Soviet Union. To facilitate the military campaign, the United States signed basing agreements with states including Tajikistan, Kyrgyzstan, and Uzbekistan, and opened discussions with others.

These arrangements immediately brought the American government into policy dis-agreement with itself, a problem that extended to Russian assistance to the effort as well (after eight years of war in Afghanistan, the Russians are a major source of intelligence on that country). The policy incompatibility pitted counterterrorism policy against human rights policy, because many of the new allies in the campaign against terrorism, including Russia, were also on the Department of State's list (as well as those of independent sources such as Amnesty International and Human Rights Watch) of states that violated the civil rights of their citizens and thus were to be sanctioned until those practices ceased.

How is the dilemma to be resolved? Is the war on terrorism such an important priority that it overrides other concerns, in this case human rights? Is there a parallel to the Cold War here? During the Cold War, the United States supported many corrupt right-wing regimes that regularly abused their citizens because their leaders professed staunch anti-Communism. Anti-Communism overrode other concerns. Is the profession of opposition to terrorism and willingness to aid in the campaign against terrorism the new anti-Communism of the contemporary age? Is it worth the price in the long run to be associated with regimes that abuse their citizens? Decide for yourself.

Albania, Bulgaria) and former Soviet states (e.g., the Central Asian republics). There was also concern about new interstate conflicts between places like Romania and Hungary, which had a territorial dispute over Transylvania. The process, as it turn out, has been less traumatic than many analysts envisaged a decade ago.

Two reasons stand out for this relative tranquility. First, the people of eastern Europe and the former Soviet Union both shucked Communist rule with ease and the absence of regret and embraced Western values. They have tried to emulate and become part of the greater world system politically and economically. Certainly this process is further advanced in some parts of the formerly Communist world than in others, but the process of assimilation has clearly been aided by the desire of most countries to become "normal" states participating fully in the world system.

Second, the system has adapted well institutionally to the challenge of assimila-tion. An umbrella organization, the Conference (now Organization) for Security and Cooperation in Europe (CSCE, now OSCE) already existed to provide a forum for the new states and the old to interact. It has been clear from the beginning that a major aspiration of most of the formerly Communist states is to partake in the greater prosperity of western Europe. Membership in the European Union (EU) is a major goal of nearly all these states. The European Union has been quite responsive to this desire and has made economic arrangements with a number of the new states. The informal criteria for membership have always been a strong, market-oriented econ-omy and a working political democracy, providing strong incentive to adopt those underlying values. Hungary, the Czech Republic, Poland, Slovenia, Estonia, Latvia, Lithuania, Cyprus, Malta, and Slovakia have all been admitted to EU.

The remaining obstacle was the extension of NATO into the formerly Commu-nist world. The interim solution in the early 1990s was a Clinton administration initiative, the Partnership for Peace (PFP). Participation in PFP, which was offered to the Eastern European states and the successor states to the Soviet Union, was a kind of partial membership in NATO, affording some benefits such as nonvoting attendance at NATO functions and participation in some NATO military exercises, but not the guarantee that the full NATO members will defend PFP countries in the event of hostilities. Most states became members of PFP in what they saw as a first step toward full NATO membership.

Expansion into eastern Europe began in 1999, when Hungary, Poland, and the Czech Republic were granted full membership in the organization, bringing the NATO total to nineteen. In Prague in November 2002, the membership was increased to twenty-six states with the admission of seven former Communist territories: Bulgaria, Estonia, Latvia, Lithuania, Romania, Slovakia, and Slovenia.

CONCLUSION: THE END OF THE COLD WAR IN PERSPECTIVE

Viewed strictly from the vantage point of the twenty-first century, the Cold War years must seem an anomalous period, one that probably should be consigned to the history books. Although many of the problems and tensions associated with the second half of the twentieth century have proven to be less enduring than those of us who witnessed them thought they would be, such a view would be shortsighted and would miss the point of how the Cold War continues to influence us.

The Cold War remains the context from which the contemporary system is emerging. Among the overarching concerns of the new millennium are the integration of the formerly Marxist-Leninist states into the globalization system, a problem that clearly could not have existed had there not been a furtive competition between ideologically defined contenders in the first place. This process of integration is being stimulated by the enlistment of former enemies as allies in the campaign against terrorism. The consequences of this initiative are uncertain but probably extend beyond the terrorism campaign itself. For better or worse, many of the difficulties with which we grapple in the contemporary world have their origins in the Cold War and can only be fully understood in that light.

There is, I think, a more fundamental reason to understand the Cold War and its ending. Most of the people in important decision-making positions in the 1990s and 2000s—and especially senior people in senior positions—have the Cold War as their formative experience, and their thinking was and continues to be influenced by the very grim, determined worldview that "working" the Cold War produced. In the Bush administration, the list of foreign and national security policy insiders with Cold War credentials includes Secretary of Defense Rumsfeld, Secretary of State Rice, and Vice President Richard Cheney, to name the most prominent.

Some of the things that happen today make more sense in the light of the experience of the Cold Warriors. Why the United States would spend as much as the rest of the world combined on defense and propose to spend even more on something like missile defense and antiterrorism makes much more sense coming from the minds of actors whose instincts tell them always to fear and prepare for the absolute worst. But if, like Donald Rumsfeld, you were secretary of defense in 1976 and returned to that same position a quarter-century later, you could not avoid bringing some baggage with you. In the Cold War, the response to the threat was greater expenditure on conventional defense. Can it come as a great surprise that essentially the same actors who made those decisions would respond similarly to the very different threat of terrorism now?

The same quality of response may not occur in ten or twenty years, when the world may have changed enough to remove the old residues and the Cold Warriors have faded away and been replaced by new decision makers for whom the Cold War is abstract history rather than personal experience. Until the system and its operators get to that point, however, the Cold War remains the context of the present.

SELECTED BIBLIOGRAPHY

Bialer, Seweryn, and Michael Mandelbaum (Eds.). *Gorbachev's Russia and American Foreign Policy*. Boulder, CO: Westview Press, 1988.

Brzezinski, Zbigniew. "The Cold War and Its Aftermath." *Foreign Affairs* 71, 4 (Fall 1992), 31–49.

Clark, Ronald W. *The Greatest Power on Earth: The International Race for Nuclear Supremacy from Earliest Theory to Three Mile Island*. New York: Harper and Row, 1980.

Claude, Inis L. *The Changing United Nations*. New York: Random House, 1967.

Fukuyama, Francis. *The End of History and the Last Man*. New York: Free Press, 1992.

Gaddis, John Lewis. *The United States and the End of the Cold War: Implications, Reconsiderations, Provocations*. New York: Oxford University Press, 1992.

Gorbachev, Mikhail S. *Perestroika: New Thinking for Our Country and the World*. New York: Harper and Row, 1987.

Mearsheimer, John J. "Why We Shall Soon Miss the Cold War." *Atlantic Monthly* 262, 2 (August 1990), 35–50.

Simes, Dmitri. "The Return of Russian History." *Foreign Affairs* 73, 1 (January/February 1992), 67–82.

Snow, Donald M. *The Necessary Peace: Nuclear Weapons and Superpower Relations*. Lexington, MA: Lexington Books, 1987.

———. *The Shape of the Future: The Post–Cold War World* (2nd ed.). Armonk, NY: M. E. Sharpe Publishers, 1995.

———. *Cases in International Relations: Portraits of the Future*. New York: Longman, 2002.

Stephanova, Ekaterina. "War and Peace Building." *Washington Quarterly* 27, 4 (Autumn 2004), 127–136.

CHAPTER 5

The Rise of Globalization

PREVIEW

This chapter introduces and traces the international dynamic competing with geopolitics: globalization. The concept of international economic phenomena as integral parts of the national security theme is of recent vintage, as is the idea of casting geopolitics (for most purposes a synonym for realism) and globalization and other nonmilitary aspects as alternate national security paradigms and considerations. As a result, the major thrust of this chapter is to introduce the international economic themes culminating in globalization and other concerns in a national security context. The method for doing this is a historical treatment of American participation in the post–World War II global economy, breaking the period into three distinct phases, including the present. The chapter concludes with some preliminary discussion of the ongoing competition between the two concepts.

Globalization and the impact of the globalizing economy were the centerpiece of the 1990s, just as terrorism has become the lightning rod of the early 2000s. During the 1990s, the international system moved away from its Cold War emphasis on geopolitically based national security concerns to a different emphasis. After the global economic recession of 1991 faded in 1992 and 1993, a period of growing economic prosperity and expansion blossomed as a trade-driven global phenomenon, and the economies of participating countries expanded in a near decade of unprecedented economic growth. This phenomenon was felt in most of the developed and parts of the developing world, but nowhere was it more evident than in the U.S. economy and for individual Americans. The U.S. economy emerged from a decade or more of relative economic listlessness to reclaim its position as the dominant economic force in the world.

This period of economic expansion induced an overreaction about the degree and depth of transformation that had occurred. Until the system endured a major shakeup in the form of the East Asian crisis of 1997 (discussed later in this chapter), there was a near euphoria about the benefits and endurance of globalization's seemingly inexorable benefits. Analysts suggested that this new phenomenon of globalization was fundamentally altering the world system. Globalization simultaneously accelerated and changed the product cycle and production system at a dizzying pace and allowed for unprecedented levels and speed of communication between governments, citizens, and firms worldwide. To its most vocal adherents, realism-based geopolitics was giving way to globalization as the dominant force in international relations. At the same time, phenomena as diverse as global warming and illicit drugs were being added to the list of conditions that affect the country's security.

The relative roles of geopolitics and globalization fit into the broader debate about America's place in the world introduced earlier and developed throughout the book. The internationalist strain in America's view of the world has always been strongly represented in the economic debate, and the United States has been a leader in the promotion of increased world trade since it emerged as an industrial power after the American Civil War. Even when the country withdrew *politically* from international affairs between the world wars into "splendid isolationism," it remained a very active member of the international economic system. The same internationalism that manifests itself in a politically activist role and an expansive view of the country's military obligations is also a part of the economic debate, the current focus of which is globalization. The so-called economic rejectionists, who have been active in disrupting pro-globalization international economic meetings in recent years, can similarly be seen as the inheritors of the tradition of those who would prefer a more limited role for the United States.

The strains of geopolitics and globalization represent different places in thinking about national security as well. The geopolitical tradition is grounded largely in the equation of national security and military affairs (the de facto emphasis of realism), with nonmilitary aspects of security taking a decidedly secondary place. The globalization perspective, on the other hand, argues that economic concerns offer the tip of the spear for a broader conceptualization of security, adding concerns as diverse as the AIDS pandemic (which President Clinton declared a national security matter in 1999), the environment, and drugs to those conditions that affect national security. The globalization perspective does not so much downplay the importance of military affairs as it adds to them.

Clearly, the two perspectives are not mutually exclusive but exist more along a continuum of relative emphasis on one element or the other. Geopolitics, for instance, may emphasize power and military force as chief elements of national security, but those elements have little meaning if not applied to the furtherance of American interests in areas such as economics, environmental degradation, or other substantive conditions that define security. At the same time, the pursuit of economic or other security conditions is likely to be incomplete, even impossible, without traditional military force somewhere in the background.

The purpose of this chapter is to create a foundation for thinking about the role and impact of economic and, to a lesser extent, other concerns on foreign and national security policy. We proceed historically from the end of World War II, dividing the American international economic experience into three distinct periods. We begin by discussing the American-dominated economic system that emerged from World War II, the Bretton Woods system. We then move to the transitional period between the American denunciation of the gold standard in 1971 and the emergence of globalism somewhere around the end of the 1980s. We conclude with the contemporary period of globalization and where it may be leading, particularly in light of the resurgence of terrorism-led geopolitics in 2001. This contemporary period has also witnessed the addition of other national security agenda items, which we note and briefly describe.

THE BRETTON WOODS SYSTEM, 1945–1971

What became known as the Bretton Woods system had its roots in World War II. It reflected perceptions about how the interwar international economic system had helped precipitate the war and about the nature of the postwar international economic situation. The result was a series of international negotiations dominated by the Americans and the British that produced an institutional framework that organized the revised and rejuvenated economic order.

The Setting

Two overarching international economic facts dominated the international scene in 1945 and were the major concerns of postwar planners seeking to recreate an international system that would not slide back to instability and yet another devastating war. First, the United States emerged from the war with the overwhelmingly largest and most robust economy in the world. It was thus the only country capable of leading a postwar reconstruction of the global economy. Second, most economic observers believed that economic policies pursued between the world wars had contributed significantly to the slide toward war. Each fact had major implications for the restructuring of the global economy.

The American economy had been rescued and strengthened absolutely and relatively by World War II. The U.S. economy had been hard hit by the Great Depression (as had Germany, and that impact was partially blamed for the rise of Hitler and thus the war). On the eve of World War II, the American industrial plant was working at only about a third of its capacity. When the United States entered the war, that unused capacity was activated to transform the country's industrial base into the "arsenal of democracy," producing the war materiel that would bring down the Axis powers. The unemployment that had been the most visible symbol of the depression evaporated in the economic and military mobilization. The American economy was thus revived by the war, and when it was over, it was ready to turn its full strength to fulfilling consumer demand that had been frustrated by the war effort. Moreover, the United States was the only major participant whose economy was not damaged militarily; thus the economy emerged untouched by the ravages of war, a fate unshared by other countries, which had at least part of their economies destroyed and which were therefore in need of rebuilding.

American economic preeminence meant the United States was the only candidate to lead any global economic recovery. Because the United States possessed an enormous amount of leverage to structure that system, it was very difficult for the other World War II participants to resist American preferences. The question was whether and how the Americans would lead the world economy to a stable new prosperity.

Answers about the direction of the global economy were worked out as part of the wartime allied collaboration that also produced the United Nations. The security problem during the interwar years had been a League of Nations that was not strong enough to enforce policies that would maintain the peace. The economic realm was even worse: an international institutional void in the area of economics allowed states to pursue policies that created an economic crisis in the 1930s that many believed led to the war.

A major culprit in interwar economics had been the punitive nature of the Versailles peace treaty that ended World War I. In 1919, Germany was forced to accept total responsibility for starting the war through the War Guilt Clause, Article 231. This provision justified sizable reparations from Germany to pay for the destruction in France (where most of the physical fighting on the western front occurred) and also to Great Britain. The reparations payments virtually ensured that Germany could not recover from the war economically. The effect was that the Great Depression hit Germany harder than any other country on the continent. Amid enormous depression-induced economic suffering in the early 1930s, the same Adolf Hitler who was laughed at and jailed when he first appeared on the political scene in the more prosperous 1920s was elected chancellor of Germany in 1932. Part of his appeal was the promise of restoring economic prosperity.

The Great Depression also set off a wave of economic nationalism that worsened matters worldwide. As the effects of the depression spread throughout Europe and threatened the integrity of industries and businesses, governments responded with protective barriers in the form of very high tariffs and other devices designed to protect indigenous industries from foreign competition by making outside goods and services artificially more expensive than domestic counterparts. These barriers reduced trade to a trickle of its pre-depression levels and added to the general animosity between countries that was greasing the slide to world war.

These perceptions helped predispose those who would take the lead in fashioning the postwar economic system. The isolationism that had been a firm part of the economic nationalism—some called it economic warfare—of the 1930s was firmly rejected. So was the notion of a punitive peace that had crippled the defeated Allies, ensured they could not fully embrace the peace settlement, and ultimately encouraged another global war.

The Bretton Woods Institutions

Formal planning for the revised economic order was a wartime enterprise dominated by the Americans and the British. Each had somewhat different perspectives on what should be done after the war ended, and each produced different blueprints for the future.

The initial international conference to craft a new set of structures was held in July 1944 in the New Hampshire resort town of Bretton Woods at the picturesque Hotel Washington nestled at the foot of Mount Washington in the White Mountains. Representing forty-four countries, the planners at Bretton Woods began by agreeing that the economic protectionism of the interwar years had contributed to the war and that protectionism had to be attacked if economic stability was to be reinstated. Specifically, they were concerned about international financial and economic practices: large fluctuations in exchange rates of currencies, chronic balance of payments problems experienced by some countries, and the high tariffs that had dominated the 1930s. All of these problems restricted the flow of international commerce, and there was a clear underlying preference for moving toward a system of considerably freer trade than had existed before the war. This free trade, internationalist position dominated the American delegation to Bretton Woods, although there remained significant protectionist sentiment within Congress and some conservative American organizations like the U.S. Chamber of Commerce.

The conferees produced agreements that created two institutions forming the core of the Bretton Woods system. At the same time, they deferred consideration of the more politically divisive issue of institutionalizing free trade until after the war was over. The institutions created were the *International Monetary Fund (IMF)* and the *International Bank for Reconstruction and Development (IBRD or World Bank)*. Both had the initial purpose of dealing with the specific problems identified as economic problems during the war. The IMF would deal with currency stabilization and balance of payments difficulties by authorizing what amounted to lines of credit to countries suffering difficulties in these areas. The World Bank was authorized to grant loans, as its formal name implied, for assisting in reconstructing war-torn economies and later developing less developed countries. Both organizations were funded by subscriptions from the members with weighted voting privileges depending on the amount of initial subscription. Because the United States had the most money to subscribe, it received the largest bloc of votes (about one-third) in both organizations.

Both institutions were heavily American from the beginning. There was strong support for both the IMF and IBRD in the United States, reflected by the votes authorizing participation in both by the U.S. Senate of 61 to 16 and the House of Representatives of 345 to 18. The permanent headquarters for the two organizations would be a city block in downtown Washington, D.C., that is a short walk from the White House and the old Executive Office Building that houses most of the White House staff. The president of the Bank has always been an American, and it is not infrequent for Americans to move freely between positions in the IMF or IBRD and agencies of the federal government like the Treasury Department.

The fate of institutionalized free trade was not so smooth, reflecting historic American debates about America's role and American economic and political independence in the world. Aside from questions of internationalism and protectionism, the desirability of the United States being institutionally entwined in free trade regimes also raised questions about impingement on state sovereignty among critics and opponents. These opposing viewpoints were as present in 1945 as they are in 2006.

The attempt to institutionalize international free trade began when the war ended but faced a perilous political course. Within the American administration of Harry S. Truman, there was great support for an institutional commitment through an organization parallel to the IMF and IBRD, thus completing the Bretton Woods institutions as a troika of international economic organizations. This idea, however, had both domestic and international opponents who effectively blocked the movement.

The Truman administration's strategy for lowering trade barriers consisted of two parts, both of which have their parallels in the contemporary debate over trade. One of these was to pursue bilateral and multilateral reductions in tariffs and quotas under the provisions of the Reciprocal Trade Agreements Act (RTAA) of 1934. The RTAA, which was passed in reaction to the extreme protectionism of the Smoot-Hawley Tariff Act of 1930, authorized the administration to reduce tariffs on specific items by up to 50 percent with other countries, but only if the reductions were reciprocal. It did not authorize the elimination of any trade barriers and thus was only a modest first step toward the administration's goal of freeing trade. It was the precursor to so-called fast-track (or what the Bush administration calls trade promotion) authority.

The heart of the free trade initiative was to be an international organization, the *International Trade Organization (ITO)*. The purposes of this organization were to promote free trade among its members and to create an enforcement mechanism to investigate and punish those who violated trade agreements into which they had entered. In order to draft a statute for the ITO similar to those of the Bretton Woods institutions, a preliminary meeting was held in 1947 in Geneva, Switzerland, to lay out trading principles under the name of the *General Agreement on Tariffs and Trade (GATT)*. The GATT was intended as a temporary umbrella, an expedient device wherein general principles could be drafted to govern the permanent ITO.

The meeting at which the ITO was proposed was held in Havana in November 1947. By the time it was convened, domestic and foreign opponents to the principle of universal free trade had organized themselves well enough to dilute the outcome. These early "rejectionists" argued against domestic and international impacts of loosening trading restrictions and for the protection of special arrangements, such as the British Imperial Preference System (which created special tariff status between Great Britain and members of the empire and Commonwealth). In addition, other national delegations refused to grant the United States the deference accorded it through weighted voting in the IMF and IBRD. Instead, they insisted that the United States would be given a single vote like any other country.

The ITO never came into being. President Truman refused to submit the ITO treaty to the Senate in 1948. He feared that in an election year, free trade, with considerable opposition in Congress and the public, might become a campaign issue. In 1949, the administration's effort to gain ratification of the North Atlantic Treaty (the first

Amplification 5.1

THE ITO AND THE ANTI–FREE TRADERS

The noteworthy failure of the Bretton Woods process was the inability to bring the International Trade Organization (ITO) into existence. The result stymied the maximum promotion of free trade, which was one of the major objectives of the architects of the Bretton Woods system. Reflecting the long-standing American ambivalence about the proper role for the United States in the international economic order, the United States both proposed the ITO to the international community and brought about its defeat by failing to ratify the ITO treaty.

As a domestic political event, the scenario was familiar. The principal backers of the ITO were in the executive branch: the original impetus for the body came from State Department planners during World War II, and when Harry S. Truman succeeded the late Franklin D. Roosevelt, his administration took the lead in proposing a United Nations Conference on Trade and Development in 1946 to draft the statute for the ITO.

Major opposition congealed in the Congress. The major elements in the protectionist coalition were Republicans who were influenced by major business and commercial interest groups that believed in protecting American products from foreign competition. Both manufacturing and farm elements were represented in this effort. At the other extreme, a number of liberal Democrats who believed the ITO statute was too timid a document in promoting free trade joined the opposition, as did conservatives who opposed the ITO on the grounds that it represented a dangerous assault on American sovereignty. The opposition successfully blocked Senate advice and consent on the matter and provided a precedent for the kind of odd-bedfellows coalition that would emerge as rejectionists at the turn of the twenty-first century.

peacetime military alliance in American history) pushed the ITO off the agenda. By the time the president submitted the treaty to the Senate in April 1950, enthusiasm for international organizational solutions to problems had cooled, and the outbreak of the Korean War in June 1950 reinforced that sentiment. In November 1950, Truman withdrew the ITO proposal from Senate consideration, and the ITO idea was a dead horse until it was revived in 1993 as the World Trade Organization (WTO).

The GATT, however, survived. Although protectionists did not like it much more than the ITO, it was less threatening to their cause. The GATT was not an organization at all, but a series of periodically convened negotiating sessions between sovereign states. This lack of structure meant that it would have no permanent investigating or enforcing staff that could enforce objectionable rules on countries and thereby infringe on their sovereignty. Also, as a series of negotiations (that became known as "rounds"), the individual states retained maximum control over what they were willing or unwilling to be bound to accept by signing or not signing individual proposals.

The GATT thus became the banner around which the free traders could congregate until the time was right for them to assert their case for a permanent international organization. In the process, the GATT developed a set of four principles that defined its operation and remain important points of reference to this day (summarized in Rothgeb, p. 75). These include *nondiscrimination* (the promotion of most-favored nation—MFN—status to all subscribing countries), *transparency* (the unacceptability of secret trade restrictions and barriers), *consultation and dispute settlement* (resolution of disputes through direct negotiations), and *reciprocity* (the idea all members should incur balanced obligations).

The free trade issues raised in the 1940s are instructive because they are parallel to and even anticipate the same kinds of debates and problems that enliven the 2000s. The debate over the extent to which free trade should be an active part of American international economic policy stands at the vortex of the issue. Generally speaking, there has been a domestic political debate with strong interbranch implications: the White House in the 1940s was the epicenter of free trade advocacy under Roosevelt and Truman, and has been for the last decade under Clinton and Bush. On the other side of the coin, organized political opposition has largely come from elements in Congress with constituencies harmed by and thus opposed to free trade. What is different is that in the 1940s, most of the organized congressional opposition was Republican, whereas much of the current opposition is Democratic.

This disagreement manifests itself in two distinct ways. One is the amount of discretion the Congress is willing to grant the executive to negotiate trade arrangements. The general outcome has been to give the president some tethered leeway. Congress granted the president limited authority to negotiate tariff reductions through the RTAA of 1934, but it restricted what he could negotiate and under what circumstances. Moreover, the RTAA was time-limited legislation that automatically expired in 1948. The Congress continued to renew the RTAA annually until 1962, but the threat of nonrenewal—presumably if the president exceeded his authority—provided the Congressional tether. A parallel exists over the so-called fast track legislation that authorized the president to negotiate trade agreements the Congress can only approve or disapprove but cannot amend. That legislation was also renewable and expired in 1993. The efforts first by President Clinton and later by Bush to get it reinstated have been an ongoing interbranch struggle with strong free trade bases that was resolved for now by extending the authority to Bush in 2002.

The other form of disagreement was over the international institutionalization of free trade. Congressional opposition effectively killed the ITO when Truman determined he did not have the votes in the Senate for ratification, and the issue remained dormant for over four decades. The call for an international organization, the WTO, emerged from the 1993 Uruguay Round of the GATT, and in a changed economic atmosphere where cutting-edge American industries in areas such as telecommunications and financial services would clearly benefit from institutionalization, the Senate passed the treaty forming the WTO (which took effect on January 1, 1995). The ITO was thus reborn as the WTO.

The other common thread of the two experiences is organized opposition to the idea of free trade. When opponents of the WTO took to the streets of Seattle in 1999 to disrupt its proceedings and carried their street tactics to meetings of organizations like the G-8 in Ottawa and Genoa and the Asia-Pacific Economic Cooperation (APEC) and the Free Trade Area of the Americas (FTAA) in Washington, they reflected a long-standing opposition to the underlying free trade values of all those organizations. The focus of those objections has changed somewhat; there were, for instance, no opponents of global warming in the 1940s. As well, the tactics and forums have changed. In the 1940s, opposition was expressed in the pin-striped suit–dominated halls of Congress, in contrast to the often rowdy street demonstrations of the 1990s and 2000s. Demonstrations accompanying President Bush's attendance at the 2005 meetings of the FTAA in Argentina and the APEC in South Korea show the continuing strength of opposition.

The Breakdown of Bretton Woods

For the first two decades following World War II, the Bretton Woods system dominated in international economics. During this time, the United States held sway over the international economic system basically because the U.S. economy was the dominant economic force in the world. Because countries needed U.S. economic resources and goods, the dollar became the only "hard" currency in the world (the only currency universally accepted in international trade). Regulating the supply of dollars in the international system provided a considerable source of leverage for the United States in international financial circles.

The attractiveness of the dollar was also enhanced because it was tied to the gold standard. As a matter of U.S. policy, every dollar in circulation was backed by gold in the amount that one ounce of gold was worth $35. The gold standard meant that, at least theoretically, anyone with $35 in cash could trade it in for one ounce of gold from Fort Knox, Kentucky, or some other federal gold depository. The gold standard was always a fiction (the United States never possessed enough gold to redeem all the dollars in circulation), but the promise of the gold standard created an aura of confidence around the value of the dollar that stabilized the entire financial system.

The strength of the Bretton Woods system was predicated on the preeminence of the American economic system and currency, and the system was bound to founder as the relative position of the United States in the world economic order faltered, which began to happen in the 1960s. Some of these changes were the direct consequence of American actions in the world; others were the result of domestically based political decisions.

Part of the change was the postwar recovery in Europe and Japan. In the late 1940s, the American economy was producing about 40 percent of all the goods and services produced worldwide. Although a remarkable testimony to American productivity, this also reflected the absence of productivity in the other traditional industrial countries, all of which were struggling to recover and rebuild from the ravages of the war.

Faced with the geopolitical Soviet menace, it had been explicit U.S. policy starting in the 1940s to assist in the recovery of the European and Japanese economies through programs such as the Marshall Plan. The motivation for this was largely geopolitical—to increase the status of these countries as anti-Communist bastions and to insure that Communism did not appeal to their citizens. Pumped up by American dollars, the European and Japanese economies did recover—as intended—and became economic competitors to the United States. In the process, the American relative share of global GNP began to shrink, moving downward to the low 20 percents in the 1970s, where it has essentially remained since. The United States did not cease to be the preeminent economic power in the world, but it no longer enjoyed the same overwhelming level of superiority it once occupied.

Since purchases of goods and services in international trade are by and large made in the currency of the country from which those purchases are made, there suddenly was a demand for currencies other than the dollar to pay for goods and services from other countries. In addition, political and economic events during the 1960s were making continuing adherence to the gold standard an increasingly impossible fiction.

Several domestic events and trends in the 1960s contributed to this problem. In the mid-1960s, President Lyndon Johnson made the fateful decision to simultaneously finance the Vietnam War and the complex of entitlement programs known collectively as the Great Society without raising taxes. The result was the first sizable budget deficits and consequent accumulation of national debt in the United States since World War II. One consequence was a decline in confidence in the American economy, which, coupled with rising inflation and competition from foreign goods and services, created a new atmosphere in which American economic predominance was actually called into question for the first time since the end of the war.

The ultimate event occurred in 1971, when adherence to the gold standard became such a millstone on the American economy that it could no longer be sustained. The inflationary spiral of the 1960s had resulted in such a flood of dollars into circulation that the fiction of redemption of dollars for gold was increasingly obviously hollow. Moreover, pegging the value of the dollar to gold resulted in overvaluation of the dollar against other currencies. That in turn made it difficult for American producers to compete with their overseas counterparts (it took too many units of a foreign currency to buy enough American dollars to purchase American goods compared to goods from other countries).

These factors combined to force the U.S. government to renounce the gold standard in 1971. Dollars would no longer be redeemable in gold. More important, the value of the dollar would no longer be determined against a set quantity of the precious metal. Instead, the dollar would be allowed to "float" against other currencies, with its value set at whatever price others were willing to pay for it in other currencies. The dollar thus essentially became a commodity like other commodities and would have to compete with other currencies in the marketplace. Almost instantly, other currencies (especially those from places such as Germany and Japan, which produced goods and services desired in world markets) became hard currencies. The global economic competition was on, and American preeminence was no longer to be taken for granted.

THE TRANSITIONAL PERIOD, 1971–1990

The renunciation of the gold standard ushered in a period of change in the structure of the international economic system. The broad theme of the period was apparent

American decline in military and political power (largely the result of the Vietnam experience), but especially in the economic realm during the 1970s, followed by resurgence by the end of the 1980s.

The 1970s was a difficult period of transition in the United States. Economic turbulence was assured by the oil shocks of 1973 and 1977. Led by its Middle East members, the Organization of Petroleum Exporting Countries (OPEC) took a series of joint actions that greatly raised the price of oil to all consuming countries. In 1973, these actions were accompanied by a boycott of countries that did not denounce Israel after the Yom Kippur War. The consequent shortages in the United States and the Netherlands (the only major states that refused to condemn Israel) resulted in long gas lines and higher prices at the pump in both countries.

The rise in the price of oil had structural effects on the global economy. Europe and Japan were rebuilt after World War II using petroleum as the basic energy source. The reason was that Middle Eastern oil was plentiful and was largely controlled by the major western oil companies (known as the Seven Sisters), thereby guaranteeing availability at a low cost ($3 to $5 a barrel). Most of Europe and Japan became heavily dependent on imported oil, since neither had domestic sources (the North Sea oil fields had not been exploited at this point). As the price of oil rose to $20 a barrel and more, the First Tier states became debtors to the oil-producing states, and successful competition in global markets to sell goods and services to buy petroleum became a serious business. Economic competitiveness in global markets became increasingly important for overall prosperity.

Other events in the United States were undermining America's normal high level of self-confidence. In 1973, the United States removed its last combat troops from Vietnam, in effect admitting its failure to prevail in that conflict. Controversy over the U.S. participation reached a crescendo of recrimination. Shortly on the heels of that withdrawal, the Watergate scandal (the break-in of Democratic Party headquarters at the Watergate apartment complex in Washington during the 1972 presidential campaign by Nixon campaign authorities and the subsequent attempt to cover up and deny presidential involvement in the affair) broke into the open. In 1974, President Richard M. Nixon, facing an impeachment trial in the United States Senate, became the only president in American history to resign from office. American faith in and support for political institutions and leaders hit rock bottom.

American Decline

Economic bad news accompanied these political mishaps. One of the apparent legacies of deficits created by financing the war in Vietnam was a high rate of inflation. By the end of the 1970s, it had become "double digit" (over 10 percent annually). Inflation eroded consumer buying power and created a sense of economic malaise. Worse yet, there was growing evidence that American industry was losing its competitive edge against other countries (especially Germany and Japan) and that the United States was in apparent economic decline. The question in the minds of many Americans was not whether this was happening, but how pervasive the losses were and how permanent the phenomenon was.

The evidence of economic decline seemed to cut across the board. American industries appeared to have become soft, no longer innovating as were competitors in Europe and Japan. American industries were losing market share in a wide variety of products from consumer electronics to heavy machinery, from hospital equipment to automobiles. Some dark predictions hinted this condition might even worsen to the point that the United States would fade into second-class status. One prediction, put forward by Yale historian Paul Kennedy (see Amplification 5.2) went so far as to prophesy that the United States would fade as a world power due to imperial overreach.

The potential national security consequences of the Vietnam "hangover" (the negative reaction to military involvement after the Vietnam conflict) and economic decline seemed to go hand in hand. If the American economy might no longer dominate the international economic system, and there was a decline in

Amplification 5.2

THE DECLINIST THESIS

The idea that the United States might be in a possibly irreversible process of national decline as a great power was most often associated in the 1980s with Yale historian Paul Kennedy, who in 1987 published *The Rise and Fall of the Great Powers: Economic Change and Military Change from 1500 to 2000*. Given American economic woes during the 1970s and 1980s, Kennedy's "declinist thesis" found many receptive ears.

In the book, Kennedy put forward as his central thesis the idea that "imperial overreach" is the trigger of national decline. Citing Great Britain and Imperial Russia as prime historical examples, Kennedy argued that great states had a tendency over time to overextend themselves militarily as they widened their imperial interests. This military burden, he contended, eventually placed such a strain on the economic underpinnings of the state that the power of the great state eventually went into decline. This, he argued, is what had happened to the British and to the Russians, and he suspected that the same overreach had afflicted the United States and quite possibly the Soviet Union. In circumstances in which the American share of production appeared to be in relative decline and there was slippage in everything from scores on standardized mathematics and science tests to health standards, many found the Kennedy thesis compelling.

Others did not, and the declinist thesis never lacked critics. One of the loudest critics was Harvard political scientist (and Clinton administration official) Joseph S. Nye Jr., who, in his 1990 book *Bound to Lead*, maintained the United States economy was much healthier than was argued by the declinists. He cited, for instance, the falsity of the amount of slippage of the American economy relative to others on the basis that the comparisons essentially "cooked the books" by comparing levels of productivity in the 1940s (when the American share was artificially inflated by postwar conditions) with the 1980s, when those levels were at more normal, and stable, levels. Time would prove Nye's projections to be more accurate than Kennedy's.

American military strength and will as well, it was not unreasonable to agree with Kennedy's pessimistic conclusions about the future. Fortunately, the dire predictions proved premature and false.

Driven by advances in high technology and changing policies and attitudes within the business and policy communities, things began to change in the 1980s. It was a quiet, virtually subterranean revolution. Much of the perception of malaise from the 1970s continued to dominate the public debate, and until the latter part of the decade, the Cold War continued to be the focal point of international concerns. One was much more likely to hear about the lack of competitiveness of American electronics or the seemingly endless military competition with the Soviets than about the crumbling of the Soviet empire or the resurgence of the American economy.

American Revival

Beginning in the 1970s and accelerating in the 1980s, policy and science coalesced to promote positive change. The policy arena of the 1980s was heavily influenced by the efforts of the Republican administration of Ronald W. Reagan in the United States and the Conservative British Prime Minister Margaret Thatcher, both of whom preached for and advocated a reduced role for government in the economic sector and a much more pure form of capitalism. Reagan's economic legacy was based on two predilections. His domestic economic program is remembered most distinctively for the huge tax reduction he pushed through Congress in 1981 that resulted in runaway government deficits and a skyrocketing debt the reduction of which became the centerpiece of Clinton fiscal policy in the 1990s. The recurring theme of the Reagan policy was "getting government off the people's backs."

Reagan and those around him also believed that the less government interference in and control over the economy, the better. It was Reagan's general belief, supported by Thatcher, that in economic matters, the private sector almost always made better decisions than did government officials and thus should be as unfettered from government intrusion as possible.

These predilections resulted in two policy thrusts. *Privatization* involved getting government out of operating businesses and turning formerly government operated functions over to private entrepreneurs and corporations. The idea was that privatization would result in increased efficiency and thus greater value for consumers. This thrust was particularly important to Thatcher because the British economy had considerably more public intrusion into economic affairs than was true in the United States. In the United States, the breakup of government monopolies such as long distance telephone service illustrated this philosophy.

Deregulation was the other shibboleth. A major perceived cause of the supposed economic decline, the Reaganites believed, was too much regulation of the private sector by the government, thereby stultifying the ability of the private sector to be flexible and to compete both domestically and internationally. By removing strictures on how business could be done, the result was to be greater efficiency in operation and hence competitiveness. Airline deregulation is a primary example of this philosophy in action.

Other forces were coming together to reinforce this set of policy predilections. A major source of change was emerging in the area of high technology, where the fruits of advances in computing and telecommunications (and the merger of these two industries to create the information age) were together changing the content and nature of what composed the cutting edge of economic and scientific activity. If the early post–World War II period had been dominated by the manufacture of goods, services and the monopoly on the most desired information came to represent the "commodity" of greatest value in the evolving economy. Figuratively speaking, software replaced steel-belted tires as the symbol of productivity.

In the period of declinist malaise, the enormous advantage of the United States in this kind of transformation was not as obvious as it is now. The chief engine of change was the computer, and the countries with the most powerful computers would lead the way in generating the knowledge and technology on which the cutting edge would be defined. The supercomputer (the most advanced computer at any point in time) was an American preserve that provided the basis for an American economic sector progressively attuned to exploiting this advantage.

The attractiveness of the American political and social system contributed to this growing American strength that became the basis for American resurgence in the 1990s. Fired by technological developments in computing, the birth of the Internet, and the like, the centers of American attraction emerged in the 1980s as magnets for the best young minds and most ambitious entrepreneurs in the world. They tended to congregate in places where there were clusters of great universities and pleasant living conditions and lifestyles. The Silicon Valley in California, nestled between and nurtured by great universities like Stanford and California–Berkeley, became the model for the further development of emerging technology, followed by places such as the Route 128 corridor outside Boston (in the shadow of Harvard and the Massachusetts Institute of Technology, among other schools), the Research Triangle in North Carolina, and others. These enclaves became the collective seedbed of America's return to preeminence.

The private sector made its contribution as well. During the period of American decline, a major criticism was that American manufacturing industry in particular had gone soft and complacent and that industries in hungrier and more ambitious countries had gained advantages, especially in the area of overseas trade. A primary example is the invidious comparison between the American and Japanese automobile industries.

This situation began to change in the 1980s, as the American manufacturing community began to reform itself by imitating the practices of countries such as Japan and restructuring the "sunset industries" (those declining in importance) through actions such as the now-familiar practice of "downsizing." As traditional American industries began to narrow the gap with their ambitious foreign rivals combined with new economic emphases in which the United States had a built-in advantage and the impact of foreign investment such as manufacturing plants on American soil came to the fore, the United States became poised for the resumption of economic leadership in the world.

Both the American decline and resurgence in the economic realm were gradual and, for the most part, not very dramatic. For those whose experience is limited to the bountiful expansion of the 1990s, it may seem difficult to think of a time when there was a more fearful, less confident United States sitting astride the world of geopolitics and globalization, but this was indeed the case during the 1970s and most of the 1980s. For those Americans who lived through that timeframe, it remains a benchmark against which to measure a return to the "bad old days" in much the same way that remembrance of the Great Depression conditioned the perspectives of older Americans.

The events that ushered in the age of globalization were political and not economic, although many of the most noticeable effects have been economic in the long run. The most obvious manifestations of change came from the end of the Cold War and the demise of Soviet and world Communism as the 1980s made the transition to the twentieth century's final decade. The end of the Cold War effectively ended the competition between economic ideologies and military machines. Socialist economics were so thoroughly discredited by the collapse of the politicoeconomic system that had enshrined Marx's and Engel's ideas that they have effectively disappeared. For the moment, at least, we are at Francis Fukuyama's "end of history" in the sense that there is no current intellectual competitor to the supremacy of political democracy and capitalist economics.

THE GLOBALIZING ECONOMY, 1990–PRESENT

The system of globalization resulted from a series of trends that came together in the 1990s rather than some traumatic economic event like American renunciation of the gold standard in 1971. The collapse of Communism provides a political benchmark of that emergence with some economic ramifications in the rise of globalism. The fall of Communism concluded the economic competition between socialism and capitalism, but the globalizing economy would probably have emerged anyway. Indeed, the economic disparities created by globalization might have been the economic force that toppled the Communist world in the 1990s, although many analysts argue that the inability of the Soviets to compete militarily was an equally or even more important factor in the collapse. Imagine the pressure on the socialist societies of Eastern Europe to join the general prosperity had they remained on the wrong side of a still-existing Iron Curtain but still could see how the West lived. Even more dramatically, imagine the trauma for China being a geopolitical enemy of the United States while simultaneously trying actively to participate in trade with this country.

The date the economic system moved from the transition period to the globalizing economy may be blurred and arbitrary, but the international economic system that it produced is, by now, reasonably well established, with a structure that clearly distinguishes it from the transitional period. For one thing, its presence in all parts of the world make it a truly global system. It is also universal in that the only alternative to participation in it is economic isolation. There are no competing images or systems providing an economic alternative—no Imperial Preference System of the interwar years or socialist world of the Cold War.

Globalization began with a distinctive set of values forged during the transition and to which the value of trade has been added as the 1990s' most important contribution to its evolution. Acceptance of the rules and values of globalization is the *sine qua non* for membership in the global economy and thus, for most purposes, participation in the prosperity that became a part of the globalizing economy in the 1990s. Those countries that reject participation must suffer the economic consequences in terms of prosperity. The pressure to become part of the globalizing economy may seem less obvious in a mid-2000s environment more closely focused on terrorism, but the pressures remain a potent force for many countries.

The emergence of the globalizing economy coincided with and helped contribute to the general global prosperity of most of the 1990s. At its height, the pressures toward globalization seemed ineluctable, and criticisms were weak and overwhelmed by advocates—even cheerleaders—such as the *New York Times'* Thomas L. Friedman. The euphoria has proven at least partially overly inflated. As chinks appeared in the armor of globalization enthusiasm, the critics came forward in increasingly public ways.

Although there has been great shock at the apparently radical nature of the objections raised by the rejectionists and their political allies, the basic arguments go back to fundamental arguments in the American political debate about the American place in the world (internationalism versus isolationism) and participation in the global economy (free trade versus protectionism), to say nothing of the parallel debate about national security (realism versus idealism). What goes around, it seems, comes around.

Characteristics and Values

The building blocks of the evolving "system of globalization" (to borrow Friedman's phrase) are central economic phenomena from the 1980s and the 1990s. The major contribution of the 1980s, as already mentioned, was the reassertion of the capitalist ethic of market-based economics. This philosophical underpinning proposed to free national economies from the government meddling and interference that it was argued had been a barrier to entrepreneurial growth and innovation. Privatization and deregulation were major tools in this policy change.

The major contributions of the 1990s represented a continuation but also a reversal of some policies with their roots in the 1980s. The continuity came in the form of the election of free trader Bill Clinton to succeed free trader George H. W. Bush as president. The result was that free trade advocacy has dominated in the executive branch of the U.S. government during most of the 1990s and beyond. The reversal in policy came through Clinton's successful commitment to wiping out budget deficits and reducing government debt as a way to improve the atmosphere in which economic entities do business in the 1990s, an emphasis largely abandoned after September 11. The combined effect was to create the so-called American model as the basis for the globalizing system.

A caveat to the legacy of the 1980s—market capitalism *within* national economies—must be added. The market capitalists rejected governmental management of economic activity, but they did *not* reject all governmental participation in providing a nurturing business environment. The specific areas of policy in which government participation is welcome is in governmental regulation, especially in overseeing the activities of financial institutions and in adopting macroeconomic policies that facilitate how business operates.

The willingness to accept some regulation of fiscal activity—especially the actions of banks and other financial institutions—has its American roots in the so-called S&L (savings and loan) scandal of the 1980s. The scandal is important because almost the same problems and solutions were encountered during the East Asian crisis of 1997 and its aftermath, when international institutions sought to enforce the same solutions on East Asian economies as the United States had adopted for itself. It will also be important as a precedent for future regulation of corporate accounting practices arising from the corporate scandals that first surfaced in 2002.

Prior to the S&L scandal, there had been very little regulation, and especially public accounting, of this part of the banking industry. The "thrifts," as they were known, were limited-purpose financial institutions specializing in activities such as home mortgages and business lending. Their attractiveness to investors was that they generally paid higher interest rates than regular banks and were thus desirable depositories for small investors to put their savings. They were not, however, subject to the same standards of reporting of activities as were regular banks, a matter that was not of great concern because savings accounts were insured by the government, and none had ever failed.

The scandal emerged when a number of S&Ls went bankrupt and threatened to dishonor investor accounts. The most famous bankruptcies were associated with the S&L empire of Arizona entrepreneur Charles Keating Jr. The investigation of a number of his institutions revealed a pattern of investor fund misuse through bad loans that could not be replayed (called nonperforming loans) and even bribes to public officials (five U.S. senators, known as the Keating Five, received favors from the banker) that had been concealed because of lax accounting rules. As the modest savings of many Americans were threatened, the U.S. Congress passed legislation aimed at guaranteeing investor confidence by insuring honesty and "transparency" (having records of transactions, the financial conditions of financial institutions, and the like publicly available for inspection) within these institutions. The reforms enacted in response to the S&L crisis restored public confidence and willingness to invest in institutions that loan funds to entrepreneurs. Over the objections of a Clinton administration that wanted them strengthened, these rules regarding accounting standards were relaxed after 1994, leading to the corporate scandals of 2002, which stimulated yet another round of reform legislation once again to create transparency.

The same rationale—bolstering public trust—applies to other forms of macroeconomic policy. Proponents of the American model believe the government has a limited useful role in the economy beyond making sure that bankers and others are honest. More specifically, the government can provide a useful service in creating a favorable fiscal climate for business and in providing services that are otherwise burdensome for the private sector.

The major beneficial macroeconomic policy of the 1990s was deficit reduction and elimination, a direct reversal of the practices of the Reagan years championed by Clinton and his closest economic advisers. A major impact of the Reagan deficits was to force large-scale government borrowing to cover obligations for which there were inadequate tax receipts. This borrowing came from the private sector, to which the government had primary access before private enterprises. Much of the money borrowed came from foreign sources (a controversial matter in its own right), but a sizable amount came from American sources. With the government in effect skimming funds available for borrowing before private firms got a chance, the result was a smaller pool of financial resources available for private firm innovation and investment. This problem has recurred and contributed to slower economic growth rates in the mid-2000s.

Reducing and ultimately eliminating deficits and beginning the process of reducing the overall debt reduction was largely the result of policies fashioned by Clinton Secretary of the Treasury Robert Rubin and enacted during the eight years of Bill Clinton's tenure in the White House. Even some of Clinton's critics have been forced to admit that it is no coincidence these policies and the prosperity of the 1990s coincided. Massive deficits have returned with the George W. Bush emphases on tax reductions and increased spending on the GWOT and Iraq.

The government also encourages entrepreneurial activity by providing the social net in the form of social security and related benefits for the general population. Doing so frees private concerns from having to develop such systems themselves, thus becoming the social net for their employees, and provides considerable flexibility for firms in their operations. Employees, for instance, are no longer tied closely to individual companies upon which they rely for things like health care and social security upon retirement. Instead, devices such as portable health insurance and government-provided pensions theoretically free companies to tailor and downsize their workforce without undue regard for the social consequences of laying off workers whose functions have been bypassed by change. The default on private pension obligations by United Airlines in 2005, followed by other companies that had also not contributed resources to pension funds in promised amounts, demonstrated that the relationship is less than foolproof.

The other policy triumph of the 1990s was the victory of free trade, a primary emphasis and legacy of Clinton. In concept, free trade represents the extension of David Ricardo's theory of comparative advantage to international economics. Politically, it represented the triumph, at least for the balance of the 1990s, of the free traders over the protectionists.

The ascendancy of free trade represented more of a practical than an ideological victory, as the negative reaction to free trade at the end of the decade and beyond showed. When Clinton came to office, one of his first priorities was the successful passage of the North American Free Trade Agreement (NAFTA) negotiated by George H. W. Bush through the Congress. The traditional coalitions had lined up in support and opposition based upon general preferences about American participation in international economics and the like. The authorizing legislation for NAFTA passed by a narrow margin in both houses of Congress (as an economic agreement rather than a treaty, it required House as well as Senate approval). NAFTA was followed by a flood of other activity supported by the free traders that, by the end of the decade, had locked the United States into a web of free trade associations from which extrication is now practically impossible. During much of Clinton's tenure, this process proceeded with virtually no organized or coordinated objections, with the major exception of the Congress's refusal to grant the administration fast-track authority (which the Bush administration has renamed trade promotion authority and has achieved) on two occasions. Demonstrations at the World Trade Organization meeting in Seattle in 1999 heralded the return of protectionist sentiment, which has continued. Why?

The broad answer is that economic circumstances had changed. When Clinton came to office, the recession of 1991 that had helped defeat the incumbent Bush in the 1992 election was lifting, replaced by an eight-year period of sustained growth

Challenge!

HOW IMPORTANT ARE A BALANCED BUDGET AND FREE TRADE?

Economic issues, and especially the structure of economic policies of the Clinton administration during the 1990s, have been under indirect assault since George W. Bush became president and especially since the terrorist attacks of September 11, 2001. The Bush administration's emphasis on the war on terrorism has pushed the emphasis on free trade to the back burner, and a combination of the 2001 tax cut and additional defense spending intended to combat terrorism have turned budget surpluses into growing deficits.

How important is free trade to the United States? When President Bush first entered office, he called spiritedly for resuming fast-track/trade promotion authority which, as noted in the text, is a prime instrument in promoting American leadership in the globalization system. When Congress balked on his proposal, he vowed to fight their reluctance, but that promise was largely submerged in his transformation into being a "wartime" president in the campaign against terrorism. In early spring 2002, he placed protective tariffs on imported steel to save American steel makers from foreign competition, while at the same time calling for trading authority, which he received. Was this a mixed message?

The same is true of balanced budgets. Before the terrorist attacks, the administration made a concerted effort to convince Congress and the American people of its commitment to a balanced budget and that the 2001 tax cut would not result in deficits. After the terrorist attacks, Bush proposed a $46 billion increase in defense spending that, combined with other initiatives, pushed the budget back into the red.

What do you think of these reversals? Are they justified by the need to combat terrorism? In the case of balanced budgets, do you think the increases can meaningfully be applied to the terrorism problem, or is terrorism simply being used as an excuse for more defense spending? Should an emphasis on free trade and balanced budgets occupy as important a place in national priorities as combating terrorism?

in the local and global economy. One can debate the degree to which Clinton was responsible for or simply the beneficiary of this expansion, but it was a period of unprecedented growth from which the vast majority benefited economically. The trade that Clinton promoted was clearly a major element in the prosperity, as cheaper foreign goods poured into the country to benefit consumers. While some American industries such as textiles suffered, in most cases there was enough prosperity to absorb most of those displaced. The argument that freeing trade was at least partially responsible for the prosperity was difficult to refute in that atmosphere, a situation that free trader Clinton nurtured and exploited.

The slowing of the economy at the end of the 1990s and the revival of opposition to free trade coincided. The results have been to reduce support for the globalization process internally within the United States and to revive political opposition that was latent during the booming 1990s. As has always been the case, free trade and protectionism have varied bases and varying arguments. Politically, the divide in the United States tends to be between the Congress and the Executive branch rather than along party lines.

Although the political context has swung back and forth on globalization, the 1990s left a legacy of policies and practices that make a reversion away from the dynamics of the global economy virtually impossible for the United States, which has been the principal proponent—and beneficiary—of the process. Part of the reason for this has been the institutionalization of globalism through a web of regional and universal international agreements and organizations.

The Mechanisms of Globalization

The process of institutionalizing globalization accelerated during the 1990s and has produced two distinct sets of institutions, agreements, and proposals. One set, to which the Bretton Woods process can be linked, involved the establishment of universal regimes promoting global economics. The IMF and World Bank are prototypes of this effort, as was the abortive International Trade Organization, the GATT, and now the WTO. At a less formal level, the G-8 also represents this tradition. The other emphasis, which has its concrete roots in the process that has evolved into the European Union (EU), has been regional. Its most prominent 1990s example is NAFTA, although it is also manifested in the APEC and more recently the proposed FTAA. With the partial exception of the European Union, the United States has been a direct creator and supporter of all of these efforts, each with the goal of increasing global economic interdependence and at least implicitly of promoting the American model of economic organization.

Both sets of institutions share the common goal of promoting the prosperity of their memberships through the reduction of barriers to trade among them. They differ in the specific qualifications for membership, geographically, politically, and economically. In some cases, the goals may seem incompatible in the sense that the regional organizations are geographically defined, may be explicitly competitive with one another, and may even discriminate against goods and services from rival regional associations. The ultimate logic of both instruments, however, is to promote globalization. The institutional network propounded by the universal organizations is a one-step approach to that end, whereas the regional organizations can be thought of as the first of two steps toward the promotion and emergence of the global economy.

The Universal Emphasis. Freeing trade was clearly one of the principal objectives of the countries that gathered at Bretton Woods in 1944. They were not, of course, instantly successful in institutionalizing this preference. At the time, protectionism was still strong enough to prevent American ratification of the ITO, forcing acceptance of the more limited and, from the vantage point of American critics of free trade, controllable GATT process.

That situation gradually changed. Over the years, the original Bretton Woods institutions expanded their roles in ways compatible with the promotion of what we now call the American model. The IBRD, for instance, went beyond merely processing loan applications to performing what amounted to audits of national economies to establish creditworthiness. Many private lenders came to base their loan decisions on World Bank ratings, thereby adding additional clout to Bank assessments. The IBRD criteria were fundamentally compatible with American economic values.

The IMF has had a similar evolution. Using its ability to issue credits to stabilize currencies as its major lever, the IMF began to inspect economies to see if they were sound enough to absorb IMF credits productively. If they were not, the IMF issued dictates about the fiscal and economic policies that had to be put in place to receive IMF assistance. Because these criteria almost always include austerity provisions, they are often unpopular, particularly in poor Second Tier countries that also argue there is little evidence that the restrictions produce their intended results.

The universalist approach is most prominently associated with the WTO. Virtually identical in purpose to the ITO, its existence is testimony to the difference in timing and political balance of the latter 1940s and the early 1990s. The objections to the two organizations were similar in both instances, but the environments were different. When the WTO proposal came out of the Uruguay Round of the GATT in 1993, advocacy of and enthusiasm about the expanding prosperity associated with globalization was on the rise, in contrast to the more restrained political atmosphere that accompanied recovery from World War II. Globalization through free trade was a much stronger force when the WTO opened its doors in 1995. The critics, who were unable to block the organization when it was proposed, did not go away, and when the global economy began to appear to falter at the end of the decade, they were waiting to raise their banners at Seattle and beyond.

An intriguing part of this mix is the Group of Eight, or G-8. It is not a formal organization at all, but rather a series of economic meetings between the world's most generally economically advanced countries—the United States, Germany, Great Britain, France, Italy, Japan, Canada, and as a kind of honorary member whose economic status does not qualify it otherwise, Russia. It began meeting in the middle 1970s, originally at a secret meeting at the Plaza Hotel in New York, and has evolved into a highly publicized twice-a-year meeting of the heads of state of the participating countries. Some of these have been little more than photo opportunities, but the fact that the most important economic powers in the world attend gives them potential clout in determining global policy across a range of subjects, including globalization.

G-8's activities have become ensnared in the general controversy over globalization, as became painfully obvious at its summer 2001 meeting at Genoa, Italy, when noisy demonstrators attempted to shut the proceedings down. The G-8 had added an important element to its deliberations by inviting a series of Second Tier heads of state to join the group and discuss their economic woes and claims on the system. While the G-8 members made no concrete promises to these leaders, they did listen and could respond in the future.

The Regional Emphasis. The other institutional thrust has been through a series of regionally based international economic organizations. The oldest and most advanced of these, of course, is the European Union, the basis for which was the Treaty of Rome of 1957 that created the original six-member European Common Market (West Germany, France, Italy and the Benelux countries). The organization has evolved to the current fifteen-member European Union and underwent expansion into eastern Europe in 2002; it has accomplished a long-sought goal of monetary union and the institution of a common currency, the euro. Its further expansion to a full-scale political union was derailed in 2005 by French and Dutch popular rejection of the treaty to charter a political union. Additional regional organizations include the APEC, encompassing most countries around the Pacific Rim; NAFTA; and the proposed hemisphere-wide FTAA (currently excluding only Cuba).

These organizations differ from the universal organizations in that the benefits of membership extend only to the member states at the exclusion and even punishment of nonmembers. The proposed FTAA would create a free trading zone for all of the Western Hemisphere, but the benefits would not extend to countries—or regional organizations—outside the membership. With the exception of the European Union, the regional organizations are also much less formalized and structured than universal organizations.

These regional solutions have several attractions. For one thing, the removal of trade barriers among the member countries is designed to stimulate trade among them. The APEC, for instance, has among its members countries accounting for over half the world's trade and including trade giants such as Japan, the United States, and China, and large potential markets like Indonesia and Russia. The FTAA, with overlapping membership with the APEC, is advertised as potentially the world's largest free trade area.

These arrangements may influence the future greatly. One way this could occur is through the expansion of membership to embrace countries generally outside the heart of the globalizing economy. The European Union, for instance, is already scheduled to embrace several countries of the former Soviet bloc (Poland, the Czech Republic, Estonia, Latvia, and Slovenia have been approved for membership), and many see the gradual expansion of the European Union as the final solution to European political division as well. The APEC has already expanded its membership to incorporate countries such as Vietnam, and the FTAA would be the most ambitious example of hemispheric cooperation ever.

These institutions may also be the stepping-stone to universal globalization. They could well become negotiating units in and of themselves, and particularly vehicles for promoting agreements between themslves. Should the FTAA be fully implemented (a prospect not to be assumed lightly), it and APEC would almost certainly merge effectively into one unit because of joint membership of countries such as the United States, Canada, Mexico, and Peru. A combined APEC–FTAA free trade area would create a powerful economic bloc that has prompted many in Europe to consider how it can make arrangements with one or both organizations.

None of this progress is preordained. The formalization of associations is going to be an extraordinarily difficult process for the fledgling associations. The APEC commitment to remove completely all barriers among the most advanced members by 2010 and among all members by 2020 and FTAA's promise of full implementation of free trade are, at this point, intergovernmental resolutions requiring concrete implementing agreements that have yet to be negotiated and do not clearly represent the highest priority of member states. The process of negotiating NAFTA among three countries revealed how complex such a process can be; negotiating implementation among the thirty-four member states of FTAA or the twenty or so states of the APEC could be infinitely more difficult. NAFTA also proves, however, that such efforts are not impossible.

The role of the United States, a key member of both APEC and FTAA, is critical in this process. Support for globalization is by no means universal in the United States on either economic or national security grounds. Economically, it is not universally agreed that the country or individual Americans necessarily benefit from globalization (arguments about which are presented later in the chapter). The national security objections are more subtle. Does globalization promote a stronger or weaker American position in the world? Or, does globalization strengthen American rivals or potential rivals like China, thereby increasing the potential for future turmoil? On the other side, proponents argue that a United States that does not maintain leadership in a globalization process it largely created may end up making itself weaker and less relevant in the evolving world order. Regardless of the position one takes on these matters, however, the sheer size of the American economy (around one-quarter of the world's total) means that American leadership is crucial to success of any enterprise.

The other side of the politics of globalization is opposition to the phenomenon and its effects within the United States and elsewhere. As the spate of demonstrations against globalization-promoting meetings in recent years has clearly demonstrated, there is a reasonably broad array of opposition. Those who believe that the process of globalization will produce more harmful than beneficial effects want "progress" in that direction made more, not less, difficult.

New Additions to the National Security Agenda

The more relaxed geopolitical environment of the 1990s also saw the addition of several other concerns to the list of items that affect national security. These new items represent an expansion of the basic concept of what constitutes security beyond its roots in protecting American soil from hostile military threats. It is raised in this chapter for three reasons related to globalization.

First, most of the elevations come from the same atmosphere of reduced military threat as the dynamic that allowed globalization to claim marquee status. With less need to concentrate our energies on military matters, there was time to concern ourselves with other matters that affect our sense of well-being, such as environmental degradation. Second, a number of the new items are themselves the result of the same dynamics that produced globalization. There could not, for instance, be a globalizing world without the increased importance and power of computers, but our very dependence on the information age makes those devices the tempting target for those who would attack the world system in the form of cyber terrorism. Third, since globalization and these new factors do extend the range of what we think of as constituting national security, there is not universal agreement that they are important—vital—enough to be considered alongside and parallel to conventional national security concerns.

No list of these new agenda items will be inclusive enough to satisfy everyone, and so no claim of inclusiveness is made here. Rather, we look at several new factors that represent the additional kinds of concerns that have been added to the national security agenda. For this purpose, we briefly examine three candidates for national security concern: energy security, environmental security, and cyber terrorism. All three have some relationship to globalization: energy consumption is the motor of economic productivity; the environment is clearly one of the concerns surrounding globalization; and the computer age has enabled globalization and created the possibility of cyber terrorism. Each topic is examined by raising three questions: How important is the issue (does it represent a threat to vital interests, the traditional criterion for military-based national security concerns)? Does its outcome affect the country's basic security, and if so, how? And what means, military or nonmilitary, are most appropriate for dealing with it?

Energy Security. The least ambiguous element is energy security, defined roughly as the guarantee of adequate energy supplies for the United States at reasonable prices. Energy security has been a staple part of American policy at least since 1980, when President Jimmy Carter declared that continuing access to Persian Gulf petroleum was a vital interest to the United States in his State of the Union address, a declaration that is known as the Carter Doctrine. The vitality of that condition has been a basic item in the national security calculus ever since, as evidenced by a permanent American military presence in the region and American participation in wars against Iraq in both 1990–1991 and since 2003. There is little question that American policy toward the Middle East would be quite different if there were no petroleum under the area's soils.

The vitality of the interest to Americans has also been well established. A harbinger of what the condition of Americans would be in the absence of an adequate flow of oil was demonstrated by the long lines at gas stations around the country during the "oil shocks" of 1973 and 1977, when OPEC members withheld their product from the market. Moreover, it is well established that energy consumption is the single best indicator of economic productivity, meaning access to energy resources is vital to the economic well-being of Americans. Energy (especially fossil fuels such as petroleum) is also likely to be an enduring source of scarcity and conflict, as additional countries (notably China and India) make increased demands for supplies.

But is energy security an entirely traditional security concern? If energy security is measured by the means used to achieve it, the answer is not clearly positive. There is a military, traditional aspect to energy security, as Persian Gulf policy clearly shows, but there are other aspects as well, such as energy conservation promotion, alternate energy source development, and even diplomatic activity to assure that producers continue the flow. These efforts require nontraditional policy means outside the realm of traditional national security means.

Environmental Security. The idea that the maintenance, protection, and promotion of a healthy, sustainable environment should be a security concern is of reasonably recent vintage and is a position held primarily by environmentalists who believe that putting the problem in this context elevates its importance and vitality. It is a position that has not been widely accepted or rejected.

The problem of conceptualizing the environment is establishing the vitality of given environmental concerns. The most obvious current lightning rod is the greenhouse effect of global warming, as exemplified in the Kyoto Protocols, of which the United States is the most prominent nonparticipant. The problem is not that anyone believes global warming is good (although some maintain it is not abnormal), but in projecting with scientific exactitude the malevolent effects. Disinterested and self-interested experts disagree about how much warming is occurring and how bad the effects will be. Moreover, the most dire predicted effects are fifty to a hundred years in the future, and the further in the future extrapolations are made, the more speculative they tend to be.

Environmental security is entirely nontraditional in terms of possible solutions. All advocacies suggest that political and economic means are the appropriate ways to attack environmental problems, providing economic resources to encourage less environmentally destructive practices and convincing countries to alter their degrading policies and practices. If environmental protection is a security concern, it is one with no real traditional military content.

Cyber Terrorism. The idea of attacking and disrupting or destroying computers with viruses or by other means that destroy or disable the information infrastructure on which modern (and notably globalizing) society rests is, of course, a product of the same dynamics as globalization itself and thus is of recent origin. As William Dyson has argued, terrorism against computers is not so much a form of terrorism per se, but terrorists are likely to use computers to aid in terrorist acts. Thus, if there is a GWOT, one of the assets that must be protected is the computing infrastructure.

Cyber terrorism evokes even more fanciful projections than environmental doomsday projections. The success of computer hackers lacking political agendas suggests that attacks on computers could seriously disrupt the ability of society and many of its institutions (banks, for instance) to function. Since undermining people's trust in societal institutions is often a terrorist objective (see Chapter 11), the potential for computer mischief climbs onto the security agenda.

The problem is how important the problem is and what can be done about it. All the scenarios about cyber terrorist acts are, at heart, no more than speculations, possibilities to be anticipated rather than concrete events on which to base proactive measures. Interestingly, a great deal of the interest in and research on cyber terrorism resides within the military, even though the problem is hardly military in a traditional military sense (e.g., what "weapons" do you use against cyber terrorists?). The speculative nature of the problem also makes it difficult to assess in terms of vitality.

Barriers and Objections to Globalization

Before the general slowdown of the global economy that began in 1999 and extended into the early 2000s took hold, opposition to globalization seemed feckless—an enterprise attempting to arrest inevitable forces and thus doomed to failure. The ability of a coalition of groups to intimidate political leaders and to slow the process has demonstrated that the logic and progress of globalization are not so inevitable and raises questions about both the desirability and the inevitability of the process. The question, Is globalization in America's best interests? was largely unthinkable five or six years ago; it is now.

The role and position of the United States as the remaining superpower is nowhere more evident than in the economic realm, and whatever position the United States takes will heavily influence the direction of the global economy. American leadership is expected and will be resented by some. Those who perceive they will not benefit from or will be hurt by globalization, both internationally and domestically, seek to influence that position. At the same time, American citizens are among the most vocal opponents (as well as advocates) of globalization, meaning the outcome of the political battle over globalization in the United States will strongly affect the global process as well.

What are the major objections? Within the international community, there tend to be three related problems raised, not so much about the desirability of extending the global prosperity but about how it is being done and the impact of imposing globalization in different places. These objections, in turn, tend to focus on the American model and the role of the United States in the globalization process.

One objection coming from the Second Tier is that the American model that has dominated participation in the globalizing economy is too rigidly American and thus cannot be imposed uniformly on very different cultures and systems. For instance, one of the major requirements of the American model is transparency, an advocacy tarnished by the scandals of 2002. Great secrecy is, however, traditional in the business practices of many Asian societies, as are activities that would be considered corrupt in western societies that, among other things, raised questions about whether the United States practiced the transparency it preached. When the values clash, which should prevail? The United States and the international organizations

Amplification 5.3

THE REJECTIONISTS

The series of protests and protesters first seen in Seattle, and a grim part of nearly every international economic event since, represents a coalition of very different groups and individuals. Unless placed in the context of the historic debate about free trade and protectionism, their grouping makes little sense. But the same coalition that has taken to the streets of Quebec City, Washington, D.C., Genoa, and elsewhere represents a long-standing tradition of opposition that was clearly present in the 1940s (see Amplification 5.1). The tactics and actors may have changed, but the underlying positions remain very similar.

Who are the rejectionists? They are a single-issue coalition bound together in their opposition to various aspects or implications of globalization that have very few, if any, other common interests. The interests they represent, however, have been present for a long time. First, there are the protectionists, who feel personally threatened by lowering trade barriers. In the 1940s, the protectionists were mostly conservative Republicans representing big business and commerce; today, they are predominantly Democrats representing the interests of trade unionists in industries that cannot compete successfully without trade protection. Second are those who feel that efforts to institutionalize globalization are too timid. Environmentalists, for instance, believe that institutions like the WTO will not adequately regulate environmental degradation by international corporations and governments (they believe that globalization is dominated by private interests with little environmental sensitivity). At the same time, others believe that the interests of Second Tier countries left out of the globalization policy are underrepresented as well. Finally, there are objections from groups that feel globalization undercuts national sovereignty.

The coalition is conceptually quite similar to the group that successfully fought the ITO over a half-century ago. The major difference is the violent, confrontational tactics that are now employed in opposition to globalization. While those tactics have not yet led to the successful blocking or slowing of the globalization process, they have succeeded in creating an atmosphere of intimidation that, among other things, caused the World Bank and IMF to shorten their annual meeting for 2001 at their Washington, D.C., headquarters to two days to minimize demonstrations.

that provide the funding and markets insist on the western way, and other cultures have been forced either to comply or remain outside the system. But for how long?

Much of that resentment, tinged with some envy, is directed at the United States. Beyond the cultural assault associated with the American-dominated economic system, there is further political resentment on other grounds. The constancy of American leadership is often raised; the United States, for instance, insists upon conformance with American financial practices but refuses to conform with globally accepted agreements on matters such as banning land mines, accepting war crimes statutes, and even honoring the Kyoto treaty on global warming. This same United States that preaches global responsibility also has historically had the highest arrears to the United Nations of any country in the world. More recently, American budget deficits have raised skepticism about American advocacy of fiscal responsibility. Which United States should the world follow: the responsible exemplar or the arrogant bully that obeys the international norms it favors and ignores those it does not? These perceptions and arguments have been made particularly sharply about the George W. Bush administration and its apparently unilateralist tendencies.

A final objection is the contribution of globalization to the growing gap between the richest and poorest countries on the globe. While no one denies that those parts of the Second Tier that have become part of the globalizing system have benefited to some extent, it is increasingly obvious that not everyone has—or is likely to—become part of the prosperity. As has been widely trumpeted, over half the world's current population lives in abject poverty, and the gap between those who are becoming richer and those who remain desperately poor has widened. This trend is especially evident geographically in Africa, where virtually the entire continent remains outside the benefits of globalization. The other side of this argument is that while benefit may be differential, virtually everyone is better off than they were before globalization—a rising tide lifts all boats, as the saying goes. Devising ways to extend globalization to those currently excluded is likely to become a major international priority.

The domestic debate is not foreclosed either. While there is little support for the basic tenets of isolationism in any pure sense, there are enough piecemeal objections to the various aspects of globalization to produce a very noisy, and occasionally effective, coalition of opponents. These objections are not going to disappear, even if there is a return to the kind of prosperity of the 1990s. There will always be, for instance, fierce advocates of the environment who will wonder how globalization subverts environmental concerns and promotes environmental degradation.

Two major domestic objections have been made recently. One surrounds accusations that globalization costs jobs, as reduced barriers to international commerce encourages sending jobs to non-American sites with lower labor costs. The outsourcing of many telemarketing and electronic service functions to overseas (especially Indian) outlets was a 2005 lightning rod for this objection. At the same time, lower trade barriers have also been tied to burgeoning American trade deficits that have the effect of lowering economic growth rates. In the first quarter of 2005, for instance, unadjusted growth rates produced by the U.S. government were at an annual rate of 4.6 percent, but when the figures were adjusted to include trade deficits, the rate dropped to 3.1 percent. American consumption of Chinese-produced consumer goods is a visible symbol of this problem.

CONCLUSION: GLOBALIZATION AND AMERICAN SECURITY

Globalization in some evolving form is simply a fact of international life in the 2000s, and the only way it could be reversed altogether would likely be as the result of some catastrophic international event such as a global war. That outcome may seem unlikely in the current context, but it is worth remembering the same thing was widely believed at the turn of the last century.

Is globalization a good thing for the United States? The question, of course, is too simply put to be answered: it assumes there is *a* globalism, when in fact globalization is an evolving condition whereby economic interconnectedness is gradually increasing. It is also too simple because the process is so multifaceted that it will almost certainly have some beneficial and some harmful effects on any country.

The real question is, on balance, does globalization add to or detract from the American place in the world and thus American security? And what can we do to improve those aspects with which we have concerns to make the process better serve those interests, including enhancing security? In the prosperous 1990s when globalization was given credit—rightly or wrongly—for helping to create and sustain prosperity, the answer was likely to be automatically positive. In the more cautious economic condition of a postmillennial era more focused on the terrorist assault on physical security, the assessment is likely to be more guarded and critical.

One aspect of the question, which also provides an intellectual bridge to the next chapter, may illustrate the difficulty of reaching expansive conclusions. It is the connection between globalization and sovereignty. As noted in Chapter 2, the retention of state sovereignty is a core realist value that has always been particularly important to the United States. Guarding our sovereignty has sometimes forced the United States out of step with the rest of the world.

By definition, the retention of effective state sovereignty is a major element of the country's national security, making the relationship between sovereignty and globalization an important matter. At the same time, if globalization contributes to the greater economic well-being of Americans, is any dilution of sovereignty that results from globalization a good bargain? Moreover, a virtue of globalization has been to impose American economic values on others, bringing them into conformance with our ideals. Should the question therefore be, Whose sovereignty is compromised?

An example may help us think about this. One part of the statute creating the WTO gives it the power to investigate allegations of trade violations by member states, and where it finds violations, to prosecute and impose mandatory sanctions against violating governments. In the ratification debate over WTO, this provision was widely condemned by defenders of American sovereignty, as it had been over a similar provision in the proposed ITO in the 1940s. The counterargument was that most of the values the WTO would enforce were American values, making vulnerability minimal and assuring that others would be forced to conform as well. Conformance to the WTO charter thus cuts both ways: it dilutes the sovereign control of countries we seek to influence, but also limits us.

The statute has indeed had both effects. A major argument for sponsoring Chinese membership in the WTO was that it would force China to reform its economic practices in ways that would loosen the ability of the Chinese government to maintain authoritarian control over the economy and ultimately, it was hoped, over the political system. While this is a difficult step for a Chinese government that

154 CHAPTER 5 The Rise of Globalization

is also a prime defender of state sovereignty, it is the price China has had to pay for full membership in the global economy. In this case, the U.S. government has used the international dilution of sovereignty to tie China more firmly into the global system and to increase American security.

But the statute does cut both ways. Shortly after the WTO came into force in 1995, the Clinton administration sought to improve its balance of payments situation with Japan by forcing the Japanese to buy more American automotive components to put into Japanese cars. To this end, Clinton announced his intention to place a high excise tax on Japanese luxury cars entering the United States that would have made them uncompetitive with domestic models. The hope was that the Japanese would cave in and agree to import more American car batteries and tires to avoid these penalties. Instead, the Japanese cried unfair trade practices and threatened to drag the United States before the WTO, where the United States would certainly have lost any judgment rendered. Faced with that likelihood, the Clinton administration withdrew the threat to exercise its state sovereignty through the excise tax.

The example suggests that the answers to apparently simple questions are rarely themselves simple. For the most part, globalization has helped the United States reassert its position in a global economic system in which it had slipped in preeminence after 1971. Whether the United States will continue to benefit depends on how we define our international interests, the degree to which we are able to influence the system in ways that benefit the most Americans, and how we react to unforeseen and sometimes unforeseeable changes.

SELECTED BIBLIOGRAPHY

Antholes, William. "Pragmatic Engagement or Photo Opportunity: What Will the G-8 Become?" *Washington Quarterly* 24, 3 (Summer 2001), 213–226.

Baker, Gerald. "The Budget Debacle." *Foreign Policy* (March/April 2005), 42–47.

Barshefsky, Charlene. "Trade Policy in a Networked World." *Foreign Affairs* 80, 2 (March/April 2001), 134–146.

Dunn, Robert. "Has the United States *Really* Been Globalized?" *Washington Quarterly* 24, 1 (Winter 2001), 53–64.

Feldstein, Martin. "A Self-Help Guide to Emerging Markets." *Foreign Affairs* 78, 2 (March/April 1999), 93–109.

Friedman, Thomas L. *The Lexus and the Olive Tree: Understanding Globalization*. New York: Farrar, Straus and Giroux, 1999.

———. *The World Is Flat: A Brief History of the Twenty-First Century*. New York: Farrar, Straus and Giroux, 2005.

Fukuyama, Francis. *The End of History and the Last Man*. New York: Free Press, 1992.

Kennedy, Paul. *The Rise and Fall of the Great Powers: Economic Change and Military Change from 1500 to 2000*. New York: Random House, 1987.

Keohane, Robert O., and Joseph S. Nye, Jr. *Power and Interdependence* (2nd ed.). Glenview, IL: Scott Foresman/Little Brown, 1989.

Levey, David H., and Stuart S. Brown. "The Overstretch Myth." *Foreign Affairs* 84, 2 (March/April 2005), 2–7.

Luttwak, Edward. "From Geopolitics to Geo-economics: Logic of Conflict, Grammar of Commerce." *National Interest* 20 (Summer 1990), 17–24.

Nye, Joseph S., Jr. *Bound to Lead: The Changing Nature of American Power*. New York: Basic Books, 1990.

Rothgeb, John M. J. *U.S. Trade Policy: Balancing Economic Dreams and Political Realities*. Washington, DC: CQ Press, 2001.

Sachs, Jeffrey. "International Economics: Unlocking the Mysteries of Globalization." *Foreign Policy*, 10 (Spring 1998), 97–111.

Spero, Joan Edelman. *The Politics of International Economic Relations* (4th ed.). New York: St. Martin's Press, 1990.

PART

II

THE CHANGING WORLD

The international environment is the setting in which national security policy is crafted to secure the country's interests in the world. In Part I, we looked at some of the historical factors that shaped how the United States looks at security matters, culminating in the rise and fall of the Cold War and the emergence of globalization after the first fault line was breached.

The second fault line of September 11, 2001, created another tectonic shift in the security environment, and in Part II, we explore various aspects of how the world is different and how those differences affect the American role in the world. Chapter 6 emphasizes the basic concepts around which security concerns revolve—security, risk, interests, and power—and how these have changed. The basic message is that interests remain largely the same as they were before, but there is a new configuration of threats to those interests, and those interests must be pursued in different ways. Chapter 7 attempts to assess the contemporary environment from the domestic perspective, how the U.S. government is organized to deal with changing circumstances, emphasizing the National Security Council (NSC) system and homeland security. The last chapter in Part II, Chapter 8, looks at the traditional military means and roles that American force has taken and how they are relevant to today's world. It examines both the changing role of nuclear weapons and conventional or traditional armed forces, including military reform and manpower.

CHAPTER 6

Security, Interests, and Power

PREVIEW

The shock of events, such as those revealed by the opening of the fault lines, tend to focus our concern on the trauma and extent of change rather than on how those events fit into the broader context of national concerns that transcend time and more strongly balance continuity with change. This chapter on the contemporary world seeks to place recent traumas into the kind of analytical context with which national security policy grapples. We analyze the impact of change on four basic categories of ongoing importance. First, what is the nature of security? Second, how has the nature and extent of risk been affected? Third, what impact has change had on basic interests? Fourth, what is the changing nature of effective power in the present and the future?

The contemporary national security environment contains elements both of continuity and change. From the vantage point of any particular point in time, including now, the unique set of forces and events of the moment may seem to predominate and draw us to emphasize change and the uniqueness of the evolving system. Thus, we are drawn to the two major fault lines of the past decade and a half and their consequent effects on highlighting globalization or geopolitics as the principal system dynamic.

At the same time, some forces that seem unique in a narrow perspective appear less so within the general evolution of the international system and our place in it. The last century began with the belief that there was little likelihood of future violence. A general optimism prevailed, based on the perception of a growing economic interdependence driven by trade that was supposed to simultaneously assure future prosperity and make the recourse to war progressively less thinkable. The shock of the terrorist attacks makes it easy to forget that on January 1, 2000, most people felt basically the same about the future as their ancestors did on January 1, 1900.

National security analysis tries to determine what it is in the environment that may provide concern for the security and well-being of Americans and citizens of the world generally and to determine what, if anything, can be done to attenuate or eliminate the sources of disturbance. We ask the same questions today that we asked fifty or a hundred years ago; it is the answers that change to a greater or lesser extent, based upon the flow of events.

The United States is clearly still in the process of reassessing the national security problem for a new century, particularly in light of our personal and intimate introduction to international terrorism, a force we had not previously had to confront in detail. Before that introduction, the environment seemed less negative than it did during the Cold War. We questioned the amount of effort we should devote to the national security enterprise and, at a more personal level, the amount of personal effort or sacrifice that should be expected of us. Those commercial airliners slamming into their targets removed the complacency about our security that had developed in the tranquil 1990s. "Everything has changed" became the mantra after September 11, 2001; "nothing will ever be the same again." Dormant security concerns have been revived and now seem permanent parts of an environment that is unalterably changed. Or is it?

We live in a period that has been called the "long peace." If the first half of the twentieth century was arguably the bloodiest period in human history, the second half was relatively benign in terms of the toll of war. The hypothetical consequences of general war may have been great during the Cold War, but the reality was that bloodshed was basically confined to the peripheries—the developing world—where the major powers only became involved when they chose to become involved, as the Americans did in Vietnam and the Soviets in Afghanistan. After 1991, breaches of the peace were basically isolated to internal war in parts of the world outside the normal range of important American interests. The terrorist attacks that killed 3,000 Americans and other nationals darkened that sunny horizon and presented a new national security imperative. But is it a temporary interruption of the long peace, or something more permanent and ominous?

Our discussion proceeds through four sequential steps. Keeping the United States and Americans safe from harm—or secure—is the basic value of national security policy, so we begin by exploring what makes us secure. Because our safety is potentially imperiled from a variety of sources that may exceed our resources, we look at the question of how we decide what to protect and what to accept as risk. Deciding where to nullify and where to accept risk is a matter of what our most important interests are, and so we return to the matter of determining levels of interest. This assessment leads to a concern about how the United States can use its powers to the service of its security in the future.

THINKING ABOUT SECURITY

Security is a variable. What makes us safe or makes us *feel* safe (the physical and psychological dimensions of security) depend upon two basic phenomena, each of which can assume different values, or can vary. The most obvious source of challenge to our security are factors that threaten the things that we value. As noted earlier, the most objective of these are physical threats, such as the ability of Russia to destroy the United States with nuclear weapons. Psychological threats—what makes us feel secure or insecure—are often less tangible and subject to individual interpretation: different people feel secure or insecure in the same situation. The degree to which we are personally threatened by the prospect of terrorist activity reflects that dimension.

This leads to the second variable about security, which is our interpretation of the environment. Does the environment make us feel secure or insecure? Thus, what actions might we contemplate to change the environment and make it less threatening (increase our sense of security)? Clearly, the two variable aspects are related to one another: a hostile physical environment will diminish our psychological feeling of security more than a benign environment where there are few adversaries posing few threats to our interests and our security.

The environmental aspect of security has apparently changed considerably since the end of the Cold War. With the demise of the Soviet adversary, the physical sense of insecurity diminished considerably for the United States. Russia still maintains a large stock of nuclear weapons but lacks any rationale to use them. The Cold War threat to American and allied security posed by the forces of Soviet Communism has disappeared and not been replaced by any worthy successor, what the initial (1997) Quadrennial Defense Review (QDR) first called the lack of a "peer competitor" (true, worthy enemy).

The discussion about these aspects of security can be divided into two related steps. We first look at the changing balance between military and nonmilitary sources of security concern. This leads to and is conditioned by the second step: the various levels of security that affect different actors in international politics. The final step is an assessment of how concepts of security may be changing.

Military and Nonmilitary Elements of Security

Historically, as noted, national security and military security have been synonymous. Although other matters might threaten the well-being of the country, those threats with which policymakers and analysts were principally worried and which fell most obviously into the category of national security dealt with military threats. Military elements were certainly the predominant form of threats during the Cold War.

The inclusion of nonmilitary elements into what was considered national security began to occur during the Cold War, particularly in the area of economic security, raised in Chapter 5. There have been previous occasions when economic and other concerns entered the national security arena—trade matters with Great Britain, for instance, had been an important part of the conduct of the American Civil War, and a major threat to the United States of a German victory in World War I was the possible exclusion of American manufactures from the European continent. Likewise, suppression of the Barbary Pirates in the early 1800s may have been the first time that responding to what we now call nonstate actors became a national security concern.

We have added nonmilitary and semimilitary elements to our concepts of security. Among the nonmilitary aspects (threats with no military component), "economic security" has been broadened to encompass environmental security, for instance. We have also added security concerns that are partly military and partly nonmilitary. A primary example of these *semimilitary* aspects of security and responses to it is the problem of international terrorism. As the campaign against the Taliban and Al Qaeda in Afghanistan has demonstrated, these problems can have a clearly military component, but significant aspects of terrorism and its suppression are also political and law enforcement concerns.

Military, semimilitary, and nonmilitary elements have melded in the post–Cold War period, in part because the purely traditional military elements of security are clearly less extensive and less intense than they were before. The virtually total absence of the danger of a major, system-threatening military conflict like the world wars or the breakdown of the Cold War into a hot war is a major characteristic of the contemporary system, even after September 11. In some sense, the long peace continues to get longer.

The nonmilitary and semimilitary elements of security have risen in relative importance as military threats have receded. For the most part, these are a series of smaller military threats, some of which existed during the Cold War but received less attention then, and some of which have emerged since. What they have in common is that none provides a direct, general threat to the United States physically in the way a potential Soviet nuclear attack did. The 2001 terrorist threat against the United States demonstrated that the American homeland has become vulnerable to harm that can kill many Americans, but these attacks do not currently place the integrity of the United States at direct risk.

Other than terrorism, the remaining security threats are at a lower level of urgency and importance, placing them squarely within the psychological dimension of security, where people can and do disagree about the importance of the threat. Some threats existed during the Cold War but paled by comparison to the larger problem. The danger and threat of the proliferation of weapons of mass destruction (WMD) to countries in the Second Tier was a problem then and now, for instance.

As purely military elements of security have declined, nonmilitary and semimilitary elements have been on the rise. Because of globalization, some of the most important nonmilitary elements are now in the area of international economics, where concerns like conditions of trade have risen to levels of concern comparable to military matters. The semimilitary threat of terrorism has occupied a special place since 2001, but it is a concern that has been long held at a lower level of intensity.

The military and nonmilitary elements of security come together in concrete ways. The situation between the United States and China is an example. China was, of course, a Cold War military adversary of the United States, even if the threat it posed was somewhat ambiguous after the split between China and the Soviet Union and the opening of Sino–American relations in 1972. Still, national security planners during the 1960s planned for two simultaneous major wars, one with the Soviets and one with the Chinese (the two-war strategy). The focus of Sino–American military rivalry was and is over the Nationalist Chinese government of Taiwan, which China periodically threatens.

After Deng Xiao-peng's announcement of the "Four Modernizations" in 1979 and its implementation during the 1980s and 1990s, an economic relationship

Challenge!

DEFINING TERRORISM AS A SECURITY THREAT

What kind of a threat does international terrorism pose to the United States? Much of the discussion of post–September 11, 2001, efforts by the United States to quell this problem has been described as constituting a "war," which suggests the problem is a military one with a military solution. The "global war on terrorism" (GWOT) is what the Bush administration initially labeled the effort, and that designation was picked up and repeated by many of the electronic and print media.

Much of the initial effort seemed to justify this designation. The insertion of American forces into Afghanistan first to help topple the Taliban government and then to try to round up and destroy remaining pockets of Al Qaeda and Taliban resistance was clearly military in content. When American forces were sent to places like the Philippines and Yemen to train local forces better to resist terrorists, this also represented a military response, albeit at the lower end of the spectrum of military responses.

This text disagrees with the assertion that countering terrorism falls within the category of military dimensions of security. Clearly, suppressing terrorism has a military element, as demonstrated by initial actions, and terrorism experts like Stephen Sloan specifically include military responses as part of dealing with terrorism. Thus, the response to terrorism clearly does not fall within the nonmilitary dimension either.

The text has placed terrorism in the category of semimilitary responses. The basic argument is that suppressing terrorism has some elements that involve various uses of military force but that the effort also clearly includes elements that are either nonmilitary or quasi-military. Gathering intelligence information on terrorist plans and activities to frustrate the terrorists and arresting and prosecuting those who engage in or plot to commit terrorist acts are also important parts of dealing with the problem, and they are not military actions.

Is the distinction of dealing with terrorism within the semimilitary dimension of security important or just a matter of splitting hairs? If the problem is only partially military in origin and solution, put another way, does the analogy with "war" hold? If it does, that helps frame the public debate—for instance, the justification for greater defense expenditures. If the effort is only partly military, on the other hand, then the rhetoric of war—questioning the loyalty of those who question the effort as unpatriotic because we are "at war"—may be excessive and run counter to democratic rule. What do you think?

emerged that began to lessen the intensity of the military rivalry. A major pillar of the modernizations was to allow the development of private enterprises in the Special Economic Zones (SEZs) of the southeastern part of the China. When the Cold War ended and the age of globalization came into full bloom, a burgeoning trade between the two countries developed and largely replaced the military rivalry.

Is China currently a national security threat to the United States? From a purely military viewpoint, one can make a small case for a "Chinese threat" in the form of a small, primitive nuclear capability and large conventional armed forces that cannot be projected far from China's shore. Taiwanese rumblings about declaring its independence regularly bring Chinese saber rattling, and incidents like the spy plane episode of April 2001 (when an American reconnaissance plane collided with a Chinese jet fighter off the coast of China) caused some concern. Balanced against those problems, Beijing will host the 2008 Olympics (a major achievement that will likely have China on its best behavior during the interim), and the Chinese Communist Party announced in August 2001 that capitalists will be permitted to join the Communist Party (a seeming oxymoron). China continues to be a major provider of consumer goods for Americans and has been further integrated into the world economy as a member of the WTO. Thus, calculating Sino–American military threats is no longer an easy or clear-cut matter as the relationship evolves to one of so-called complex interdependence.

The Chinese example is not the only one in which the intersection of military and nonmilitary aspects of security become blurred. Not all are directly American. One source of insecurity is and always has been over access to important resources. Among these issues, access to water could provide a similar dynamic in the relatively near future, as Amplification 6.1 suggests.

Amplification 6.1

ISRAEL, SYRIA, THE GOLAN HEIGHTS, AND WATER

One of the ways in which concerns over security have been changing in the contemporary environment is the expansion of situations and conditions about which states may feel insecure and thus feel the need to take action to ensure their security. Military security has, in other words, been augmented by economic security, environmental security, energy security, and a variety of other concerns.

One scarce resource that will assuredly climb to the top of the agenda of security concerns in some places is access to adequate supplies of potable water. Nowhere in the world is this concern more evident than in the arid Middle East, where very few states have adequate supplies, particularly to service populations expected to grow in the future and place additional demands on dwindling supplies (Turkey is the exception to this rule). Although it receives little publicity outside the region itself, the problem of water remains a major barrier to the ability of Israel to reach an accord with the last of the countries that has opposed it in war, Syria.

The major remaining issue between the Israelis and the Syrians is the return of the Golan Heights to Syria. Before the 1967 Six Days' War, Syria had used the Heights, a series of low mountains that border on northern Israel, to launch mortar and artillery attacks on the Israeli settlements in the valley below. As a result, when Israel was occupying territories of its neighbors because of the war (the West Bank from Jordan, the Sinai Peninsula and Gaza Strip from Egypt), it also occupied the Golan Heights to assure that Syria could not physically resume its attacks.

The Golan Heights are also important because of water. Much of the water that Israel (and Jordan) uses comes from the Jordan River, the source of which is the Sea of Galilee. As the map shows, the eastern shore of the Sea forms the border between Israel and Syria when Syria possesses the Golan Heights, thereby affording the Syrians the physical ability to interfere with that source of Israeli water. The problem is moot with Israel occupying the Heights, since the Syrians are physically kept away from the seashore. Return of the Golan Heights to Syria is the *sine qua non* for a peace settlement between the two countries. Before Israel agrees to transfer the territory back, however, it must have an iron-clad agreement covering military attacks from the Golan Heights and, perhaps more important, assuring that Syria will not interfere with Israel's water supply.

Levels of Security

The previous discussion centered on the idea of state security, which is the primary focus of concern in a system where the realist paradigm predominates. This focus is one of the more controversial consequences of a realist paradigm world and has caused many reformers to suggest that there should be a more balanced approach to legitimate security concerns both below and above the level of the state.

Competing levels of security arguments run closely parallel to the debate about sovereignty. The idea that there could be a source of superior authority to the state was, of course, a major issue in the Thirty Years War in the clash between sectarian authority and secular authority and dynastic and territorial claims. There are parallels within the contemporary assertion that the security of subnational groups and individuals should be primary considerations. This assertion reflects the notion of popular sovereignty first put forward by political thinkers such as Locke and Rousseau that also heavily influenced the writers of the American Declaration of Independence and Constitution. It is at least implicit in the rationale of other democratic systems (minimally, the idea that power and authority flow from the people).

The arguments are more than academic. Some of them, of course, reflect assaults on the sovereign base of the state system and tend to emphasize the negative consequences of a state-centered system with state security as its underlying first principle. Others assert the need for and positive consequences of a reorientation of security around the individual or supranational concerns.

One line of reasoning questions the consequences of states acting principally out of their own security concerns while ignoring other levels. A most basic formulation of this concern is something known as the *security dilemma*. In this construct, states may act in ways—such as building up levels of armaments—to increase their security against real or potential adversaries regardless of the effect on the larger international system. The response of those targeted by the original action may be to respond in kind (building their levels of arms), which may result in an arms spiral wherein, in the end, all parties are left feeling less secure than in the beginning. Security dilemma situations represent the perspective of *international security*, the security of the overall system.

The security dilemma is not an abstract problem but can be seen in ongoing, concrete situations. Currently, the debate over American construction of a missile defense system shows the dynamic in action. The national missile defense (NMD) is clearly an American *national* defense proposal aimed at solving a perceived American security problem, the future vulnerability of United States territory to missile attacks by states possessing small numbers of missiles armed with WMD. Other states may, however, feel threatened by the U.S. WMD system. China is a prime example. It has a very small nuclear arsenal, which it maintains to threaten retaliation should the United States launch a nuclear first strike against it (no matter how far-fetched such an attack might seem). They are concerned the NMD is designed to intercept and destroy an attack of about the size and nature the Chinese might be able to mount after absorbing a first attack. Thus, the Chinese deterrent is compromised, and the Chinese are left to ponder how to respond if NMD deployment occurs. One obvious response would be to build enough additional rockets to guarantee overcoming the

NMD regardless of the effectiveness of the American first strike. The result could be to make the United States more vulnerable to China than before NMD deployment—the security dilemma in action. India, the state that feels most threatened by Chinese weapons, might then feel the need to respond to a Chinese buildup, a ripple effect that could then extend to Pakistan, further destabilizing the system.

The American terrorism campaign also raises levels of security concerns. The American military response in Afghanistan was clearly framed in terms of American state security—removing the source of a threat to the American homeland. Very few in the world argued with this campaign. When the United States threatened to widen the campaign to other sources of potential threat—notably Iraq's suspected WMD program and the incumbency of Saddam Hussein—leaders from France's Jacques Chirac to Jordan's King Abdullah in effect raised the security dilemma in objection. American actions to strengthen its own security, they (and others) argued, could so destabilize the Middle East as to leave everyone worse off.

The other level of concern is that of *individual security*, a primary orientation of security around individuals and groups. This emphasis is most often associated with the protection of the safety of people within states. The problem arises from traditional interpretations of the absolute power state sovereignty provides for the state over its population. The consequences of this power become an international concern in the post–Cold War environment of internal wars that involve atrocities against victim populations and groups within populations.

Traditional definitions of sovereignty give the state total control over its territorial base, including the treatment of individual citizens and groups, and makes illegitimate any outside efforts to affect that treatment. In the cases of particularly tyrannical regimes, the result has often been state-sponsored or state-conducted campaigns against their own citizens, which the international community technically cannot prevent or alleviate; it is none of anybody else's business how a state treats its citizens.

An assertion of the validity of individual security challenges that assumption. It is related to the assertion of popular sovereignty, since presumably no one would delegate authority to the state the right to abuse them. The history of individual security, however, is relatively recent and based in two post–World War II phenomena: reaction to the Holocaust and the emergence of notions of individual, enforceable human rights.

The Holocaust was a terribly traumatic event for the international community and gave a black eye to advocates of the notion of total sovereign control. Among other things, it revealed the lengths to which unrestrained governments might go in mistreating their citizens—state sovereignty had run amok. Yet, in the early war crimes trials at Nuremberg, a prominent participating American jurist opined that Nazis could be tried for killing non-German Jews and Gypsies (among others), but not German Jews or Gypsies, since they had sovereign authority over their own populations.

Reaction to the Holocaust boosted advocacies of universal human rights after the war and helped result in a number of international treaties asserting that individuals everywhere had certain rights that could not be denied by governments.

Since nondemocratic governments existed and routinely denied and repressed these rights, individual rights and a concept such as individual security reinforced one another.

Once again, the importance of this distinction is not abstract in the post–Cold War world. Although mass atrocities occurred during the Cold War (e.g., the Khmer Rouge slaughter in Cambodia during the 1970s), brutal civil wars have been a major part of post–Cold War violence. Ethnic cleansing, the displacement or extermination of ethnic, religious, and other groups, and the violent suppression of human rights have been a focus of violence within the international system, a problem discussed in Chapter 11.

The question of security—what makes us secure—is not as simple as thinking about military force and military threats. Security does take on different forms—military, semimilitary, and nonmilitary. And different entities—individuals, states, even the international system—have security concerns. When these are combined, objects of security are both complex and numerous. It is a long list of entities that can be threatened in different ways, and all the resources necessary to remove all kinds of threats to security are not always available. In that circumstance, we must make choices, raising the problem of risk and its management.

RISK AND RISK MANAGEMENT

In an ideal world, we would have the means available to remove all our sources of insecurity. In the real world, however, the threats that we face—or potentially face—always outnumber the resources we have available to negate those threats to our safety. The gap between the threats we face and the resources to nullify those threats is *risk*, and it can be depicted in the suggestive formula: risk equals threat minus capability.

Since risk is calculated on the basis of threats to security, it is also a variable quantity. How much we are forced to endure is, according to the formula, the result of two factors, each of which can vary. The first and most elastic of these quantities is threat. As already explained, the degree of threat we encounter is the result of physical and psychological aspects of security. Primarily, this means that the amount of potential risk we face is the result of what makes us *feel* secure or insecure, and people differ on what frightens them and must thus be countered to reduce insecurity. For instance, we all agree that international terrorism threatens the United States; we disagree on what potential aspects of the terrorism problem are most dangerous and immediate and thus threatening.

Threat can also vary depending on the amount of exposure we have to potentially threatening forces, and this element of threat is partially controllable either by exposing ourselves to the security problem or by avoiding it. A global power like the United States will have more threats to its security than a smaller state with more parochial interests, for instance, meaning the threat to the United States will exceed that of most others. On the other hand, the way we treat potentially threatening opponents can increase or decrease the amount of threat we must try to nullify. For instance, American policy toward the Democratic People's Republic of Korea (DPRK, or North Korea) during the 1990s had largely convinced the North Koreans not to pursue their nuclear weapons program that now concerns us. The North Korean threat in 2005 is considerably larger than it was in 1995; changes in U.S. policy could conceivably reduce that threat to its previous level. This problem is explored in Amplification 6.2.

Amplification 6.2

WHAT SHOULD THE UNITED STATES DO ABOUT NORTH KOREA?

For the past several years, the United States has been involved in a direct confrontation with the government of the Democratic People's Republic of Korea (DPRK, or North Korea). It is, of course, not the first time the two countries have been at odds: America's first major military conflict of the Cold War occurred in 1950 when the North Koreans invaded the Republic of Korea (South Korea), and the United States intervened to restore South Korean sovereignty in a war that lasted over three years and cost over 37,000 American lives.

The DPRK is one of the most destitute, remote countries in the world. It shares with Cuba the distinction of being one of the two remaining countries practicing Communist ideology both politically and economically (the other Communist states, China and Vietnam, have effectively renounced socialist economics). Politically, the country has had only two leaders, the late Kim Il Sung and, since the self-designated "Great Leader" died in 1994, his son Kim Jung Il. The country is among the poorest in the world and suffers periodically from harsh famines because it does not produce enough farm products to feed itself.

The long-standing source of controversy between the United States and the DPRK surrounds the North Korean nuclear program. Although the North Koreans have been members of the Nuclear Non-Proliferation Treaty (NPT)—whose members vow not to develop nuclear weapons—Pyongyang has maintained an active nuclear research program and has the material to build nuclear weapons. Additionally, it has an active missile program, which could become a delivery capability should they produce nuclear weapons.

During the 1990s, relations between the two countries had reduced tensions. In 1993, the DPRK became the first country to announce its intentions to withdraw from the NPT, which produced a flurry of activity. In 1994, the North Koreans suspended their withdrawal in an interim agreement with the United States that called for American assistance to the regime, and in 1999, a further agreement reduced, among other things, travel restrictions between North Korea and the world. This was followed by the first open relations between North and South Korea and with Japan. North Korea was viewed as a relatively minor risk.

That changed with the election of George W. Bush. In addition to designating North Korea a member of the "axis of evil" (along with Iran and Iraq), the administration suspended bilateral contacts with the Kim Jung Il regime. Slighted by these actions, North Korea angrily announced its resumption of efforts to produce nuclear weapons. At American initiative, six-power talks (North and South Korea, China, Japan, Russia, and the United States) have attempted to quell this development but with only limited success. Since 2001, North Korea has been a considerable source of threat and risk.

What should the United States do about North Korea? One answer is to go back to bilateral diplomacy, which proponents of current policy say were demeaning and ineffective. Another is to continue the six-party talks, which the North Koreans do not like because they prefer bilateral negotiations. A third alternative is for the United States to use military force to deprive North Korea of the ability to make nuclear weapons, an action that could provoke another war on the peninsula that no one wants. The final option is for the United States to ignore the situation and leave it to regional solution. None is an overwhelmingly obvious solution. What do you think?

Capability, defined as the capacity to take actions that nullify threats, is also a variable, although not an infinitely elastic or expansible one. Capability is generally defined in terms of various kinds of power available to insure that threats cannot be successfully carried out against us. In the simplest terms, for instance, the existence and structure of the United States armed forces is designed to insure that any foreign military invader would be repulsed, thereby nullifying the threat of invasion and conquest of the United States. The semimilitary threat of harm posed by terrorists, on the other hand, is so diverse and diffuse that it is not clear what resources are needed to nullify entirely the risks posed by terrorist threats to do us harm.

In general terms, it is almost always true that threats will exceed the capability to nullify them, and this observation is particularly true in the current context of international terrorism. There are so many potential targets for terrorist attacks on American soil and overseas (see Chapter 10 for a discussion) that removing all of them from harm's way is, as a practical matter, impossible. This means that choices must be made about which threats we will nullify and which targets we will leave at risk. Since the potential list of what makes us feel safe or unsafe is subjective, it is always more expansible than the capabilities we might marshal to protect everything.

Those threats that we do not nullify (although we do not admit that there is such a list or what is on it, for obvious reasons) constitute risk. Determining what risks will and will not be nullified is the job of policymakers, who regularly engage in what amounts to the triage of risk reduction and risk management. Risk reduction, as the name implies, consists of those actions that maximize the threats that are nullified. Which threats will be nullified and which will remain risks is the realm of risk management.

Risk can be modulated by manipulating either element of the formula. One way to reduce risk is to redefine those things that threaten us. Illegal immigration poses a threat that needs to be addressed only if we define such immigration as a problem. If we were to declare that it is no longer a problem, then the threat is reduced and we are no longer at risk. This particularly controversial example is cited purposely, since any attempt to define away risks will almost always be highly controversial.

The other way to reduce risk is to increase the capability to address and attack threats. In political terms, this means increasing the resources allocated to the particular problem. To continue the illegal immigrant example, if continued illegal immigration is defined as a threat to the United States, the obvious risk-reducing response would be to make our borders more impermeable—for instance, by hiring additional border guards or immigration and border patrol employees. That solution would cost money, opening political debates on taxes, deficits, and the reallocation of resources from some other functions—for instance, guarding national parks or monuments from potential terrorist attacks.

THINKING ABOUT INTERESTS

Where we accept risk and where we do not depends on the hierarchy of things we value, or our interests. Questions about the role and implications of interests mirror differences over what constitutes security in the contemporary order. The interplay of interests—whose are realized and whose are not—are central to the dynamics of international relations organized around the realist paradigm. The interests at the base of these calculations are invariably state interests. Constructed in this manner, the military aspects of security are prominent because force is one of the options available to achieve the state's most important (or vital) interests.

For better or worse, interest-driven calculations remain the criteria by which states operate in the anarchical international system. When the interests of states come into conflict, the question of which states' interests will prevail also arises, and this leads to trying to determine how important interests are, where and how they are threatened (at risk), and thus what means will be employed to attempt to achieve them. Thus, the question of levels of interest must be addressed, although within a somewhat different context than the question of security. These levels, in turn, suggest different national security and military and nonmilitary implications, including economic implications connected to the theme of globalization. Finally, the challenge to traditional concepts of national interest in the form of broader variants of what constitute vital interests are addressed.

Levels of Interests

The various levels and intensities of interest introduced in Chapter 2 need not be repeated here. The heart of that discussion, however, dealt with the critical traditional national security question of the boundary between *vital* interests and those that are deemed less than vital. The salience of that boundary is that it is theoretically the demarcation point of when the state will contemplate the use of military force to realize its goals. Interests failing the test of vitality (major or peripheral interests) imply the use of means of lesser intensity than those that are vital. Most of

Figure 6.1: Interest Levels and Security Means Dimensions

		Interest Level	
		Vital	Less-Than-Vital
Security	Military	Cell 1	Cell 2
Means	Semimilitary	Cell 3	Cell 4
Dimension	Nonmilitary	Cell 5	Cell 6

the economic methods of achieving goals that are compatible with globalization presumably are useful for less-than-vital interest realization. There are instances when economic weapons may be applied to vital interests, such as the boycott and economic isolation of Saddam Hussein to gain his compliance with international norms of WMD inspection, but such actions have a very limited success rate and are relatively infrequent. In the case of semimilitary threats, the invocation of vital interests may suggest both military and nonmilitary responses.

This conjunction between interests and security can be depicted in matrix form, as is done in Figure 6.1. Cells 1 and 6 are the easiest to describe. It is the heart of the realist formulation that when vital interests are threatened, force may become an option if the situation is solvable by using force (military security, as depicted in cell 1). At the same time, when less-than-vital interests come into conflict, they are normally solved nonmilitarily because military force is either inappropriate or more drastic than the situation dictates (cell 6). An imminent attack on one's territory would be a clear cell 1 situation; a dispute over tariff schedules would clearly fall in cell 6. When vital interests are involved, the first inclination is to try to use nonmilitary means to resolve the differences—maintaining force as a "last resort" if all else fails (cell 5). Applying economic sanctions would be an example.

The real debate is over the situation in which vital interests are not engaged but military aspects of security may be contemplated because they are the only means that may bring about a satisfactory resolution (cell 2). A strict interpretation of the realist paradigm is very restrictive in this regard: if American vital interests are not threatened, for instance, then American use of force should not be contemplated. This was the basic stance taken by the Bush campaign in 2000 when it argued that the United States should not be the "world's 911"; that stance was arguably relaxed when the United States invaded Iraq in 2003.

The continued application of realist criteria for using force rages in cell 2 with strong national security and military implications. Because the United States possesses such an overwhelming amount of force, there is some temptation to apply it to a variety of situations. As Clinton Secretary of State Madeleine Albright once said, "What is the point of having armed forces if you never use them?" The retort from the realist paradigm is that you only use them when the situation is really important (vital interests) and when force is appropriate. Whether the removal of Saddam Hussein was important enough to justify invading Iraq is a cell 1–cell 2 dispute.

The role of force is more complicated in cells 3 and 4 (semimilitary dimensions). Where vital interests are at stake, force is justified to the extent it can be effective.

The military aspects of the war on terrorism is a clear cell 3 application. The questions revolve around how much of a role force plays when it may be a necessary, but not sufficient, condition for success. The war on drugs arguably represents cell 4, since drug use is an important but probably not system-threatening (vital interest) problem. In this case, questions can be raised about whether the problem is severe enough to invoke force and whether the use of force is appropriate for dealing with the problem.

Remember that the boundary between military and nonmilitary dimensions (vital and major interests) is not a fixed line. It is more like a movable confidence interval of changing widths and locations. Where the line should be and just how wide the interval around it ought to be is the heart of the national security debate about using force. It is a highly political debate about which reasonable people can disagree over specific situations and that changes location as time passes and circumstance change. While there will always be high levels of consensus on some vital items, there will equally always be disagreement about the exact location of the intellectual barrier separating those situations that do and do not justify the employment of American armed forces. The existence of semimilitary situations only further blurs the distinction.

The debate within cell 2 and in cells 3 and 4 can thus be seen as a question about how much the change in the international environment of the post–Cold War world has moved the width of the band surrounding what is and is not vital and the extent and role of force in semimilitary situations. During the Cold War period, the location was relatively clear. The United States could and would use force when Soviet-inspired or Soviet-directed Communist movements threatened to come to power at the expense of American friends and allies. The clearest cases were those in which the United States had clearly important interests— western Europe and northeast Asia (Japan and Korea)—and, of course, in which the Soviets could threaten the United States directly with nuclear weapons. In cases that put the physical survival or independence of the American homeland or the territory of our closest friends at stake (the physical dimension of security), it was clear that military security was at stake and that force would be used (cell 1).

Even during the Cold War, the demarcation was an interval, not a line, and this was most clearly seen in places that might be of interest to the United States in Communist–non-Communist terms but where otherwise the United States had few other interests. Those situations occurred most often in developing world areas such as Africa and much of Asia, and the American assessment became more debatable, falling within the psychological dimension of what makes us feel secure and about which reasonable people can disagree. These are the instances that fall into cell 2.

Two potentially similar situations on which opposite conclusions were reached illustrate this relationship between interests and security. The first is the American involvement in Vietnam. When the United States replaced France as the principal barrier to Communist victory there after the Geneva Conference of 1954, there was relatively little debate about American direct interests in the outcome of that conflict. Rather, the prevailing criterion for some level of involvement was opposition to Communist expansion globally, of which Southeast Asia happened to be the then most current example. Opposition to Communism as a general proposition was viewed as important enough to ask the question, How will American interests be affected by the worst possible outcome (the unification of the country under Communist control)?

In retrospect, it is probably unfortunate that the specific question was not raised in the public debate and fully considered at the time, because quite likely the assessment would have been negative. In the end, the worst possible outcome did occur, but except for the self-inflicted angst the country experienced because we "lost" the war, American interests otherwise were hardly affected at all—the answer to how interests were affected was "not very much." What looked at the time like a cell 1 situation looks much more like a cell 2 or even cell 6 situation in retrospect.

The other example is Nicaragua in the 1980s. How important Sandinista rule was to the interests of the United States was argued both as a matter of the competition between the Communist and non-Communist rule and on the basis of geography. At one level, a Marxist Nicaragua provided a foothold for Communism on the mainland of the Americas through which Soviet assistance could be funneled through Cuba into Nicaragua and on to destinations such as El Salvador, where the pro-American government was facing a Marxist insurgency. At another level, an activist Nicaragua might stir up trouble generally in the region, possibly eventually threatening control of the Panama Canal and even destabilizing the southern part of Mexico, where there was an incipient antigovernment insurgent movement active.

Did the Nicaraguan situation rise to a threat to a vital interest, justifying a military response (cell 1), or were the interests less than vital, in which case a military response might or might not be appropriate? There was disagreement between the White House and the Congress on this question, and the ultimate decision was to treat it as either a cell 2 or cell 6 situation, one not requiring the employment of American military forces—a determination vindicated when the Nicaraguans voted the Sandinistas out of office in 1990.

Why engage in such a lengthy discussion of the relationship between security dimensions and interest levels? For one thing, it illustrates that in the real world, such determinations are difficult and ambiguous. Were the world made up exclusively of clearly cell 1 or cell 6 situations, making and implementing national security policy would be simple. In fact, one of the sources of nostalgia about the Cold War is that the central confrontation between the United States and the Soviet Union was such a precisely cell 1 instance. Because of that, building security policy from that central construct was intellectually straightforward and relatively noncontroversial. Having said that, the United States never used military force during the Cold War in an unambiguously cell 1 situation (the closest possible exception may have been Korea); Americans *deployed* forces to deal with cell 1 contingencies (NATO forces in Europe), but they were *employed* in situations more closely associated with cell 2.

The post–Cold War world is composed almost exclusively of situations that cause debate about where the boundary between vital and less-than-vital interests should be placed and what kinds of responses—military, semimilitary, or nonmilitary—are most appropriate. Because of the interest–threat mismatch, there are hardly any clear cell 1 situations for which to prepare and around which to ground planning. If international terrorism truly threatened the physical integrity of the United States and was a force appropriate for military eradication, it might rise to cell 1. American military preponderance makes it difficult even to think of potential cell 1 situations in the near future because no state or coalition of states poses a threatening symmetrical threat.

The ongoing environment exists outside the realm of vital interests—in cells 2, 3, 4, and 6. Part of the problem involves determining which of those cells is appropriate to describe any given concrete situation and to suggest appropriate ways to deal with them. At the same time, arguably vital interests are engaged in areas outside of national survival and where semimilitary solutions may be appropriate. Also, economic well-being such as terms of trade with Japan demonstrate situations in which nonmilitary aspects of security are clearly more appropriate (cell 5). There are, in other words, more ambiguous decisions to be made than there are clear-cut determinations such as whether the country should be prepared to defend a Soviet invasion through the Fulda Gap in Germany.

Security and Interests in the Contemporary Environment

It is an old saw that national interests rarely change but that threats to those interests change. A stable, free western Europe, for instance, is just as important to the United States today as it was a half-century ago; what is different today is that there are no realistic threats to the security of the countries of western Europe. At the same time, new (or apparently new) threats to long-term interests may emerge, as the terrorist threat to American territory exhibits. In the terrorist case, interests and threats converge, and the only question is how to deal with them.

This situation creates an intellectual bind for those who think about and plan for national security, especially the military dimension of national security. While there may be situations that potentially engage American vital interests, the only one that has activated American interest has been Iraq. When Saddam Hussein invaded and conquered Kuwait in 1990, he threatened American guaranteed access to Middle Eastern oil, a clear American vital interest. When he was alleged to have been stockpiling WMD and consorting with terrorists in 2002, the red flag of vital interests was raised again. Similarly, it is still possible that North Korea might try to cross the 38th Parallel into South Korea or that China might venture across the Straits of Taiwan to annex the island into the Chinese polity, but neither of these contingencies is especially likely.

Potential conventional military threats to vital American interests are unlikely in the short or medium terms. Countries may and do have major disagreements with the United States on a variety of issues, but because of the enormous advantage the United States has in symmetrical capabilities, it is implausible that any state or group of states would or could challenge the United States in conventional arms. Iraq's de facto nondefense against the American invasion of 2003 is testimony to this calculation.

The Korean and Taiwanese scenarios are similar. Despite being one of the most secretive, reclusive regimes in the world, the North Koreans are showing steadily increasing interest in closer relations with the much more prosperous South Korea, and a reprise of the 1950 invasion could only destroy the economic base in the

South that is the North's best (and possibly only) source of assistance in relieving the overwhelming poverty of that country. Based on any objective reading of the situation, it is much easier to project peaceful reunification of the Korean peninsula than it is to imagine an attempted reunion by the sword or North Korean nuclear aggression.

A forceful Chinese annexation of Taiwan is similarly implausible. The Chinese lack the naval assets for an amphibious invasion (especially with the American Seventh Fleet interfering with the operation—a virtual certainty in the event). While China could reduce Taiwan to rubble in a rocket attack, it is hard to see the point, since virtually all the Taiwanese investment capital flowing onto the mainland would be destroyed in the process. Moreover, even limited military action against Taiwan would have serious repercussions—especially in trading—with the rest of the world on which Chinese prosperity depends. As mentioned earlier, the Chinese likely will be on their best international behavior between now and the 2008 Olympics for fear that misbehavior would cost them the Olympic games they worked so hard to obtain (the Chinese remember the Western boycott of the 1980 summer Olympics in Moscow after the Soviet Union invaded Afghanistan).

One may, of course, question any of these arguments and concoct a set of circumstances that is more negative and forbidding than described here. Under any circumstances, it is difficult to fashion a threat scenario for any of those situations to which one would attach other than a very low order of likelihood.

The terrorist attacks of 2001 and the continuing campaign to eradicate terrorism—the second fault line—adds a new element to the mix. Protecting the homeland is clearly a vital interest, but the threat is asymmetrical in size and only semimilitary in response. At one level, interests and threats converge, but at another level they remain mismatched. Although overthrowing the Taliban and disrupting the bin Laden network's sanctuary in Afghanistan was a fairly traditional military mission, the post-Afghanistan campaign against terrorism is not being conducted on any battlefield with a climactic confrontation. Rather, it must be conducted against an opponent using unconventional methods, including acts of terror (asymmetrical warfare). Beyond the direct attacks on American soil on September 1, 2001, the earlier pattern of actions carried out by bin Laden probably represent the nature and scale of response that the United States faces. Bin Laden's intent is to harm as many Americans as he can. His means of doing so has been to commission acts of terror against select American targets, such as the U.S. embassies in Dar es Salaam, Tanzania, and Nairobi, Kenya, and the suicide attack against the USS *Cole* in a Yemeni port. He was also involved in the attack against the World Trade Center towers in New York in 1993.

What defines these acts is their size and responses to them. The African embassy attacks killed around two dozen Americans (as well as hundreds of Kenyans and Tanzanians), and seventeen sailors died on the *Cole*. While these losses were tragic, they were not on a scale that threatens the basic integrity of the United States. It is also not clear how to respond to these kinds of acts. The United States retaliated for the embassy bombings by launching cruise missiles against suspected terrorist training camps in Afghanistan run by bin Laden, but they failed either to kill the Saudi expatriate or to slow down his activities. A major conceptual problem arises from the Al Qaeda lack of a territorial base that can be attacked, which is a main use of conventional force in symmetrical war situations.

How to use armed forces when the kinds of situations for which they have traditionally been employed (securing vital interests) are basically absent or partially appropriate is a major agenda item in the current debate about national security. Clearly, many of the real threats to American national interests fall on the less-than-vital side of the demarcation line. The clear implication is that there is not clear guidance about what military forces, and especially conventional forces, should do in these situations. What, then, are the implications for the constellation of American instruments of power, including military force?

How do we deal with such circumstances? One way is to enforce the realist paradigm and accept the decreased saliency of regular military force in the current milieu. If American forces are to be used only when vital interests are at stake, then they will be used relatively infrequently in the near future, or they will only be a variable part of responses to worthy threats. The other solution is to broaden the criteria under which force employment is allowable. This amounts to moving the line between vital and less-than-vital interests more into the less-than-vital category of actions. The primary "beneficiary" of such a movement comes currently in the form of deployments of American forces into peacekeeping missions in places such as Bosnia and Kosovo under the justification of so-called *humanitarian vital interests*, to which allusion was made in the introduction of this book.

APPLYING INSTRUMENTS OF POWER

The anarchical nature of international relations requires that states engage in self-help in order to realize their interests. A recourse to some superior source of authority before which they could adjudicate conflicts of their interests with those of others does not exist. There is no such authority, of course, because states have vital interests that might not prevail if some outside authority decided the outcomes of conflicts of interests. Since, by definition, a state will not willingly accept denial of its most important interests, the solution is to avoid having any body that can make adverse rulings that would probably be disobeyed.

This depiction is at the heart of the operation of the realist paradigm of the international system. In such a system, states achieve their goals to the extent of their ability to coerce or convince others to comply with their goals or interests. Whether one applauds or decries that situation is interesting but, for present purposes, irrelevant in the sense that this is the dynamic that energizes the system in the absence of some fundamental reform that has yet to occur.

Instruments of power (introduced in Chapter 2) generically refer to the array of methods a state possesses to gain conformance with its interests. Power situations (in which one state seeks to get another to do what it does not want to do) involve situation-specific relationships. That means that what will work to gain compliance in one situation will not necessarily have the same result in another, because power interplays involve discrete relationships between the players. Therefore, the more varied and robust the instruments a state has, the more likely and it is to prevail more of the time. Operationally, a state's rank among the powers refers to both the variety and depth of its power across the spectrum of instruments.

Using the Instruments

The instruments of power do not exist in a vacuum but gain their meaning in terms of whether their application accomplishes the purposes for which they are used. For an instrument to be potentially effective, it must possess two traditionally defined characteristics, to which we add an implied third. First, a state must possess the physical wherewithal to take the actions it proposes, what is known as *capability*. The absence of capability renders a threat ineffectual if the threatened party recognizes the deficiency. A Chinese threat to close the strategic Straits of Malacca by interdicting shipping transiting the straits would be ignored because China lacks the long-range aircraft (and refueling capability) or navy to sustain such action. Second, objects of threats must believe the threatening state would actually employ those capabilities in the ways it says it would in order to accomplish its ends, what is known as *credibility*. Based upon his perceptions of post-Vietnam unwillingness to use force, Saddam Hussein wrongly believed the United States would not use force to reverse his conquest of Kuwait. Beyond capability and credibility is the ability to apply the instrument in a manner that achieves the sought-after goal, or what we can call *efficacy*.

These characteristics are clearly interrelated. Capability and credibility are linked. At the most obvious level, no state is going to believe a threat based on a capability the threatening state does not possess. Nicaragua, for instance, cannot threaten to invade Mexico because it lacks the military capability to do so. Conversely, however, the ability to carry out a threat does not imply the willingness to use that power. The United States becomes annoyed with France frequently over France's attempts to keep symbols of American culture, such as American popular music and films, out of the country (or to limit the amount of penetration of French culture). While it is physically possible for the United States to threaten a nuclear attack against France to force it to lift these restrictions, no one would believe such a threat, meaning it lacks credibility. At the same time, a country may possess—and employ—a variety of instruments that will not achieve the goal for which they are intended. The American economic boycott against Cuba for the past forty years has not accomplished its principal goal of removing Fidel Castro from power or of lifting Communist rule from the island state.

Orchestrating the uses of the instruments of power is a delicate activity, one that involves considerable uncertainties arising from the fact that whether power is effectively applied is largely a complex psychological exercise. At one level, it is a duel between the state threatening to employ an instrument and the state receiving the threat. Assuming the threatened party knows whether the threatener has the capability to do what is proposed (which the threatening party may seek to obscure), it then has to assess whether the threat is credible, which is an exercise in mind reading. There may be some evidence based upon how the threatening state has acted in similar circumstances in the past to provide an indication of the threatener's will, but since no two situations are identical, that evidence may or may not be conclusive: Will he or will he not?

The threatening partner must also make a psychological assessment of the party against whom it is seeking to apply power in a situation of less-than-perfect knowledge of the other party's mental state. Will the other party believe I would carry out the threat or call my bluff? At the same time, will the threat gain compliance without having to be carried out (the best possible outcome, since carrying out threats normally involves some harm for all parties)? If not, will carrying out the threat convince the other party to do what I wanted done in the first place, or will it fail?

The answers to these questions are generally not cut-and-dried in real-world situations. The calculations sound like the reasoning in a poker game, where capabilities are defined by the hands the players hold but where part of the hand is obscured (capability), where betting is a form of indicating credibility, and the success of maneuvers such as bluffing measure the efficacy of the threats that raising bets represent. Employing power in the real world, however, has added complications, such as the emotions of the interplay of national pride, different and largely nonmeasurable (at least in advance) factors such as national resolve, and the importance of outcomes to all the players.

During the Cold War, much of this calculation had been worked out, and the dynamics were reasonably clearly defined. Among the instruments of power, the military instrument was conceded to be of the greatest importance, at least in the relations among the contending superpowers. The economic instrument was clearly more important in the relations within the developed countries headed by the United States, but economic sanctions and rewards had virtually no impact on East–West relations. The greatest ambiguities about which instruments had efficacy were in the developing world, both in the extension of the East–West confrontation and in relations over matters like political and economic development.

How does the end of the Cold War alter the constellation of efficacious applications of power? One indication of change has been the reduction of military budgets for all the major powers (other than the United States). At the same time, the economic instrument seemed to become more important as globalization spread, but how will that instrument be affected by the international economic turbulence that has accompanied the return of geopolitics to the center of international concern? How does the rise of terrorism as an instrument of power wielded by nonstate actors affect the environment?

The Contemporary Balance of Instruments of Power

Whether there is a real change in how international relations occur today is largely a matter of the state of the third criterion identified for applying instruments: efficacy. The question of change can be rephrased to ask whether other, nonmilitary forces induce change in the post–Cold War world more than did those (normally military) in the Cold War era. Assertions of dramatic change will almost inevitably overshoot the truth, but there may be some discernible differences.

The efficacy of the traditional military instrument has clearly become more restricted. Military threats or actions among the major powers of the developed world absolutely lack credibility. This is really not a change, however, because it was equally unlikely that the western allies (including the market democracies of Asia) would have fought one another during the Cold War. If there is a difference, it is that what President Clinton liked to call the "ring of market democracies" has been gradually enlarging, including the addition of former authoritarian foes from the old Communist world. In these cases, positive military inducements may have supplanted threats as the instrument to advance American interests in spreading market democracy. Actions such as military arms sales, training programs, and membership and participation in military alliances like NATO are means to induce formerly nondemocratic countries into the general peace.

The use of military force in the developing world has similarly undergone only modest, peripheral change. Most of the violence in the world occurs within (as opposed to between) developing world states, as was generally the case during the Cold War. What has changed are the incentives for outside involvement in these conflicts. During the Cold War, the motivation was to prevent the victory of Communist elements, and the calculus included the likelihood and intolerability of Communist success. In the contemporary environment prior to 2001, the incentives tended to cluster around humanitarian concerns. The calculus involved whether any lasting good could be achieved by physical involvement and what levels of sacrifice are tolerable to accomplish various levels of good. These were less compelling interests that fighting Communism. Blunting and suppressing terrorism has provided a firmer basis for applying the military instrument; as a semimilitary concern, striking a balance between the use of military and nonmilitary instruments is the problem.

The major contraction in the efficacy of military force surrounds the avoidance of major war with potent and threatening adversaries. Only the utter failure of market democracy in a major state such as China or Russia could produce the underlying animosities necessary to produce a new peer competitor for the United States. Such a transformation would, of course, be carefully monitored from the beginning, and actions would certainly be taken to reduce or contain such developments. Moreover, the reversion could occur only by the failure of the very economic modernization on which a potent military is built. Russia, for instance, cannot afford the military forces it has today. Were the Russian system to fail to the point of reaching a Faustian bargain to return to authoritarianism, what kind of military could such a totally failed system afford?

What this suggests about the military instrument is that its efficacy has shrunk in the most important and costly area it occupied formerly. If that is the case and the likelihood of a returned equivalent threat is unlikely, then those facts should have major implications for the capability component of the capability/credibility/efficacy equation that energizes the instruments of power.

It is easy to overstate how much the economic instrument has undergone change. Globalization has clearly expanded the arsenal of economic instruments of power. The emphasis on trade and the removal of trade barriers creates opportunities for countries with large markets such as the United States to obtain leverage among those who wish to compete in the American domestic market. Membership in the various universal and regional trading associations can provide the ability to influence economic decisions in various countries, and the ability of the International Monetary Fund (IMF) and other international monitors to guide the development of developing economies has clearly been enhanced as well. The desire to share in the general prosperity creates opportunities to shape the behavior of states outside but wanting into the global prosperity.

Three cautionary points should be made about too rhapsodic an assessment of the positive impacts of globalization. First, the enhancement of instruments of economic power is really the extension, possibly intensification, of powers that were already there. Special economic preferences have always been part of foreign economic policy, for instance, and the IMF has been influencing governments for a long time. Second, the amount of leverage that globalization creates will be significantly related to how positively the phenomenon is perceived in the future. The decade of the 1990s was one of unrestrained enthusiasm and clamoring for inclusion—at almost any cost—until economic turmoil at the end of the century and the recession of 2001 took hold. How badly new members want in and what they are willing to do to get in will depend on how well the system operates and produces prosperity in the future. Finally, there are and continue to be countries that resist the process and that are thus impervious to its influence. This resistance is particularly strong wherever fundamentalist Islam is a major force.

New forms of power may blossom in the future. The telecommunications revolution has been a particularly potent force in economic expansion, information explosion, and a variety of other areas. The positive expansion of the information age to nonparticipants is an enormous positive inducement to influence behavior. This positive aspect, however, has a darker side in the form of threats to disrupt the very fragile systems on which the telecommunications revolution rests. Cyber terror, a prospect raised in Chapter 5, may become an all-too-familiar instrument of power given the increasingly electronic dependency of the international system.

CONCLUSION: THE CHANGING NATURE OF INFLUENCE

In this chapter, we raised and examined four related concerns about contemporary international politics and the transition from the Cold War environment to the present. The first concern was with security and asked how a changed environment affects American national security in both a physical and psychological sense. Is American security enhanced or detracted from due to changes that have occurred? The second concern was how the changed security environment affects the kind and amount of risk the country must endure and the problem of risk reduction and risk management. Is the world a riskier place? The third concern was with national interests, phrased in terms of whether the most important interests were more imperiled or reinforced today. Can the United States better realize its interests today than previously? The fourth concern was with how those interests are realized in the form of changes in the effectiveness of the various instruments of power. Are different instruments more efficacious than they were before for realizing interests in the changed environment?

Overall, the major conclusion one must reach is that the post–Cold War world, despite the intrusion of international terrorism, is a more secure, less threatening place than before for the United States, and one in which the country is basically better able to realize its interests. One can easily overstate both the pervasiveness of change and the improvement of the situation, but at least in a marginal sense, the generalizations seem to hold, even if the one major source of insecurity that terrorism represents is factored in.

The chief cause of improvement is, of course, the end of the Cold War and thus the removal of the largest challenge to security, the possibility of a general systemic war in which the nuclear-armed superpowers confront one another on the battlefield with the fate of civilization in the balance. The vulnerability of American territory to terrorist attacks remains a significant threat, but not on the scale of World War III during the Cold War.

As large-scale military power has depreciated in value, economic leverage arising from globalization has expanded in the quiver of elements of national power. The reassertion of a robust American economy that remains the world's premier market (chronicled in Chapter 5) provides the United States with considerable leverage to promote an international economy and national economies and policies based on the American value of market democracy. The world economic downturn in 2001 has dampened some of the more effusive enthusiasm about how much globalization has transformed the international system, but globalization continues to be a positive force that benefits the United States.

What could cause a deterioration of the current situation and the American place in it? A cataclysmic turn of the global economy like the Great Depression of the 1930s would certainly represent the worst possible case. One of the fears surrounding the emergence of international terrorism was the prospect that it might trigger a general economic downturn, for instance. Hardly anyone expects that to occur, but there are still potential dangers on a lesser scale.

Reaction to American supremacy probably represents the greatest potential for negative change. Many commentators have pointed out that the current epoch is remarkable because, unlike other historic periods when a single political entity dominated the world scene, no competitor or coalition of competitors has arisen to oppose and counterbalance American power. Initially, this seemed to be the case because, unlike other states, the United States was rarely viewed as a threatening power in the system. As time has passed, however, erosive influences have emerged in the form of reactions to what are perceived as American inconstancy and even arrogance in its dealings with the rest of the world.

Where these concerns may become most evident is through the resurgence of American unilateralism, a trend most evident since the election of 2000 and even within American responses to terrorism. Such responses run counter to one of the contemporary trends in the international system, which has been to internationalize efforts, in the United Nations, through regional and universal economic associations and through treaty obligations. This trend has all been part of a sort of democratization of international relations generally, giving all states the opportunity to participate in decisions about international norms and their implementation. This trend can be seen in subject areas as diverse as lowering tariffs, banning land mines, and raising air quality standards. For the United States (or anyone else) to exercise leadership and thus to maximize its influence over matters within its interests that enhance its security, it must be a prominent part of that internationalization or be perceived as an arrogant, even overbearing, outsider.

SELECTED BIBLIOGRAPHY

Burton, Daniel F., Victor Gotbaum, and Felix Rohatyn (Eds.). *Vision for the 1990s: U.S. Strategy and the Global Economy*. Cambridge, MA: Ballinger, 1989.

Flanagan, Stephen J., Ellen L. Frost, and Richard L. Kugler. *Challenges of the Global Century: Report of the Project on Globalization and National Security*. Washington, DC: Institute of National Strategic Studies (National Defense University), 2001.

Luttwak, Edward N. *Strategy: The Logic of War and Peace*. Cambridge, MA: Belknap, 1987.

Pfaff, William. "Invitation to War." *Foreign Affairs* 72, 3 (Summer 1993), 97–109.

Pilat, Joseph F. "Reassessing Security Assurances in a Unipolar World." *Washington Quarterly* 28, 2 (Spring 2005), 159–167.

Rogov, Sergei. "International Security and the Collapse of the Soviet Union." *Washington Quarterly* 15, 2 (Spring 1992), 16–28.

Sloan, Stephen. *Beating International Terrorism: An Action Strategy for Preemption and Punishment* (rev. ed.). Montgomery, AL: Air University Press, 2000.

Smith, W. Y. "U.S. National Security after the Cold War." *Washington Quarterly* 15, 4 (Winter 1992), 21–34.

Snow, Donald M., "'Let Them Drink Oil': Resource Conflict in the New Century?" in *Cases in International Relations: Snapshots of the Future*. New York: Longman, 2002.

———. *When America Fights: The Uses of U.S. Military Power*. Washington, DC: CQ Press, 2000.

CHAPTER 7

The Foreign and Domestic Environments

PREVIEW

How environmental changes affect policy and our approach and response to national security challenges is more than just an abstract matter. In this chapter, we begin to see how the influences of the international and domestic political environments have an impact on political processes and outcomes. Because there is some difference in generalized view of whether the environment is essentially benign or hostile (which has strong implications for viewing globalization or geopolitics as the dominant paradigm), we begin by presenting and trying to reconcile two competing popular conceptualizations. We then turn to the question of how internal political processes affect and are affected by national security changes. In particular, we examine the chief institutional response to international terrorism, the Department of Homeland Security, and its enigmatic evolution.

The way in which the United States (and other countries) deal with the world is a combination of a number of factors. One is an assessment of the international environment: Is it generally hostile or benign, and what, if anything, can and should the United States try to do to help create a world more to our liking? Generally speaking, the United States prefers an international environment wherein peace and stability hold and, ideally, where the American ideals of political democracy and market economics are taking hold more widely. This was, by and large, the environment of the 1990s, when globalization was the rising force in the world. But that generally benign set of conditions contained circumstances in which radical international terrorism festered and grew and man-made disasters like the genocide in Rwanda scarred Africa.

Deciding what to try to do about the world begins by assessing the environment. Our view has been jaundiced by the terrible events of 2001, which have rearranged our national priorities and arguably distorted our overall view of the world. Beyond the focus on terrorism, there is less agreement about critical elements of the environment now than during the 1990s and before. In the wake of the terrorist attacks of 2001, the GWOT became the major pivot around which many problems were conceptualized to revolve. How long will that focus remain?

The international environment provides contrasting images and impressions. The unifying influences of commerce and communications were the apparently ascending forces of the 1990s. How could one not look favorably on a world where a Starbucks coffeehouse had been set up inside the walls of the Forbidden City of Beijing? At the same time, optimism was conditioned by negative phenomena such as the pestilence of AIDS that ravaged much of sub-Saharan Africa and vicious civil conflicts that dotted the map of much of the developing world.

The confusion over the environment is also reflected in domestic politics. Partly, the debate is a philosophical discussion about the extent of American activism in the world that reflects an assessment of what the world out there is really like and the degree to which the United States has some role, obligation, or ability to affect the environment. The 1990s was a period largely of American internationalism and activism under the Clintonian foreign policy sobriquet "engagement and enlargement."

The domestic equation changed after the 2000 election, and even more dramatically after September 11, 2001. The new Bush administration initially professed a more limited approach to the American role in the world than its predecessor, arguing the United States neither could nor should attempt to involve itself everywhere and that it was willing to act unilaterally when it felt it needed to do so. The inclination to limit activism was doused by the actions of Al Qaeda. Unilateralism temporarily gave way to an international effort to combat the problem, but it returned when the international community disagreed with aspects of the American approach, as much of it did over the forceful removal of Saddam Hussein and the general war effort in Iraq.

Competing visions of the world and the American place in it spill directly onto the substantive national security question and its implications. The debate occurs in a circumstance where there is broad agreement in the national security community that the environment has changed enough to require rethinking and even restructuring American capabilities and approaches to confront that world. Responses to the terrorist attacks have added the concept of homeland security to the lexicon of central national security concerns and has resulted in major institutional adaptation.

COMPETING IMAGES OF
THE INTERNATIONAL ENVIRONMENT

There is substantially less agreement about the international environment today than there was a decade ago and certainly during the Cold War. Our Cold War image was of a menacing and threatening world of confrontation and potential nuclear holocaust that gave way to a more benign image in the 1990s. Terrorism reintroduced menace to our environment that continues to globalize. Which image predominates?

A view on these matters is influenced by the vantage point from which one looks. Part of that vantage point is geographical. If one concentrates on the Pacific Rim as the direction of the future, the impression is of a basically benign international system of spreading commerce and cooperation, only slightly blemished by geopolitical concerns such as the China–Taiwan relationship. A Pacific Rim focus is likely to be optimistic about the future and to upgrade the role of globalization at the expense of geopolitics. If, on the other hand, the focus is primarily on the poorest parts of the developing world outside the globalizing economy, then the shocking violence, poverty, and hopelessness of the situation is likely to result in a much more negative view, in which geopolitics rise to the fore. The areas of despair and discontent form the cauldron from which terrorism has emerged, we have had to begin to confront it.

Two sharply competing views of the general direction of the international system from the 1990s represent the geopolitical and globalization perspectives. For exemplary purposes, these can be represented by two international journalists, Robert D. Kaplan and Thomas L. Friedman, each of whom has traveled and written extensively about international trends but reached diametrically opposed conclusions about the human condition.

Kaplan: The Coming Anarchy

Robert D. Kaplan is a long-time international correspondent, most of whose work has appeared in the *Atlantic Monthly*. His travel and coverage have been concentrated on the poorest parts of the world, those generally outside the developed world and remote from the growing international economic activity associated with globalization. In particular, much of his reporting has been on Africa and the multiple calamities faced on that continent. Some of his more dramatic observations are contained in a slender volume composed of his essays and called *The Coming Anarchy*.

Kaplan's presentation is dramatic and provocative in its observations and conclusions, but much of it is shared by other analysts as well. Moreover, many of the dynamics he describes apply clearly to conditions in parts of the Middle East that have produced international terrorists. His basic thesis is that the international system is becoming increasingly "bifurcated" between "societies like ours, producing goods and services that the rest of the world wants, and those mired in various forms of chaos." In terms used in this text, he divides the world into roughly the countries participating in the globalizing economy and the countries that, due to extreme underdevelopment or rejection of globalization values, stand outside the process. He argues that not only does a gulf exist between the two but it is progressively widening.

As such, this thesis is not exceptional. In the past few years, there has been increasing publicity about the divide between the rich and the poor states, a recognition given greater urgency by the outbreaks of particularly vicious internal fighting and killing in places like Sierra Leone and, more recently, the recognition of the enormity of the AIDS pandemic throughout Africa.

Whereas many analysts point to the humanitarian tragedy of Africa and the moral and humanitarian obligations the rich countries have to alleviate the suffering, Kaplan sees the situation as a security problem for the international community. A major part of this emphasis is based on what he sees as an expansion of the security menu not unlike what was suggested in Chapter 5 and elsewhere. He believes much of the source of instability and violence in the world will come from unconventional problems already present in Africa, such as "environmental scarcity, cultural and racial clash, geographic destiny, and the transformation of war." In the latter category, he sees a continuation of the very chaotic, transnational forms of internal violence that have marked a number of African countries since the end of the Cold War that could spread more widely in a geographic sense. This analysis applies equally well to places like eastern Pakistan and Afghanistan, which have been the breeding ground for organizations like Al Qaeda. Rioting and destruction by developing world immigrants in the suburbs of Paris in late 2005 offer a somber view of possible future developments.

The implications he draws from these trends make Kaplan's analysis provocative. Many analysts see environmental and other pressures such as population expansion as sources of future world problems and even of potential violence as scarcity increases along with demands for resources. Where Kaplan and his critics (who are numerous) part company is in the implications of change for the developed world. Many Africanists, for instance, believe that the heart of African tragedy is the extreme marginalization and isolation of the continent from the rest of the world. As a result, African problems are left to be solved by Africans who lack the wherewithal for the effort. In this view, the gulf will steadily widen, but Africa will simply be left out, with no recourse that will allow Africans to join the general prosperity.

Kaplan believes quite the opposite. He argues the response to worsening conditions in the developing world will be their transfer to the developed countries. As the misery in the least developed countries becomes more intolerable, he believes the result will be massive migration by the disaffected to the seats of power and prosperity—to the most developed countries. He states this thesis in predictably dramatic form:

> It is time to understand the environment for what it is: *the* national-security issue of the early twenty-first century. The political and strategic impact of surging populations, spreading disease, deforestation and soil erosion, water depletion, air pollution, and possibly rising sea levels . . . will prompt mass migration and, in turn, incite group conflicts [that] will be the core foreign-policy challenge from which most others will emanate.

Rather than silently suffering in isolation, in other words, those most deprived will share their misery with the rest of the world in hopes of improving their condition. The French now recognize this problem.

Kaplan's thesis is controversial in at least two ways. First, it is possible to argue that he overstates the case factually, that things are not and will not become as dire as he predicts. There is evidence on both sides of the issue. If, however, he is correct or partially so, the other question his prognosis raises is what to do about the problem. The broad policy options follow the general contours of the U.S. debate over its role in the world. The internationalist response suggests a concerted effort to alleviate the conditions before they reach the proportions that could trigger the dire consequences that Kaplan prophesies. A more minimalist, isolationist approach suggests we have no business interfering in these natural conditions and that we lack the resources or will to do much about them anyway. At any rate, Kaplan projects a very grim, geopolitically centered view of the world.

Friedman: Globalization

New York Times foreign affairs correspondent Thomas L. Friedman has been among the loudest and most consistent champions of the phenomenon of globalization and what he likes to describe as the transition of international relations from the "cold war system" to what he calls the "globalization system." The most elaborate description of this "system" and its operation is found in Friedman's 1999 book *The Lexus and the Olive Tree* and more recently in his 2005 sequel, *The World Is Flat.*

Friedman's basic argument can be summarized in his own words: "The driving force beyond globalization is free-market capitalism—the more you let markets rule and the more you open your economy to free trade and competition, the more efficient and flourishing your economy will be. Globalization means the spread of free-market capitalism to virtually every country in the world." Since that spread means the adoption of a uniform economic philosophy that implies movement to a common political idea—democracy—the virtues of globalization include that it integrates the countries into a commonality that should spread and reinforce peace and stability.

If the claims of the advocates of globalization are accepted, the result should be a more secure, peaceful world in which the recourse to violence will gradually subside in the mutual acceptance of the mantra of market capitalism. Countries will have progressively more in common than what may separate them, thereby moderating international sources of conflict. States that accept the rules of globalization will become prosperous and thus peaceful. Globalization will triumph over geopolitics in this happiest of all possible outcomes.

The most optimistic descriptions and advocacies of the system-transforming effects of globalization are products of the 1990s and focus on Asia. Friedman, for instance, presents a majority of his evidence from Asian examples, and when he shows how embracing globalization can transform countries not currently part of the global economy, most of his examples come from Asia and the non-Persian Gulf region of the Middle East, not from the parts of Africa that Kaplan decries.

The ongoing globalization process defines the future global (including geopolitical) competition. The symbolism of a "flat" world is that the knowledge base on which globalization builds has spread around the world, leveling the global playing field and allowing countries like India and China to compete for global leadership in the globalization system. Friedman argues that economic, and thus geopolitical, advantage will go to those countries most adept at producing the most profound science and technology to fuel the evolution of globalization and that the outcome of that competition is by no means foreordained.

There are several arguments against the Friedman formulation. One argument is that we have heard all of these claims before, and they have always fallen short of fulfilling their promise in the past. The argument that states can be brought into a system from which they benefit to the point that old-fashioned geopolitics and the recourse to violence disappears is the basic argument made by the functionalists (such as David Mitrany) in forming the specialized agencies of the United Nations. (The idea was that having UN agencies provide basic services such as health would cause people to abandon loyalty to the state as the functions of states were replaced by international providers.) It is also the basic argument of the advocates of complex interdependence (see Nye and Keohane), and globalization is, in a very real linear sense, the current manifestation of that hope. At the same time, others point out that we have had periods resembling what we now call globalization before, and they have not lasted.

A second argument is that globalization does not have the universal appeal its apologists claim. Some countries and regions reject the cultural intrusion and destructiveness of globalization for local cultural, religious, or other practices. Strict Islamic countries are most often cited in this regard, and although advocates such as Friedman would argue such resistance consigns those countries to the dustbin of the modern system, it is hard to see how many countries in the region could become part of globalization without a great deal of trauma, probably including major violence. Another group of rejectionists are those countries that, for a variety of reasons, are unlikely ever to be competitive enough economically to become members of the system. Friedman calls these countries the "turtles," implying they cannot gain the momentum to become full participants in the system. The most obvious examples are the very African countries that concern Kaplan and may mean that globalization is not the answer to the problems Kaplan hypothesizes.

There is further question about the inevitability of globalization. It has been argued that historical evidences of globalization are cyclical and tied to periods of monetary expansions and contractions. When money supplies are expanding and investors are optimistic, then globalization is fed by supplies of capital that flow into the developing world. If history is any guide, however, cycles of monetary expansion are followed by cycles of contraction, when investor confidence wanes and resources are pulled from international markets. The result has been a decline in globalization.

Finally, there is the argument that globalization ultimately harms the state by undercutting state sovereignty. If the erosion of some amount of state sovereignty on the altar of globalization is accepted, the question of whether or not the benefits outweigh the costs is raised. If, on the one hand, globalization leads to a more peaceful, prosperous world with decreased security concerns, then the bargain may be an acceptable—even good—one. If, on the other hand, globalization is subject to fluctuation, reversal, and thus instability, then the same bargain may not seem so good at all.

Reconciling Worldviews

These two 1990s assessments contain common and divergent points. They largely agree that problems within the international arena occur primarily in the most unstable parts of the developing world, which of course is hardly anything new. Internal conflicts within Africa and parts of Asia are the core military problem facing the contemporary scene as well as they did in the last decade. What is different in the assessment is the severity of the problem and how to deal with it.

The globalization approach is inherently internationalist and activist. It sees the problem of world politics and instability primarily in economic terms and the solution in the gradual spread of the process of globalization to those parts of the world that are not current participants. This was the essence of the Clinton policy of engagement and enlargement, but it came with a caveat. The Clinton formulation said the United States should promote market democracy in those places where it had the best chances of taking hold and then hope that it spread beyond those bounds. It was not very specific about how that spread would occur in those areas—like most of Africa—that are most removed from the process of globalization or are the least able to compete (Friedman's turtles). It is also not clear how viable the strategy is if globalization falters.

The coming anarchy assessment is more cautious and pessimistic in its approach. Kaplan projects a basic hopelessness about conditions in the poorest parts of the world and a virtual inevitability about the negative consequences he foresees. This tone does not suggest that the levels of activism that are likely will make much difference and thus lends a more restrained approach toward reforming the system. Rather, we can read a sort of neo-isolationist message of trying to build up barriers against the onslaught that Kaplan sees in the future. The difference between the two visions is how fatalistic one is about conditions in the most wretched parts of the world and what can or should be done about them.

These arguments lost much of their abstract nature on September 11, 2001. The sources of the attacks came from the very kind of circumstances that Kaplan describes: backwardness, poverty, and hopelessness in a hostile world (even though most of the actual 9/11 suicide/martyr terrorists were Saudis). With the immediate problem of terrorism contained—if not eliminated—we now move toward the question of how places like Afghanistan and Pakistan can be made impervious to terrorist appeals in the future. Can they be drawn into the globalization system, or are they hopeless turtles that can never make the grade? How important is the effort to find out?

THE IMPACT OF DOMESTIC POLITICS

National security policy is, for a number of reasons, among the most contentious political areas within the American federal system. For one thing, the content of national security policy is potentially very important, ultimately including decisions that can affect the very physical survival of the country and, less dramatically, decisions about when Americans may be compelled to put themselves in harm's way to defend American interests.

National security policy is also highly political because it involves the expenditure of very large amounts of money. Currently, defense spending is the second-largest category in the federal budget, behind spending on entitlements (social security, Medicare, and the like) and just ahead of service on the interest on the national debt. Historically, defense has been the second-largest category of expenditures during the Cold War, involving roughly a quarter of the federal budget and 5 to 6 percent of gross national product (GNP). In the mid-1950s, before many of the entitlement programs were enacted, it accounted for nearly one-half of federal spending. Currently, it is over one-fifth of the federal budget.

Defense spending is highly political for other reasons as well. One of the important characteristics of the defense budget is that it is the largest *controllable* element within the federal budget. One way to distinguish items in the federal budget is to divide them into controllable and uncontrollable elements. A controllable element is one that must be appropriated annually; an uncontrollable element is one that is automatically appropriated unless there is specific legislation altering or rescinding the appropriation (social security is the best example). Nearly two-thirds of the controllable money in the federal budget comes from defense, meaning that attempts to increase, decrease, or alter the pattern of federal spending often begin with the defense budget.

The political nature also reflects the impact of national security spending on Americans. Not only is a lot of money spent on defense but those expenditures are made in a large number of physical locales, wherever concentrations of military installations and defense industries are found. The competition for defense contracts or the locations of bases or posts is a highly competitive process wherein the financial health and prosperity of communities can be vitally affected by the effectiveness of congressional delegations able to win federal contracts for their states and districts.

National security spending is also contentious because much of the money is spent on highly durable procurements. The decision, for instance, to build an aircraft carrier not only involves appropriating several billion dollars for its construction (money that is fed into the local community wherever the ship is built, of course) but also involves investment in a weapons "platform" that is expected to be in the arsenal for 30 years or longer. Procurement decisions affect not only the arsenal characteristics of whatever administration commissions them but also the military capability available to a commander-in-chief a quarter-century or more in the future. The same is true of procuring new fighter or bomber aircraft, a new model of main battle tank, and the like.

There is an old saw that "policy is what gets funded," and that truism holds for the national security area generally and is particularly true in the current milieu. Two things are coming together to create a sharp poignancy for the political, and especially budgetary, elements of the national security decision process. One is the nature of the current military arsenal. The military characteristics of the current force include the fact that it was largely shaped to confront a Soviet military threat that no longer exists and is not being replicated by any emerging potential adversary. Moreover, the force is getting old, and much of it needs replacement. A major question is how to modernize the force. One group, led by Secretary of Defense

Donald Rumsfeld, argues for the application of the *revolution in military affairs* (*RMA*), applying very sophisticated technologies to warfare to produce such a qualitatively superior force as to be unassailable. Others argue against such a heavy investment on the grounds that it would be excessive to any actual or likely threat facing the United States, and that the United States could decrease military spending and enjoy a "peace dividend" (savings) such as was promised but never really delivered in the 1990s. Allies worry that the American force has already become so comparatively sophisticated as to render their own forces obsolete and expendable.

The other side of this debate is over spending priorities more generally within the federal government. As the budget surpluses generated during the 1990s have been transformed into record-setting deficits in the early 2000s because of tax reductions and increased defense spending, all areas of federal spending have come under close scrutiny. While the Bush administration has argued for enhanced spending on national security, the amount and direction of that spending has become intensely controversial. Because of the inherent vulnerability of the defense budget (its controllable nature), it will remain the subject of considerable political concern. The GWOT and the Iraq War have muted this debate for now, but it will certainly return.

The politics of national security are played out at various levels that come together in the budget process. One level is within the executive branch of government, where the representatives of various government agencies and functions compete for priority within federal policy, including the budget. This competition extends to the legislative branch, where the same kind of competition occurs within the various layers of the committee system in hammering out what budget the executive will ultimately have to spend. Ultimately, decisions involve the interaction of the two principal legislating branches of the government (a process in which the judiciary is rarely involved).

The Executive Branch

National security policy within the executive branch of the government operates on two separate tracks that are, in some ways, paralleled conceptually within the Congress. The day-to-day conduct of national security (as part of overall foreign policy) occurs within the federal agencies with authority in the field, such as the State Department, Department of Defense (DOD), and the Central Intelligence Agency (CIA), at the direction of the president. Policy decisions are coordinated and implemented through the *interagency process*, the chief vehicle of which has been the National Security Council (NSC) and its subordinate bodies. New institutional actors, such as the Department of Homeland Security (DHS) and the Director of National Intelligence (DNI) are being integated into this system. This process of policy development and implementation is conceptually similar to the role of the authorizing committees of the Congress. The other track is the competition for funding, which is the heart of the budgetary process, and it pits parts of the national security community against one another and against competing functions of the government. The framework for this interaction, of course, is the constitutionally mandated roles for the various branches of government laid out by the Founding Fathers.

Amplification 7.1

THE PRESIDENT, THE CONSTITUTION, AND NATIONAL SECURITY

Because the Founding Fathers did not anticipate a level of involvement in international affairs that even mildly resembles the extent to which the country interacts with the rest of the world today, the U.S. Constitution does not lay out an elaborate list of powers for the president in the area of national security or foreign policy. Such specific powers as are provided are found in Article II of the Constitution, and as we shall see in a subsequent Amplification, essentially all are counterbalanced by contrary powers given to the Congress as part of the "checks and balances" system that characterizes the entire document. The result is an "invitation to struggle" (see Crabb and Holt) intended to make the two branches coequal in this area.

The Constitution lists six powers for the president that directly apply to national security and defense policy. They are the positions of chief executive, chief of state, commander in chief of the armed forces, treaty negotiator, nominator of key personnel, and recognizer of foreign government.

Chief Executive. In this capacity, the president is designated as the major presider over the executive agencies of the government, all of which report directly to the president. In the area of foreign and national security policy, these agencies include the departments of State and Defense, the Central Intelligence Agency, and the various economic agencies, including the Departments of Treasury and Commerce and the U.S. Trade Representative. These agencies collectively are the chief repositories of the expertise of the federal government on foreign matters, and the president's access to them provides an important advantage in dealing with foreign and national security matters.

Chief of State. In this largely symbolic role, the president is designated as the chief representative of the United States government to all foreign governments. This means, for instance, that officials of foreign governments (ambassadors, for example) are accredited to the president, and when the heads of other states interact with the U.S. government, it is with the president or a representative of the president.

Commander in Chief. The president is designated as the commander in chief of the armed forces of the United States. This means, among other things, that he is the highest military official of the government to whom all members of the armed forces are subsidiary and that it is the president's authority to employ the armed forces in support of various public policies, including the commitment of force in combat (although this power is circumscribed by congressional limitation).

Treaty Negotiator. Only the president of the United States or his or her specified representative (known as plenipotentiary) is authorized to enter into negotiations with foreign governments leading to formal relationships and obligations on behalf of the U.S. government. Although only a small percentage of agreements between the United States and foreign governments come in the form of formal treaties, this nonetheless sets the precedent for presidential leadership in all arrangements with foreign governments.

Appointment of Key Personnel. The president alone has the power to name key officials of his or her administration. Most of the important appointments are at the Cabinet levels (the various secretaries of executive agencies), the National Security Council, and the deputy and assistant secretaries, such as those who serve on the various committees of the National Security Council system.

Recognizer of Foreign Governments. Only the president has the authority to extend or remove formal recognition of foreign governments by the U.S. government. This is one of the few powers of the president that does not require some form of formal supporting action by the Congress.

The Interagency Process. The foundation of what has evolved since the Eisenhower administration in the 1950s as the interagency process was the National Security Act of 1947. In addition to creating the CIA as the country's first peacetime intelligence-gathering agency, a consolidated DOD, and an independent Air Force, the Act created the NSC to coordinate foreign and national security policy.

The act was of great symbolic importance. It symbolized the growing importance of the United States in the world and the need for some formal mechanism to assist the president in dealing with this new, expanded role. It also implicitly boosted the centrality of defense matters within the hierarchy of foreign policy concerns by making the new Secretary of Defense (SECDEF) a coequal permanent member with the Secretary of State (the president and vice president are the other permanent members). In addition, the Act established the Director of the CIA and the Chairman of the Joint Chiefs of Staff (CJCS) as statutory advisors to the NSC, and others who have been added subsequently. At a more informal level, the model and function of the NSC set the precedent for presidents to coordinate and focus on other policy areas. President Clinton created the National Economic Council in 1993 to emphasize his commitment to economic matters. President George W. Bush created the Homeland Security Council (which closely resembled the NSC in structure) in the wake of the 2001 terrorist attacks, which became the institutional springboard for the cabinet-level Department of Homeland Security. Reform of the intelligence community, based on recommendations of the 9/11 Commission, began in 2004. Its most notable accomplishment to date has been the creation of the DNI.

The NSC system in its present form as the interagency process came into being during the 1980s, and it is a fairly elaborate system. The NSC itself consists of the four permanent members and whomever else the president may designate to attend and participate for any particular purpose. The White House Chief of Staff is normally always included, and on military matters, so is the CJCS and the National Security Advisor (NSA). The purpose of the Council is purely advisory. The members offer advice to the president that he is free to accept or reject. No votes are ever taken, ensuring that the president will not be swayed by what the majority may favor.

Directly below the NSC itself is the *Principals Committee (PC)*. This group is composed of the same membership as the NSC itself, except the president does not attend. There are two basic occasions when the NSC meets as the Principals Committee. If there are matters that do not require direct presidential involvement and thus intrusion on his busy agenda, the others may meet without him. At the same time, the president will occasionally absent himself in order to facilitate a more frank exchange of views than might occur when he is present, and he feels the other members might be unwilling to champion views they think he might oppose. This latter reason was used by John F. Kennedy during portions of the Cuban Missile Crisis when the Principals Committee was known as the ExComm (Executive Committee).

The next layer in the system is the *Deputies Committee (DC)*. As the name suggests, this group is composed of the principal deputies of the members of the NSC. The meetings are traditionally chaired by the president's principal deputy for national security, the National Security Advisor, although in the early days of the Bush administration there was an apparently unsuccessful attempt by Vice President Richard Cheney to usurp that role from then NSA Condoleeza Rice. The Deputies Committee is more of a working-level body, and its roles include formulating policy proposals for action by the NSC or Principals Committee or figuring out how to implement decisions made in those bodies. Other members of the Deputies Committee include the undersecretary of state for political affairs, the undersecretary of defense for policy, the deputy director of central intelligence, and the vice chairman of the JCS. Full implementation of the 9/11 Commission reforms could alter this structure somewhat, especially in the intelligence area.

These levels of the process normally labor outside the public eye. When *Time* magazine revealed that plans for countering Al Qaeda had been developed in the Clinton administration but had become bogged down in the pre–September 11 Bush regime, the Deputies Committee and Principals Committee were specifically singled out as institutional loci where the plans languished, a rare public exposure of the workings of the interagency process.

At the bottom of the process are the *Policy Coordinating Committees (PCCs)*. This is a series of committees formed along both functional and geographic lines. The functional committees are chaired by the assistant secretary (or equivalent) from the cabinet department with the most direct and obvious responsibility. There are, for instance, functional PCCs for defense, intelligence, arms control, and international economics. The geographic PCCs are all chaired by the assistant secretaries of state for the particular regions. It is the role of the PCCs to monitor their areas of responsibility (the PCC for the Near East and East Asia keeps tabs on the activities of Iraq, for instance), to provide options to the Deputies Committee and above on assigned problems, and to carry out the detailed policies adopted elsewhere in the process.

Reflecting his own interests and perceptions about change in the international environment, President Clinton created a parallel body, the *National Economic*

Council (NEC), by executive order in January 1993. It differed from the NSC in that it was not created by legislation and thus could be dismantled without congressional action. Clinton gave it four charges that parallel the duties of the older body: (1) to coordinate the economic policymaking process with respect to domestic and international economic issues; (2) to coordinate economic policy advice to the president; (3) to ensure that economic policy decisions and programs are consistent with the president's goals; and (4) to monitor implementation of the president's economic agenda.

The NEC was a prominent and important part of national security policy during the Clinton years between the fault lines and reflected the paramount importance of economic policy during the 1990s. The NEC was chaired personally by Clinton, and in addition, it had its own Deputies Committee and staff capability through the Trade Policy Review Group and the Trade Policy Staff Committee. The first task assigned to the first director of the NEC, Robert Rubin (later secretary of the treasury), was Clinton's comprehensive budget reduction plan, which succeeded in balancing the budget in 1998, and the NEC was prominent in trade policy and multilateral negotiations on trade promotion. When he came to office in 2001, President George W. Bush threatened to do away with the NEC as an unnecessary relic from his predecessor but has retained it at a much lower level of visibility and with much less personal involvement.

How the interagency process works is largely a matter of how the president wants it to operate. The NSC is assisted by the NSC staff, all of whom are members of the president's personal staff and thus not subject to congressional confirmation, review, or scrutiny. Because they serve at the president's pleasure, they are highly loyal to the chief executive and generally closely reflect the president's views. The degree to which the president utilizes this asset depends on presidential prerogative. Richard Nixon, for instance, had a long and deep-seated distrust of the State Department. State Department officials have civil service protection and cannot be fired (except in extreme circumstances), and most generally opposed Nixon's policies. As a result, he enlarged the NSC staff and used it in effect as an alternate State Department to ensure his policy preferences would be implemented. Presidents who are highly activist in foreign affairs, such as George H. W. Bush and Bill Clinton in his second term, rely heavily upon the NSC to carry out their desires, whereas those with less interest (such as Gerald Ford) use the NSC less and rely more on the executive agencies to conduct policy on their own.

Funding Security. The other dimension of policymaking within the executive branch focuses on the competition for resources to fund various government functions and programs. The principal manifestation of this political battle is the formation of the presidential budget request to the Congress and how that is translated into the working budget of the federal govenment of the United States. The budget process is one of the most complicated, arcane, yet fundamental political activities of the government. If one accepts the notion that policy is what gets funded, it is also the heart of the political process.

The complexity of the process of allocating public monies for the various things government does goes well beyond the purposes of this volume to unravel in detail.

Instead, we look briefly at two aspects of the politics of national security budget-making, the competition among the services for resources, and the competition between defense and other government functions in the formation of the executive branch's request to the Congress (some of the politics of the congressional response to the president's budget request is found in the next section of this chapter).

Budgeting is an ongoing, continuous process within the United States government. At any point in time, the DOD, for instance, is working on at least three different budgets: the budget for the current fiscal year, which has been appropriated and is being expended; the budget proposal for the next fiscal year, which has been proposed to Congress and to which the Congress is responding; and the next year's budget proposal, which is being formulated for presentation to the Congress in the following fiscal year. In addition, some long-range programs are funded over several years, meaning funds appropriated in earlier budget cycles are also being spent at any given time (known as "out years").

The competition between the services and between defense and nondefense spending is closely related to this process. Under the provisions of the Planning, Programming, Budgeting, and Spending (PPBS) system first introduced by the McNamara Pentagon in the early 1960s, initial planning for a budget begins approximately two and a half years before the first money is spent (assuming the Congress and the executive branch agree on a budget before the beginning of the fiscal year in which spending is to occur). Thus, planning for spending in Fiscal Year 2006 (which began on October 1, 2005) began in January 2004, when initial planning requests were sent to operational units within the DOD and elsewhere in the government. In spring 2004, the requests from defense units such as the military services were compared with other equivalent requests and reconciled with one another, then processed through the programming and budgeting phases during the late summer and fall of 2004. In turn, the DOD's proposal was compared with requests from other executive agencies and reconciled into a budget request that would accompany the president's State of the Union address to the Congress in January 2005. Legislative enactment would occur between January and September 2005, and if all went well, there would be a budget agreed to by both branches of the government that would go into effect on October 1, 2005. While legislative action was going on in 2005, the planning process for the Fiscal Year 2007 budget was set in motion, and the Defense Department was spending resources from the Fiscal 2005 budget.

Much of the politics within the executive branch occurs during the initial phases, when the president's budget request is being formulated. At the beginning, the military services are asked to formulate their individual requests. All units know that the aggregated requests (what is sometimes known as the "wish list") of the services will exceed by some large order of magnitude the resources that will actually be available to the services. Nonetheless, each makes the request for everything it wants regardless of funding expectations, for two reasons. First, doing so creates a record of what, say, the Army feels it really should have to carry out its mission most effectively. Second, since all the services know their requests will be cut—and, based on experience, approximately by what percentage they are likely to be cut—submitting a request that combines what the services think they will actually receive plus what they assume will be cut reasonably ensures that after cuts are made, the services will get roughly what they expected. Submitting a more modest and realistic request and having it cut probably means getting less than expected and needed.

The politics of interservice competition is particularly important over military procurement of new equipment, and especially for major weapons systems. During the process of proposal and negotiations, it is fair to say the services provide a valuable public service to the budgeting process by offering detailed critiques of the requests of the *other* services in order to find weaknesses in the other services' requests that might be turned to their own advantage. The motivation combines self-interest and civic-mindedness, and it serves the useful purpose of providing a kind of informal check and balance within the process through expert monitoring of rival service requests.

Once the defense request has been formulated, the national security budget comes into direct competition with other spending priorities within the federal budget. As in the internal defense process, the requests from agencies representing the range of government activity invariably exceed the total amount of money the Congress is likely to be willing to appropriate in any given year, meaning budget compromises must be negotiated to get the total budget request within realistic parameters.

The defense budget is especially vulnerable during this phase of the process. The first and most obvious source of vulnerability has already been mentioned: the defense budget contains the largest controllable elements within the total federal budget and is thus a tempting target for budget cutters with other priorities. Increases in social security benefits are mandated and automatically appropriated in the absence of specific legislation changing those benefits; the funding for new fighter aircraft for the Air Force must be expressly appropriated each year. At the same time, despite colorful political campaign rhetoric to the contrary, there is relatively little "fat" in other budgets that can easily be used to compensate for other priorities.

The politics of budgeting in the executive branch was dramatically demonstrated in the first year of the Bush administration in 2001. The new president inherited a budget request formulated in 2000, when Bill Clinton was president, and which reflected Clinton's priorities (as well as Al Gore's, who would have inherited the request had he been declared winner of the election). This formulation contained modest but real increases in defense funding, much of which the military planned to invest in force modernization. As is always the case, the new administration had a short period to alter budget priorities before sending its request to Capitol Hill as part of the State of the Union. Usually these alterations are relatively minor, and it is normally assumed that the second year's budget (in this case, the budget request for January 2002) would be the first "true" budget of a new administration.

President Bush had different ideas. Inheriting a budget request that emphasized federal debt reduction (through maximizing government surpluses to retiring the debt) and bolstering social security, he introduced new priorities. The most dramatic of these, of course, was a massive tax cut that the critics said would reduce the surplus dramatically and mean curtailing of other budgetary priorities. Bush, however, proposed budget increases in funding for education and for national missile defense and insisted he would not compromise on either goal.

These changes had a direct impact on budgeting within the DOD. Secretary of Defense Rumsfeld, intent on implementing the president's NMD proposal, combed the defense budget as part of the QDR process in order to force the services to find ways to save money that could be diverted to the NMD. This change of emphasis meant potentially unraveling earlier budget agreements and modernization commitments that had been hammered out the preceding year for a missile defense program that had very little support within the uniformed services anyway. The result was a major, if temporary, confrontation between a new administration that had campaigned partially on increased support for the military and a military establishment that felt it had been rudely jilted by its former suitor.

The confrontation was defused by the terrorist attacks, which directed attention away from both the budget battle and the QDR. Defense budget increases became part of the homeland security effort in the fiscal year 2003 budget presented to Congress in 2002 that included a $46 billion increase above projected levels in previous budgeting cycles. The result was that the services received most of the modernization requests from previous wish lists.

The Congress

The parallel process within the U.S. Congress is theoretically simpler and more compact than within the executive branch. The structure for considering the budget request of the administration is more direct, consisting of three prescribed steps rather than the multiple steps in the formulation process within the executive branch. Compactness is facilitated because the Congress does not have to develop a budget on its own. It only has to respond to a presidential request, which it can accept, reject, or modify. At the same time, the two Houses of Congress are in fact two large and often unruly committees, consisting of 100 highly independent senators and 435 equally independent members of the House of Representatives. Unlike the politically appointed officials of the executive branch, they are divided politically by party and by political philosophy. Moreover, the disposition of the defense budget is particularly important to individual members because defense dollars are spent in individual congressional districts and states. Members of Congress thus have an acute built-in self-interest in the outcomes. The result is quintessential politics.

The heart of congressional action in the area of national security is through the budget process. The process is important because it produces the resources that fund efforts to ensure the national security and thus provides much of the shape and nature of the national security effort. The budget process is also of particular importance to the Congress because it is the power imbedded in the American constitution that gives it the most leverage over the executive branch in matters pertaining to national security.

The Committee System. Because of its size and consequent unwieldiness, the Congress does relatively little of its most important business acting as overall houses of

Amplification 7.2

THE CONGRESS, THE CONSTITUTION, AND NATIONAL SECURITY

The U.S. Constitution is similarly as compact in its enumeration of congressional responsibility over foreign and national security affairs as it is with the executive branch. The powers of the Congress are enumerated in Article 1 of the Constitution. Some of these are direct responses to and limitations upon presidential powers, and others derive from the application of more general congressional authority to the national security arena. These powers include lawmaking power, the power of the purse, war-making power, confirmation, ratification, and general oversight of the executive branch.

Lawmaking Power. Nearly all of the actions taken by the government are the result of the passage of legislation by the Congress or the application of previous legislation. As noted in the text, all legislation must begin in one house of the Congress or the other and must have the concurrence of both houses. The president may, of course, veto any legislation he or she deems unacceptable.

Power of the Purse. The Constitution specifies that all authorization of the expenditure of public funds must be initiated in the House of Representatives and have the specific concurrence of both houses of the Congress. Particularly in the area of national security, this is a significant power because of the large amounts of money spent on national security and because most of those funds are controllable and must therefore be appropriated each year.

War Powers. Although the president is the commander in chief of the armed forces, the Congress has important countervailing powers. The Congress sets the size and composition of the armed forces (promotions for officers, for instance, must formally be approved by Congress before they can take effect). The president can have no larger armed forces than the Congress authorizes. Moreover, the Congress is the only agency of government that can declare war. While this provision has only been used five times in the country's history, it remains a strong limitation on the president's practical ability to place American armed forces into harm's way.

Confirmation of Officials. Presidential appointees to high offices in the administration (with the exception of the National Security Council staff, who are considered part of the president's personal staff and thus are exempt) are subject to confirmation by the U.S. Senate. The purpose of this provision is to insure that the president does not appoint personnel who are personally obnoxious or politically objectionable in a policy sense.

Ratification of Treaties. Although the president is the only official who can negotiate agreements with foreign governments, none of these can take force until they have the positive advice and consent of two-thirds of the United States Senate. This limitation is necessary because a ratified treaty is coequal to laws passed by the Congress. Because of the sheer volume of the relations between the United States and other governments, only a small portion of the dealings with other governments are in the form of treaties (most are executive agreements that do not require senatorial ratification), but most of the more important relationships are in the form of treaties.

Oversight. Although it is not specifically enumerated in the Constitution, the power to review how laws are implemented by the executive branch and to examine how well executive agencies operate has long been an accepted form of congressional limitation on executive actions. The chief mechanism for this oversight is through the various congressional authorizing committees that mirror major executive branch functions (the Armed Services Committees and the Department of Defense, for instance).

Congress. The real, detailed business of the Congress is performed by the committee system, wherein smaller groups of senators and congressmen, all of whom have volunteered for the committees on which they serve (although by no means do all members get membership on all the committees they desire) hammer out congressional positions, oversee the activities of the executive agencies they parallel, and respond to presidential budgetary and policy initiatives. When the Congress is working properly (which it does not always do), the agreements that are reached in committee are ratified by the overall bodies.

One might reasonably ask why committees are so important and powerful within the Congress. For one thing, the various committees (including their staffs) are the major repositories of congressional expertise on the area of their focus. Congressional members typically volunteer for committee assignments in which they or their constituents are interested or in which they have particular expertise. Thus, a congressional district with a large concentration of military facilities or defense contractors will produce congressional members who will develop an interest in and knowledge of defense matters because the outcomes of defense issues may affect their constituents. The longer members of Congress stay in the Senate or House and remain on the armed services committee, for instance, the more expertise they acquire and the more influence they develop. The most prominent and knowledgeable members attain the status of congressional leaders in their area of expertise. Former Georgia Senator Sam Nunn, who served as chair of the Senate Armed Services Committee during the 1980s and early 1990s, developed a particular reputation as a defense intellectual both within and outside Congress.

These experts—especially the chairs and the ranking members of the minority party (who become chairs if their party attains majority)—become chief congressional spokespeople in their area of expertise. Members with less expertise than the experts tend to defer to the judgments of these leaders (especially members of the same party) and vote the way the chairs recommend. The same is true of the major subcommittees of the major committees, where the chairs develop great expertise in their narrower subject area (military manpower, for instance). The rise in partisanship and especially ideological division within both houses of Congress during the 1990s has made members more independent of their leaderships and thus decreased some of the deference paid to the chairs, but their impact on legislation remains formidable. It has also hardened along party lines on important matters.

Another reason the committee system is so powerful is because of the smaller and more manageable size of committees compared to the full houses of Congress. It has often been said of the houses of Congress themselves that their size and organization make them great debating forums for the discussion of public policy, but that they are so large and unwieldy as to be terrible places to enact and especially to frame legislation. The major committees of Congress, normally with memberships of twenty or fewer members, are more compact and can give more thorough and knowledgeable consideration to matters of legislative review, including such things as calling for and considering the views of expert witnesses. The recommendations of the appropriate committees thus have a considerable impact on how the Congress as a whole acts on matters that come before it. If one wants to get a sense of what the Congress thinks about a particular matter, the person to listen to is the chair of the appropriate committee.

The Budget. The budgetary process is the essence of the congressional committee system in operation. It consists of three steps. The first comes reasonably early in the legislative session that convenes in January and consists of actions leading to a *budget resolution*. When the president's proposed budget is submitted to the Congress, the budget committees of the two houses receive and analyze the request, both overall and by budget category (one of which is national defense). The review establishes likely budgetary ceilings for the overall budget and for each category. When the committees of the two houses reach agreements on these general goals and their acceptability is acknowledged by the executive, the result is the joint budget resolution.

This resolution is a nonbinding agreement about the general shape of the budget that is supposed to guide other congressional committees in legislating the details of the budget package. Sometimes the final budget conforms fairly closely to the guidelines, but often it does not. In 2001, for instance, President Bush did not include unusual funding for missile defense in his original budget proposal, and it was not included in the budget resolution. When he added it later, many in the Congress cried foul and maintained this addition invalidated the original agreement (a position that was probably disingenuous given the President's quite public advocacy of NMD in the 2000 campaign and subsequently). The 2001 budget resolution was passed in April.

After the budget resolution is in place, the serious work of budgeting begins in the Congress. This process is depicted in Figure 7.1. This process is, in a sense, both simpler and more complicated than it may seem. The second and third steps in the congressional budgeting process occur through the actions of the authorizing committees of each house, the Senate and House Armed Services Committees (SASC and HASC) and the appropriations subcommittee on defense of each house. The role of the authorizing committees in budgetary action is programmatic: they review the programs requested in the budget and decide which of these to authorize and at what level of support. They do not, however, make specific recommendations about

Figure 7.1: The Budget Process

House		Senate
	President's Budget Request	
Budget Resolution		Budget Resolution
	Joint Budget Resolution	
Authorizing Committee (HASC)		Authorizing Committee (SASC)
Appropriations Subcommittee		Appropriations Subcommittee
	Conference Committee	
House		Senate
	President	

how much should be spent on individual programs and the overall budget, although there are clearly budgetary implications in areas such as procurement—approving a program for a given quantity of a particular weapons system costs has predictable budgetary consequences.

Actual recommendations on the size of the budget and on what can be spent is made by the appropriations committee of each house and, in the case of defense, the appropriations subcommittee for defense. The role of the overall appropriations committee is to develop the total congressional version of the federal budget, and the subcommittees, one of which parallels each functional authorizing committee (including defense), is to make recommendations for that function that are aggregated in the overall budget.

The process becomes political and controversial when there is disagreement among the various initiating and reviewing bodies, as there normally is. These disagreements can come about in three basic ways. First, the authorizing and appropriating committees in either or both of the houses can disagree on both programmatic priorities and budgetary size. The result is a mismatch between approved programs and resources to fund them. Second, the committees in the two houses, when each reaches accord on its vision of the budget, can disagree. The results can be different programs or appropriations between houses. Third, the president can disagree with the overall outcome. The more these possible points of disagreement come into conflict, the more contentious the overall process becomes and the more problematic is the outcome.

The authorizing and appropriations functions theoretically should be sequential. In a totally rational world, the authorizing committee would review the budget request programmatically and decide which programs are meritorious and worthy of funding. They would then pass their recommendations along to the appropriations subcommittees, which would allocate appropriate funding. In fact, the two forms of committee actions occur more or less simultaneously and independently within each house and with little formal coordination either within or between the houses. The result is often four more or less conflicting recommendations that require reconciliation before a budget bill can be passed along to either house for enactment.

If this seems a disorganized approach to enacting a budget, the reasons derive from the consequences of the outcomes. Members of appropriations subcommittees, like their counterparts on authorizing committees, commonly represent constituencies with interests in the outcomes and hence want to be certain their interests are thoroughly represented. This is not only true regarding the defense budget, but has parallels in every other area of budgetary and policy concern—the agricultural committees and subcommittees in both houses, for instance, overwhelmingly have members from farm states who want to protect the interests of their constituents.

When differences exist between the authorizing and appropriations subcommittees within the two houses, they are resolved by joint meetings whose purpose is to produce accommodations and compromises acceptable to all. Normally, there is informal contact with the parallel committee leaderships in the other house. In some cases, the president may well invite the leaderships of the committees to the White House to "jawbone" them into reaching agreements as close as possible to his position.

The ultimate outcome unfolds from this interaction. Each house passes a defense budget allocation based on the interaction of the authorization and appropriations committees. If these are identical (which they rarely are), they go directly to the president. If they are different, they are sent to a conference committee composed of members of the appropriate committees of the two houses to reach agreement on identical bills, which are then sent back to the individual houses to be voted upon. When each house has approved the bill, it is then sent to the president for his signature. The president may accede and sign the budget, veto it, or ask for revisions.

This process has become especially turbulent, as the 2001 session of Congress demonstrated. The new Bush administration proposed major revisions in the budget it inherited from its predecessor, including changes at odds with the preferences of the military. The QDR produced some unconventional views of the threat and how to counter it that had strong budgetary implications. In 2002, the atmosphere of extreme partisanship was exacerbated by the fact that the two houses were controlled by different parties (meaning conference committees featured a Democratic Party–led delegation from the Senate and a Republican-led House delegation). Since the Iraq War began, it has become administration practice not to include full funding requests for ongoing operations in the regular budget process, arguing exact projections in a war zone are impossible. Consequently, periodic supplemental requests inflate the overall figures to what some feel are unacceptable levels but cannot be resisted, because doing so would appear to demonstrate nonsupport for the troops.

APPLICATIONS: THE HOMELAND SECURITY RESPONSE TO THE ENVIRONMENT

The interaction between the changing international environment and the vagaries of domestic politics can best be demonstrated by looking at actual policy arenas where the two come into play. In the post–September 11 context, the major change in emphasis has been in dealing with terrorism. The GWOT has been concentrated in military efforts to track down and suppress foreign terrorists. The greatest domestic change has been in the creation of the DHS as the institutional response to organizing and coordinating efforts aimed at reducing the risks posed by terrorists. As we shall see, it has been a mixed success.

The Department of Homeland Security

One of the most important questions raised after September 11, 2001, was the institutional adequacy of the United States government in the face of terrorism. In the days and months following the attacks, information became available that there had been intimations of the impending attacks circulating at lower levels of the government in the months before the actual attacks and even a planning document held over from the Clinton administration specifically aimed at Al Qaeda. And yet, the attacks appeared to come as an awful surprise. Why? In order to answer the question and to make some sense of the process, we examine three aspects of homeland security: the historical evolution of our concern with homeland security, its institutionalization as DHS through the Homeland Security Act of 2002, and problems of the homeland security effort.

Background and Evolution

Although the term *homeland security* appeared abruptly after September 11 and thus seemed to be a very new kind of phenomenon; it is not. If homeland security is defined as that part of the national security effort focusing primarily on the protection of the physical territory and citizens of the United States, then homeland security has been a major, if largely implicit, cornerstone of American national security policy since the formation of the republic.

As suggested in Chapter 3, however, what we now call homeland security has not been a major operational problem for the United States throughout our national history. The reason, of course, has been the accident of geography that provided the United States with nonthreatening neighbors and broad oceans that protected us from harm. The vulnerability of the American homeland to attack was not a problem until the latter 1950s, when Soviet nuclear-tipped missiles became capable of attacking and destroying the American homeland. That danger, of course, remained theoretical and abstract throughout the Cold War; the terrorist attacks of September 11 made the problem concrete and immediate. The impact of the attacks was to create an equation between homeland security and a concrete threat, that of terrorism.

The modern evolution of homeland security has proceeded along two policy thrusts. The first of these is emergency management. Largely associated at the federal level with the actions of agencies such as the Federal Emergency Management Agency (FEMA) and at the state and local levels with first responders like police and fire agencies, this effort had two major emphases: protection against and reaction to natural disasters (hurricanes, tornados, earthquakes, etc.) and man-made disasters. Problems with the former were vividly illustrated by responses to Hurricanes Katrina and Rita; the latter was associated primarily with civil defense efforts in the event of a nuclear attack against the American homeland.

The suppression of terrorism was added to the homeland security portfolio during the 1980s, although at a much more muted level of publicity than the current effort. During the 1980s, a number of actions were taken within the federal government to create federal capabilities in the areas of antiterrorism and counterterrorism and to elevate and attempt to coordinate the efforts of the principal federal agencies with responsibility for terrorism: the CIA, FBI, and INS. Operational responsibility for dealing with on-site efforts when terrorists might strike remained at the state and local levels.

The two efforts have remained parallel, although with some tensions that were apparent from the beginning but which lacked enough urgency before September 11 to compel rationalization. Terrorism suppression is primarily a federal function, for instance, whereas emergency management is mostly state and local in execution. Operationally, the federal government is more interested in preventing disasters like terrorist attacks and is secondarily concerned with dealing with the consequences of disasters; the order of emphasis is reversed for the emergency managers. These differences are manifested in allegations of poor communications between the federal and state and local levels and in the competition for funding for homeland security. FEMA, with responsibilities in both areas, has become something of a whipping boy for problems of coordination.

The process of trying to organize the government to deal with these matters dates back to the Reagan administration. In 1986, President Reagan issued National Security Directive (NSD) 207, which did three things. First, it created the Interagency Working Group (IWG) under the National Security Council. Second, it designated the IWG as the mechanism to coordinate responses to terrorism. Third, it established the lead agency designation (the federal agency with primary responsibility) of the State Department in regard to international terrorism and the FBI over domestic terrorism.

The Clinton administration was also active during the 1990s. In 1995, Clinton issued Presidential Decision Directive (PDD) 39, with three emphases: preventing terrorist acts, responding to terrorist acts and provocations, and managing the consequences of terrorist attacks. The FBI was given broader responsibility domestically, including the formation of domestic emergency support teams to act in the event of significant problems. Clinton also authorized the suspension of *posse comitatus* (which prevents the use of the military for domestic police functions) during emergencies and designated FEMA to lead "consequence management" efforts. Clinton issued two other relevant documents in 1998. PDD 62 created the Office of the Coordinator for Security, Infrastructure Protection, and Counterterrorism, and PDD 63 added the problem of cyber terrorism specifically to the agenda under the designation of "information infrastructure." (Much of this evolution is detailed in Richard Clarke's *Against All Enemies*.)

The point of this discussion is not its details but that there was governmental activity in the area that has become homeland security for at least a decade and a half before September 11, 2001. The potential for terrorism was known within specialized parts of the federal government, but the efforts were low-key and generally low priority, as terrorism remained, for the most part, a peripheral concern for most Americans despite overseas instances of terrorist attacks against Americans and American facilities (the African Embassy bombings of 1998, the attack on the USS *Cole* in Yemen in 2000) and despite even the 1993 attack on the Trade Towers in New York. During this time period, the dual emphases on terrorism suppression and emergency management were established, and homeland security was largely equated with terrorism as a military and law enforcement problem. These efforts, however, remained at the peripheries of the public agenda until a compelling event caused them to be thrust on center stage.

The Homeland Security Response to September 11

The Al Qaeda attacks against New York and Washington instantly elevated the concept of homeland security to the heart of the national political process. The initial institutional reactions included the creation of a Homeland Security Council parallel in structure to the National Security Council, the establishment of an Office of Homeland Security, and the appointment of a director for the effort. Militarily, the DOD established a Northern Command (from the old Force Command) to coordinate military responses to threats against the American homeland. This process ultimately resulted in the passage of the Homeland Security Act of 2002, which President Bush lauded as the single most important and sweeping reorganization of government in fifty years (a comparison with the National Security Act of 1947). The DHS came into existence in 2003 as a result of that legislation. Its role and structure are still evolving.

The initial response to the September 11 problem was the creation of the Office of Homeland Security within the White House and the appointment of former Pennsylvania Governor Tom Ridge as its director. Ridge was given a position conceptually similar to that of the National Security Advisor (at least in terms of purported access to the president) and was charged with rationalizing and coordinating improved government capabilities for dealing with terrorism. Critics at the time maintained that Ridge's position left him as little more than a figurehead who could not compel agencies to do anything, especially to cooperate with one another.

In June 2002, the administration proposed a stronger way to institutionalize the effort—the creation of the DHS. The new department, with full Cabinet status, was legislated into being in November 2002 and mandated to perform four functions: border and transportation security; emergency preparedness and response; chemical, biological, radiological, and nuclear countermeasures; and information analysis and infrastructure protection. To accomplish its tasks, the president proposed pulling resources from a number of existing agencies under the control of the new department.

Virtually no one opposed either the general proposition of this effort or its implementation in principle. As is often the case, however, the devil has proven to be in the details of implementation. The kinds of reorganization authorized by the Act moved over 170,000 employees from twenty-two major federal agencies under the umbrella of DHS. Such a movement in and of itself is daunting, as many agencies, individuals, and organizations with contrasting work cultures and methods of operation and little or no tradition of interaction and coordination are suddenly thrust in positions in which they are expected to work as a team acting in a common effort. At the same time, there have been significant "turf wars" over which agencies (and their budgets) will find their way into DHS and which should remain within their traditional homes. These political problems have spilled significantly over into the oversight relationship between DHS and the Congress.

The first and most difficult problem was which agencies would be drawn into the new department and which would not. As already suggested, there are three federal agencies with primary responsibility operationally in the terrorism field that form a kind of golden triangle of federal efforts. Ideally, the CIA (which, until legislation establishing the DNI passed in 2004, was an independent agency) has primary responsibility for discovering and monitoring the existence and activities of overseas terrorists; the INS (part of the Department of Justice) has responsibility for monitoring and intercepting aliens entering the country; and the FBI (also part of Justice) monitors and arrests terrorists committing acts within the country. Within this relationship, the CIA should tell the INS who is attempting to enter the country, and when suspicious aliens do come into the United States, the INS should then inform the FBI so it can begin its role of monitoring. In order to maximize the likelihood that this relationship is seamless and effective against terrorism, it follows that all three agencies should be included in DHS.

They are not. The INS and Customs Service are part of Homeland Security (mostly because INS has had so many political problems that Justice was glad to get rid of it), but the CIA and FBI remain independent, with only directions to coordinate with the DHS. Why? Both the CIA and FBI argued, apparently effectively, that terrorism is only one part of their responsibilities. Virtually all the agencies that might be included in the new department could make the same argument that they had terrorism as only part of their portfolios, but the FBI and CIA were sufficiently powerful that their arguments succeeded while other failed. In the process, of course, the traditional budgets of the FBI and CIA were protected as well.

The amalgamation of agencies into DHS has been analogized to a similar process that created the Department of Energy (DOE) in 1977. Both agencies share three major commonalities. First, they were both created as responses to national emergencies: the oil shocks of the 1970s led to demands for a DOE, just as the terrorist attacks of 2001 created the momentum for the DHS. Second, both departments represent attempts to reorganize the federal government by rearranging the federal organization chart, pulling agencies and responsibilities out of existing structures and putting them under the umbrella of the new agency. As we have seen with regard to DHS, this is a daunting task internally. The analogy with DOE, however, provides another invidious political comparison that has plagued both agencies—the problem of congressional oversight. Third, both were done "on the cheap." The Bush administration initially argued that the DHS would require no added funding because resources would be made available by agencies contributing people and other resources to the DHS (which proved largely false). Underfunding remains a problem: the DHS budget for 2004, for instance, was under $30 billion.

Each function of the executive branch of government is overseen for programmatic and budgetary purposes by committees and subcommittees of the two houses of Congress. The oversight function is a significant part of the power base of the members of Congress because it provides real clout in determining who receives and does not receive funding under whatever function they may control. As a result, members of Congress are quite jealous of their prerogatives with regard to oversight and are particularly resistant to the idea that a function over which they have some control might move from the department their particular committee oversees to a committee created to oversee a new department like DOE or DHS, on whose committee they do not serve. Reform at the executive level, in other words, threatens the power of members of Congress. The result is resistance to change of the effective structure that can make the work of the new agencies all the more difficult.

DOE is a miniature version of the congressional problem faced by DHS. The DOE solution in Congress was largely to leave budget and programmatic aspects of agencies included in DOE under their previous committee purviews. The result is that the DOE secretary must report to seventeen committees and subcommittees of the Congress, a daunting and time-consuming way to get policy advice and funds. Moreover, since most of these bodies do not have energy per se as their sole or even primary focus, the advice and funding recommendations are likely to be at odds with one another. No one recommends the DOE precedent as the right way to organize a new department.

The DOE's problem with Congress is child's play compared to that faced by DHS. In aggregating the various agencies into the DHS organization chart, the responsibilities of no fewer than eighty-eight committees and subcommittees in the two houses are affected by the transfers. When the DHS came into being in 2003, a survey showed that *all one hundred* senators and all but twenty members of the House were on committees whose jurisdictions were potentially affected by the reorganization. While everyone could agree in abstract principle that the new DHS would face the smoothest possible sailing in admittedly troubled waters if there was a single authorizing committee and single appropriating committee in each house (which is the case for traditional departments), the potential consequence of moving toward that ideal end was to erode the power of virtually every member of the Congress by removing some power from a committee or subcommittee he or she sits on. This potential erosion of power has caused sufficient opposition to reforming the congressional part of the relationship that there is no permanent Homeland Security Committee in the Senate and a committee with largely symbolic value in the House of Representatives.

Two other important problems attended the creation of DHS. One was with regard to funding. The Homeland Security Act was passed at the same time that President George W. Bush was pushing for additional tax cuts beyond those he had achieved during his first year in office, and one consequence of this emphasis was that he did not want to appear to be increasing funding in other areas of the federal budget at a time when he was arguably reducing revenues. As a result, the decision was made that the new effort would require no additional funding, since the funding of agencies and functions moving out of their old agencies into DHS would simply follow them into the new agency and provide the budgetary base for DHS. This assertion was, of course, a fiction: as noted, agencies would fight tooth and nail to maintain their budgets, and the new mandates given DHS clearly required new funds. The precedent, however, was set, and DHS attempts to gain additional resources have suffered from the albatross created by the original fiction.

There has been the additional problem of mandate. At one level, protecting the American homeland from foreign enemies—notably terrorists—would seem to be a fairly straightforward task, but in operation it has proven to be complicated. Securing American territory encompasses a wide range of duties, from monitoring who comes into the country through customs to border security to the protection of specific potential terrorist targets to port security. Each of these duties requires different skills and puts demands on the system for additional resources, not all of which have been available, particularly if one aggregates all of these sources of threat and tries to eliminate them. Put in a way raised in Chapter 6, achieving an acceptable level of risk reduction and risk management has been a difficult task for the planners at DHS. Funding and other resource deficiencies associated with the DHS response to Hurricane Katrina (largely through FEMA) illustrate the consequences of assuming this risk.

Despite all its problems, the DHS has, of course, come into being. The Process of building a new agency to deal with a complex set of tasks that were poorly handled in the past has proven to be a daunting task, the eventual success of which has yet to be determined. As long as international terrorism remains a top priority in Washington, the DHS will remain an important work in progress.

Ongoing Problems and Controversies

Some of the difficulties associated with the evolution of the new DHS can be attributed to growing pains. Whether one accepts the claim of the monumental stature of the Homeland Security Act as accurate or as political hype, it has created the basis for a very large governmental overhaul in a large, high-priority area of concern. As suggested, the effort has become politicized, and this has made accomplishment of the ambitious goals set forward for the new agency even more difficult. Only a few months into his tenure as the replacement for Tom Ridge as secretary of DHS, Michael Chertoff announced his firm intention to engage in a massive reform of the agency, notably its intelligence capabilities, in June 2005. No one thought this task would be easy to accomplish; some thought it was essentially impossible.

Several ongoing questions and controversies surround the DHS and its mission. For our purposes, we mention and briefly examine four of them: the emphasis of the agency between the federal and the state and local levels, with special attention to budgetary and political concerns; the evolution of the critical intelligence function both within DHS and in its dealings with other agencies; the division of responsibilities between DHS and other agencies, a subject on which the 9/11 Commission has weighed in; and the extent to which the DHS effort collides with the rights of citizens.

Mission and Political Emphasis. Although it was the stated intention of the homeland security legislation to elevate this important governmental function above the political fray, that effort has not been altogether successful. The reason, simply enough, is that setting priorities and emphases has budgetary implications, and that means politics inevitably intrudes.

Beyond the question of moving funding among federal agencies, this question of emphasis has come to center on the debate over relative emphasis on combating and preventing attacks against the United States (the federal emphasis) and emergency management by first responders (the state and local emphasis). Originally, the pattern was for the federal government to mandate actions by the states and localities, for which they were to find funds (unfunded mandates)—a way to maintain the fiction that homeland security required no new funds. As concern with avoiding new spending has ebbed, however, funding has become available for the first responders, mostly in the form of equipment grants and funding for emergency plans and the like. The availability of these kinds of funds, in turn, provides opportunities for members of Congress to endear themselves to their constituencies by gaining funding for new ambulances, fire trucks with hazardous materials (hazmat) capabilities, police communications capabilities, and the like. To some observers, provisions like this are evidence of a commitment to first response; to others, they are pure "pork" (needless expenditures). Benjamin Friedman, writing in *Foreign Policy*, cites 2003 allocations of $725,000 for port security in Tulsa, Oklahoma, and $1.5 million in federal funds to Fargo, North Dakota, to purchase trailers equipped to respond to nuclear attacks and "more biochemical suits than it has police officers." Secretary Chertoff has responded with a plan to base future allocations on the basis of risk (the higher the threat to a potential target, the greater its priority for funding), to which first responders (and their congressional supporters) respond that this is a disguised way of promoting federal programs.

Improving Intelligence. There has been universal agreement since September 11 that a major component in the disaster was a failure of the intelligence community to penetrate the conspiracy and allow it to be prevented. The 9/11 Commission was particularly critical of the intelligence breakdowns that permitted the attacks to occur, recommending major reforms to the overall process. In addition to the creation of a National Counterterrorism Center (NCTC), the Commission recommended a consolidation of the fifteen federal agencies engaged in intelligence activities and the creation of the position and office of the Director of National Intelligence. The structural reforms recommended by the commission are summarized in Amplification 7.3, Recommendations of the 9/11 Commission.

The DHS was also given responsibilities for intelligence analysis, and personnel were assigned within the agency to develop the capability to analyze raw intelligence and analysis generated from other agencies in terms of the DHS mandate.

Amplification 7.3

RECOMMENDATIONS OF THE 9/11 COMMISSION

In assessing why the September 11 tragedy occurred, part of the view of the 9/11 Commission was that structural deficiencies had contributed to the government's inability to predict and prevent the disaster. To deal with that problem, the Commission made a number of structural recommendations, three of which stand out.

First, the Commission called for the creation of the National Counterterrorism Center (NCTC). The NCTC is to be the central focus for joint planning and operations in dealing with terrorism. It is to be headed by a director appointed directly by the president and whose position is equivalent to that of Deputy Secretary (second in command) in a Cabinet-level agency. The director is to be confirmed by the Senate and required to testify before the Congress (subject to subpoena). This provision has been implemented.

Second, the Commission recommended creation of the DNI. The DNI is to oversee the operation of all other intelligence agencies and is to have power over all intelligence budgets. The DNI is to have three principal assistants: the Director of Central Intelligence for foreign intelligence, the Undersecretary of Defense for Intelligence for defense-related intelligence, and the Undersecretary of Homeland Security for domestic matters. Control over budgets, especially those in the Defense Department (which controls 80 to 85 percent of all intelligence funds), has been a sticking point in the total implementation of this provision. This job description of the DNI closely parallels the original role envisioned for the DCI in 1947; it remains to be seen whether the DNI will be allowed politically to perform all these tasks in the face of predictable bureaucratic opposition.

Third, the Commission calls for congressional reform, notably the creation of a single Homeland Security Committee and a single Appropriations Subcommittee for Homeland Security in each house to reduce reporting and budgeting problems. As noted in the text, this recommendation has been fiercely resisted within the Congress.

Secretary Chertoff maintains that the department has not done a good job of "collecting, piecing together, and sharing" the intelligence it receives and analyzes, and he promises reform of the intelligence function as a major part of his reforms of DHS. One possibility that he has raised is the creation of the position of a deputy director for intelligence within the agency.

Homeland Security and Terrorism Mandates. While the idea of DHS was to consolidate governmental efforts in the homeland security area within a single governmental location, the 9/11 Commission also argued that this has not truly been the case. As noted earlier, of the three core agencies in identifying and dealing with terrorist threats to homeland security (CIA, INS, and FBI), only one (INS) is part of the DHS structure. The CIA and FBI remain in their customary positions within

Challenge!

THE "ANGRY LIBRARIANS" AND CIVIL LIBERTIES

While a number of provisions of the PATRIOT Act have been the subject of opposition and even derision, one provision, Section 215, has come to symbolize what critics believe is most egregious about it. Because it deals partly with governmental access to library records of individuals, it has been given the nickname, "the attack of the angry librarians."

The section contains three provisions its detractors find obnoxious. First, it permits government investigators access to a wide range of information about suspects, including what library books they have checked out (which critics view as invasion of privacy). Second, secret subpoenas that cannot be contested in court (should someone find out about them) can be issued to gain access (thus denying the right to contest the subpoenas). Third, there is no requirement that the government disclose its investigations to those under scrutiny (thereby denying rights of due process). All the provisions are justified as necessary national security actions in the "war" on terrorism.

Are such actions justified by the homeland security threat? In the absence of the assertion of a national security basis for them, they would unambiguously be declared unconstitutional, violations of fundamental rights guaranteed to all Americans. The government's counterargument is that in the state of war between the United States and terrorism, they are necessary and appropriate actions. Do you agree? How much individual freedom can and should be sacrificed in the name of security? What do you think?

government. In addition, the DOD has independent intelligence responsibilities and control of special operations and the Central and Northern Commands. The State Department maintains primary responsibility for international policy coordination and cooperation, and the NSC and Homeland Security Council stand outside the control of DHS. Among other things, this diffusion of responsibility puts a strain on the fairly narrow talent pool available in the homeland security area.

Homeland Security and Civil Rights. A fairly muted but significant level of concern has been raised about the impact of homeland security efforts on the civil rights of American and other citizens. The problem of potential infringements on people's rights has not been specific to DHS but has tinged the entire problem. Much of the concern centers domestically on provisions of the PATRIOT (Provide Appropriate Tools Required to Intercept and Obstruct Terrorists) Act of 2001, most of which were renewed in 2005. Critics argue the Act's provisions represent an unreasonable infringement on civil liberties, and supporters contend the provisions are necessary for the successful pursuit of terrorists (see the *Challenge!* box, The "Angry Librarians" and Civil Liberties). Internationally, the open-ended detention of suspected terrorists and their sympathizers at Guantanamo Bay, Cuba, has added to the global concern about the problem.

Conclusion: The Environment Since September 11, 2001

Thinking about and dealing with the environment was set on its head by the events of September 11, 2001. Suddenly, a mostly benign and tranquil environment was revealed to have a very dark and hostile side that had heretofore been the subject of adventure motion pictures and novels. Before the attacks on major symbols of American military and financial power, the only instances of foreign-inspired and foreign-committed acts had been small and relatively primitive—the most notable example was the 1993 attack on the World Trade Center towers by a single truck laden with explosives that killed six people. The scale of the 2001 attacks and the enormous loss of life revealed a level and quality of vulnerability that few Americans had imagined in their worst of nightmares. The body politic was thrown into convulsion about how it could have happened, how it could be avoided in the future, and how to punish those behind the atrocity.

The shock of the attacks and the ambiguity about appropriate responses confused the debate, raising doubts but few obvious solutions. The conventional debate was particularly muddied. National security planning has concentrated on dealing with the concrete, conventional military threats posed by other sovereign states or groups within states. Although the importance of those threats and hence how to counter them was tinged by a certain level of implausibility, at least the discussions could proceed within a common frame of reference that all parties understood. Suddenly, the area of homeland security moved to the center of our attention; as the preceding discussion has suggested, fashioning an organizational and policy response is still a work in progress.

The massive attacks by nonstate actors engaging in the most unimaginable forms of "warfare" did not fit within standard categories. Shadowy, private terrorist organizations that do not represent states and that have small, elusive units (or cells) do not lend themselves to conventional military responses. The idea of using commercial aircraft heavily laden with jet fuel essentially as cruise missiles to attack urban, civilian targets had no precedent within military doctrine or practice and could only be found in escapist fiction (Tom Clancy's *Badge of Honor* revolves around using an airliner to attack the national capitol). How do we define such a threat? Moreover, how do we develop forces and capabilities that can counter and negate this kind of problem? The answers were and are not clear, but it was evident that one had to move beyond conventional thinking to formulate responses.

Selected Bibliography

Clarke, Richard. *Against All Enemies: Inside America's War on Terror*. New York: Free Press, 2004.

Crabb, Cecil V., Jr., and Pat Holt. *Invitation to Struggle: Congress, the President, and Foreign Policy* (2nd ed.). Washington, DC: CQ Press, 1984.

Flynn, Stephen. "The Neglected Home Front." *Foreign Affairs* 83, 5 (September/October 2004), 20–33.

Friedman, Benjamin. "Think Again: Homeland Security." *Foreign Policy*, July/August 2005, 22–29.

Friedman, Thomas L. *The Lexus and the Olive Tree: Understanding Globalization*. New York: Farrar, Straus, & Giroux, 2000.

Fullilove, Michael. "All the President's Men." *Foreign Affairs* 84, 2 (March/April 2005), 13–18.

Harty, Maura. "U.S. Visa Policy: Securing Borders and Opening Doors." *Washington Quarterly* 28, 2 (Spring 2005), 23–34.

Hilsman, Roger. *The Politics of Policy Making in Defense and Foreign Affairs: Conceptual Models and Bureaucratic Politics* (3rd ed.). Englewood Cliffs, NJ: Prentice Hall, 1993.

Kaplan, Robert D. *The Coming Anarchy: Shattering the Dreams of the Post–Cold War World*. New York: Random House, 2000.

Keohane, Robert O., and Joseph S. Nye, Jr. *Power and Interdependence* (2nd ed.). Glenview, IL: Scott Foresman/Little Brown, 1989.

National Commission on Terrorist Attacks upon the United States. *The 9/11 Commission Report: Authorized Edition*. New York: W.W. Norton, 2004.

Rothkopf, David J. "Inside the Committee That Runs the World." *Foreign Policy*, March/April 2005, 30–41.

Snow, Donald M. *United States Foreign Policy: Politics Beyond the Water's Edge* (3rd ed.). Belmont, CA: Wadsworth, 2005.

CHAPTER 8

Traditional Military Problems

PREVIEW

Thinking about and planning for large-scale war between armed forces as they were developed for and fought in World War II—conventional forces for symmetrical warfare and strategic nuclear war—predate and postdate September 11, 2001. The traditional purposes for which these forces were developed largely disappeared with the end of the Cold War, and only the United States retains a robust traditional capability that it proposes to augment through force modernization. At the same time, critics say these large, European-style forces are anachronisms in a world of shadowy asymmetrical threats. Before assessing these criticisms, it is necessary to describe traditional forces and missions, first nuclear forces and then conventional forces and the residual problems associated with each that have a continuing impact. The chapter concludes with some assessment of the relevance of these forces in the future.

The past, it is sometimes said, is the prologue of the future, and nowhere is that observation more applicable than in the area of military forces. War is an ancient institution, and it has evolved and changed over time, but it retains significant continuities in how and why it is fought. Doctrine—beliefs about the best ways to accomplish military ends—has a long past, and much of the doctrine we employ today is rooted in the cumulative world view that existed before September 11. The past is thus relevant to the future.

What do we mean when we refer to traditional problems and conventional forces and solutions? Basically, we are describing the structure of the American armed forces in the European style that evolved through the formative period of the American military experience and congealed in World War II. The structures of armies, navies, and air forces armed with nuclear and nonnuclear (conventional) weapons are designed to confront and defeat similarly armed and organized opponents in symmetrical warfare. These forces remain the backbone of American capabilities. A major question against which they must be measured is their relevance in a world of asymmetrical threats. This chapter describes those forces; Chapter 9 assesses their relevance.

Why is this description important? There are four reasons. First, these forces and uses have been important in the past. Second, they are still major components of the package of forces with which the United States confronts the world—the components military planners best understand and are most comfortable with. Third, modernizing and enhancing the capabilities they represent is a major part of the added defense expenditures proposed by the current administration. Finally, it may be necessary to use these forces again in the future against some currently unforeseen or foreseen foe. Any of these reasons is sufficient to warrant a review and analysis of the traditional security components of national security; collectively these reasons are compelling.

In this chapter, we examine the inheritance of two major functions of armed forces during the Cold War competition: thermonuclear forces and the strategies governing their potential use, and so-called conventional armed forces. Both capabilities were developed explicitly for a Cold War confrontation and environment that no longer exists, but the capabilities and plans for their use remain essentially intact today and influence the current national security debate. Moreover, these forces frame what the United States can and cannot do militarily in the world and especially in the most militarily stressful situations we may face. Their continued relevance in a world where hardly anyone else has a counterpart force is a major question.

The relevance of these traditional uses of armed force was a matter of debate before September 11, 2001. The series of events set in motion by those tragedies quickly added the semimilitary nature of terrorism to the menu and made us aware of an entirely different kind of war that a few analysts had been predicting for a decade or more but which had by and large been downplayed within the national security community.

In this chapter, we examine the traditional problems of national security sequentially. We begin with nuclear forces and deterrence, the historically unique military problem of the Cold War. The possibilities of nuclear Armageddon, however remote, were of such enormous potential consequence as to receive the highest priority in defense planning and thinking.

The other side of the traditional balance is the continuing utility of conventional (or nonnuclear) forces. The Cold War's military competition featured very robust nonnuclear forces—large, heavily equipped armies; highly capable surface, subsurface, and aerial navies; and sophisticated bomber and fighter-based air forces—developed to deter and, if necessary, fight the "central battle" in Europe. The preparations undertaken came from a vision of an even larger and bloodier reprise of World War II. Of the two massive forces that conducted that competition, only American forces remain as large and configured with the kinds of capabilities the Cold War dictated.

These two types of forces continue to exist, although their traditional roles have largely been overcome by events. There are, however, residual issues arising for each type. For nuclear forces, these include the problems of nuclear proliferation and missile defenses. For conventional forces, military manpower and military force reform are important residues.

NUCLEAR FORCES AND DETERRENCE

The nuclear age was formally born in the predawn hours of July 16, 1945, when the first atomic explosion lighted the skies around ground zero at the Trinity Site at White Sands, New Mexico. The light from the explosion could be seen as far away as Albuquerque, New Mexico, a hundred miles or so away. Robert Oppenheimer, the physicist considered the "father" of the atomic bomb, was so overwhelmed by the event that he said later, "There floated through my mind a line from Bhagavad-Gita, 'I am become death, the shatterer of worlds.' " General Lesley Grove, the military commander of the Manhattan Project that produced the bomb, intoned, "This is the end of traditional warfare," as he viewed the explosion. His view was, of course, over-stated, and traditional warfare continued despite this monumental change in destruc-tive capability. The clear difference, however, is that wars are now conducted with nuclear escalation as a possibility, especially when nuclear-capable states are involved.

The thought surrounding nuclear weapons has its rich, distinct history, much of which has faded from public view and policy concern. The "shadow of the mushroom-shaped cloud" is, however, a remaining artifact of the second half of the twentieth century, and thus it is worthwhile briefly sketching its dynamics, highlighting those with continuing relevance.

Seminal Events of the Nuclear Age

The nuclear age did not burst upon us suddenly at White Sands. Scientific research into nuclear physics went back nearly a century through more-or-less independent in-vestigations in Europe and North America. The impending clouds of World War II and intelligence reports that Nazi Germany was attempting to harness and weaponize nuclear physics alarmed Albert Einstein to the extent that he wrote a letter at the be-hest of more politically active colleagues like Enrico Fermi to President Franklin D. Roosevelt warning of the potential problem such weapons could pose in the hands of the Nazis. Roosevelt's response was to commission the Manhattan Project, which be-gan the crash program that produced nuclear bombs shortly before the end of the war.

The first operational atomic bombs were, of course, used against Hiroshima and Nagasaki, Japan, on August 6 and 9, 1945, to shorten the war in the Pacific by forc-ing Japanese capitulation short of an anticipated bloody invasion of the Japanese home islands. (This vision was made especially vivid by the spirited Japanese defense of Okinawa which, interestingly, included Japanese soldiers wrapping themselves with explosives and committing suicide by blowing themselves up.) When the second bomb exploded, the American arsenal was temporarily exhausted; for the last time, the world had no nuclear weapons. In the next quarter-century, the nuclear world evolved from those primitive days through the cumulative impact of a series of nuclear events.

The Atomic (Fission) Bomb. The successful conclusion of the Manhattan Project was, of course, *the* seminal event of the nuclear age, since none of the other sophisti-cations would have been possible without having taken the first step. The original atomic bomb was what is known as a fission device—the basic physical reaction that makes the bomb explode and produce its deadly effects occurs through the breaking apart (or fission) of atoms of certain elements, in this case unstable isotopes of uranium. The atomic bomb represented a quantitative change in the deadliness of war. The delivery of an atomic bomb over a target could produce deadly effects that otherwise could only have been produced by literally hundreds or thousands of attacks by conventional bombardment. The campaigns against Dresden, Germany, and Tokyo with incendiary bombs (both of which were more destructive than the atomic attacks) had required attacks by many hundreds of aircraft, because the characteristics of those bombs were insufficient to create an undeniably qualitative change in warfare. Atomic bombs made bombardment incredibly more "efficient" than it was in the prenuclear age.

The Hydrogen (Fission-Fusion) Bomb. The second major event was the successful development of a qualitatively larger form of nuclear explosive, the fission-fusion or hydrogen bomb. Known as the "Super" at the time because of the orders of magnitude increase in deadly effect that it had, a prototype of the hydrogen bomb was successfully tested by the United States in 1952. The Soviet Union followed suit a year later. As the name implies, the physical reaction behind this new form of nuclear explosion involves two steps—the explosion of a small fission "trigger" to induce the second step, which is fusion. This reaction involves the fusion of atoms of heavy hydrogen (deuterium or tritium), which produces the release of an enormous amount of energy far in excess of that possible with a fission reaction.

The effects of a thermonuclear explosion are awesome. Fission bombs produced yields that were the equivalent of thousands of tons (kilotons) of TNT; fission-fusion devices produced explosions with destructive effects measured in *megatons (MT)*, or the equivalents of *millions* of tons of TNT. During the Cold War, the Soviet Union was reported to have tested a fission-fusion device that produced an 85 MT blast.

The entry of thermonuclear bombs into the arsenals of the two sides altered the calculus of nuclear weapons and their use in two ways. First, it altered the calculation of survivability in a nuclear war. A society might endure grievous damage as the result of an attack with atomic bombs, but it could reasonably anticipate surviving such an attack. The same attack with thermonuclear bombs—a quantum leap in destructive capability—made survivability questionable and meant the new weapons represented a *qualitative*, rather than a quantitative, increase in the deadliness of war. Second, during the early 1950s, scientists achieved considerable success in designing bombs that were more compact and much lighter than the Hiroshima and Nagasaki prototypes. This made possible the delivery of these deadly weapons by missiles, a further qualitative change.

The Intercontinental Ballistic Missile (ICBM). The effort to weaponize rocketry began in the period between the world wars, when the first rockets were developed and tested in Germany and the United States, among other places. In World War II, the first prototypes, the V-1 "buzz bombs" and the V-Rockets, were used against Great Britain in a desperate act by the Germans to break British will. These early designs were so grossly inaccurate as to have little impact on the war, and rockets were considered little more than terrorist weapons. By the 1950s, advances in rock-etry allowed nuclear weapons to be transported over intercontinental ranges and land close enough to their targets to destroy them.

The result of these advances fundamentally altered the impact of nuclear weapons on war more than any of the other seminal events. The reasons were (and are) profound and cumulative. The thermonuclear bomb had removed the ability to calculate surviving a nuclear war if a large number of these devices were used. The ICBM produced the perfect delivery device for such weapons, since there was (and arguably still is) *no known defense capable of defending against a nuclear rocket attack.* The result is total societal vulnerability to nuclear devastation, and when both sides have this offensive capability, the condition is known as *mutual societal vulnerability.* In this situation, the only way to avoid being killed in a nuclear war was to avoid having such a war at all. Nuclear war avoidance (or nuclear deterrence) became a prime value and concern.

The Multiple Independently Targetable Reentry Vehicle (MIRV). The fourth development was a major increase in the deadliness and extensiveness of nuclear arsenals—the perfection of a means to dispense more than one nuclear bomb (or warhead) from the tip of a single rocket. The military capability was achieved by the United States in 1970, when it began to add MIRV capability to its arsenal; the same feat was achieved by the Soviet Union in 1975.

The MIRV had two major effects on the nuclear equation. The first was to multi-ply the size of nuclear arsenals without increasing the number of nuclear missiles within those arsenals, a phenomenon known as "fractionalization," which meant that a single rocket's capacity could be increased by the number of additional warheads that the MIRV permitted to be added (or fractionated). The MIRVing of superpower arsenals had a second, anomalous effect. During the 1970s, arms control negotiations with the purpose of reducing the likelihood of nuclear war between the superpowers were particularly active, and one of their purposes was to place limits on the size and capabilities of the two offensive arsenals. MIRVs, however, had been excluded from those discussions by the Soviets (who lagged in the technology and did not want to negotiate away their chance to catch up), and the process of converting arsenals to MIRV status meant that the number of warheads actually increased greatly during the decade. The MIRV was the reason.

Ballistic Missile Defense (BMD). The fifth seminal event—defenses against missile attacks—has not yet occurred but is instead a residue of the Cold War. It has been a high priority of the Bush administration (although one sidetracked by the war in Iraq) and could, in certain circumstances, alter the nuclear calculus as much as the others. The current round of debate about missile defenses is nothing new. In fact, investigation of how to try to destroy incoming ballistic missiles proceeded parallel to the development of offensive applications of rocketry, and all the theoretical prob-lems of missile defense had been solved before the first ICBM was launched in 1957.

The problem has not been the concept; the difficulty has been, and continues to be, execution of the proposed mission, as we shall see later in the chapter.

Why would the development of effective defenses represent a seminal event in the nuclear age? The answer is that an effective system should be capable of intercepting and destroying all of an incoming nuclear missile attack (it is not clear it would function against attacks by other than missile delivery). A truly effective, reliable defense would thus remove dependence on deterrence as the only basis on which to prevent the ravages of a missile-launched nuclear war. Rather than relying on the threat of robust retaliation after absorbing an attack (the basic threat under theories of deterrence as they have been practiced), a defensive system that worked could render such an attack ineffective and futile and make nuclear weapons "impotent and obsolete," in Ronald Reagan's depiction of the purpose of his Strategic Defense Initiative. A truly effective defense would rank with the ICBM in importance in nuclear evolution and change the way we thought and think about nuclear weapons.

Theories of Deterrence

As the nuclear balance evolved, two broad conceptualizations of deterrence emerged to dominate theorizing and defense planning in the United States, including the development and deployment of nuclear arsenals. Both positions were first articulated in two works published in 1946, one very famous (Bernard Brodie's *The Absolute Weapon*) and one not so well known (William Liscum Borden's *There Will Be No Time*).

These formulations sound strange, even macabre or bizarre, when taken out of the context of the times. Brodie's formulation evolved to the strategy of assured destruction, which a detractor modified by putting the word "mutual" in front of it to produce the acronym MAD. Borden's position evolved by the 1980s to a strategy known as limited nuclear options (LNOs) or countervailance; a detractor gave its adherents the title Nuclear Utilization Theorists, or NUTS. The intellectual debate about what best deterred a nuclear attack thus became a dialogue between those who were MAD and those who were NUTS.

Assured Destruction. The title of Brodie's book gives its thesis away. According to Brodie and his associates at Yale University who collaborated on *The Absolute Weapon*, nuclear weapons fundamentally changed the nature and calculation of war. The destructiveness of those weapons was so great that, in Brodie's opinion, conventional war—which could escalate to nuclear war—was now obsolete. Thus, the only reason states could have for maintaining military forces (including nuclear weapons) was to avoid their use against them—in other words, deterrence. Borden disagreed, arguing that nuclear weapons were weapons, after all, and that weapons are eventually used. From this premise, Borden argued that the secret was to be sure these weapons were only used against military targets, thereby limiting their horror. Thus, the debate over the usability of nuclear weapons was joined, but not resolved, in 1946.

Much of the debate lay fallow for over a decade. The event that enlivened the question of deterrence, of course, was the successful testing and deployment of ICBMs in the latter 1950s. Since the only way to guarantee not being killed in a nuclear war when ICBMs were present was to make certain that a nuclear war did not occur, the question became, What kind of nuclear strategy best assured the avoidance of nuclear hostilities?

The Brodie position was the first answer to dominate the debate and was articulated in the early 1960s as assured destruction. The first premise of the strategy, which came directly from Brodie himself, was that all sides would lose in any nuclear war, meaning that only war avoidance was acceptable. The question was how best to assure that no one could ever miscalculate the possibility of succeeding in a nuclear war and thus decide to start one. The answer was the assured destruction threat.

The basic assured destruction threat was that any Soviet nuclear attack would be met by a fierce and destructive American retaliation that would destroy the Soviet Union and rob it of any possible calculation that it had "won" anything. ICBMs guaranteed the condition of mutual societal vulnerability under which such a retaliation would occur against an initial attacker; and the upshot was that launching a nuclear strike became the equivalent of committing national suicide.

The implementation and implications of assured destruction are ghoulish and created a lively opposition. In order to reinforce to Soviets the suicidal nature of an attack, the strategy features *countervalue targeting* by American retaliatory forces against Soviet targets. This antiseptic term means aiming weapons at the things people value most, notably their lives and the conditions that make life commodious. The prototypical countervalue target is an urban complex, the larger the better, since the purpose is to convince the adversary's leadership and population they will die if they attack the United States.

As the critics were quick to point out, this strategy amounts to no more than a promise to commit genocide in response to an initial attack, hardly a praiseworthy goal. Supporters replied in two ways. First, they argued that if a nuclear war ever began, both sides would likely become so vengeful that the assured destruction outcome would probably occur even if it was not the conscious basis for planning. Second, the threat was purposely hideous to insure that no one could miscalculate: assured destruction maximizes deterrence by guaranteeing the hideousness of its failure.

Limited Nuclear Options. The murderous implications of assured destruction did not go unnoticed or uncriticized. Arguing that such a threat was both gruesome beyond belief and incredible because of the ghoulish consequences, a second strand of thought emerged within nuclear strategy circles suggesting a different role for nuclear forces. In the curious world of nuclear weapons and deterrence, the argument began with the belief that the assured destruction threat was unbelievable because of the moral abyss that implementation of the strategy promised, and then posed a supposedly more humane alternative. Thus, nuclear planning must contain ways to use nuclear weapons that do not necessarily entail Armageddon.

This basic idea, extrapolating from Borden, became known as limited options in the 1970s and 1980s and posited proportionality as the basis of deterrence. The defenders began by arguing that the assured destruction threat was believable only in the event of an all-out Soviet first-strike attack against the United States. Since the Soviets knew the consequences of such an attack, it was the least likely form of attack for them to undertake. Thus, any nuclear attack they might actually contemplate would be less than all-out, leaving the president with only the options of doing nothing or launching the entire arsenal. As a result, the assured destruction threat emerges from this analysis as a credible threat against the least likely form of nuclear aggression and an ineffective threat against other and, by definition, more likely forms of provocation.

Limited nuclear options remedies this deficiency by creating within the Single Integrated Operational Plan (SIOP, the actual plan for implementing nuclear attacks) a series of options short of all-out response (hence the name limited options). The idea is to provide the president with a whole array of possible responses proportional to the original attack by the Soviet Union. Thus, for instance, if the Soviets were to launch twenty to thirty missiles against U.S. ICBM fields in North Dakota, the United States should have the capability and plan to respond by taking out a similar target in the Soviet Union. Presumably, the threat and ability to do so would have two salutary effects. First, a proportional response would be more believable than an all-out counterattack. Second, knowing the United States could effectively play tit-for-tat in the event of any provocation, they would realize that any action they might initiate would be countered effectively; their attack would be trumped and provide no advantage.

As might be expected, adherents of assured destruction disagreed with this assessment. They argued that contemplating the use of nuclear weapons in less than the direst situations might actually lower the inhibition on using them in the first place (the major goal of deterrence), since it was possible to calculate surviving a limited exchange. Moreover, the calculation of limitation could prove wrong. It was possible the exchange could be limited to a single attack and counterattack. It was also possible that the initial attack, of whatever proportions, would so inflame passions on both sides that an inexorable spiral to the all-out assured destruction would occur. Assured destruction adherents argued the cruelest irony would be to act on the assumption that an exchange could be limited when in fact it could not. The only reliable way to avoid nuclear destruction was to avoid nuclear exchange altogether, which the absolute known horror of assured destruction would best guarantee.

The debate between advocates of assured destruction and limited options continued inconclusively for decades, because there was no hard evidence to conclude which construction produced deterrence best. The central contention always boiled down to the question of whether nuclear war could be limited. Happily, the debate between those who were MAD and those who were NUTS did end indecisively with the end of the Cold War and thus the end of the reason for the competition. In the end, deterrence prevailed in the sense that nuclear war was in fact avoided. Whether this success was an act of enormous insight and persistence or the mere avoidance of what would have been the stupidest (and possibly last) decision in human history is a judgment to be left to the reader and to history.

Nuclear Residues

Nuclear weapons may have lost the prominent role they played during the Cold War, but that does not mean nuclear considerations have simply disappeared from national security concerns. Indeed, there are at least two related concerns about nuclear weapons that remain on the agenda: problems of nuclear proliferation and the alleged need for BMD. Each is a concern of long standing. The spread of nuclear weapons to states that do not currently have them was one of the earliest worries of nuclear thinkers in the 1960s, and the prospects of and debates about missile defenses predate the actual deployment of the missiles that the defenses seek to stymie.

Nuclear Proliferation. The proliferation of nuclear weapon capability to new state or nonstate actors—also known as horizontal proliferation—has been a concern of the United States and other nuclear states for some time. This concern arises from the general assumption that the more states that have nuclear weapons capability, the greater the chances that someone will use nuclear weapons, with unknown consequences for the rest of the system. When proliferation occurs, it often comes in the spread of the weapons to historical rivals, such as India and Pakistan in 1999, raising the prospects that their ongoing military conflict could escalate to nuclear exchange.

In the current context, the more urgent problem deals with the possible spread of nuclear weapons to states considered unreliable, unstable, and hostile to U.S. interests. At the top of the list of such states stand Iran and North Korea. Although the North Koreans very publicly renounced the intention to try to operationalize a nuclear capability in 1994, they became involved in a diplomatic imbroglio with the United States over resumption of nuclear activity that could lead to weapons capability in early 2003 that continues to the present. The fear about Iran was not only that it is a rogue but that it may develop connections with nonstate groups such as Usama bin Laden's Al Qaeda, with whom it is feared that Iran might share a nuclear device to aid in their terrorist campaign against the United States. These dual fears provided much of the official rationale for the American invasion and occupation of Iraq in 2003.

The proliferation question is controversial. No one—with the exception of countries attempting to obtain the weapons—thinks that proliferation is a good idea or that the world would be a better place with more nuclear weapons–possessing states. At the same time, there is disagreement about *how much* of a problem it is. At least four different points are made regarding the nature and seriousness of the proliferation threat.

One argument is that the problem is essentially overblown. While the undesirability of proliferation has been bemoaned for forty years or more amid dire predictions of the number of states that might attain these weapons, in fact very few have. The list of nuclear weapons states stands at eight—the United States, the Soviet Union, Great Britain, France, China, Israel (which does not officially admit possession but is universally regarded a nuclear state), India, and Pakistan—and only the last three have joined the nuclear "club" in the past forty years. Lists of potential proliferators have routinely suggested the prospects of twenty to thirty new nuclear states, and these predictions have simply been incorrect.

A second argument is that much of the gist of the proliferation argument is insulting, even racist. Implicit in arguments to prevent nuclear weapons spread is that it is all right for current possessors to keep their weapons, while it is destabilizing if other states obtain them. Despite pompous rhetoric to the contrary, this conceit is also included in the Nuclear Non-Proliferation Treaty's provisions, which state that nonpossessors should abjure trying to get the weapons while possessors should move toward nuclear disarmament (which none of them have). At the bottom line, however, is the implicit statement that current possessors are more responsible with the weapons than the states that might gain them. Such an assertion is arguably true but is both condescending and insulting.

Third, the rationale for stifling the spread of nuclear weapons is that proliferation will make the world a more unsafe place because it increases the number of "fingers on the nuclear button" and increases the likelihood of nuclear war. This concern is greatest if "rogue states" or, even worse, nonstate terrorists obtain nuclear capability. But is that rationale justified by experience? The world has, after all, witnessed seven instances of proliferation (the Soviet Union was the first to join the American "club"), but there has not been a single instance of nuclear weapons usage. In fact, a case can be made that gaining nuclear weapons actually stabilizes situations, either because that possession makes countries feel less vulnerable (China, for instance) or because mutual possession by historic enemies sobers them about the consequences of future conflict (India and Pakistan).

There is a fourth and very ironic argument about proliferation in the current context. It is that countries seek nuclear weapons in order to guard against being attacked by their enemies—a deterrence argument. Nuclear weapons possession, it is argued, provides status and respect from potential predators: no state in possession of nuclear weapons has ever been attacked. The irony is that this argument is currently voiced most prominently as a reason for gaining nuclear weapons in Iran and North Korea, and the country they seek to deter with those weapons is the United States.

A question increasingly asked is whether concepts of deterrence developed in the Cold War competition can be translated into ways for dealing with nascent nuclear powers. Does the threat of nuclear retaliation dissuade a leader like Kim Jung Il or bin Laden in the same way that Soviet and American leaders were deterred during the Cold War? Or is the new breed of enemies so different—including being suicidal—that traditional deterrence concepts will be ineffective? Answers about the dynamics of what deters were highly conjectural during the Cold War, and they may be even more debatable regarding the spread of these weapons to developing countries. This uncertainty strengthens the urge to look for a hedge in case deterrence does not offer one, and one alternative to traditional deterrence is the ability to defend oneself from attack, missile defense.

Missile Defenses. The Bush administration proposal to build a missile defense is not a new idea. In fact, the *national missile defense (NMD)* is the third generation of advocacy for developing and deploying a defense against ballistic missile attack. The first proposal was put forward in the latter 1960s and early 1970s as the Sentinel and later as the Safeguard system. Its purported purpose was to guard against a Chinese nuclear capability that was projected for the future, and as such, it was similar to the current NMD plan in intent (see Amplification 8.1, The China Threat).

In 1983, President Ronald Reagan proposed a much more ambitious system, the *Strategic Defense Initiative (SDI)*. The Reagan SDI had the grand purpose of providing

Amplification 8.1

THE CHINA THREAT

Current proposals to deploy a national missile defense (NMD) bear an eerie resemblance to similar arguments made nearly forty years ago when the People's Republic of China's fledgling nuclear capability was the major objective of the United States' proposed Sentinel and later Safeguard antimissile systems. What critics of NMD argue was particularly instructive about the comparison was that the "threat" posed by China was, at the time, potential rather than actual. At the time, China had nuclear warheads but no ballistic missiles capable of delivering them against the United States. The projected problem was the assertion that China would soon acquire such a capability and that missile defenses were needed to deter a Chinese launch against the United States when they indeed acquired the capability.

In retrospect, the arguments appear nearly hysterical, although the state of U.S.–China animosity in the late 1960s made them appear more plausible than they do today. In 1967, after all, the United Sates had no formal relations with the Chinese (and had not since the Communists assumed power in 1949), and this country had fought Chinese "volunteers" in the Korean War (Chinese forces sent to Korea were officially designated as volunteers to avoid a direct legal and political confrontation between the two countries). Moreover, Chinese leader Mao Zedung had publicly proclaimed after China joined the nuclear weapons club that China's huge population meant it was the only country that could physically survive a nuclear war.

The irony of the rationale was not only that the projections of Chinese acquisition of delivery capacity against United States targets were premature, but that the capability has never been meaningfully achieved. As of 2005, the Chinese arsenal, although undergoing modernization, remains minuscule, consisting of a handful of unreliable liquid-fuel land-based and sea-based missiles that cannot be kept at a high state of readiness because their means of propulsion cannot be stored in the rockets and would have to be "gassed up" before a launch. These missiles arguably pose a potential threat to neighboring Taiwan but not the United States. The question is whether potential acquisition of delivery capability by "axis of evil" states such as Iraq and North Korea may be as fanciful as the Chinese "threat" against which the first missile shield was proposed.

a comprehensive, totally effective shield against a massive launch of nuclear weapons (essentially an assured destruction attack) by the Soviet Union. The impenetrability of the SDI screen would render nuclear weapons "impotent and obsolete," in Reagan's own words. Reagan's longer view was that such a shield would make nuclear weapons themselves irrelevant and thus lead to nuclear disarmament, his real goal. The SDI program lost focus during the first Bush administration and was formally scuttled by President Clinton. What remained after the demise of SDI was research on a more limited form of defense. The current NMD proposal came from this ongoing program.

The Clinton White House never showed great enthusiasm for missile defense, and the program was kept alive largely because of congressional interest. President George W. Bush took up the cause of missile defense in his 2000 campaign and continued that advocacy once elected. The events of September 11, 2001, temporarily sidetracked what had been active attempts both to gain support for the program and to overcome foreign (notably Russian, but also Chinese) objections to deploying such a system. The antiterrorist campaign has since been used to argue both the greater necessity of a missile screen and its relevance as a tool to frustrate terrorist organizations from attempting to use a nuclear weapon against the United States.

The idea of missile defense is inherently appealing. That appeal arises from the realization that deterrence can in fact fail (or a nuclear terrorist attack can be launched). In that event, the absence of some form of defense leaves the population absolutely vulnerable to being killed, a decidedly unappealing prospect and one against which it is appealing to try to hedge. In some advocacies, it is further suggested that it is immoral not to try to mount a defense against a missile attack.

There are several objections to developing and deploying the NMD, almost all of which have been raised against its predecessor proposals as well. The first and most fundamental objection is *workability*. Although the theoretical principles for missile defenses had been worked out before the first ICBM was fired successfully, developing a system that actually could shoot down missiles with any proven reliability has been and remains illusive. In fact, critics counter the claim that it is immoral not to mount a defense by asserting it is crueler and more immoral to build a defense that would not work than it is not to build one at all. The Bush administration itself has demonstrated some public ambivalence on this issue. At times, it has said it would not deploy an NMD until a design had proven "workable," which presumably means that it has succeeded in knocking down offensive missiles in numerous, realistic tests (something it has not yet accomplished with any reliability). At other times, Secretary Rumsfeld has argued that demonstrated workability is not a defining criterion in a deployment decision. The deployment of elements of the NMD shield in Alaska that began in 2004 proceeded without any operational demonstration of the system's effectiveness.

A second critique deals with the *need* for a defense. As Amplification 8.1 points out, the original Sentinel/Safeguard system was designed to thwart a projected Chinese nuclear threat to the United States that has yet to emerge more than thirty years later. While no one questioned that the Soviets posed a threat for which an effective SDI might provide a remedy, the NMD proposal is more similar to Sentinel/Safeguard than to SDI. The NMD is not designed as a counter to an existing threat but rather as a hedge against the emergence of a threat by rogue states or, in the wake of the September 11 terrorist attacks, by nonstate actors. Critics argue that, as in the 1960s, this threat may never emerge, and if it does, it is far enough in the future to wait until a truly effective system can be designed.

The third objection is *cost*. A major characteristic of all three missile defense proposals has been widely diverging speculation about how much a system designed to fulfill its mission would cost. The numbers are always high. The most extreme case was the comprehensive SDI, the most ambitious of the proposals. The cost of deploying

SDI was estimated at anywhere between $500 billion and $2 trillion over a ten-year deployment period. Estimates for the NMD run upwards of $60 billion.

Controversies over cost vary with estimates of effectiveness and need and are conditioned by assessments of the state of the economy and thus the ability to bear the costs. Clearly, a costly defense the effectiveness of which is unknown is harder to sell than a system of known high-quality performance, and the costs are easier to justify against a real and menacing threat than in a more uncertain environment. The increased defense spending deployment would entail (unless those costs are absorbed by cutbacks elsewhere in defense) is easier to justify in a vibrant economy such as that of the 1990s than it is in the softer economic conditions of the early 2000s. Moreover, most estimates conclude that BMD schemes can be thwarted by building additional offensive forces to overwhelm the defenses, and that such offensive increments are cheaper to field than additional defenses.

The various missile defense proposals have had different fates in the face of these objections. Deployment of the Safeguard system actually began in the early 1970s but was submarined by the Congress on the dual bases of cost effectiveness and the absence of a demonstrable threat. The SDI advocates had no trouble identifying a problem but were ridiculed on the question of workability and the enormous and uncertain costs of the program. The NMD has been under scrutiny on all three dimensions: workability, given the highly uneven results of testing; analogies with the Chinese threat that never materialized; and the current projected threats that also may not exist. It has also been derided as a waste of money, particularly given other priorities. According to John Pike of the Federation of American Scientists, which has opposed missile defenses consistently over time, the NMD is a "system that won't work against a threat that does not exist."

Two other problems have affected NMD. The first comes from the international political environment. Virtually all countries (Israel being a notable exception) oppose deployment of the system as destabilizing and cite Bush administration insistence on building it as evidence of American unilateralism. The Bush administration mounted a massive diplomatic initiative in 2001 to overcome those objections with some limited success, such as gaining a limited agreement with Putin to allow the United States to test and develop the system while holding Anti-Ballistic Missile (ABM) Treaty prohibitions on testing in abeyance. Much of the international objection was based in the fact that deploying the system would force the United States to abrogate the ABM Treaty, which is viewed as the symbolic apex of Cold War arms control success. American announcement of its intention to withdraw from the treaty in 2001 has, however, created little fanfare in the international community. Similarly, when the administration announced its intention to begin construction of the first elements of the NMD system in Alaska in late 2002 and began construction in 2004, there was no more than muted adverse reaction.

The other problem is the impact of the terrorist campaign against the United States begun on September 11, 2001, and the need for missile defenses. Advocates of NMD argue that the willingness of terrorists to attack American soil directly demonstrates the need for comprehensive defense of the homeland, including protection against possible future missile attacks. This kind of reasoning underlies much of the rationale for the "axis of evil" designation of Iran, Iraq, and North Korea, as already noted. Critics counter that the NMD would have had no effect on preventing the attacks that occurred against New York and Washington, so the attacks actually prove the irrelevance of NMD in light of real threats. Terrorists, in other words, are unlikely to have missiles against which the NMD might be a response, but they would likely smuggle into the country on a ship or truck a device against which the NMD would have no effect. Moreover, critics argue, coping with terrorism will require a broad range of national efforts that will put large demands on government resources, and NMD should not occupy a high place on any list of priorities.

CONVENTIONAL FORCES AND THE FUTURE

Both of the fault lines highlight the question of the future of conventional forces. As already noted in the introduction to this chapter and in Chapter 4, the bulk of American conventional military forces and the expenses associated with them were devoted to maintaining and modernizing a force that was largely designed and configured to fight World War III in Europe. The end of the Cold War made this kind of a conflict extremely unlikely, and no realistic substitute has emerged to confront the United States in traditional symmetrical warfare (both sides fighting stand-up western-style war), nor is one likely to emerge in the near future. Saddam Hussein challenged the United States on its own military terms in the Persian Gulf War in 1990–1991, and he failed miserably. His experience was instructive for all who might challenge the West, and especially the United States, on its own terms in the future. The end of the Cold War started the process by which the United States' conventional power has become so great that it has made itself virtually obsolete, a kind of self-fulfilling prophecy in which American prowess has eliminated the problem for which it was devised.

The campaign against terrorism has simply accentuated this situation. Following the fairly conventional first phase (overthrowing the Taliban), the campaign in Afghanistan has witnessed a very different way of waging hostilities and raises some further questions about the continuing relevancy of traditional military forces to deal with these kinds of problems. Where do conventional forces fit in this environment? In the remaining pages of this chapter, we look at the traditional roles such forces have played and the fate of attempts to reform those forces, the question of force modernization in light of environmental changes and revised missions for the military caused by dynamics associated with fault lines, and the impact of recent events on the equation.

Traditional Roles

World War II was the major formative period for American conventional military forces as they now exist and are configured today. The purpose of that conflict was the defeat of Nazi aggression by large, heavily armed, mechanized forces fighting European style, and the United States and its allies responded with symmetrical forces. Although the structure of active-duty forces was largely dismantled in the years immediately after that war, it served as the model for the Korean conflict, with some peripheral modifications to reflect technological innovations (such as jet aircraft and helicopters). Since this force remained in being after Korea rather than following the

American tradition of mobilization for war and then rapid demobilization at war's conclusion, the conventional force for the Cold War was one with which veterans of World War II were comfortable and familiar. Only the adversary changed, and since the Soviets were similarly organized and were likely to fight symmetrically, the model seemed vindicated. This force structure has largely survived reductions in size since the end of the Cold War but is under more intense scrutiny in a new century. Indeed, the 2001 Quadrennial Defense Review (QDR) had raised the question of force restructuring before September 11, and a streamlined force was and is a top priority of Defense Secretary Donald Rumsfeld. The terrorist attack and the Iraq War have consigned this debate to the back burner, but it will return. When it does, there are, in broad terms, two models available for future structure.

The Heavy Force Model. The bulk of the American nonnuclear armed forces can be reasonably accurately described using two adjectives, *heavy* and *conventional*, that define what the military like to refer to as *legacy forces*. The term *heavy* refers to the way the force is configured and how it is equipped to perform its mission. More specifically, it describes a force designed to fight large-unit, concentrated-firepower combat by mobile mechanized units against a similarly configured opponent in brutal, positional land, air, and naval warfare. The symbols of heavy warfare are tanks and mobile artillery on land, bombers with large payloads in the air, and large capital ships (battleships, aircraft carriers) on the sea. By contrast, *light* forces feature more lightly armed and mobile forces capable of engaging in a variety of forms of warfare and generally not preferring the kinds of direct confrontations between armies, navies, and air forces typical of heavy forces.

Heavy forces are designed to fight *conventional* warfare, which is the style that was perfected during World War II and that we have called European. Sometimes referred to as the "Western way of war," its military purpose is to overcome adversary "hostile ability" (the capacity to resist the other side's armed forces physically) through the direct confrontation of armed forces. The military purpose is to destroy "in detail" or to break the cohesion of enemy armies, sink enemy navies, and shoot down enemy air assets. Collectively, the objective is to gain military superiority over an adversary in order to impose political objectives on that enemy by overcoming its physical ability to resist that imposition. Warfare employing heavy forces is most closely attached to wars of total political purpose (in which the objective is the overthrow of the enemy government) such as World War II, although in some circumstances these forces are effective in lesser contingencies. Heavy forces are designed and best suited for confronting similar forces possessed by the opponent. They are the tools of symmetrical warfare.

A heavy force was appropriate for the Cold War confrontation with the Soviet Union and its allies. United States and Soviet armed forces were virtual mirror images of one another physically, and both shared similar plans in the event of war. The doctrines of both sides emphasized mass (having more force at the point of engagement). A war between them, it was assumed, would resemble World War II except that it would be much bloodier and more violent, and one side or another would exhaust its weaponry and its ability to continue first. Moreover, such a war would likely be total in purpose, with one side or the other having its government overthrown (unless, of course, the war escalated to system-destroying nuclear war, in which case both sides would lose). The heavy model proved durable for fighting and winning World War II and confronting the Soviet Union short of war during the Cold War.

The prospects of this kind of war have not survived the end of the Cold War. With the collapse of the Soviet Union, the United States and to a lesser extent its NATO allies stand alone in possessing heavy forces, and no country or conceivable coalition could mount a force that could challenge the American heavy force combination or is likely to try. In a very real sense, we have perfected conventional warfare to the point that no one can (or will) fight one with us, a point previously made but worth reiterating. At the same time, the sheer size and mass of a heavy force may be useful in other situations, such as an extended occupation where hostile elements are present and must be controlled (Iraq).

The Light Force Model. The alternative approach to building heavy military forces is the light force model. Light forces generally refer to military structures that de-emphasize large military equipment and that, at the extreme, are largely limited to equipment (e.g., rifles, small caliber mortars) that can be carried physically by soldiers on foot or transported by helicopter or similar conveyance. The emphasis of light forces is on speed, maneuver, and surprise. They are not designed to confront and "slug it out" with heavy forces, against which they stand little chance in symmetrical warfare. Rather, they are forces best adapted to rapid movement, to special assignments for which speed and deception are critical, and to accomplishing missions that heavy forces cannot because of their relative lack of speed and flexibility—capturing fugitives or rescuing hostages, for instance.

In the developing world, light forces have been associated with guerrilla warfare, particularly in the jungles of the mountainous "green belt" surrounding the Equator, where it is easy for such forces to maneuver, and especially to engage in hit-and-run tactics in the face of more firepower-intensive heavy forces. The Viet Cong during the Vietnam conflict were classic practitioners of this style of warfare, and it consistently frustrated the efforts of much more heavily armed American regular forces.

The light model has always been a part of the Western tradition, although its relative importance has varied. Some might suggest that the cavalry tradition is the prototype for light forces in the American system, comparing the cavalry on horseback with helicopter-borne "air cavalry." Special Forces and Rangers are also examples of the light force model.

A major criticism of light forces is their inability to match up with heavy forces in direct combat; a soldier with a rifle stands little chance against a tank. This criticism is valid and carries considerable weight when the opponent is heavy, in which case heavy forces are the necessary counterweight. A light force facing a heavy force can only deal with it successfully by avoiding the kind of direct confrontations in which the superior firepower of heavy force can be brought to bear to "frame" and destroy the lighter force. This was the lesson painfully learned by Taliban light forces that remained massed in the face of American air forces in 2001. Heavy forces, however, have not always prevailed over light forces in unconventional asymmetrical warfare, as Vietnam provides ample evidence. If the future is likely to hold more asymmetrical than symmetrical foes, then the primacy of heavy forces is not to be taken for granted.

Light or Heavy Futures? If the heavy model served the United States well in the twentieth century, is it equally durable and serviceable for confronting the environment of the twenty-first century? Clearly, the environment within which the use of armed forces is contemplated has changed. The prospect of fighting a symmetrical war against heavy forces using conventional means has all but disappeared. In the words of the original 1997 version of the QDR, the United States lacks a "peer competitor," or foreseeable adversary that poses the kind of military threat for which those forces would be historically appropriate. The question becomes whether this type of force and style of warfare is appropriate for the challenges ahead. The experience of the United States in Afghanistan, where both heavy and light forces were employed in both symmetrical and asymmetrical settings and ways, does little to clarify this debate, as Amplification 8.2 explains. However, there is nothing really new in the debate, nor is it likely to be resolved definitively anytime soon.

Amplification 8.2

LIGHT AND HEAVY FORCES?

For a country with considerable resources available to it, the debate over heavy or light forces is not an either-or proposition. Very poor countries may have no affordable alternative to lightly armed forces. The United States, on the other hand, can afford both kinds of forces, and although there will always be a debate over which kind to emphasize at different times and in differing situations, one form or the other is extremely unlikely to disappear.

There are several good reasons why the debate is over emphasis, not the exclusive existence of one kind of force or the other. First, keeping both kinds of forces is politically the easiest solution, especially in the relations between civil authorities and the military itself. An emphasis on light forces has considerably more support within the civilian community than it does within the career military, most of whose leaders have emerged from backgrounds in "heavy" military specialties. Considerable political capital is preserved by arguing the need for both kinds of forces.

Second, it is difficult to argue for the elimination of either emphasis in an uncertain environment. As military apologists are quick to point out, for instance, no one foresaw as little as a few months before the fact that Iraq would invade and conquer Kuwait. In order to oust the Iraqis, heavy forces were clearly necessary to confront and defeat a heavy Iraqi opponent. Had the choice been made in advance to draw down American heavy assets, the effort would have been considerably more difficult and expensive. A wide variety of forces, in other words, are a hedge against unforeseen contingencies.

Third, eliminating or drastically cutting back heavy armed forces would eliminate the principal military advantage the United States possesses in the world. Confronting the United States frontally in symmetrical combat may be unthinkable under current circumstances, but if the United States self-abnegated its advantage, then such warfare might once again emerge as a real and lively problem.

The arguments over what kinds of forces are preferable in any given environment are endless, and they are almost certainly going to be inconclusive. Heavy forces may arguably be anachronistic today, but that does not mean they always will be. Both light and heavy forces have long traditions in the American and other militaries. Neither is likely to disappear.

The experience in Iraq offers another, different "lesson" about heavy and light forces. The force used to invade and conquer that country was basically light, a highly maneuverable, rapidly mobile force that darted around and through bewildered Iraqi defenders, a very effective application of "shock and awe." These forces were not, however, obviously well configured for the hostile occupation that followed. Highly mobile force vehicles like Hummers had very little (if any) armor. Stripped of armor, they could move rapidly on the attack, but patrolling at low speeds as occupiers, they were vulnerable to enemy snipers and improvised explosive devices (IEDs). To make the occupation less deadly for the occupiers, it became necessary to import more heavily armored vehicles (e.g., Bradley fighting vehicles) to protect the troops. The lesson may be that light forces are effective for capturing territory, but heavy forces are necessary for keeping it. If the future holds conquest and occupation, both kinds of forces may be necessary.

TRADITIONAL RESIDUES

The proper types of traditional military forces and their applications in today's environment remain in question, and the experience of the United States in Iraq and Afghanistan further clouds the outcome. In fact, this evolving experience has called into strong relief two related residual questions about these forces that must be answered for the future application of traditional forces. One question centers on military manpower: how many forces will be needed for what purposes, and how will we acquire them? The other question surrounds military reform and centers on what kind of forces the United States will need or be able to develop to confront the environment in the future.

Military Manpower

In the middle of 2005, the United States faced a mounting manpower problem that threatened to become more acute, to the point of jeopardizing the American military ability to meet current and future military obligations. The major symptom of this crisis was the inability of the armed forces to meet recruiting goals (numbers of recruits necessary to replace retiring members) for several months in a row. The major questions this crisis raised were why and how the problem emerged, and what might be done to remedy it.

The crisis was, in its most general sense, the result of the reversal of two trends from the 1990s. The first is greater utilization of the force, increased operational tempo (or op tempo in military jargon), than in the 1990s. Some increase in force deployment and employment is a natural outgrowth of the attacks of September 11 and the increased need for military force in places like Afghanistan. The principal cause of increased deployment, of course, is the war in Iraq, which is also the cause of much of the manpower crisis. This increase in op tempo is in some ways ironic; when George W. Bush campaigned in 2000, one of his criticisms of the Clinton administration was its overuse of military forces in places like Haiti and Bosnia—deployments that pale in comparison to the Iraq commitment. The other trend has been the beginning of the transformation of the force along the guidelines of the Rumsfeld streamlining of the American military (described in the next section). One consequence of these reforms is a smaller physical combat force than in the past. These trends congeal in a smaller armed force being asked to do more.

The Iraq commitment has brought the manpower problem to a head. As of late 2005 (before scheduled Iraqi elections), nearly 160,000 American forces remained in that country as part of the occupation—a much larger physical commitment than the administration apparently anticipated in its prewar assessment of the situation (although purely military estimates called for an occupation force of 250,000 to 300,000. In order to have a rotation schedule that is not destructive of troop morale, there has been a heavy reliance on Guard and Reserve units, some of which were experiencing second and third deployments in Iraq that they had not expected when they enlisted.

The result, of course, is the manpower crisis that emerged in spring 2005. It has two major components and one major implication for the United States. One component is recruiting shortfalls—all of the services have, at one time or another, failed to meet their recruitment goals, and in some cases the deficits have been substantial. The problem is most acute for ground forces—the so-called combat arms—as is normally the case. The most commonly cited reason that eligible young Americans are not enlisting is their reluctance to serve in Iraq. The combat arms problem is especially acute in the Guard and Reserves. The other component is lower than normal reenlistment rates for current military members. Once again, the greatest part of the problem is in the Guard and Reserves, where non-reenlistment rates are approaching 50 percent in some cases. As long as this situation continues (and the United States maintains a significant force in Iraq), the implication is clear: American armed forces are effectively tied up in that Middle Eastern country, and it would be difficult to organize and mount major military operations elsewhere in any timely fashion.

What can the United States do about this problem? The answer is parallel to the discussion of risk. One way to reduce risk is to increase capability to deflect risk; the parallel for the military would be to increase the size of the armed force. The question is, how? One way is to increase recruitment, by creating greater incentives to join (e.g., more money for college tuition, signing bonuses) or offering better terms of service (e.g., shorter enlistment periods, fewer overseas deployments). The problem

Challenge!

MILITARY SERVICE AFTER IRAQ

No American who was not at least eighteen years old on January 1, 1972, has ever been subjected to the possibility of involuntary conscription into the United States armed forces. One of the consequences of that condition—the result of negative reactions to the Vietnam War—is that few young Americans have had to give serious thought to the prospect of military service. Since exemption from involuntary service now spans two generations, this means that relatively few Americans in what used to be the "draft eligible" age pool of eighteen to twenty-six years old even have fathers who served voluntarily or involuntarily.

The attacks on the World Trade Center and the Pentagon produced a spike in interest in enlistment in the armed forces from young men and women across the board, including college students, who were heretofore among the least likely to enlist. This proved to be a temporary reaction—enlistments by college students did not rise appreciably after September 11. The problem of enlistment is more acute regarding Iraq.

What will the post-Iraq situation be like? Prior to our invasion, had military service occurred to you? If it had, what did you conclude about joining one of the services? Has your attitude changed because of the Iraq War? More specifically, has your view changed enough that you give more consideration or less to the services than before?

in the current context is the opposition of parents to their children's enlistments—opposition that incentives are unlikely to change. The other way to increase the force, of course, is through involuntary service—conscription or the draft—a prospect that is politically suicidal.

Another way to reduce risk is to reduce the threat. In military manpower terms, the parallel would be a decrease in op tempo for the force. With fewer overseas deployments, for instance, major objections to enlistment would be eased, and more current members would likely reenlist (especially Guard and Reserve elements). Clearly, the way to decrease op tempo most dramatically would be a major reduction of the force in Iraq, a move that would have enormous policy implications. The accompanying *Challenge!* box explores this future.

If the administration is unwilling to reduce its commitment to Iraq or to contemplate reinstating the draft—both likely—what is left? One answer is to keep doing what we are doing and hope that circumstances—stabilization in Iraq, for instance—allows a reduction in commitment and thus the ability to heal the manpower wound. Another possibility is to dramatically improve the *quality* of the force through applications of military technology that make individual soldiers more effective or capable—what are known as force multipliers. This is the mission that Secretary Rumsfeld has been trumpeting since he became Secretary of Defense in 2001. It is largely an exercise in military reform.

Military Reform

Changes in how and what the military does—military reform—come in several forms, not all of which are relevant for present purposes. Reform may, for instance, refer to changing rules about who can join the military (females, gays) and for what purposes (women in combat roles). It can refer to proper military conduct or the relationship between civilian and military authorities, and a broad variety of other areas of military concern.

For our purposes, we limit our consideration to the questions of military missions and the appropriate and most efficiently configured forces to carry out those missions. The questions, generally speaking, are logical and sequential. The first concern is what kinds of situations the military will be forced to confront and what outcomes are likely. The second is whether current forces are appropriate for achieving current and future assigned missions, and if they are not, what changes should be made to better align missions and forces. (One could, of course, reverse the sequence of these concerns and determine what to do based on what can be done, but that would be a self-limiting approach more appropriate for a smaller and weaker state with more limited goals in the world than for the United States.)

Military reform in this context is a dynamic and ongoing process, since situations are always changing, as is the ability to deal with the changes that occur. Military reform, however, is an especially wrenching task for military professionals to undertake. The nature of the problem for which military forces are developed is profoundly serious, ultimately the protection of the population from harm, even their survival. That mission tends to make the military conservative in approach, more prone to "tried and true" methods than to untested innovations that might fail at critical points. Institutionally, most military professionals get into positions where they may be charged with assessing reform proposals only after they have served long careers in specific warfare specialties to which they have great allegiance and loyalty and which they believe are necessary to the successful prosecution of war. Moreover, the "American way of war" emphasizes the Western tradition in warfare and has been relatively successful in prosecuting warfare fought by forces with similar values and rules of war (what are sometimes called conventions of war). Military traditions and values are simply resistant, if not impervious, to reform efforts unless truly traumatic experiences force change upon the military establishment of the day. This observation is not intended to be demeaning or insulting to those charged with reform but only to reflect sources of and reasons for resistance.

The history of military reform efforts since the end of World War II reflects this resistance. The first systematic effort was convened by new Secretary of Defense James Forrestal in 1948 at Key West, Florida, to rationalize military roles and missions. In the early 1990s, President Clinton's first defense secretary, Les Aspin (a former chair of the House Armed Services Committee) commissioned the "Bottom Up Review" (BUR) to conduct an exhaustive review of how the military should operate with the collapse of the Soviet threat. When that effort failed to produce meaningful reform, a frustrated Congress pushed through legislation requiring the QDR. The initial report was produced in 1997. When the George W. Bush administration entered office in

January 2001, one of the first assignments facing Secretary of Defense Rumsfeld was to complete the 2001 QDR by September 30 of that year. Overwhelmed by the terrorist attacks of September 11, the new QDR was issued without fanfare on October 1, 2001.

Those formulating the 2001 QDR were faced with two major challenges. The first was to describe a national security environment that had changed markedly since the Soviet Union collapsed but which remained murky, shapeless, and difficult to describe adequately. The events of September 11, which occurred after the document was in final draft, seemed to add a new dynamic to that environment. The operational implications of this "new kind of war" were not immediately obvious but were clearly unconventional, adding to rather than clarifying the essential amorphousness of a threat environment that was suddenly more compelling but no less confusing than before.

At the same time, the American military stood at a junction point in terms of force modernization. Critics of the Clinton administration had argued for several years that the numerous deployments of American forces in places like Somalia, Haiti, Bosnia, and Kosovo had come at the expense of modernizing and reequipping a force in desperate need of replenishment and updating. Each of the services had impressive arrays of new and potent weapons systems they were anxious to field to increase their effectiveness. In the months before September 2001, however, the administration argued for economy and the devotion of new resources to missile defenses, leaving the military leadership with the disquieting impression that many of their force modernization needs would go unmet.

The political reactions to terrorism radically changed the fiscal situation for defense. Concerns about the contributions of increased defense spending to returning the country to deficit spending (which had originally been raised over the Bush tax cuts earlier in the year) simply evaporated in the patriotic fervor the attacks created among Americans. Suddenly resources for the war on terrorism were not in short supply. But what to spend the newly available resources on? And for what purposes should the military receive these rewards? The QDR was intended to provide major guidance in answering both of those questions.

The 2001 QDR does not so much provide answers to the questions of reform and the future shape and character of American forces as it raises more questions. The document readily acknowledges that we are in the midst of a process of change from which a different kind of force will likely emerge. In order to accommodate the notion of change, it develops a series of analytical categories by which to organize thinking about the changes it predicts will occur. However, apart from acknowledging there is still no peer competitor and endorsing the national missile defense system, it provides little guidance about the direction the future is taking and how we should respond to it.

Part of the reason for this reluctance to predict future developments may reflect the political context from which the document emerged. When the Bush administration first entered office, Secretary Rumsfeld made a very public point of saying that he was undertaking a basic reevaluation of the defense sector and that the results of this investigation would provide basic reforms that would be reflected in the QDR. Since President Bush had campaigned on the promise to rejuvenate a military establishment whose needs he alleged had been neglected by his predecessor, the services took this to mean that the new administration would be highly sympathetic to their needs. In this spirit, the Joint Chiefs of Staff put together a wish list of new—and mostly heavy—equipment and systems they felt they needed, with a ten-year price tag of an additional $50 billion to $100 billion per year.

The new administration, more interested in tax cuts and missile defense than in force modernization, did not respond warmly to this initiative. Rather, to many in the service departments, it seemed the purpose of Secretary Rumsfeld's review was to find places in the service budgets to *cut* and reduce programs to free up funds to spend on missile defenses. The grumbling grew within the Pentagon to the point that many serving officers were predicting, with some anticipation, that Rumsfeld would be the first Bush Cabinet member to be relieved of his duties. His emergence as the highly articulate, tough-talking chief spokesman for military efforts in Afghanistan to fight terrorism stilled such speculation, as did the Iraq War.

The confrontation between the services and the defense secretary—and thus over the contents of the QDR—were, in a sense, saved by the terrible events of September 11. The QDR document was in final draft form and under final review, but reactions to the terrorist attacks pushed the review off the agenda. At the same time, the reaction to September 11 included a newfound willingness for large defense expenditures in the Congress, enough to assuage the president's interest in missile defenses and the services' interests in upgrading their conventional forces. A QDR with a vaguely worded vision of the future and responses to it served everyone's interests at the time it was released to the public.

The QDR document is best understood in this light. That it does not offer a detailed blueprint of force modernization should not come as a surprise. The proposals being made by the various services are numerous and complex, and the new administration was forced to issue its report less than nine months into its term. Instead of trying to do what was probably the impossible by picking and choosing among specific proposals, it instead offers an alternative framework within which future decisions can be made.

Using the terrorist incidents of September 2001 as its context, the document offers an assessment of the threat environment in which decisions will be made, a situation of considerable uncertainty. As the report puts it, "The attack on the United States and the war that has been visited upon us highlights a fundamental condition of our circumstances; we cannot and will not know precisely where and when America's interests will be threatened, when America will come under attack, or when Americans might die as a result of aggression." The Cold War comfort of a potent but known opponent has been replaced by lesser, but also less predictable, potential foes. As a result, the report argues the need "to establish a new strategy for America's defense that would embrace uncertainty and contend with surprise."

This assessment of the environment changes the context within which questions of force modernization must occur. During the Cold War, forces were developed on the basis of known, concrete threats that needed to be negated. Threat-based capabilities were matched to Soviet capabilities in a relatively straightforward manner—when the Soviets built more tanks, for instance, the United States responded by building more antitank weapons.

With no concrete opponent, there is no measurable threat against which to develop capabilities. Instead, "the United States is likely to be challenged by adversaries who possess a wide range of capabilities, including asymmetric approaches to warfare, particularly weapons of mass destruction." With uncertainty as the backdrop, force planning will thus be based on capabilities rather than threats in the face of a potentially diverse set of requirements.

A capability-based approach to force development works in two ways. First, it attempts to identify the range of likely problems the country may confront and to develop forces to nullify that range of threats. An example is the projected problem of possession of weapons of mass destruction by rogue states or nonstate actors like Usama bin Laden. The national missile defense system is advertised by its champions as an example of a capability-based response to this potential threat. At the same time, the approach is also designed to exploit American technological superiority in weapons development through the revolution in military affairs. The environment, the report argues, "requires the transformation of U.S. forces, capabilities, and institutions to extend America's asymmetric advantages well into the future." As an example of exploiting advantage, the Bush administration's first announced modernization (other than its stated commitment to NMD) involves buying three thousand units of the Joint Strike Fighter, a versatile fighter-bomber that will be used in various modified versions by the U.S. Air Force, Navy, and Marines to guarantee American air superiority well into the century.

One of the more interesting questions not fully discussed in the QDR regards military manpower. The numbers of Americans on either active duty or in the reserves and National Guard has shrunk from Cold War numbers by about one-third. Partly in response to these reduced overall numbers, the armed forces have turned to the reserves for a variety of tasks formerly assigned to active forces. Reserves were prominent in the Persian Gulf War (the first major reserve activation since Korea), and they have played a major role in Iraq, as noted. As Amplification 8.3 explains, this increased role was also a conscious Army response to Vietnam.

Amplification 8.3

CREIGHTON ABRAMS AND THE ROLE OF THE RESERVES

In its postmortem of the military experience in Vietnam, one of the questions the U.S. military, and especially the Army, asked was why the military lost the support of the American public for the war effort. Putting the argument in Clausewitzian terms, the trinity of unity between the people, the government, and the army—which the Prussian had argued was essential for successful prosecution of war—had been severed as public support for the war eroded to the point that American withdrawal from the war became inevitable. The question was both why this had happened in Vietnam and how the Army could avoid a recurrence in the future.

The answers were sequential. After carefully reviewing the record, the Army concluded that what allowed the tie between the Army and the public to fray and eventually break was that the public had never been asked to commit to the struggle when the war was contemplated, and that lack of commitment eventually turned into outright opposition. The only overt display of political support for military action in Vietnam was the Gulf of Tonkin Resolution of 1964, when the Congress (acting as the people's representatives) overwhelmingly provided President Lyndon B. Johnson with the authority to take appropriate military action in retaliation for alleged attacks against American warships in the Gulf of Tonkin—a dubious mandate for an eight-year military excursion. The Army, under the leadership of Army Chief of Staff General Creighton B. Abrams, further concluded that the reason public support was not solicited was the fear that the public would voice opposition that would effectively veto the military action before it could be mounted. There was no World War II–style call to war to which the population could reply "yea" or "nay," and Abrams and his colleagues concluded that parallel situations might arise in the future, potentially creating the same problem as occurred in Vietnam.

The Army had a solution: the reserves. They reasoned that one effective way to insure that the public had a chance to voice its opinion about potential military deployments was through the prospect of reserve activation in future conflicts. The prospect that reserves would be among the first forces called to action meant the people, through their elected representatives, would in effect be asked to voice their approval or disapproval through their willingness to see their friends, neighbors, and loved ones activated and sent off to war. To insure that reserve activation would have to occur, the Abrams-led Army took the lead in transferring critical tasks exclusively to the reserves so that future deployments would be impossible without reserve participation. Thus, mostly noncombat functions such as medical care, transportation, civic affairs, and aerial refueling are now reserve responsibilities, and when deployments occur, the reserves are among the first to be called upon in the defense of their country.

Such deployments have, of course, become routine in the 1990s and 2000s, but they were not when they were proposed in the 1970s. The gap between the Persian Gulf War and the major deployment involving reserves in Korea was a span of forty years. That reserves have become a routine part of deployments in places like Somalia, Bosnia, Kosovo, Afghanistan, and Iraq since 1990 is a testament to the conviction by Army leaders in the wake of the Vietnam experience that they would never again be caught without public support.

The QDR is essentially mute on the question of force size and the relative mix of active-duty and reserve forces, other than to say that these questions will be part of the "ambitious transformation" of U.S. forces "to sustain U.S. military advantages, meet critical operational goals, and dominate future military competition." Presumably, the American experience in the campaign against the Taliban and Al Qaeda in Afghanistan will provide useful guidance for future substantive force modernization and reform considerations. Force modernization meanwhile remains very much a work in progress with less than totally predictable outcomes.

The process of force modernization has largely been put on hold since the United States invaded Iraq in 2003. Within the services, attention has obviously been focused on the conduct of hostilities. At the same time, the war itself is a laboratory of sorts for testing concepts about the kinds of forces we will need in the future, and the postwar assessment of "lessons learned" will have major implications for future reform.

A new QDR produced in early 2006 largely failed to change this calculus by offering an alternative view of the environment. A radically different assessment was unlikely, however, since the same people who drafted the 2001 document are basically in office now and because, evidence from Iraq notwithstanding, the Bush administration continues to contend the world has not changed much since 2001.

CONCLUSION: THE CONTINUING RELEVANCE OF TRADITIONAL FORCES

There is clearly much more agreement that change is occurring in the role of military force than there is about its actual direction. In a speech in early November 2001, Secretary of State Colin S. Powell went so far as to declare not only that the Cold War was over but that the post–Cold War period had been surmounted as well. He did not, however, tell us the new era into which we are entering.

What seems clear is that the military requirements of the post–September 11 defense environment are considerably different than those of the Cold War. We have moved decisively away from the large end of the scale of threat with huge arsenals of nuclear weapons and massive conventional forces facing one another in what could have been mankind's most destructive, and possibly last, war. Russia, the successor to the menacing Soviet Union, is now virtually an American ally; Vladimir Putin and George W. Bush have, in some ways, become faster friends than Bill Clinton and Boris Yeltsin. The titanic clash that once seemed inevitable now seems a more fanciful possibility. The military artifacts of that confrontation seem oddly archaic as well.

We have moved toward the small end of the scale with no "peer competitor" directly in front of us or on the horizon. Instead, the threats to American security come from more remote places where American interests are less engaged and where the scale and nature of American involvement are less well defined but generally more limited. The terrorism of bin Laden against the American homeland is the apparent exception to that rule, but it is not yet entirely clear whether his, or some other, form of terrorism will fill the center stage of our concern or prove to have been a historical aberration. We begin to explore those possibilities in the next two chapters.

How relevant are the military concerns and forces of the Cold War for the present and the future? Certainly, the conventional forces and structures inherited from that era proved to be highly useful during the Persian Gulf War of 1990–1991, which helps explain why a more thorough critique of future roles has not been undertaken. The defenders of tradition received a reprieve in the Kuwaiti desert. As the United States began to conduct military operations in Afghanistan in the fall of

2001, those forces seemed adequate to the task as well. Whether either experience was reminiscent of the past or a harbinger of the future is less certain. Iraq fielded a symmetrical Russian organized and equipped force in 1990 and apparently learned its lesson and did not stand to fight in 2003. Will future opponents be cooperative and fight by American rules? Our analysis to this point suggests they mat not.

The huge nuclear arsenals and the elaborate constructs for their deterrent roles seem particularly anachronistic, which is partly why Putin and Bush are moving forward on largely dismantling them. Nuclear weapons are not completely irrelevant, of course, because several states possess them and others, including terrorists, may attempt to get them. Both the United States and Russia will clearly maintain arsenals adequately large to promise that an aggressor contemplating attacking either one with weapons of mass destruction will be given pause to face the suicidal consequences of such actions. In the meantime, the emphasis will be on arsenal reductions, the security of remaining forces from undesirable hands, and whether the threat from those undesirable others is sufficient to undertake highly expensive defenses against ballistic missile delivery of WMD.

The structure of conventional forces is also questionable. As noted, the heavy composition of American (and most other Western) forces was designed for a massive, Western-style World War III clash with like forces from the Soviet world. Now, the only countries that possess those kinds of forces are American allies or friends, and it is not clear how adaptable those forces are for other contingencies, especially the kinds of asymmetrical wars that may be the future. If we need any preview of how well conventional forces perform in the contemporary environment, we have only to look at Russian performance in Chechnya, where it has pummeled a rag-tag guerrilla force with everything in its conventional arsenal for nearly a decade but has been unable to bring the Chechens, reinforced with *mujahadeen* from other Islamic countries in the region, to their knees. American conventional forces are undoubtedly more capable than their Russian counterparts, but the question remains. Iraq is the current testing ground.

Conventional forces are buffeted from both ends of the spectrum. On one hand, their relevance in the face of unconventional forces bent on devising ways to negate their advantages has not been proven. If technological proficiency and mass always prevails, the United States must have won in Vietnam. At the same time, we may well produce capabilities that make current capabilities obsolete or vulnerable. Although not reflected in the 2001 or 2006 QDR, candidate Bush talked about simply leapfrogging a generation of weapons procurement for this reason—for instance, not building a new generation of manned fighter aircraft, but waiting for the technology to provide unmanned drone aircraft to do the same things fighters do without endangering human pilots. In the same vein, some naval critics see aircraft carriers becoming as obsolete as battleships did in World War II. Just as aircraft flying off carriers reduced battleships from dreadnaughts to targets, so too may advanced cruise missiles reduce current carriers to vulnerable targets.

If the continuing relevance of traditional forces is coming into question, there remains considerable uncertainty about what threats we face and how we must respond to them in the future. The assertion that the future will be different has to be addressed in terms of *how* it will be different.

SELECTED BIBLIOGRAPHY

Borden, William Liscum. *There Will Be No Time: The Revolution in Strategy*. New York: Macmillan, 1946.

Brodie, Bernard. *Strategy in the Missile Age*. Princeton, NJ: Princeton University Press, 1959.

Carter, Ashton B. "How to Counter WMD." *Foreign Affairs* 83, 5 (September/October 2004), 72–85.

Clark, Ronald W. *The Greatest Power on Earth: The International Race for Nuclear Supremacy from Earliest Theory to Three-Mile Island*. New York: Harper and Row, 1980.

Clausewitz, Carl von. *On War*. Princeton, NJ: Princeton University Press, 1976.

Deutch, John. "A Nuclear Posture for Today." *Foreign Affairs* 84, 1 (January/February 2005), 49–60.

Gabel, Josiane. "The Role of Nuclear Weapons after September 11." *Washington Quarterly* 28, 1 (Winter 2004–05), 181–195.

McNamara, Robert S. "Apocalypse Soon." *Foreign Policy* (May/June 2005), 28–35.

Payne, Keith B. "The Nuclear Posture Review: Setting the Record Straight." *Washington Quarterly* 28, 3 (Summer 2005), 135–152.

Perkovich, George. "How to Be a Nuclear Watchdog." *Foreign Policy* (January/February 2005), 28–35.

Quadrennial Defense Review. Washington, DC: U.S. Department of Defense, September 30, 2001.

Snow, Donald M. *The Necessary Peace: Nuclear Weapons and Superpower Relations*. Lexington, MA: Lexington Books, 1987.

PART

III

NEW CHALLENGES

The contemporary environment described in Part II has created a new set of security problems with which the United States must wrestle in order to secure itself in the world. The purpose of Part III is to examine these problems, why they are important to the United States, and how they individually and collectively produce opportunities and challenges for the United States.

In the wake of the terrorist attack of September 11, 2001, Chapter 9 explores systematically what is sometimes called the "new kind of war." While fighting against nontraditional opponents may appear to provide some unique problems, the basic argument is that nontraditional, asymmetrical warfare is not something new but the repackaging of ideas and approaches that have given the United States and other countries problems in the past and will continue to do so in the future. The Iraqi insurgency is the latest instance of this problem. Chapter 10 looks at what has been identified as the most dangerous military and semimilitary problem the United States faces—terrorism—and what the country can do to reduce the risks caused by terrorists. One of the consequences of conflicts that are dominant in the world today is the need to rebuild and rehabilitate countries after the fighting stops. Because of this, Chapter 11 looks specifically at the problems of peacekeeping and state-building in war-ravaged countries. Chapter 12 concludes Part III, looking at how the dynamics of globalization fit into the geopolitical pattern of the contemporary environment and into the solutions of contemporary problems.

CHAPTER 9

Asymmetrical Warfare: The "New Kind of War"

PREVIEW

The events of September 11, 2001, reintroduced the United States to a form of warfare it had experienced in the past, most recently in Vietnam nearly forty years ago. Because the United States prefers to engage in traditional, conventional (symmetrical) warfare and has had an undistinguished history against unconventional foes, the attacks were all the more difficult to comprehend. Had we, indeed, discovered a new kind of war that represents the future? Or had the emergence of the United States as the world's premier symmetrical warrior forced others to adopt asymmetrical warfare as the only way to confront American might? To answer these questions, we first define and describe asymmetrical and symmetrical warfare, with an emphasis on the more unfamiliar former. Following that examination, we look at asymmetrical futures in the forms of fourth-generation warfare and the new internal wars (NIWs). The chapter concludes by looking at how "new" this kind of war really is.

The horrendous events of September 11, 2001, revived the public debate over the uses of American military force for the future. In the decade following the end of the Cold War, important American interests at which armed force might be employed were largely unchallenged, and as a result, the debate over how and when to use force had been largely muted. The principal international dynamic in a national security sense was indeed the interest–threat mismatch in which American vital interests were hardly threatened anywhere and the threats that did exist were so peripheral as to be hardly interesting. No country on Earth appeared to pose a meaningful threat to basic American security. The only remaining superpower reigned supreme, and the only apparent needs for American armed forces were in "deployments of choice" (situations in which the United States elected but was not compelled to employ armed forces) in remote and obscure locales such as Haiti, Bosnia, and Kosovo to quell humanitarian disasters.

This seeming tranquility did not mean that questions were not being asked about the future of American military activity. Within the professional defense intellectual community, the future was a lively concern that centered on two related questions. The first question was the kind of circumstance in which Americans might have to bear arms, and the answers tended to suggest that the most likely scenarios were nontraditional conflicts occurring in the developing world. A few writers, as we will see, were even predicting the kinds of concerns that have been raised since September 11, 2001, although their exhortations were clearly not prevalent during the 1990s. The other question was how the United States should prepare for future contingencies, and it was focused on issues of force modernization and possible restructuring, introduced in Chapter 8.

The future came home with a literal crash with the terrorist attacks against New York and Washington, D.C. The events themselves were galvanizing and shocking enough to raise basic concerns about national security. As the reaction to the airplane attacks settled in our collective consciousnesses, an immediate victim of the exposure of the second fault line was American complacency about a supposedly tranquil and nonthreatening environment. At the bottom line, the attacks revealed that the United States was indeed vulnerable to attack. Even if we lacked a major foe that could imperil our survival, our previously assumed invulnerability to harm was shown to be false and could not easily or quickly be restored, and we lacked any clear consensus on the larger meaning of what had happened and what could be done about it.

In our immediate, shocked response, the analogy that dominated descriptions of our new situation was that of "war." President Bush rapidly described the bombings as acts of war equivalent in their infamy to the Japanese attack on Pearl Harbor sixty years earlier. The media, and especially the electronic news networks, promptly seized the analogy, with Cable News Network (CNN), for instance, proclaiming the "new kind of war" as the masthead of its news coverage for months after the fact.

Our shock masked an important dynamic of the new environment. In the decade or so since the Cold War, the United States had developed the most powerful conventional (symmetrical) armed forces in the world, forces that were compared to the Roman Legions. These forces were so potent at symmetrical warfare, as demonstrated against Iraq in 1991 and 2003, that no other country could face the Americans on their own terms and hope to succeed. The United States had become a military juggernaut that could not be defied.

The result was that we failed to see the inevitable reaction to our prowess. Realizing that a symmetrical response to the Americans was suicidal, our opponents did what groups have always done: they adopted approaches to fighting—what we now call asymmetrical warfare—that negate the American advantage. The unrecognized consequence of American strength was to negate its application: we became so good at symmetrical warfare that, in a classic self-fulfilling prophecy, we made it obsolete. No one will (or should) play the game the way we want to play it.

The law of unintended consequences was at work here. The United States developed its prowess to advance its interests in the world, but the world responded by changing the nature of the competition to give itself a chance against the American behemoth. The unintended consequence of American power is that we are now confronted by a new problem, asymmetrical warfare, that we have not historically been very good at confronting.

It is not a problem likely to disappear anytime soon. The simple fact is that asymmetrical warfare does succeed in leveling the playing field and gives what appears to be a hopelessly outmanned force a chance to compete, even to succeed. The Iraqi insurgency is only the most recent instance of this dynamic.

The extension of the antiterrorist campaign to Afghanistan and the effort to remove the Taliban government shielding Al Qaeda from capture added to the conceptual confusion. In Afghanistan itself, forces loyal to the Taliban were waging a very traditional civil war against a series of opponents led by the Northern Alliance. It was traditional, or *symmetrical*, warfare in the sense that both sides were fighting in similar manners and for the traditional goal of maintaining or gaining control of the government. When the United States entered that situation, we were indeed involved in what quite properly could be described as a war, where American airpower and special forces were employed in absolutely traditional ways to help overthrow the Taliban government. When the Taliban was overthrown and the objective returned to rooting out Al Qaeda from its hideouts in the caves of the Tora Bora mountains, the enterprise moved away somewhat from traditional warfare. The Afghan campaign thus mixed symmetrical and asymmetrical elements and helped obscure the emergence of the distinctive asymmetrical problem. We are still trying to clarify exactly what the new face of war is like.

The attacks of September 11 set a tone by which we now listen to and think about asymmetrical war. Terrorism (the subject of Chapter 10) is an extreme form of asymmetrical warfare, although it is not exactly "war" even in the unconventional manner so much as a semimilitary problem. The attacks were obviously successful, however, and led the United States to seek retribution against a real and concrete opponent, the Taliban government of Afghanistan that was physically providing sanctuary for the Al Qaeda terrorists.

These are not merely academic concerns, and they must be taken in the context of the debate that was ongoing before the terrorists violated American soil. The future face of war has, for instance, very strong implications for the future evolution of American forces and missions. As the war in Afghanistan began to take shape, American Special Operations Forces (SOFs) became very prominent in the early going, serving as advisors to the anti-Taliban forces and as spotters directing American air strikes to their targets. Later they helped organize and conduct operations against remnants of the Taliban and Al Qaeda hiding in caves in the Afghan mountains. Is the future one in which SOFs occupy a much more central place in the Army than they did in the past? Because the Taliban forces chose not to abandon conventional war when the American bombers arrived, they were left in concentrated, vulnerable positions. American airpower had its most successful showing since the Persian Gulf War, killing and helping to destroy the cohesion of those Taliban who maintained their positions along traditional military lines and ended up serving as fodder for the bombers. Does this mean the future lies in the greater decisiveness of airpower, as its proponents have long argued?

The aftermath of September 11 raises more questions than it answers, but it has provided a new emphasis for the debate about war in the future. What is clear is that the menu of violence has changed in at least two ways. First, the likelihood of American involvement in classic conventional war has been reduced dramatically (there is no one who will fight us this way), meaning any involvements we do experience will in some way be asymmetrical. Second, the asymmetrical pattern will—by definition—change. Asymmetrical warfare is an approach to war, not a set of instructions for making war. The asymmetrical warrior fights in whatever way works at any place and point in time, and that is an evolving process of experience and adaptation.

SYMMETRICAL AND ASYMMETRICAL WARFARE

A basic consideration in thinking about the nature of warfare is through the conceptualizations of war that the different participants have. For most of the American experience, our wars have been fought by traditional, conventional military forces, where both sides were organized in pretty much the same way, had largely the same (if opposing) purposes, served as representatives of sovereign states (or of groups seeking to gain or maintain control of states), and accepted the same general conventions (or laws) surrounding proper and improper ways to conduct war. A term we have used to describe warfare among similar opponents is *symmetrical warfare*, in the sense that the contending sides resemble or mirror one another along the axes of organization, purpose, affiliation, and intent. The world wars represent the epitome of symmetrical wars.

Symmetrical warfare suggests the existence of its opposite. One of the newer terms to enter the public debate is *asymmetrical warfare*. In its broadest connotations, asymmetrical warfare represents the opposite of symmetrical warfare. In this form of combat, one side fights conventionally while the other side organizes itself differently, may or may not share the same objectives as its opponent, may or may not represent a government or a movement aspiring to become a government, and rejects the conventions or laws of warfare propounded by the conventional side.

In the current context, symmetrical warfare is associated with the Western military tradition associated with modern Europe and, more recently, North America and other parts of the world that have adopted its norms. The salient characteristics of countries operating in this tradition include the fielding of mass armies, navies, and air forces that are similarly organized and configured (e.g., wearing regular uniforms, organized in traditional rank orderings), follow Clausewitzian principles regarding the subordination of war to its political purposes, fight as representatives of state governments seeking to realize the interests of states, and accept common rules about what is permissible and impermissible in war (e.g., treatment of prisoners, acceptability of purposely targeting civilians). While not all wars fought in this tradition completely mirror all of these characterizations, it is the general and expected means of war. Those who hold these values view adherence to them as honorable and deviation from them as somehow less than honorable.

In the current debate, asymmetrical approaches are more closely related to what is described as the Asiatic (including Middle Eastern) approach to war. This tradition goes back to the beginning of recorded theories of war and is currently manifested in military conduct in which at least one of the opponents is organized in a manner different from a standard armed force (guerrilla fighters, for instance), may or may not have gaining or maintaining government control as its central purpose, may not represent governments or insurgents, and do not accept or practice warfare (especially limits on permissible actions) in accord with Western conventions.

There is nothing new about asymmetrical warfare other than the name. Its underlying motivations are clear and have deep roots. As already argued, asymmetrical approaches to warfare are attractive to those who cannot compete successfully using conventional methods and whose only chance for success requires changing the playing field so that they do have a chance. As Vincent Goulding Jr. put it in a recent article, it is the approach by which "weaker opponents have sought to neutralize their enemy's technological or numerical superiority by fighting in ways or on battlefields that nullify it." If you cannot win fighting one way, it makes sense to find another way at which you can at least hope to succeed. The principle is as old as the first armed group that faced a superior enemy it could not possibly defeat if it fought according to the accepted rules of the day.

Put a slightly different way, asymmetrical warfare is unconventional warfare. Symmetrical warfare is the preference of those entities that are advantaged under accepted forms of war, whereas asymmetrical approaches are appealing to those who cannot compete successfully within the constraints of those rules. In the current environment, the world's most vociferous champion of symmetrical warfare is quite understandably the United States, whereas its opponents are inexorably drawn to asymmetrical approaches.

Evolution of Asymmetrical Warfare

As already stated, the term *asymmetrical warfare* is much newer than the general phenomenon it describes. Methods of warfare displaying some or all of this style of warfare have a long history, have been described with a variety of names, and have long been at least a small part of the American military tradition.

The idea of trying to negate the advantages of opponents fighting the conventional warfare of the day is as old as organized warfare. Although styles and tactics have changed, conventional warfare has almost always been conducted by massed, uniformed armies divided into ranks who used their weight and firepower to confront and overwhelm opponents. It is how the Roman Legions generally fought, although Belfigio (see *Selected Bibliography*) points out that they also occasionally engaged in what we would now call asymmetrical methods as well, and it is how the various combatants in World War I and II conducted war. Normally, this style of warfare is conducted in conformance to some broad set of rules of engagement that specify acceptable and unacceptable conduct in battle. Through history, there have been, of course, notable exceptions to this depiction—the Mongol Hordes substituted maneuver for mass and ignored conventions on the treatment of prisoners, for instance. The tradition of this style of warfare, what we now are calling symmetrical warfare, is highly Western in content and values. More to the point, it is key to the "American way of war."

Normally, an opposing force that lacks the mass of a conventional armed force in either quantitative or qualitative terms cannot successfully confront a conventional force on its own terms and prevail. In that circumstance, the options available to the inferior force are either to quit the contest and surrender, to stand before and be destroyed by the superior force, or to adopt a style of warfare that negates the advantages of the superior force and provides an opportunity for success. In other words, the only possible avenue for victory is to fight asymmetrically.

The asymmetrical tradition is most associated with Asian styles of fighting. The original Chinese military manual, Sun Tzu's *Art of War*, is a virtual primer on how to shift the advantage from a superior to an inferior force. Many of the principles originally laid out by Sun Tzu were adapted and operationalized by Mao Zedung in his campaigns against the Guomintang led by Chiang kai-Shek in the twenty-plus years of the Chinese Civil War and were in turn adapted by the Vietnamese historian-turned-general Vo Nguyen Giap in his campaigns first against the French and later

Amplification 9.1

SUN TZU ON ASYMMETRICAL WARFARE

Little is known about Sun Tzu, a Chinese military thinker who advised several warlords in China approximately 3,000 years ago. Some argue he did not exist at all, but that the work attributed to him was the collection of experiences of others. His classic military manual *The Art of War* (similar in intent to Machiavelli's political manual *The Prince* for Italian leaders in the sixteenth century) was little studied in the West until it became known that it was one of the sources of inspiration for Mao Zedung in his campaign to seize control of China over a twenty-year period ending in 1949.

The heart of Sun Tzu's military advice, which would be familiar to practitioners of what is now called asymmetrical warfare, was knowing when and how to fight. His philosophy of indirection and asymmetry is best stated in his advice to military leaders of his time: "When the enemy advances, we retreat; when the enemy halts, we harass; when the enemy seeks to avoid battle, we attack; when the enemy retreats, we pursue." In addition, he adds that the victor on the battlefield has a superior understanding of his opponent that allows him to deceive and thus alter favorably the battle: "All warfare is based on deception. . . . To subdue the enemy without fighting is the acme of skill. Thus, what is of supreme importance is to attack the enemy's strategy." Echoing that sentiment 3,000 years later, Goulding adds, "War might usually favor the side with the heaviest battalions, but it *always* favors the smartest." Does war really change?

against the Americans between 1945 and 1975. Hundreds of years earlier, the Vietnamese successfully evicted Kublai Khan and the Mongols from Vietnam during the thirteenth century using similar techniques.

The style of warfare represented by the asymmetrical tradition has known different names across time. A parallel term is guerrilla warfare, used to describe a particular style of warfare involving highly unconventional tactics employed for the traditional end of gaining control of government. Unconventional warfare is to conventional what asymmetrical is to symmetrical. Terms like *partisan* or *people's war* have also been used as synonyms. The purpose of saying this is not to confuse the reader but to point out that asymmetrical warfare has known many names and that the names change more than the underlying principles on which they are based.

It is also part of the American military tradition as well, beginning in the earliest days of white settlement of North America. Most of the Indians whom the settlers encountered fought unconventionally at the tactical level, engaging in ambushes, hiding behind trees and rocks, and otherwise behaving in ways that did not conform to the tactics of linear warfare practiced in Europe. When the American Revolution began, it quite quickly became apparent that the fledgling Continental Army could not successfully contest the British Army in linear battles, and some of its tactics moved from the symmetrical to the asymmetrical. America's first great victory in the Revolutionary War, at Saratoga in 1777, was a classic linear clash, but its success was largely the result of attrition of the British expeditionary force coming down from Lake Champlain by American militiamen fighting Indian style. By the time General Burgoyne's army finally reached Saratoga, attrition had reduced it to about half the size of its American counterpart. Francis ("the Swamp Fox") Marion in South Carolina and George Rogers Clark in the Northwest Territories were notable practitioners of this form of warfare during the revolution. The United States faced asymmetrical opponents in the Seminole Wars in the 1820s in Florida, in the campaigns against the Western Indians after the Civil War, in the Filipino Insurgency at the turn of the twentieth century, and against Pancho Villa in New Mexico and Arizona in the 1910s.

The United States' most extensive and traumatic encounter with an opponent practicing a form of asymmetrical warfare was, of course, in Vietnam. The basic situation conforms neatly to the distinctions we have already made and, as we shall see, has some parallels in the ongoing campaign against the remnants of the Taliban in Afghanistan.

Consider the basic structure of the military situation in Vietnam. The Vietnamese insurgents (the North Vietnamese and Viet Cong) faced an American-organized and hence thoroughly conventional South Vietnamese opponent. Following the basic outlines of the Maoist mobile-guerrilla warfare strategy (see Snow, *Distant Thunder*, Ch. 3, for a description), the North Vietnamese Army (NVA) and the Viet Cong (VC) had worn down the Army of the Republic of Vietnam (ARVN) through a guerrilla war of attrition and, by 1964, had gained such a military advantage that it converted to conventional warfare, confronting the ARVN in a symmetrical fashion for the purpose of destroying the ARVN and seizing political power.

The United States entered the fray with combat forces in 1965. The South Vietnamese were in desperate straits when intervention occurred, but American conventional military power quickly reversed the military situation. This change was first demonstrated in the two-day Battle of the Ia Drang Valley in November 1965, an encounter vividly captured in Moore and Galloway's *We Were Soldiers Once . . . and Young* (which was the basis of the motion picture *We Were Soldiers*). On the first day of the battle, an NVA conventional force encountered and engaged an American force in a conventional battle. The overwhelming American advantage in firepower (mass) turned the confrontation into a deadly shooting gallery in which the NVA was severely bloodied. On the second day, however, the Americans began a march to the staging area from which they were to be evacuated that stretched the troops single file over three miles, and the NVA responded by reverting to guerrilla tactics of ambush and hit-and-run attacks by small units that could avoid American concentrated firepower. The result was a defeat for the Americans.

Although largely unrecognized at the time, the Ia Drang experience was a parable of sorts for understanding the dynamics both of Vietnam and of symmetrical and asymmetrical warfare. Prior to the American intervention, the NVA and VC were fighting symmetrical (conventional) war against the ARVN, and they were succeeding (the ARVN continued to fight that way because although they were losing, it was the only way they knew how to fight). When the United States entered the contest, however, the much more modestly equipped NVA and VC realized they could not compete with American firepower in symmetrical combat, leaving them the choices of surrender, loss, or changing the rules to provide them with a chance of success.

The asymmetrical style they selected was the guerrilla phase of mobile-guerrilla warfare. Instead of standing toe-to-toe with the Americans, they reverted to guerrilla tactics such as ambush and avoidance of concentrations of American forces. Capturing and holding territory ceased to be a central concern; instead, they sought to wear down the American forces, to drag out the war until the Americans wearied of the contest and public opinion demanded they leave. It was the classic Vietnamese approach that they had used seven hundred years earlier to rid themselves of the Mongols, and it ultimately worked equally well against the Americans. And, of course, when the Americans left in 1973, the NVA abandoned asymmetrical methods and returned to conventional, symmetrical warfare to finish off the job the Americans had interrupted during their stay.

The Contemporary Setting

If the American military experience in Vietnam was a harbinger of our encounter with asymmetrical warfare, and post–Cold War and post–September 11 environments have reinforced that precedent. The 1990s witnessed the emergence of the United States as the military hyperpower: although U.S. troop strength declined during this period, the forces of other countries declined even more. At the same time, the application of electronic technology to warfare, the revolution in military affairs, was added to the American arsenal. The result was the overwhelming and growing military disparity between the most advanced countries—and especially the United States—and the rest, including the developing countries in which violence most often occurs. This trend was made evident to all serious observers originally in the Persian Gulf War, and it was reinforced in the campaign against the Taliban and Al Qaeda. The major implication of the trend has been an increase in the adoption of asymmetrical methods when confronting Western—and especially American—forces.

The Impact of the RMA. The growing gap in qualitative military capabilities is largely the result of the revolution in military affairs (RMA). Without going into diverting detail, the idea of an RMA (there have been several of them historically) is the impact of a particular technology or series of technologies on the battlefield when those scientific discoveries are applied to warfare. The classic study of how new weaponry changes the nature and outcome of war was the Brodies' *From Crossbow to H-Bomb*. A good twentieth-century example of the effects of applying new technology to warfare was the impact of the internal combustion engine, which allowed the development of weapons such as the tank and the armored personnel carrier and made possible the *blitzkrieg* tactics introduced by the Germans in World War II and widely employed by all combatants in that war.

The current RMA features the application of advances in computing and telecommunications to modern warfare. The "computer revolution" was first applied by the United States in the Vietnam conflict in ways such as using electronic sensing of VC and NVA troop movements. At the time, the applications were fairly primitive (for example, the VC stymied the sensors by hanging sacks of human waste above the sensors, which emitted heat and chemical signatures that caused the sensors constantly to record troops going by when none were), and there was an inadequate appreciation of the strategic implications of the application of technology to the war. The early attempts in Vietnam, however, were no more than the tip of the iceberg of contemporary applications.

The "weaponization" of high technology began to mature in the years following Vietnam. Although technology has had a pervasive influence, it has been most dramatic in two related areas that have most widened capability disparities: reconnaissance and weapons accuracy. Reconnaissance has been enhanced dramatically by satellite imagery which, when wedded with the most modern telecommunications equipment, allows the location of both friendly and adversary forces over a wide area and in considerable detail. To aid in visualization of the battlefield, for instance, high definition television (HDTV) was subsidized by the U.S. Department of Defense to produce the most vivid, detailed pictures of combat areas possible. Particularly when this kind of information is available to one side but not the other, the result is a considerable advantage for the possessor and almost insurmountable disadvantage for the side lacking the capacity. In its most extreme manifestation, the possessor knows where the opponent is and can target him all of the time, whereas the nonpossessor never knows where the enemy is or when and how that enemy is likely to strike.

The second advance has been in guidance capabilities that allow the precision delivery of munitions—usually airborne from cruise missiles or bomber aircraft—over long distances with astonishing accuracy. This capability makes it possible for the possessor, once the enemy is found, to attack promptly and with a very high degree of success. Because the munitions normally can be fired from distances outside visual range and at speeds such that they cannot be seen, the victim is helpless to protect himself. Reconnaissance and precision delivery are just two of the more important aspects of the current RMA. All these applications have the effect of being *force multipliers*, or enhancers of the effectiveness (lethality) of the force that possesses them. In addition, they all reduce dramatically the vulnerability of the warriors who possess them, thereby dramatically reducing casualty rates for the possessing state while increasing the rate for the victims.

The resulting technology gap becomes an illustrative problem that the asymmetrical warrior must negate. Electronic surveillance works only when the target can be found, and thus the asymmetrical warrior will likely take countermeasures (like hiding) to avoid detection. It does not matter how accurate a weapon is if it cannot find its target, so denying "target acquisition" is a major asymmetrical objective. The feckless campaign to locate and capture or kill Usama bin Laden demonstrates that the asymmetrical warrior can sometimes succeed in foiling the fruits of the RMA.

The Persian Gulf War Example. The first application of this growing disparity occurred in the Persian Gulf War of 1990–1991. After the Iraqi invasion, conquest, and threatened annexation of tiny Kuwait in August 1990, a military coalition was organized to reverse that outcome. The United States took the lead in organizing the effort under United Nations auspices and eventually brought together a coalition of twenty-five states, including some Islamic countries from the region, to oppose Saddam Hussein.

At the time, there was great concern about how difficult the military task of dislodging the Iraqis from Kuwait would be. Iraq possessed the fourth largest army in the world, it was pointed out, and it was a battle-tested force, having fought for eight years in the Iran–Iraq war that ended in 1988. In those circumstances, many predicted a stout defense by the Iraqis, and speculations abounded about, among other things, the level of casualties the United States would incur.

Those who predicted large numbers of casualties, of course, were proven wrong, as the war turned out to be a walkover in military terms. The applications of the RMA to the forces of the major Western powers had created such a technological disparity between the two opponents that the Iraqis stood no practical chance against the coalition troops. Saddam Hussein also misperceived American will (he believed the United States was still so traumatized by Vietnam that it would not react decisively) and the relative strength of his forces arrayed against the Americans and their allies. As a result, he engaged his Soviet-trained and Soviet-styled armed forces in conventional, symmetrical warfare fought on the terms of the coalition, against which he could not prevail.

The major difference was the RMA. When the air war commenced, the Americans attacked and destroyed the Iraqi radar and communications infrastructure on the first day. For the rest of the campaign, the United States had uncontested control of the skies while the Iraqis were limited in their ability to monitor activities of the coalition literally to what they could see standing on the ground. Meanwhile, satellites provided detailed images of Iraqi locations and movements that Iraq absolutely lacked. As an example, the global positioning system—or GPS—meant Americans always knew where they were in the featureless Arabian Desert, whereas the Iraqis were never certain of their own, much less the enemy's, location. At the same time, the Americans were able to locate Iraqi targets and to direct precision munitions to them well out of range of Iraqi retaliatory capabilities. Although subsequent assessments have indicated that some of the more dramatic claims of superiority were inflated, nevertheless, the results were an overwhelming coalition victory with very few coalition—and specifically American—war deaths (less than 150, not all of which were the result of hostile action). The implication for future developing countries taking on the United States symmetrically using American rules was clear to all concerned.

The Afghanistan Reprise. The same dynamic occurred again in 2001 when the United States broadened its response to the terrorist attacks of September 11, 2001, to include the deposing of the Taliban government of Afghanistan. In order to achieve its underlying purpose—the destruction of the bin Laden organization, Al Qaeda, which was being shielded by the Taliban regime—it was determined that a prefatory step had to be the overthrow of the Afghan regime that refused to turn over bin Laden and his followers to the United States for prosecution. The result was to involve the United States in what had been a reasonably conventional civil war between the Taliban and opposing factions, notably the Northern Coalition.

Prior to the United States' entry into the conflict with SOFs and airpower, the Taliban had been engaged in a conventional civil conflict with their opponents. Success and failure in that conflict was measured by territory controlled, and the clear purpose was for one side to maintain or the other to gain political power territorially defined—clearly traditional purposes. The fighting itself was reasonably conventional, with thrusts and parries in one direction or the other and fortified lines facing one another across the harsh Afghan vista. It was war the way it had been fought for centuries among Afghan factions, and it was a war in which the Taliban were holding their own or winning.

Enter the Americans. After the Taliban leadership refused to capture and relinquish bin Laden and his followers into international custody, the United States began to mount a military campaign the purpose of which was to force the Taliban to comply and turn over the terrorist or, failing in obtaining that goal, physically to assist in the overthrow of the regime, thereby removing that barrier to bringing the terrorist to justice.

The military campaign involved the use of both conventional and unconventional forces. SOFs were among the first dispatched to Afghanistan, coordinating efforts with anti-Taliban rebel forces, securing crucial staging grounds such as airfields (a task for which Marines were also used), and acting as spotters directing the bombers to their targets. The real hammer of the operation, of course, was airpower, both from fixed-wing aircraft relentlessly bombing Taliban and later Al Qaeda positions and from helicopter gunships strafing suspected concentrations of enemy forces.

The Taliban apparently did not anticipate either the fury or the deadly effect of the American action. It is arguable that the Taliban failed to anticipate American actions because they believed bin Laden's assessment of prior American responses to terrorist attacks. In those cases, bin Laden had publicly argued that the United States had either done nothing in retaliation, as occurred after the Khobar apartments attack in 1996 and the attack on the USS *Cole* in 2000, or had carried out a symbolic but ineffective response, as in the cruise missile attacks on supposed terrorist training camps in Afghanistan in 1998 after the bombings of the American embassies in Dar es Salaam and Nairobi. Bin Laden had also suggested in various of his pronouncements that he believed the Americans were obsessed with avoiding casualties under any circumstances and that they clearly would not put American forces in harm's way.

Whatever the basis of their assessment, the Taliban were clearly wrong and did not respond appropriately to the American aerial assault. Past experience has suggested (at least to some) that airpower can be devastating to concentrations of exposed forces (in other words, forces fighting Western-style symmetrical warfare), but that it loses some of its effect if its targets take evasive action, such as dispersing and retreating into more impregnable positions, like the Afghan mountains (in other words, adopt asymmetrical methods). To do this, of course, the Taliban forces would have had to abandon the lines they used to protect the physical areas under their control to the advancing Northern Alliance and other opponents.

The Taliban options were devil's choices. Beyond the option of surrender, they could either continue the war as they had been fighting it, which meant symmetrically, or they could stage a Maoist reversion to asymmetrical warfare. In either case, they were likely to lose, either by being pounded into submission by their airpower-aided opponents in a continuation of the conventional war or by retreating into the mountains, where they would become the hunted opposition that had abandoned the territory they controlled. They initially chose to stand and fight, leaving themselves ready targets for American bombs. The effect was predictable: in addition to killing a large number of Taliban fighters, the sheer shock effect of the bombing apparently destroyed the cohesion of the Taliban forces, sapping their morale and will to continue fighting. With the Taliban bombed into disarray, they and the remaining Al Qaeda fighters retreated to the mountains, where they have managed to regroup and mount a resistance to the Afghan government by adopting long-held asymmetrical tactics such as evasion.

The Iraq War. The impact of the RMA, combined with *blitzkrieg*-style maneuver techniques, was also felt dramatically in Iraq. The Americans and the British were able to sweep through the country virtually unopposed except in a few cities like Basra. In addition to the "shock and awe" effects of massive precision bombing, the heart of the success was the extreme speed with which the coalition forces moved, demoralizing and dispiriting their Iraqi foes.

There was, of course, an apparently unanticipated development—the Iraqi resistance. While the regular Iraqi forces did not mount a spirited defense and eventually capitulated, some of their colleagues instead went underground to prepare for the asymmetrical campaign that has been going on ever since. According to our analysis, this was probably the logical—and only—way the American occupation could be opposed with any hope of success.

The Strategic Effects. The dual lessons of the Persian Gulf War and the Afghanistan campaign should be clear, and so should their implications be clear for likely uses of

American force in the future. The assessment is not without irony, as already noted. At the bottom line, the United States and its closest allies have become so proficient at conventional warfare that they are likely to be able to engage in such methods only against extremely foolish or masochistic opponents. At the same time, the maintenance of such force will continue to be necessary to remind potential future opponents of the folly of challenging the United States symmetrically and to perform the kinds of tasks for which such forces are adept, such as military occupation.

The two experiences clearly reinforce the gap in conventional capabilities that has been widened to a chasm between RMA-proficient forces and conventional forces that do not share those capabilities. In Kuwait, Afghanistan, and Iraq, the opponents of the United States both stood and to some extent fought symmetrically in circumstances where they realistically had no chance of prevailing, and in all cases, their conventional forces were thoroughly and efficiently routed. This gap in capability between the military "haves" and "have nots" will only widen further in the future, meaning the consequences will remain in the future as well.

Much has been said since Vietnam about the failure of American will, especially the American aversion to accepting casualties. Two factors from the Kuwait, Afghanistan, and Iraq experiences should mitigate this perception and thus temper future assessments of how or if the United States will respond when provoked. One of the consequences of American conventional dominance that was first demonstrated in Kuwait and reinforced in Afghanistan has been the ability to greatly reduce American casualties through the application of technology. The mass of American firepower and the distance from which it can be employed not only devastates its opponents if they try to confront it directly but also saves American lives. The old perception (foretold by American actions in Lebanon and Somalia) that an opponent can force an American withdrawal by killing a few American soldiers is very difficult to achieve fighting symmetrically with the Americans. The current testing ground of American willingness to incur losses is the ongoing Iraqi resistance.

The Afghanistan experience provides another rejoinder about American willingness to accept battle losses. The reaction to the terrorist attacks reminded us of another factor, that Americans have always been willing to put lives at risk *if the cause was sufficient*. The question of the unacceptability of casualties has arisen when people thought the cause was insufficient to justify the sacrifice, as in places such as Somalia. In that sense, the analogy between the terrorist attacks on September 11, 2001, and Pearl Harbor are apt: the United States may be reluctant to respond when the situation does not clearly dictate a response, but we will when the reasons are obvious and compelling.

The lessons of these combined experiences for future potential American (or more broadly Western) opponents should be fairly obvious. The most obvious lesson, of course, is that it is fool's work to challenge the Western powers at their own game; symmetrical warfare with the West is suicidal. It has been suggested that one way for weaker states to level the playing field would be to introduce WMDs such as chemical or biological weapons on the battlefield. Such a suggestion misses the essential point and actually reinforces the disparity. Should Saddam Hussein have introduced chemical or biological agents into the Gulf War (as it has been suggested he contemplated doing), the overwhelming Western advantage in WMD would have simply made his defeat all the more decisive, with the United States, for instance, responding to a chemical attack against its forces with a more or less controlled nuclear response. Fortunately for most potential opponents of the West, they lack the military resources for a symmetrical challenge anyway.

The other obvious lesson is how to fight the West if a clash becomes inevitable. The overwhelming weight of American and other Western might means a challenger cannot confront that power directly and only has some chance of success by changing the rules. Vietnam again provides a model of sorts. The North Vietnamese government understood shortly after the American intervention that it could not defeat the United States symmetrically, so they reverted to an asymmetrical style (guerrilla warfare) that negated the American advantages in technology and firepower. Instead, they attacked the American will to continue the contest by inflicting a large enough number of casualties on the Americans (although the numbers were trifles compared to the casualties they incurred themselves) to convince the American public and its leaders that persevering was not worthwhile. What ultimately undermined the American campaign was not, as Saddam Hussein and Usama bin Laden apparently concluded, American unwillingness to incur losses; it was our unwillingness to do so in what we concluded was a *less than worthy cause*. The fate of the Iraq campaign will likely ultimately be decided in those terms: Will Americans conclude that Iraq was worth the amount of sacrifice that it entailed?

This assessment leaves some ironic implications for American preparation for the future. On the one hand, the only countries that could possibly confront the United States in conventional, symmetrical warfare are our closest allies (NATO) and other countries with which we have developed such close relations that war is unthinkable (Russia, China). All realistic potential foes either lack an armed force that could challenge us directly or realize such a force would lose. Thus, the very kind of application of force at which we most excel is the least likely kind of force we will have occasion to use in the near future.

That does not mean, however, that conventional force can be abandoned, dismantled, or substantially diminished. While one can argue about whether current American forces deter *all* kinds of attacks on the United States (future terrorist assaults, for instance), they certainly do deter conventional attacks that might be contemplated in their absence. At the same time, both Kuwait and Afghanistan demonstrate that periodically situations can arise in which such forces can be brought to bear with decisive effect.

What this analysis suggests is that, in the future, most of the situations in which the United States will have the opportunity to use force will be against an opponent adopting asymmetrical methods to try to obviate the American dominance in conventional warfare. This would suggest an emphasis on light forces (see Chapter 8) and on special purpose forces, such as SOFs, as well as precision airpower. At the same time, it is equally clear that asymmetrical opponents will continue to make adaptations to the means they employ against us, thus requiring flexibility in countering new methods they devise.

ASYMMETRICAL FUTURES?

The asymmetrical approach to warfare—changing the rules to negate disadvantages—is ancient, even if some of the tactical means of applying asymmetrical warfare principles are new and evolving. In order to get a better idea of what the dynamics of asymmetrical warfare are and how they may affect the future, we look at two models. One of them is a more or less theoretical construct predicting what some analysts during the 1990s thought about the likely future of warfare and providing a generic description of that future—what has been called *fourth-generation warfare*. The other, about which I have written in *Uncivil Wars* and other works, is a description of the empirical nature of a series of chaotic civil wars of the 1990s and beyond that I have called the *new internal wars*. They are basically similar depictions, with NIWs essentially serving as concrete examples of how the fourth generation of warfare may look in parts of the world. These constructs are important to examine in terms of the context of whether they will become the dominant form of future conflict or just an additional element of the pattern of war.

Fourth-Generation Warfare

A body of thought among military historians and other analysts has for some time argued that conventional, Western-style warfare, especially warfare conducted along Clausewitzian lines, represents an aberration rather than a universal phenomenon. In particular, these analysts maintain the kind of warfare we have described as symmetrical is a temporal oddity. Among the champions of this position has been the British historian John Keegan, who argues there has been a kind of Clausewitzian interlude beginning with the Napoleonic era and ending with World War II when the trinitarian relationship between the people, government, and armed forces was dominant and Western norms of warfare prevailed. Keegan argues that era has passed and that the dominant pattern of warfare in the future, as it was in the past before the Napoleonic period, will be what we have identified as asymmetrical warfare. A persistent band of contemporary analysts agrees; for some of them, the dominant analogy is fourth generation warfare.

Fourth-generation warfare represents a conceptual and physical departure from the dominance of Western-style warfare. One of the earlier depictions of this change, described by a group headed by a former aide to Senator Gary Hart, William Lind, examines the evolution of warfare from the Napoleonic period forward in an article published in the October 1989 *Marine Corps Gazette*. The authors maintain that the first generation of warfare was dominated by linear formations of armies clashing in open fields where the dominant weaponry was the smooth bore musket. This form of fighting favored the offensive actions of the conventional armies in combat. The second generation was the result of the introduction of much more accurate rifles and muskets that made the charges of tightly configured formations suicidal. The trench warfare of World War I is the epitome of this kind of defensively dominated war. With the weaponization of technologies like the truck and tank and the storage battery (for propelling submarines), the pendulum swung back to the offensive advantage, as maneuver was reintroduced onto the battlefield. The epitome of this style of warfare was the *blitzkrieg* style of fighting mastered by Germany in World War II.

What is notable about these three generations is how geopolitically and militarily traditional they are. In all three cases, they describe warfare fought by Western national armies organized conventionally and with clear and identifiable political purposes for their actions. The changes from generation to generation are not radical but largely the result of changes in weapons technologies and adaptation of strategies and tactics that reflect those changes. At the same time, this Western-style warfare features the clash of armies frontally when the major purpose of conflict is for one side or the other to defeat the enemy on the field of battle as a necessary preface to imposing its political will on the vanquished. It is fundamentally a Clausewitzian vision of war.

Those who suggest a new kind of war, whether or not they use the fourth-generation analogy, maintain that we are entering a period of radical change in warfare. One of the apostles of this change is the Israeli analyst Martin van Creveld, who described the magnitude of the change he foresees in 1991 in his *The Transformation of War*. His basic argument is that the Western paradigm of war is being broken. The Clausewitzian base, for instance, is shattered because, "should present trends continue, the kind of war that is based on the division between government, army, and people seems to be on its way out." The result will be the crumbling of conventional nationally based military forces. As he puts it, "Much present-day military power is simply irrelevant as an instrument for extending or defending political interests over much of the globe."

What replaces conventional, trinitarian warfare in the van Creveld scheme? He argues the change is fundamental in terms of the units that wage war, the methods of combat they use, and the purposes for which they fight. In his words, "In the future, wars will not be waged by armies but by groups whom we today call terrorists, guerrillas, bandits and robbers. Their organizations are likely to be constructed on charismatic lines rather than institutional ones, and to be motivated less by 'professionalism' than by fanatical, ideologically based loyalties." The new kind of war, in other words, turns the traditional warfare of the first three generations on its head both organizationally and in terms of its underlying purposes. It also describes Al Qaeda and the Iraqi resistance well before they existed.

The arguments surrounding this alleged transformation are, of course, controversial. While they have been made for a decade or more, most of the discussions have been confined to places like the war colleges, where they have been extensively debated and dissected. The events of September 11, 2001, have brought these arguments out of the shadows and onto center stage. The actions by bin Laden and his cohorts clearly meet parts of the description of future war described by van Creveld, and the popularization of the term *new kind of war* has sent many scrambling to find out what this newness is. There is no consensus at this point.

We cannot settle all the controversy here. What we can do is describe what the champions of the new form of war claim about it. Because the terrorist attacks and the subsequent campaigns against the Taliban, Al Qaeda, and the Iraqi resistance proved the stimulus for consideration of the fourth generation, we can also ask how an assessment of that experience reinforces or undercuts the claims of those arguing fundamental change.

Characteristics of Fourth-Generation Warfare. Although there are other depictions available that differ in detail, the framework of Lind and his colleagues is useful for describing what people mean when they talk about fourth-generation warfare. What is interesting about their analysis is that it not only argues the change that marks the fourth generation but it also points out how important elements of the new environment have their roots in the past and evolving kinds of war.

Lind and his colleagues argue that there are a series of characteristics of fourth-generation warfare that can be traced to the past. In terms of the conduct of hostilities, for instance, they maintain in the future there will be no distinctions between civilians and military forces in terms of targeting: society is the battlefield in the new environment. There will be an absence of definable battlefields or fronts, and the places where fighting occurs will be dispersed and undefined: everywhere and nowhere is the front lines. The result is a much more fluid military situation in which traditional concerns like logistics and measures such as land gained or lost will largely lose meaning as measures of military success.

The purposes of fighting will also change, at least for those who adopt the methodologies of the fourth generation. The goal will not be traditional military defeat, but instead the internal political collapse of the opponent and its will to continue. The manipulation of the media will be a skill that is highly sought by practitioners of the fourth generation, and the targets of much of this activity will be popular support for the government or whatever force against which the campaign is waged.

To this point, the description of fourth-generation warfare is still not terribly innovative. While one can see elements of it in the terrorist attacks (not distinguishing between military and civilian targets, for instance), almost all of these characteristics could easily be ascribed to the NVA and VC asymmetrical campaign against the United States a third of a century ago. In fact, this part of the description is largely attributable to the postmortem of the American experience in Vietnam.

Lind and his colleagues extend these characteristics in trying to describe the basic nature of the fourth generation. First, they argue explicitly the non-Western, Asiatic (including Middle Eastern) basis of this form of warfare. In an article published in October 2001, Keegan embellished this connection:

> The Oriental tradition, however, has not been eliminated. It reappeared . . . particularly in the tactics of evasion and retreat practiced by the Vietcong against the United States in the Vietnam war. On September 11, 2001, it returned in an absolutely traditional form. Arabs, appearing suddenly out of empty space like their desert raider ancestors, assaulted the heartlands of Western power in a terrifying surprise raid and did appalling damage.

Second, they argue that terrorism is a standard tactic of practitioners of the fourth generation. Because they are militarily weaker in the traditional (symmetrical) sense, terrorist tactics provide an asymmetrical way to bypass the conventional strength of

Western militaries and to strike at the homeland. They are aided in accomplishing these acts by the very openness of free societies that makes them more easily penetrable. Third, a major objective of fourth-generation practitioners is the disruption of target societies, what Lind and his colleagues call the "culture of order," which is the direct objective of the attacks. Finally, they argue that movements adopting fourth-generation warfare will often not be nationally based governments but will have a transnational and, on some occasions, even a religious base.

These descriptions, published twelve years before the September 11 attacks, have an eerily prescient ring in terms of what happened in New York and Washington. Van Creveld adds (once again, in 1991) another evidence of similarity: "There will be a tendency to treat leaders as criminals who richly deserve the worst fate that can be inflicted on them. Hence, many leaders will probably decide to remain unattached and lead a semi-nomadic life."

The Fourth Generation and September 11, 2001. The descriptions of the nature and implications of fourth-generation warfare seemed virtually to predict the terrible events of September 11, 2001, a decade or more ago, which is, in large measure, why they are reproduced and quoted in some detail. Imbedded in these discussions, however, is the further assertion that nonstate-based warfare fought using asymmetrical methods and for nonconventional purposes will become the dominant form of warfare in the future. Implied in that prediction is the further assertion that traditional, Western national military forces will become obsolete relics because of the new form of warfare.

Does the experience of the terrorist attacks and responses to them bear out these implications? In some ways, they clearly do. The attacks against the Pentagon and the World Trade Center towers clearly fit the descriptions and motivations of the purveyors of this new "model" of warfare. Not all the attributes were new, of course—terrorism is a decidedly old tactic, and terrorist acts committed by nonstate actors are hardly novel in the American or international experience. What sets the attacks apart in the contemporary context is their audacity and scale. Terrorist attacks by individuals and groups with no formal state affiliation that kill a relatively small number of people are, if not common, not entirely uncommon. When thousands of innocent people are killed in such attacks, then the problem achieves another order of magnitude.

Did the attacks and the subsequent campaign to overthrow the Taliban, destroy the Al Qaeda, and capture bin Laden vindicate the apostles of the fourth generation of warfare? In other words, were the attributes of how America's asymmetrical foes fought sufficiently frustrating to the United States that we felt the need to reformulate how the military goes about its business in the face of future repetitions that may become the norm for future violence?

The short-term answer would seem to be overwhelmingly in the negative. Admittedly, the Taliban did not engage in a campaign of asymmetrical warfare after the Americans entered the civil war to bring about their ouster, which was a major mistake caused by the irony of their situation. At the same time, part of the reason for their defeat may also have been a seething, if repressed, hatred for their rule, which meant most of their countrymen offered them neither aid nor comfort when they came under the relentless fury of the American bombers. Some of the ease with which the Taliban were dispatched, in other words, stemmed from their lack of popular support at home.

Al Qaeda, on the other hand, did attempt to fight asymmetrically, and it did them more good. While the Taliban remained in their conventional lines providing target practice for the bombers and the Northern Alliance, the Al Qaeda fighters headed for the cave-pocked mountains, where they went into deep hiding, emulating their earlier Viet Cong predecessors.

Ultimately, Al Qaeda ended up in the Tora Bora Mountains and beyond, where they were pounded by the combined conventional might of the Americans and the various Afghan factions, but not entirely broken. All the adherence to apparently novel forms of warfare did not keep them from being forced to go deep underground, and bin Laden and his closest cohorts evaded the dragnet out to snare them. Conventional force and counterterrorist actions were able to reduce Al Qaeda to a shadow of its prewar status but have not been able to destroy it completely. The resilience that Al Qaeda has demonstrated will, in all likelihood, be part of the model for future asymmetrical warriors.

New Internal Wars

While the events of September 11, 2001, have quite understandably caught our attention more fully, another form of warfare has been raging over the last decade or more in parts of the developing world in the form of often grotesque and hideous conflicts that I have identified as the new internal wars (NIWs).

These kinds of wars broke onto the public scene during the 1990s, although there were a few internal conflicts during the Cold War that met all or most of the criteria for classification as NIWs. What sets these conflicts apart is their disorderliness and the extreme violence and apparent senselessness of the suffering being exacted mainly against civilian populations by their countrymen. Moreover, although they have occurred most often in places far from the geopolitical spotlight, the unrelenting eye of global electronic mediation has focused upon them as the "warts" in what, until September 11, 2001, had appeared a very benign international environment, at least in terms of threats and violence. The genocide in the Sudan has brought NIW-style conflicts back into at least limited public attention.

The end of the Cold War contributed to the emergence of the NIWs as a major phenomenon in the pattern of world violence. Internal conflicts were, of course, the dominant form of war during the Cold War, and in that sense, the NIWs represent a continuation of the pattern that occurred during the period of superpower competition. At the same time, civil conflict during the Cold War generally had the character of traditional insurgency, where the structure of the violence featured a government seeking to maintain itself in power and supported by one of the superpowers (usually the United States) and an insurgency employing some form of mobile-guerrilla war model that sought power and was supported by the other superpower (usually the Soviet Union). Superpower presence layered an often irrelevant Communist–anti-Communist aspect to contests more properly understood in other terms (ethnic or tribal dominance, for instance), but it also brought restraint to the fighting, since neither superpower wanted its client (and by extension, itself) charged with atrocities.

The war in Cambodia in the 1970s between the Khmer Rouge and its opponents was the major exception to this rule (the contending sides were sponsored by the Soviet Union and China), and in many ways, it was the prototype for the NIWs. The brutal, genocidal campaign by the Khmer Rouge government to transform Cambodian society into a pastoral, docile condition produced a litany of horrors that war crimes investigators are still unraveling. They also provided a frightening portent of the future of internal war that was largely ignored at the time.

The list of the most prominent instances of these new internal wars is familiar. The post–Cold War prototype occurred (and in limited form is still going on) in Somalia, where a combination of a long drought and the use of international food supplies as weapons in the clan-based conflict for power threatened to result in massive starvation until an international peacekeeping force intervened to interrupt the suffering. "Ethnic cleansing" was added to the language of international politics as Serbs, Croats, and Bosnian Muslims struggled to partition the Bosnian successor

Amplification 9.2

THE "BATTLE" FOR SIERRA LEONE

The civil conflict that has wracked the small west African country of Sierra Leone for a decade and which has only recently been terminated by the insertion of a United Nations–sponsored peacekeeping force UNAMSIL (United Nations Mission in Sierra Leone) is, in some ways, the epitome of the phenomenon of new internal war.

First, it is not a war in the common sense of the reasons for which war is fought. At various times, three different groups have been involved in shifting coalitions with one another: a weak and unsupported government, an equally weak Sierra Leone army, and the Revolutionary United Front (RUF). The objective of the war was only indirectly control of the Sierra Leone political system, especially for the RUF. The real objective was political destabilization of the country so that there is no legitimate authority that can interfere in the criminal exploitation and smuggling of the country's primary resource, diamonds.

Second, the war was not military in any recognizable sense. The RUF did not even pretend to be soldiers, rather preferring the designation of "fighters," and there have been no battles between the sides worthy of the name. The principal distinguishing mark of the RUF, before the peace was imposed, consisted of more or less random acts of terror against members of the population. The preferred form of terror has been amputation of hands and feet, leaving Sierra Leone with an enormous prosthetics need that nongovernmental organizations (NGOs) such as *Medicins sans Frontieres* (MSF, translated into English as Doctors without Borders) have only recently been able to begin to deal with. The result of the "battle" over Sierra Leone has been to leave a helpless, prostrate country that it will take years of concerted effort to rebuild.

state to Yugoslavia, and that phenomenon was reprised a half decade later in Kosovo. Between those Balkan conflicts, the United States intervened in Haiti, and the Rwandan nightmare was added to the list in 1994. Simmering NIWs dot the map of Africa, notably in places like Sierra Leone.

Arguably the dominant form of warfare in the 1990s, the NIWs sent contradictory signals to an international system enjoying peace and prosperity for the major powers and the apparently inexorable spread of globalization into the developing world. On the one hand, almost all the NIWs occurred outside the band of countries participating in the global economy. That created in those victimized countries a certain sense of marginalization that suggested they could be ignored: Is it any of our business what goes on in East Timor or the Sudan, for instance? On the other hand, global television gave full-blown coverage to the human suffering associated with these hideous conflicts and made them difficult to ignore altogether. Who could not be moved by the distended bellies of the starving children of Somalia? the gaunt faces of Bosnian detainees so reminiscent of the German concentration camps? the hacked bodies of Rwandan women and children? the hopeless, helpless visages of Kosovar refugees? the pitiful amputees of Sierra Leone? the starving Sudanese refugees in makeshift camps in Chad? The security question of the 1990s was what the international community should do about these human tragedies, if anything. Although that question has been pushed from the center of the agenda by the terrorist acts of 2001 for a time, the ongoing evolution of the situation in Afghanistan provides a bridge of sorts. Afghanistan was not an NIW (although it had some characteristics of one), but the solution selected for Afghanistan—state-building—is also the prescribed solution for states in which NIWs have occurred, as discussed in Chapter 11.

Characteristics of New Internal Wars. The characteristics ascribed to NIWs are derived differently than those for fourth-generation wars, making any precise form of comparison difficult. As noted, the *Marine Corps Gazette* article from which the list of fourth-generation characteristics was derived combined historical observation of trends with extrapolations into the future. While some of the characteristics of NIWs also come from past experiences, I have limited my characterizations to experience to date with more contemporary instances of NIWs and have not tried to extrapolate those trends forward.

The characteristics can be divided into political and military categories. At the political level, the most striking feature of these wars is their nearly total reversal of the kinds of goals found in traditional insurgencies. Unlike traditional civil wars, the control of government is often not the clear objective of both sides. In a number of cases of NIWs, the "rebel" force articulates no political objectives or statements of ideological principles about how it would organize itself to rule. The Revolutionary United Front (RUF) of Sierra Leone, for instance, never issued a manifesto of any kind, and this is not unusual. The apparent reason for this is that the RUF movement has had neither the intention nor desire to gain control of and govern the country, and this is not unusual in NIWs. Rather, in a number of cases, the highly nontraditional political purpose is anarchical, in the sense of seeking to destabilize the country from governmental control by anyone. Creating anarchy is, of course, a political goal, but not one that is accorded legitimacy in a state-centered, Westphalian world. In these cases, most notably the narco-insurgencies of South America and some parts of Asia and the criminal insurgencies of parts of Africa, the real goal is to create a sense of total lawlessness that maximizes the group's ability to enrich itself either through thievery and worse or by controlling or protecting narcotics trafficking. Such groups often adopt splendid political ("revolutionary front") or otherwise high-sounding (the "Lord's Army" of Uganda) names to mask the basic criminality that forms their purpose.

There is another political characteristic that also helps differentiate NIWs from traditional internal wars and explain the savagery that often dominates these conflicts. Traditional civil wars, as noted, are fought for control of the government of a country, and a central factor in which side prevails is the loyalty of the country's population—the so-called "hearts and minds" of the people. This "center of gravity" is a point of competition for both sides, and neither wants to drive the people into the other side's arms by committing hideous and unacceptable acts of violence against the population. The need to appeal to the people thus moderates the violence, especially against noncombatant civilians.

Since the goal in NIWs is not to govern but to intimidate or kill those members of the population who might be in opposition, there is no such motivation toward moderation. In Bosnia during the first half of the 1990s, Bosnian Serbs did not seek to appeal to Bosnian Muslims or vice versa; rather, their aim was to drive people from their homes, move in, and claim the land by virtue of possession. Similarly, the Rwandan Hutus were clearly not appealing politically for the support of the Tutsi as the rampage proceeded; they simply wanted to kill as many people as possible. The religious purification of the Sudan by murdering non-Muslims is similar. This absence of a shared center of gravity that needs to be nurtured makes NIWs effectively like wars between states (interstate wars) rather than internal wars (intrastate wars) politically. Like interstate wars, the purpose is to subdue, not to win over, the opponent. Unlike traditional intrastate wars, there is no battle for the "hearts and minds of men" to moderate the slaughter.

The military characteristics of NIWs follow from these nontraditional political characteristics and provide a close parallel with the military characteristics of fourth-generation warfare. Since there are no clear political objectives for these affairs, they do not translate into strategic guidance to form conventional military objectives and operations. The military units that conduct these forms of hostilities are typically highly irregular, not uniformed or organized into coherent rank orderings of officers and enlisted soldiers. They are poorly trained, if they have received any military training at all, and are unaware or contemptuous of normal conventions of war. Similarly, they normally lack a sense of military order or discipline. It is not unusual to have these troops referred to not as "soldiers" but as "fighters," since that is what they truly are. In a number of instances, these fighters have been little more than children, with members of the ranks reportedly no more than ten- to twelve-year-olds, often kidnapped and forced into service by the fear of personal or family consequences if they refuse (the Lord's Army of Uganda, for instance, kidnaps children from orphanages and threatens to kill them if they resist becoming "soldiers").

Given these characteristics of the forces, the savagery and atrocity associated with these wars should come as little surprise. Echoing the fourth-generation lack of distinction between civilians and military targets, they are marked by high incidences of attacks by fighters against unarmed civilians, notably women and children, the elderly, and other similarly helpless beings (atrocities in the Sudan are a particularly gruesome example). In most NIWs, there are rarely any encounters between the organized armed forces of the two (or more) contending sides. The large reason for this pattern is that the sides are not organized into military forces that can contend against other organized forces; attacking, mutilating, or killing helpless, innocent civilians is their form of asymmetrical warfare.

The Prospects for NIWs. One of the notable aspects of NIWs is where they occur. For the most part, internal violence, of which the NIWs are a prominent part, happen in the poorest parts of the world where the lives of average citizens are among the most miserable and where there is little sense that things can get much worse. This is also the description of the places that have been the breeding grounds of some terrorists—notably, the recruitment grounds for a number of the fighters associated with Al Qaeda and other terrorist organizations. While the practitioners of asymmetrical warfare may be motivated by different end states and aspirations, they do share a fairly common breeding ground (this is discussed in the terrorist context in Chapter 10).

Before September 11, 2001, refocused our attention, there was a policy debate about whether it was wise for the United States to involve itself in these situations. A major observation about NIWs is that they generally cannot be ended internally, because neither the government nor its opposition possesses the physical capability for toppling the other (which the "insurgents" may not want to do, preferring to have an ineffectual government to the prospects of an effective successor). It then becomes a question of whether there is sufficient outside interest in trying to do something to end whatever atrocity is occurring. This is an ongoing problem that is examined in its operational and philosophical aspects in Chapter 11. The point is that the prospects for future NIWs, not unlike terrorism, are as good as is the amount of suffering in the world. The question is whether we care as much, less, or more about the prospects now as we did before asymmetrical warfare landed directly on our doorsteps.

CONCLUSION: NEW FORM OR NEW FACE OF WAR?

We conclude by going back and asking the question raised at the beginning of the chapter: Is the kind of warfare that America faces literally something new? Or is asymmetrical warfare a "back to the future" proposition, borrowing from the title of Goulding's article in the U.S. Army's journal, *Parameters*? As the analysis has sought to demonstrate, in a purely military sense, what is now called asymmetrical warfare does not represent a great change in war but is instead the approach that has been taken throughout history by weaker protagonists when facing superior forces. The American reintroduction to this kind of warfare in Vietnam did not, however, prepare us for an opponent who would change the rules of engagement so radically as to attack and destroy the kinds of civilian targets that were attacked on September 11, 2001. The innovation was not the dynamics of war, it was the physical object of attack.

If asymmetrical warfare as a generic concept is nothing really new, its manifestations in fourth-generation warfare and NIW does pose some differences from past experience. Clearly, the high level of irregularity of the forces we face—in terms of composition, style, methods, and objectives of fighting—is a factor we have not encountered before. At the same time, fighting not directed at political goals of gaining or maintaining governance is a novelty in our experience that creates wartime difficulties of sorting out the sides and postwar difficulties in reconstructing a peace. We understand people who fight like us for the reasons we fight; we are not quite so certain how to deal with people who accept neither our methods nor our ends. It is not clear that we have either the military or political solutions to this phenomenon.

We had better anticipate, however, that we will face more asymmetrical foes in the future. One of the other clear characteristics of the contemporary environment is the huge and growing chasm of conventional military capabilities between the countries of the West and the rest of the world. The RMA means, to repeat, that no developing world country or movement has any military chance against the United States or its friends and allies if they fight on our terms (symmetrically). The Iraqis did not understand that in 1991 and paid a price they were unwilling to pay again in 2003. The Taliban either did not understand it or could not adapt quickly enough when confronted with Western airpower in 2001. Not many others are going to make the same mistake.

That leads to the conclusion that, at a minimum, future opponents are likely to confront the United Sates with highly unorthodox, unconventional, and unanticipated problems. If what we learn from September 11, 2001, is how to combat terrorism (see Chapter 10) and no more, we will have missed the real novelty of the "new kind of war," which is the need to change and adapt and to be ready for the unexpected. The alternatives are unattractive. As Goulding puts it, "Military force like those of the United States and its allies who constitute the bulk of 'well organized and well paid regular forces' and generally play by the rules may, in their next battles, wish fervently that it was against soldiers of their own ilk they were fighting."

If the concepts underlying asymmetrical war are hardly new, the ways in which it is conducted are constantly evolving and adapting to changed physical and political circumstances. The tactics that worked in the Vietnamese mountains and jungles are not directly applicable to arid Iraq, and so the Iraqi resistance to the American occupation fights differently to rid themselves of the Americans than did the Vietnamese. Future asymmetrical opponents will also seek to present us with novel problems for which we are unprepared. The secret to confounding asymmetrical warriors is anticipating and preparing for what they will do before they can do it.

Challenge!

IS THERE A NEW KIND OF WAR?

The initial, highly emotional reaction to the terrorist attacks of September 11, 2001, in the United States suggested that these were somehow an unprecedented phenomenon, and the rage and smoldering desire for revenge could most easily be translated into the analogy of militarily crushing those who had committed these atrocious acts. The idea that we were faced with a new kind of war was born of this conjunction of the apparent uniqueness of the act and the desire for a military reaction.

Is the analogy accurate? The burden of much of the analysis in this chapter has been that it is not. The central point has been that terrorism has long been a central manner in which weak groups attempt to assert their will over stronger groups. A major thrust of these efforts involve changing the rules of engagement between contending forces to remove some of the advantage the stronger party has and to, in effect, level the playing field or tilt it in the weaker party's favor. Since part of that leveling entails rejecting the rules and conventions under which the dominant player operates, the result is likely to be outrage when the weaker party attacks. This dynamic of fourth-generation or asymmetrical warfare dates back to antiquity. The uniqueness of the current application is its scale and the fact it has been visited directly against the American population. Would we have the same sense of rage and the same depth of reaction if airliners had attacked the 1,381-foot Jin Mao building of Shanghai in China? Or the world's tallest buildings, the 1,483-foot tall Petronas towers in Kuala Lumpur, Malaysia?

The question asked in the title of this *Challenge!* is really two related questions. Is the form of activity in which the United States is engaged properly described as a form of war? And is that activity something new? The answer to the second question is fairly clearly no, but the answer to whether this is a form of war is not so clear. Is it more useful to think about this kind of campaign in warlike terms, or is some other framework more useful? What do you think? If you believe war is not the best way to think about countering terrorism, what do you think is a better way?

Countering terrorism is not the only form that asymmetrical warfare has taken or will take. Clearly, for instance, the Iraqi resistance is also a form of asymmetrical war in which urban guerrilla warfare in the form of ambushes and random bombings using improvised explosive devices (IEDs) are the primary tools of combat, and leading the United States to conclude that it is not worth the pain being caused is the method chosen to force the Americans to abandon their quest. Is it worth it for the United States to persevere? Should we have anticipated this problem? What do you think?

Selected Bibliography

Belfigio, Valentine J. *A Study of Ancient Roman Amphibious and Offensive Sea-Ground Task Force Operations.* Lewiston, NY: Edwin Mellen Press, 2001.

Boot, Max. "The Struggle to Transform the Military." *Foreign Affairs* 84, 2 (March/April 2005), 103–118.

Brodie, Bernard, and Fawn M. Brodie. *From Crossbow to H-Bomb: The Evolution of Weapons and Tactics of Warfare.* Bloomington: Indiana University Press, 1973.

Dobbins, James. "Iraq: Winning the Unwinnable War." *Foreign Affairs* 84, 1 (January/February 2005), 6–25.

Gallagher, James J. *Low-Intensity Conflict: A Guide for Tactics, Techniques, and Procedures.* Harrisburg, PA: Stackpole Books, 1992.

Goulding, Vincent J., Jr. "Back to the Future with Asymmetrical Warfare." *Parameters* XXX, 4 (Winter 2000–2001), 21–30.

Haass, Richard N. "Regime Change and Its Limits." *Foreign Affairs* 84, 4 (July/August 2005), 66–78.

Keegan, John. *A History of Warfare.* London: Hutchison, 1991.

Lewis, Bernard. "Freedom and Justice in the Modern Middle East." *Foreign Affairs* 84, 3 (May/June 2005), 36–51.

Lind, William S., Keith Nightengale, John F. Schmitt, Joseph W. Sutton, and Gary I. Wilson. "The Changing Face of War: Into the Fourth Generation." *Marine Corps Gazette*, October 1989, 21–26.

Luttwak, Edward N. "Iraq: The Logic of Disengagement." *Foreign Affairs* 84, 1 (January/February 2005), 26–36.

Mao tse-Tung. *Mao tse-Tung on Guerrilla Warfare* (translated by Samuel B. Griffith). New York: Praeger, 1961.

Moore, Harold G., and James L. Galloway. *We Were Soldiers Once . . . and Young: Ia Drang: The Battle That Changed the War in Vietnam.* New York: Harper and Row, 1993.

Snow, Donald M. *Distant Thunder: Patterns of Conflict in the Developing World* (2nd ed.). Armonk, NY: M. E. Sharpe, 1997.

———. *Uncivil Wars: International Security and the New Internal Conflicts.* Boulder, CO: Lynne Rienner Publishers, 1996.

———. *When America Fights: The Uses of U.S. Military Force.* Washington, DC: CQ Press, 2000.

Sun Tzu. *The Art of War* (translated by Samuel B. Griffith). Oxford, UK: Oxford University Press, 1963.

Van Creveld, Martin. *The Transformation of War.* New York: Free Press, 1991.

CHAPTER 10

Terrorism

PREVIEW

The most dramatic form that asymmetrical warfare presents to the United States is terrorism, and more specifically, the international religious terrorism represented by organizations like Al Qaeda. The terrorist attacks of September 11 galvanized public attention on this problem, and American national security policy has had the global war on terrorism (GWOT) as its central focus ever since. In this chapter, we investigate the nature of the terrorist problem, how it is changing, and what can be done about it. We begin by examining the dynamics of terrorism: what is it, what do terrorists seek to do, who are they, and what causes people to become terrorists? We then move to how terrorism has evolved as a problem since September 11 and what kinds of efforts we can mount against it. Based on this information and perspectives raised throughout the case, we conclude by suggesting some elements of a comprehensive terrorism suppression strategy.

Terrorism and the well-publicized GWOT have dominated the national security agenda in the United States since the September 11 attacks by Al Qaeda against New York and Washington, D.C., targets. The problem of terrorism was not unknown within the government and expert communities before September 11, and we know after the fact that there had been premonitions and even fairly specific warnings that Al Qaeda would attempt something like what they did. Because terrorism had heretofore been an apparently minor problem that had captured the central attention of neither the public nor top political leaders, the warnings went unheeded and American vulnerability was revealed in shocking, bloody relief.

The problem of terrorism is unique and enigmatic. It is an ancient practice that most historians date back at least to biblical times, and it has recurred episodically and persistently ever since to the point that it is not unfair to characterize the phenomenon of terrorism as a permanent feature of the international environment. Individual terrorists and their causes come and go, but terrorism remains. At the same time, terrorism is one, arguably the most extreme, form of asymmetrical warfare and thus an important part of the overall national security environment we introduced in Chapter 9. Finding a way to deal effectively with terrorism is thus a central factor in modern, post–September 11 defense policy.

The GWOT, as the central organizing device for dealing with this problem, is now roughly five years old. It has had some successes, notably in capturing or otherwise suppressing elements of the old Al Qaeda network, but the problem of terrorism has not abated. The apparently monolithic threat posed by Al Qaeda itself is smaller than it was in 2001, but the problem of terrorism itself is not: new permutations have arisen that are, if anything, more provocative and dangerous. Most share radical Islam as a foundation, but from Chechnya to Indonesia, new and different organizations have emerged as new challenges: international terrorism has become a hydra-headed beast.

Before turning to the examination of the phenomena, four related observations are necessary to condition the comments that follow. First, although we speak of a GWOT, the use of the term *war* is unfortunate, deceiving, and distorting. As the term is normally used, war refers to armed combat between combatants organized as states or states versus organized oppositions within states. War, in other words, is an action that pits people against other people and the groups attack one another to impose their will on those other people. Terrorism, on the other hand, is a more intangible idea, a method by which people seek to accomplish goals. We cannot attack and subdue an idea. What we can do is to oppose and subdue people who act from ideas—we can make war on terrorist organizations like Al Qaeda (although their lack of a territorial base makes subduing them difficult); the best we can do with an idea is to discredit it.

The second observation flows from the first: the war analogy is further flawed because it implies that the opposition can be defeated—that the purpose of the war is to suppress and eliminate the opposition. Terrorism is an ancient practice that transcends efforts to suppress and defeat individual manifestations—defeating Al Qaeda or any other terrorist organization will not eliminate the phenomenon, just particular practitioners. There will always be terrorists somewhere, and the realistic purpose of those opposed to terrorism is to *contain* the problem, not eliminate it. The Bush administration tacitly admitted these kinds of problems in 2005, when it began to refer to the Global Struggle against Violent Extremists (GSAVE).

Third, because terrorism cannot ever be eliminated altogether, efforts in opposition to it are exercises in *risk reduction*, not risk elimination. Risk, as already noted in Chapter 6, is the difference between threats to our interests and our capabilities (or resources) to counter, contain, or eliminate those threats. Although the level of terrorist threat ebbs and flows across time, it is essentially always potentially greater than the resources available to effectively thwart all manifestations of the threat. Terrorism, to paraphrase ex-German chancellor Helmut Schmidt, is a problem to be worked, not solved for once and for all. Any strategy or policy that is aimed at "smashing" or "defeating" terrorism is bound to come up short.

Fourth, terrorism is not only an international, and thus national security, problem. Domestic terrorists also pose a threat to the safety of Americans, as evidenced by Timothy McVeigh and Theodore Kaczynski (the Unabomber). Up to now, however, most domestic terrorism has been carried out on a comparatively narrow basis that constitutes more of a criminal than a national security problem. The long terrorist campaign by the Ku Klux Klan against selected Americans is the major exception to this rule. Thus, our discussion largely centers on the international terrorism level, although we also incorporate domestic terrorism examples in the discussion.

In order to facilitate our discussion, we largely use three different organizations or movements that have been deemed terrorist as examples. For obvious reasons, a good deal focuses on Islamist (more properly *jihadist*) Middle Eastern groups featuring Al Qaeda and its successors. Because they burst on the international public stage with such fury in 2004, the Chechen separatist movement is also mentioned. To a lesser degree, the Indonesian terrorist movement Jemaah Islamiyah is also included.

DEFINING TERRORISM

The first step in coming to grips with terrorism is defining the term. It is an important consideration because so many phenomena in the contemporary international arena are labeled terrorist. For some (including many in government), terrorism has become the sobriquet for anything or anybody we oppose. This makes a definition particularly important as a means to measure whether a particular movement or act is terrorist or not. Without a set of criteria to tell us what does and does not constitute terrorism, we are left disabled in trying to make a determination.

This is not merely a semantic exercise. Take, for instance, the current emphasis on Chechen separatists and their campaign that the Russian government has called terrorist. Certainly, actions such as enlisting suicide terrorists to blow up two Russian airliners and the brutal siege of the school in Beslan in the Caucasus were hideous, brutal acts that comport with an understanding of terrorism, but is it correct to label the movement that commissioned and carried out the acts terrorist as a result? In context, when the Russian government of then-President Boris Yeltsin used the Russian army to attack Chechnya in 1995 to wipe out the secessionist movement there (among other things, leveling the capital of Grozny) and current President Vladimir Putin renewed the campaign in 1999, there were widespread international accusations the Russian government was terrorizing the Chechens and engaging in crimes against humanity (acts of state terrorism). So who is the terrorist here?

Having an agreed definition of terrorism would help answer this and similar questions about other potentially terrorist activities, but unfortunately, such an agreement does not exist. Rather, there are virtually as many different definitions as there are people and organizations making the distinctions. There are also some commonalities that recur across definers, which allow us to adopt a definition for present purposes. A few arguably representative examples aid in drawing distinctions.

The U.S. Department of State offers the official governmental definition, which is applied in its annual survey of international terrorism. Its definition of terrorism is "premeditated, politically motivated violence perpetrated against noncombatant targets by subnational groups or clandestine agents, usually intended to influence an audience" (quoted in Krueger and Laitin). In *Attacking Terrorism*, co-author Audrey Kurth Cronin says terrorism is distinguished by its political nature, its nonstate base, its targeting of innocent noncombatants, and the illegality of its acts. Jessica Stern, in *Terrorism in the Name of God*, defines terrorism as "an act or threat of violence against noncombatants with the objective of exacting revenge, intimidating, or otherwise influencing an audience." Alan Dershowitz (in *Why Terrorism Works*) offers no definition himself but notes that definitions typically include reference to terrorist targets, perpetrators, and acts.

These definitions and similar ones from others in the field differ at the margins but have common cores. All of them share three common points of reference: terrorist acts (illegal, often hideous and atrocious), terrorist targets (usually innocent noncombatants), and terrorist purposes (political persuasion or influence). The only difference among them is whether they specify the nature of terrorists and their political base: the State Department, Cronin, and Dershowitz all identify terrorist organizations as nonstate-based actors. Cronin in particular emphasizes that "although states can terrorize, by definition they cannot be terrorists."

My own definition incorporates the three components of terrorist acts, targets, and purposes but not the criterion of terrorist organizations as nonstate actors. Historically, states have been leading terrorists either through the actions of government organizations like the secret police or by creating, commissioning, or controlling the activities of terrorists. In the contemporary setting, almost all terrorist organizations are nonstate based, and this fact is at the heart of our difficulty in dealing with them. Defining terrorism as a nonstate-based activity, however, removes an important category of past (and conceivably future) activity from the definitional reach of terrorism. The nonstate basis is a characteristic of modern terrorism, not a defining element.

Based on these distinctions, terrorism is defined as "the commission of atrocious acts against a target population normally to gain compliance with some demands the terrorists insist upon." Terrorism thus consists of three related phenomena, each of which must be present in some manner for something to be considered an act of terrorism. If all three elements are present, so is terrorism. If one or more elements are missing, the phenomenon is not terrorism but something else. Discussing each helps enliven an understanding of what constitutes terrorism.

Terrorist Acts

The first part of the definition refers to *terrorist acts*, which are the visible manifestation of terrorism and the part of the dynamic of the phenomena with which most people are most familiar. Several comments can be made about terrorist acts.

Terrorist acts are distinguished from other political expressions in that they are uniformly illegal. Terrorist acts are intended to upset the normalcy of life through destructive acts aimed at either injuring or killing people or destroying things. Regardless of the professed underlying motives of terrorists (normally couched in lofty political terms), the actions they commit—and especially their focus on noncombatants whose only "guilt" is being part of the targeted group—break laws and are subject to criminal prosecution. By raising the rhetoric of terrorist actions to acts of war (currently holy war, or *jihad*), terrorists may seek to elevate what they do to a higher plane ("one man's terrorist is another man's freedom fighter"), but the simple fact remains that terrorist acts are criminal in nature.

The general purpose of terrorist acts is to frighten the target audience: indeed, the word terrorism is derived from the Latin root *terrere*, which means "to frighten." The method of inducing fright is through the commission of random, unpredictable acts of violence that seek to induce such fear that those who witness the acts (or learn of them) will conclude that compliance with terrorist demands is preferable to living with the fear of being future victims themselves. Acts of terrorism are not particularly aimed at the actual victims themselves (who are normally randomly selected and whose individual fate does not "matter" to the terrorist) but at the audience who views the actions. As Brian Jenkins puts it, *"Terrorists want a lot of people watching and a lot of people listening, and not a lot of people dead"* (emphasis in original). The dynamic of inducing this fright is the disruption of the predictability and safety of life within society, one of whose principal functions is to make existence predictable and safe. Ultimately, a major purpose of terrorism may be to undermine this vital fiber of society, a goal shared with fourth-generation warriors.

Beyond frightening the target audience, individual terrorist acts are committed for a variety of reasons, not limited to the normally expressed political goals of particular terrorist organizations. Al Qaeda, for instance, says its most fundamental goal is the expulsion of the West (especially the United States) from the holy lands of Islam and that its acts (especially those serving bin Laden's *fatwa* calling for killing Americans everywhere) are intended to further that goal. But that is not the only motivation for particular actions.

Terrorists may also act for a variety of other reasons. Jenkins provides a list of six other, generally less lofty, purposes for terrorist actions. First, terrorist actions may be aimed at exacting special concessions, such as ransom, the release of prisoners (generally members of the terrorist group), or publicizing a message. The capture and threatened (or actual) beheading of foreigners by Iraqi resistance groups to force countries to withdraw their nationals from Iraq is a case in point in the use of terrorist actions for gaining concessions. In that case, the capture of foreign nationals was at the base of demands for prisoner release and to force foreign countries to withdraw from the international relief effort in that country. Jemaah Islamiyah carried out its 2004 attack on the Australian embassy in Jakarta, Indonesia, and promptly announced that it would perpetrate similar attacks if its leader Abu Bakar Bashir was not released from prison.

Second, terrorists may act to gain publicity for their causes. Before Palestinian terrorists kidnapped a series of airliners and then launched an attack on the Israeli compound at the Munich Olympics in 1972, hardly anyone outside the region had ever heard of the Palestinian cause; the terrorist actions got them global awareness of that cause. The publicity may be intended to remind a world that has shifted its attention away from a particular group and its activities that it is still active and that it is still pursuing its goals. One of the apparent reasons for the spate of Chechen violence in 2004 for which Chechen leader Shamil Basayev claims credit was to remind the world that the Chechen movement to gain independence from Russia is still alive.

A third, and more fundamental, purpose of terrorist acts is to cause widespread disorder that demoralizes society and breaks down the social order in a country. This, of course, is a very ambitious purpose and one that presumably can only be undertaken through a widespread campaign that includes a large number of terrorist acts, and it is the kind of objective most likely to be carried out by governments or semigovernmental actors. The suicide terror campaign by Hamas against Israeli civilians (and the Israeli counterattacks against Palestinians) provides an example of terrorism for this purpose.

A fourth, more tactical use of terrorism is to provoke overreaction by a government in the form of repressive action, reprisals, and overly brutal counterterrorism that may lead to the overthrow of the reactive government. This was a favorite tactic of the Viet Cong in the Vietnam war and evoked the ironic analogy among Americans of building schools during the day (as a way to pacify the population) and then bombing those schools at night (because they became the source of Viet Cong actions after nightfall). It is not clear whether some of the acts committed against American forces in Iraq by the resistance have been to try to elicit American overreactions and thus fuel anti-Americanism among Iraqi citizens.

A fifth purpose of terror may be to enforce obedience and cooperation within a target population. Campaigns of terror directed by the governments of states against their own citizens often have this purpose and are often assigned to a secret police or similar paramilitary organizations. The actions of the KGB in the Soviet Union, the Gestapo and other similar organization in Nazi Germany, and the infamous death squads in Argentina during the 1960s and 1970s are all examples of the use of government terror to intimidate and frighten their own population into submission. At a less formal governmental level, many of the actions of the Ku Klux Klan during the latter nineteenth and early twentieth centuries against Black Americans qualify as well.

Jenkins's sixth purpose of terrorist action is punishment. Terrorists often argue that an action they take is aimed at a particular person or place because that person or institution is somehow guilty of a particular transgression and is thus being meted out appropriate punishment for what the terrorists consider a crime. Although the Israeli government would be appalled at the prospect of calling its counterterrorist campaign to bulldoze the homes of the families of suicide terrorists (or bombing the homes of dissident leaders) acts of terror, from the vantage point of the Palestinian targets of the attacks, they certainly must seem so.

Stern adds a seventh motivation that is internal to the terrorist organization: morale. Like any other organization, and especially terrorist groups in which the "operatives" are generally young and not terribly mature, it may be necessary from time to time to carry out a terrorist attack simply to demonstrate to the membership the continuing potency of the group as a way to keep the membership focused and their morale high. As Stern puts it, "Attacks sometimes have more to do with rousing the troops than terrorizing the victims." Improving or maintaining morale may also have useful spin-off effects, such as helping in recruiting new members to the group or in raising funds to support the organization's activities.

A final comment about terrorist acts is whether, or to what degree, they are successful. The answer is rather clearly a mixed one that has to do with the scale of the actions and their intended results. In some cases, terrorism has been highly successful, but usually in relatively small ways where the terrorists' purposes were bounded and compliance with their demands was not overly odious. To cite one example, terrorist demands to release what they view as political prisoners (usually jailed members of their group) have, on occasion, been complied with, although some countries are more prone to comply than others. Likewise, the Iraqi resistance's campaign of kidnapping and threatening to execute foreign nationals if the countries did not leave Iraq has been somewhat successful and will almost certainly be duplicated in the future by other asymmetrical warriors who include acts of terrorism in their operational repertoires.

It is when terrorists make large demands and follow them up with sizable actions that they tend to be less successful. When terrorists come to pose a basic perceived threat to the target country (often because of the audacity of what they have done or the perceived obnoxiousness of what they propose), the reaction by the target may be, and usually is, increased resolve rather than compliance. The September 11, 2001, attacks, after all, did not result in a groundswell of sentiment for the United States to quit the Middle East (especially Saudi Arabia) as bin Laden and Al Qaeda demanded; rather, it stiffened the will of the country to resist (by late 2005, American troops had, in fact, left the Saudi Kingdom). This poses something of a quandary to the terrorist: the more ambitious a group becomes, the more likely it is to increase opposition to achievement of its goals. On the other hand, sizing terrorist acts downward to levels that will not increase resolve may result in less positive, and less than satisfying, outcomes.

What this discussion of terrorist acts seeks to demonstrate is that, like virtually everything else about the subject, the acts that terrorists commit occur for a variety of reasons. Some of these are more purposive and "noble" than others, but it is not clear what may motivate a particular action. Moreover, different reasons may motivate different groups at different times and under different circumstances. Knowing that a terrorist attack has occurred, in other words, does not necessarily tell you why it has been committed.

Terrorist Targets

Akin to the military objectives in more conventional war, the targets of terrorists can be divided into two related categories. The first is people, and the objective is to kill, maim, or otherwise cause some members of the target population to suffer as an example for the rest of the population. The second category is physical targets, attacks against which are designed to disrupt and destroy societal capabilities and to demonstrate the vulnerability of the target society. The two categories are obviously related in that most of the physical targets worth attacking contain people who will be killed or injured in the process. As well, attacking either category demonstrates the inability of the target population to provide protection for its members and valued artifices, thus questioning the efficacy of resisting terrorist demands.

There are subtle differences and problems associated with concentrating on one category of target or another. Clearly, attacks directly intended to kill or injure people are the most personal and evoke the greatest emotion in the target population, including the will to resist and to seek vengeance. From the vantage point of the terrorist, the reason to attack people (beyond some simple blood lust) is to attack the target population's will to resist the demands that terrorists make. In Snow and Drew, we refer to this as *cost-tolerance*, the level of suffering one is willing to endure in the face of some undesirable situation. In the case of terrorist targeting, the terrorist seeks to exceed the target's cost-tolerance by making the target conclude that it is less painful (physically or mentally) to accede to the terrorist's demands than it is to continue to resist those demands. The terrorist seeks to exceed cost-tolerance by maximizing the level of fear and anxiety that the target experiences because of the effects (often hideous) of attacks on other members of the target group. The terrorist wants the target group to become so afraid of being the next victim that they cave in and accept the terrorist demands. If cost-tolerance is exceeded, the terrorist wins; if the target remains resolute, the terrorist does not succeed (which may not be the same thing as saying the terrorist loses).

Recognizing that producing fright is the objective reinforces Jenkins's observation about the murderousness of those committing terrorist acts against targets. It is, after all, impossible to frighten dead people, nor can the victims of murder capitulate and accede to demands. Only survivors who view the carnage and wonder if they will be next can be so manipulated, and the terrorist has a vested interest in keeping enough around to buckle to terrorist demands.

Overcoming cost-tolerance is not an easy task, and it usually fails. For one thing, terrorist organizations are generally small with limited resources, meaning that they usually lack the wherewithal to attack and kill a large enough portion of the target population to make members of that population become individually fearful enough to tip the scales (blowing up people on airplanes may be a partial exception). One of the great fears associated with terrorist groups obtaining and using weapons of mass destruction is that such a turn of events would change that calculus. For another thing, attacking and killing innocent members of a target group (at least innocent from the vantage point of the group) may (and usually does) infuriate its members and increase rather than decrease the will to resist. That was certainly the case during World War II in Germany, where constant aerial bombardment failed to destroy the German peoples' will to survive and may actually have strengthened their will to resist.

Standing up to terrorist attacks on human targets is not always easy, as the example of hostage-taking in Iraq shows. In such cases, officials are placed in an obvious quandary. On one hand, when hostages are taken and their execution threatened if some demands are unmet, there is an obvious and understandable instinct to try to save the hostage(s); and in the absence of an ability to rescue them physically (which, in the Iraqi cases, was apparently impossible), the only means available is to accede to the terrorists' demands (have cost-tolerance exceeded). On the other hand, doing so means the terrorists succeed and are likely to be emboldened to do the same thing again, as was the case in Iraq when several countries pulled their workers out after some of their nationals were kidnapped and threatened with execution. The

Amplification 10.1

THE MORALITY OF SAVING TARGETS

Dealing with terrorists always poses difficult moral dilemmas that different people and countries handle in different ways. One of the most difficult dilemmas is what to do in instances when terrorists capture hostages and demand concessions that, if not honored, will result in the execution of the hostages.

There are two ways to respond to such occurrences and demands. One, prominently associated with the American and British governments, is to refuse categorically to negotiate with terrorists. The rationale is that if governments do negotiate, and especially comply, with these demands, the terrorists are somehow legitimized and, at a more practical level, encouraged to repeat the kidnapping. The refusal also usually condemns the kidnapped to execution, bringing pain and grief to their families and friends, who are also fellow countrymen. As the Iran-Contra scandal revealed, this principle is sometimes ignored.

The other way to respond is to take notice of the terrorist demands, negotiate with them, and potentially agree to the demands the terrorists make. This solution has the likely humane outcome of saving a human life or lives, but it also represents capitulation to the terrorists and the success of their action. In the context of the war on terrorism, it amounts to nearly a surrender to the terrorists.

In principle and in the abstract, the refusal to give in to terrorist demands has overwhelming appeal because it is a more virile response than negotiating with terrorists. At the same time, that refusal amounts to signing a death warrant for the victim, and that is not always politically or morally acceptable. Because of the moral dilemma, governments react in both ways on different occasions.

Americans and British refused to accede in these demands, and a number of their citizens were executed. In those cases, the terrorists did not prevail, but they also did not visibly lose, since (at this writing) none of them had been captured and brought to justice for their deeds. This situation is difficult for policymakers, as discussed in Amplification 10.1.

When the targets are physical things rather than people per se, the problems and calculations change. When the target of terrorists is a whole society, the range of potential targets is virtually boundless. In attacking places, the terrorist seeks to deprive the target population of whatever pleasure or life-sustaining or life-enhancing value the particular target may provide. The list of what we used to call *countervalue* targets when speaking of nuclear targeting (things people value, such as their lives and what makes those lives commodious) covers a very broad range of objects, from hydroelectric plants to athletic stadiums, from nuclear power generators to military facilities, from highways to research facilities, and so on. Compiling a list for any large community is a very sobering experience. The problem is further complicated because acting to protect one class of targets may simply cause terrorists to move on to another class (a process known as target substitution).

It is unreasonable to assume that the physical potential target list for any country can be made uniformly invulnerable. There are simply too many possible targets, and the means of protecting them are sufficiently discrete that there is little overlap in function (protecting a football stadium from bombers may or may not have much carryover in terms of protecting nuclear power plants from seizure). As a result, there will always be a gap between the potential threats and the ability to negate all those threats, and the consequence is a certain level of risk remaining: realistically, protecting targets is an exercise in risk reduction, not elimination.

Terrorist Objectives

The final element in the definition of terrorism is the objectives, or reasons, for which terrorists do what they do. These objectives, of course, are directed against the target population and involve the commission of terrorist acts, so the discussion of objectives cannot be entirely divorced from the other two elements of what constitutes terrorism.

For present purposes, our discussion of terrorist objectives refers to the broader outcomes that terrorists seek (or say they seek) to accomplish. Objectives are the long-range reasons that terrorists wage campaigns of terrorism. In the short run, terrorists may engage in particular actions for a variety of reasons, as already noted (group morale or recruitment, for instance). What they seek ultimately to accomplish is the province of terrorist objectives.

It is useful to distinguish among types of goals terrorists pursue. The major objectives of terrorists, their ultimate or strategic goals, refer to the long-term political objectives to which they aspire. For Al Qaeda, for instance, the removal of Americans from the Arabian Peninsula is a strategic goal, for Chechen separatists, independence from Russia is the ultimate objective. At the same time, terrorists also pursue interim, or tactical, goals, which generally involve the successful commission of terrorist acts against the target population. The purpose, in the case of tactical objectives, is to demonstrate continuing viability and potency, to remind the target of their presence and menace, and to erode resistance to their strategic goals.

Because most terrorist groups are ultimately political in their purposes, terrorist objectives are political as well. To paraphrase the Clausewitzian dictum that war is politics by other means, so too is terrorism politics by other, extreme, means. Likewise, the objectives that terrorists pursue are extreme, at least to the target population if not to the terrorists themselves. Sometimes terrorist objectives are widely known and clearly articulated, and at other times they are not. Ultimately, however, campaigns of terror gain their meaning in the pursuit of some goal or goals, and their success or failure is measured by the extent that those goals are achieved.

As a form of asymmetrical warfare, terrorism is, of course, the method of the militarily weak and conceptually unacceptable. The extremely asymmetrical nature of terrorist actions arises from the fact that terrorists cannot compete with their targets by the accepted methods of the target society. Terrorists lack the military resources to engage in open warfare, at which they would be easily defeated, or in the forum of public discourse and decision, because their objectives are unacceptable, distasteful, or even bizarre to the target population. Thus, terrorists can neither impose their purposes on the target nor persuade the target to adopt whatever objectives they want. These facts narrow the terrorist group's options.

The fact that terrorist objectives are politically objectionable to the target sets up the confrontation between the terrorists and the target. Normally, terrorist goals are stated in terms of changing policies (Palestinian statehood or the right to repatriation within Israel, for example) or laws (releasing classes of unjustly detained people) that the majority in the target state find unacceptable. Since the terrorists are in a minority, they cannot bring about the changes they demand by normal electoral or legislative means, and they are likely to be viewed as so basically lunatic and unrealistic by the target audience that it will not accord seriousness to the demands or those who make them. To the terrorists, of course, the demands make perfect sense, and they are frustrated and angered by the treatment their demands are given. The stage is thus set for confrontation.

Terrorists achieve their objectives by overcoming the will of the target population to resist, or cost-tolerance. The campaign of terrorist threats and acts is intended to convince the target population that acceding to the terrorist demands is preferable to the continuing anxiety and fear of future terrorism. If the target population concludes that giving in to the terrorist demands is better than continuing to resist, cost-tolerance has been exceeded and the terrorist wins. If continuing resistance (even increased defiance) is the outcome, then cost-tolerance is not exceeded and the terrorists do not succeed.

The failure to achieve strategic objectives is not the same thing as total failure, however. The successful terrorizing of a large society by a small group of terrorists is a tall order, one for which the terrorists (almost by definition) do not have the resources to achieve. At its zenith, after all, Al Qaeda consisted of probably fewer than ten thousand active members, who could hardly bring the United States to its knees. Terrorism is, after all, the "tactic of the weak," and there are real limitations on the extent of the danger such groups can physically pose. The degree to which we inflate—even overinflate the extent of the threat is, arguably, an indicator of terrorist success.

Determining whether terrorists achieve their goals or fail is complicated by the contrast between the tactical and strategic levels of objectives, making the compilation of a "score card" difficult. Modern terrorists have rarely been successful at the strategic level of attaining long-range objectives. Al Qaeda has not forced the United States from the Arabian Peninsula (although American presence is declining), Russia has not granted Chechnya independence, and Jemaah Islamiyah has yet to achieve a sectarian Islamic state in Indonesia. At the same time, the terrorist record at achieving tactical objectives (carrying out terrorist attacks) is, if not perfect, not a total failure either. As long as terrorists continue to exist and to achieve some of their goals, they remain a force against the targets of their activities. Thus, the competition between terrorists and their targets over the accomplishment of terrorist objectives continues to exist within a kind of netherworld where neither wins or loses decisively and thus both can claim some success: "We do not give in to terrorism," defined as resisting terrorist strategic objectives, versus "We succeed by killing the infidels," defined as the successful commission of acts of terrorism.

PERSPECTIVES ON AND CAUSES OF TERRORISM

For most of us, terrorism is such an alien phenomenon that we have difficulty conceptualizing exactly what it is and why people would engage in acts of terrorism, up to and including committing terrorist acts that involve their own planned deaths (suicide). And yet, the historic and contemporary public records are strewn with enough instances of terrorism as to make confronting the conceptual "beast" necessary for understanding and coping with the reality around us and devising strategies and policies that will combat it.

Terrorism is too complex a phenomenon to capture entirely in a single chapter, but we can gain some insights into it by viewing it through two lenses. The first is by examining three perspectives that try to capture terrorism and its place in international politics. The second is to look at three of the explanations commonly put forward to answer the question, Why is there terrorism?

Three Perspectives

Where does terrorism fit into domestic and international politics? Is terrorism ever a legitimate enterprise, or is it always something outside the realm of legitimacy? Answers to these questions depend on one's perspective, as captured in a typecasting of terrorism as legitimate or illegitimate behavior. Two polar opposite perspectives are generally the basis for such a discussion: terrorism as crime and terrorism as war. To these two distinctions, we add a third that we have developed throughout our discussions, which is terrorism as a specific kind of warfare, asymmetrical war.

The basic distinction serves two purposes. On the one hand, it speaks to the legitimacy of terrorism: a depiction of terrorism as crime clearly stamps it as illegal and thus illegitimate, whereas depicting it as war (of one sort or another) raises its status among actions of states and groups. The distinction also suggests the appropriate approach to dealing with terrorism either as a legal system or military problem, which is also a contentious matter.

The *terrorism as crime* perspective focuses on terrorist acts and their acceptability, with an emphasis on their illegality. It is primarily the perspective of the victims of terrorism. All terrorist acts against people and things violate legal norms in all organized societies: it is against the law to murder people or to blow up things, after all, regardless of why one does so. If acts of terrorism are, at their core, criminal acts, then terrorists are little more than common criminals and should be treated as such. Terrorism thus becomes at heart a criminal problem, and terrorists are part of the criminal justice system subject to arrest, incarceration, trial, and, where appropriate, imprisonment or execution.

Terrorists simultaneously reject and embrace this depiction. They reject the notion that what they do is criminal, because their acts—while technically illegal—are committed for what they believe to be higher political purposes. Terrorists kill people, but they do not murder them. Terrorists are not criminals; rather, they are warriors (in contemporary times, "holy" warriors). Thinking in this manner elevates the status of the terrorist from criminal to soldier, a far more exalted and acceptable position. At the same time, terrorists prefer for target societies to think of them as criminals in those situations in which they are captured and brought to justice (assuming the capturing society adheres to its own criminal procedures, which is not always the case). The reason is simple: at least in the West, criminal procedures are considerably more stringent in procedural and evidentiary senses than military law, affording terrorists greater protections under the law and making their successful prosecution more difficult. Attempts in the United States to relax criminal safeguards regarding terrorists seek to change that status but have created controversy in civil rights and liberties terms.

Terrorists prefer the second perspective, *terrorism as war*. This viewpoint emphasizes the political nature of terrorism and terrorist acts, in essence adopting the Clausewitzian paraphrase that "terrorism is politics by other means." If one accepts the basic premise of this perspective, then terrorist acts are not crimes but acts of war and, as such, are judged by the standards of war (broadly defined, since asymmetrical warfare commonly succeeds by ignoring conventional rules that disadvantage them) rather than by criminal standards. The interactions between terrorist organizations and their targets are thus warlike, military affairs. Killing outside situations of war is always illegal, but within war it is permissible, at least within certain bounds regarding who and in what conditions killing is deemed permissible.

The current global war on terrorism implicitly accepts this perspective, if not its implications. Within the GWOT, the term *war* is used rather loosely and almost allegorically rather than literally, and almost all apostles of the designation do not view terrorists as warriors but rather as wanton criminals to be brought to justice or their demise. Within the antiterrorism campaign in Afghanistan, for instance, members (or alleged members) of Al Qaeda were not treated as prisoners of war, which would have afforded them certain legal rights under the Geneva Conventions on War, but instead under the legally vague designation of "detainees," who apparently do not possess Geneva Convention protections.

The problem of treating terrorism as crime or as war is that, in most cases, it is both. Terrorists do engage in criminal acts, but they do so for reasons more normally associated with war. This suggests that there should be a third way of depicting terrorism, which we will call *terrorism as asymmetrical war*. Asymmetrical warfare is different from the conventional forms of warfare that are covered by the traditional laws of war; indeed, a major characteristic of asymmetrical warfare is the rejection of traditional norms and rules as part of the attempt to level the playing field of conflict. As noted in Chapter 9, for instance, the asymmetrical warrior does not distinguish between combatants and noncombatants, just as the terrorist considers all members of the target group equally culpable and thus eligible for attack.

Terrorism as asymmetrical war is a hybrid of the other two perspectives. The terrorists' rejection of accepted rules means they can treat their actions as acts of war while the target society rejects this contention and can continue to consider their actions crimes against mankind. The status of asymmetrical warriors as warriors may be ambiguous within the rules of war, but leaving their actions within criminal jurisdiction satisfies the target society's depiction while affording captured terrorists the legal protections they seek. This perspective also allows terrorism to be depicted both as a criminal *and* a military problem, which it is, and thus allows both law enforcement and military responses to terrorists. The only difficulty is in determining the appropriate mix of criminal justice and military responses generally and in specific situations.

Three Causes

The motivation to become a terrorist and to engage in the often gruesome and dangerous acts that typify terrorism is also the source of considerable speculation and disagreement among experts and lay observers. Much of the difficulty in making such assessments derives from the absolute inability most of us have in imagining why anyone would become a terrorist and kill people who, from our perspective, are innocent. Whatever leads people to become terrorists is so alien to us that we cannot draw analogies from our own experiences or those arising in our society as we know it (which has, of course, produced its fair share of terrorists).

Three vantage points on what causes people and groups to adopt terrorism are often put forward, reflecting in some ways the disciplinary vantage points that various students of the phenomenon represent. Most of these explanations surfaced during the 1960s and 1970s, during the third or "New Left" wave of modern terrorism, according to David C. Rapoport (the first two were anarchism and anticolonialism; the fourth and present wave is religious). This is worth noting because the 1960s and 1970s tended to be more tolerant of, even sympathetic to, politically aberrant movements than is true today. At any rate, terrorism is typified as primarily a societal, a psychological, or a political problem. The three explanations are neither mutually exclusive nor agreed upon.

The *societal* argument is that social conditions provide the breeding grounds for terrorism. Societies that consistently underachieve, that fail to provide adequate material or spiritual advances or hope for their people, and in which the citizens live in an unending and hopeless condition of deprivation provide a kind of intellectual and physical "swamp" in which terrorism "breeds" a ready supply of potential terrorism followers who are willing recruits for causes that promise to bring meaning and direction to their lives. These "failed societies" may even oppress specific groups that are even more prone to the appeals of terrorism recruiters and may prevent other groups from achieving the goals to which they aspire (what Gurr calls "aspirational deprivation"). A variant of this argument also suggests that some societies' values may be better suited than others for producing terrorists. In the contemporary setting, for instance, some observers note that Islam has a more prominent, positive role for religious martyrdom than do other religions, making the terrorist path, and especially suicide terrorism, more acceptable than it would be in other places.

If this argument is substantially correct, it leads to a potential solution to the terrorism problem: if the wretched (or frustrating) conditions are removed and the society ceases to be a failed one, then the conditions that breed the terrorists may also be removed. These failed societies are not necessarily the poorest societies (which tend to produce criminals but not terrorists), but those where opportunities are limited or missing. This is the heart of the argument for "draining the swamp" as a way to combat terrorism. The tool for doing so is the infusion of (probably massive) amounts of developmental assistance to create the physical basis for greater prosperity and a sense of meaningful futures: people do not volunteer for potential self-immolation (such as suicide terrorist missions) if they have hope for a more positive, promising future. In the current debate, feeding resources into the Pakistani education system to create a peaceful alternative to the religious *madrassa* schools that teach anti-Americanism is a prime example of the application of the societal argument.

Critics point to a hole in this explanation of what creates terrorism. They argue that many modern terrorists are not the product of objective societal deprivation, but of aspirational deprivation. Sixteen of the nineteen September 11 terrorists, after all, were Saudi citizens who could hardly be accused of coming from abjectly deprived backgrounds. Such an observation is obviously true, but it does not completely negate the argument that inferior societal conditions produce terrorists. Rather, the observation conditions the argument by saying that *not all* terrorists come from physically deprived backgrounds. Most terrorist leaders, it appears, and some of their followers come from middle-, even upper-class backgrounds (bin Laden, for instance), but a lot of their followers indeed emerge from the "swamp."

The second explanation moves from the group to the individual. Rather than focusing on failed societies, the *psychological* argument shifts the emphasis from the failed society to failed peoples. The psychological argument is not entirely divorced from the societal argument in that it basically contends that certain traits in people, certain psychological states, make them more susceptible to the terrorist appeal and thus more willing to commit terrorist acts than is true in other individuals. Since not everyone who possesses these traits becomes a terrorist (lots of people are frustrated but do not react by blowing themselves up, for instance), there must be triggering societal conditions that activate these tendencies.

Terrorist profiling is a clear example of the psychological explanation of terrorism. In many contemporary arguments, for instance, it has been observed that many of the individuals who perpetrate religious-based terrorism from Middle Eastern settings share several characteristics. Most of the terrorist followers (as opposed to the leaders who recruit, train, and direct them) tend to be teenaged boys with high school educations who do not have jobs at all, or if they do, their jobs pay them sufficiently poorly that they have few prospects. They tend to be unmarried with few prospects of finding a wife (often because they cannot support them). They also tend to have low self-esteem intermixed with a high sense of helplessness and hopelessness about their futures. These perceptions lead to a high sense of humiliation, embarrassment, and impotence toward the future. Individuals with this kind of profile are believed to be especially vulnerable to recruitment by terrorist leaders who promise to restore meaning and purpose and thus a sense of self-esteem. A particularly troubling

Amplification 10.2

PROFILING SUICIDE TERRORISTS

The problem posed by terrorists willing to kill themselves to commit their terrorist acts burst on the scene during the clash between Israel and the Palestinians that erupted in 2000 (*Intifada* II) and has been given further publicity by the suicidal actions of some Iraqi car bomber members of the Iraqi resistance. Suicide/martyr terrorism is neither truly new nor unique to the present: Americans, for instance, encountered suicide bombers during the conquest of Okinawa in World War II, which was one reason they sought to avoid an invasion of the Japanese home islands. The whole idea of self-immolation, especially by the young people associated with Palestinian suicide terrorism, is, however, totally alien to most of us.

The Israelis (as reported in Stern) have developed a profile of these terrorists. They tend to be young, often teenagers, and they are generally mentally immature. In nearly all cases, they are under pressure to get a job but, due to a lack of connections, are unsuccessful in doing so. As a result, they have no money or reasonable prospects to improve their situations. Among other things, they cannot afford girlfriends or fiancées, and marriage is not an option for them. They thus feel a profound sense of helplessness and hopelessness. For many, God and the Mosque are their only refuge.

Becoming a suicide terrorist remedies some of these problems. Being a member of a terrorist organization can restore a sense of purpose and self-esteem: the recruit is now an important person, and his willingness to make the ultimate sacrifice only adds to his social prestige and acceptance. Martyrdom reestablishes his worth.

What is frightening (and was mentioned earlier) is that the population bulge in the Middle East means there are a large number of young men (and increasingly women) who meet the profile. Unless steps—whatever they may be—can be taken to reverse the conditions that give rise to suicide terrorists, we can expect more in the future.

recent trend has been the emergence of females with similar profiles in terrorist roles. The terrorist profile is discussed in Amplification 10.2.

The implications of this profile are particularly disturbing because the Middle East has a population "bulge," which includes a large number of young males who meet the basic enabling characteristics described in the profile. Moreover, the societal conditions in most Middle Eastern states offer few prospects for reducing these conditions, notably of employment, that can turn the situation around. As long as life does not contain meaningful prospects that can prevent the triggering of psychological processes leading to terrorism, there will be fertile breeding grounds for new generations of terrorists. It might be added that far fewer studies suggest similar profiles for terrorist leaders, except that they come from higher socioeconomic situations.

The third explanation is *political*, that failed governments produce the societal and psychological conditions in which terrorism emerges or produce conditions in which terrorists emerge or are nurtured. Although it hardly exhausts the possibilities, state action can lead to terrorism in two ways. First, state oppression (indeed, including the use of terrorism *by* the government) may lead to political opposition that must be clandestine and resort to terrorism as their only means of survival (terrorism as the tool of the asymmetrical warrior). The Chechen resistance would certainly view itself in this manner. In other cases, the government may be so inept or ineffective that it provides a haven for terrorists to exist without being able to do anything about it. The ineffectiveness of the Pakistani government in suppressing remnants of Al Qaeda and other sympathetic groups in the mountainous areas bordering Afghanistan is an example. In yet other cases, sympathetic governments may even provide refuge and sanctuary for terrorist organizations. The relationship between Afghanistan's Taliban regime and Al Qaeda is a frequently cited example.

As with the other explanations, the political model also suggests remedies. If it is bad governments that create, put up with, or consort with terrorists, then there are two ways to deal with the problem. One is to convince the government to abandon the terrorists, quit creating them, or apprehend them, using either positive inducements (military or economic assistance) or threats of some form of sanctions to induce compliance. This has been the basic American strategy with Pakistan. If those efforts fail, a second option may be to replace those governments with more compliant regimes. That is at least part of the rationale for the American invasion of Iraq. The effectiveness of these solutions is, of course, open to question.

As noted, these explanations are not mutually exclusive. Failed governments have failed societal conditions as one of their causes and consequences, and it is failure at these levels that may create the triggering conditions for psychological forces that activate terrorists. It may be, as well, that these explanations are not comprehensive but may be characteristic of the 1960s and 1970s variants of terrorism, which were, among other things, noticeably secular rather than religious. Strategies for dealing with the terrorism problem must sort out the influences of various explanations and how well they apply to the current and evolving forms of terrorism.

TERRORISM SINCE SEPTEMBER 11

The events of September 11 understandably focused national attention on a specific terrorist threat posed by Al Qaeda. The focus was natural given the audacity and shock value of the actual attacks, by the novelty of an organization such as Al Qaeda, and by the underlying hatred of Americans that they revealed. To the extent that Americans had much of an understanding of terrorism, it was associated with more "classical" forms, such as highly politicized anticolonialist movements like the Irish Republican Army (IRA), with state terrorism in the form of suppression by totalitarian regimes like Hitler's Germany or Stalin's Soviet Union, or with isolated anarchist assassinations or individual acts like the bombing of the ʲ ᵗᵃʰ Federal Building in Oklahoma City.

Understanding the nature of the threat has been difficult for at least sons. First, the contemporary form of terrorism appears very different from we have encountered before. It is nonstate-based terrorism that does not arise from specific political communities or jurisdictions but instead flows across national boundaries like oil slipping under doors. It is therefore conceptually difficult to make terrorism concrete and to counter it. It is also religious, showing signs of fanaticism that are present in all religious communities (including our own, historically) but are alien to our ability to conceptualize. Slaughter in the name of God goes beyond most of our intellectual frameworks. It is also fanatically anti-American and thus in sharp contrast to the general pro-Americanism that we at least believed dominated the end of the twentieth century. It also employs methods such as suicide terrorism that, if not historically unique, are deviant enough to go beyond most of our abilities to conjure.

Second, our understanding is made more difficult by the extremely changing nature of contemporary terrorist opponents. The Al Qaeda of 2001 was hard enough for us to understand, but it has evolved greatly since then. Partly this is because international efforts since 2001 have been quite effective in dismantling the old Al Qaeda structure by capturing and killing many of its members. This success, however, has caused the threat to disperse and transform itself into forms that we find even less recognizable and thus more difficult to identify and attack. A discussion of organizational evolution is necessary to clarify the nature of the current terrorist threat.

Jessica Stern, in *Terrorism in the Name of God*, lays out the requirements for a successful terrorist organization. The effectiveness of a terrorist organization is dependent on two qualities: resiliency (the ability to withstand the loss of parts of its membership or workforce) and capacity (the ability to optimize the scale and impact of terrorist attacks). The larger the scale of operations the terrorist organization can carry out without large losses to its members through capture or death, the more effective the organization is. Conversely, if an organization can carry out only small, relatively insignificant acts while having large portions of its membership captured or killed, it is less effective.

Resiliency and capacity are clearly related. For a terrorist organization to carry out large operations such as the coordinated attacks on Spanish commuter trains in 2004, it must devise a sophisticated, coordinated plan involving a number of people or cells who must communicate with one another to both plan and execute the attack. The Achilles' heel in terrorist activity is penetration of the organization by outsiders, and the key element is the interruption of communications that allows penetration into the organization and movement through the hierarchy to interfere with and destroy the organization and its ability to carry out attacks (in other words, to reduce its resiliency). The most effective way for the terrorist organization to avoid penetration is to minimize communications that can be intercepted, but doing so comes at the expense of the sophistication, coordination, and thus extent of its actions (reduction in capacity).

The result of the interplay of these contradictory factors is a dilemma that is changing the face of contemporary terrorist organizations. Historically, according to Stern and others, most terrorist organizations have followed an organizational form known as the *commander-cadre* (or *hierarchical*) model. This form of organization is not dissimilar to the way complex organizations are structured everywhere: executives (commanders) organize and plan activities (terrorist attacks) and pass instructions downward through the organization for implementation by employees (cadres). In order to try to maintain levels of secrecy that improve resiliency, terrorist organizations structure themselves so that any one level of the organization (cell) knows only of the cell directly above and below it (which, of course, distinguishes them from more conventional complex organizations).

Commander-cadre arrangements have the advantages of other large, complex organizations. They can coordinate activities maximizing capacity (the African embassy bombings, for instance); they can organize recruitment and absorb, indoctrinate, and train recruits; and they can carry out ancillary activities such as fund raising, dealing with cooperative governments, and engaging in commerce and other forms of activity. The disadvantage of these organizations is that they may become more permeable by outside agencies because of their need to communicate among units. Modern electronics becomes a double-edged sword for the terrorist: things like cell phones facilitate communications in executing attacks, but those communications can be intercepted, leading to resiliency-threatening penetration. In fact, elec-tronic surveillance of terrorist communication has been extremely helpful in the pursuit of Al Qaeda to the point that the old organization of the 1990s, which basically followed the commander-cadre model, has been reduced in size "from about 4,000 members to a few hundred," according to Gunaratna in the Summer 2004 *Washington Quarterly*.

The result of the campaign against Al Qaeda has been to cause it to adapt, to become what Stern calls the "protean enemy" that has "shown a surprising willingness to adapt its mission" and to alter its organizational form to make it more resilient." Al Qaeda is no longer a hierarchically organized entity that plans and carries out terrorist missions. Instead, it has adopted elements of the alternate form of terrorist organization, the *virtual network* or *leaderless resistance* model and has dispersed itself into a series of smaller, loosely affiliated terrorist organizations (Jemaah Islamiyah is a prime example) that draw inspiration from Al Qaeda. The announcement by Iraqi resistance leader Abu Musab al-Zarqawi of allegiance to bin Laden's goals in October 2004 (Zarqawi is sometimes mentioned as a possible successor to bin Laden) may be another case in point of this evolution. If it ever was a monolithic dragon, Al Qaeda has instead become a hydra-headed monster.

The virtual network organizational model was apparently developed in the United States by the Aryan Nation hate group (many argue the prototype is found in the anarchist movement in the late nineteenth century). Its problem was that its membership was constantly being penetrated and disrupted by law enforcement organizations like the FBI, which used extensive electronic surveillance (wire tapping) to uncover and suppress illegal Aryan Nation activity and to prosecute both the planners and executioners of its actions. The solution for Aryan Nation, recently adapted and adopted by international terrorist organizations like Al Qaeda, is the virtual network or leaderless resistance.

The core of this model is the reduction of direct communications between the leadership and its members. Rather than planning operations and instructing operatives to carry out those plans, leaders instead exhort their followers to act through public pronouncements (for instance, through the use of Web sites). Leaders may issue general calls to action, but they have no direct communications with followers that can be intercepted or used as the basis for suppression or conspiracy indictments. The leader has no direct knowledge or control of individual terrorist acts, which he or she may inspire but not direct.

The "Army of God" movement in the United States is an example; its leaders condemn doctors who perform abortions and suggest to followers that they should be suppressed, even through use of physical violence. The hope is that a devoted follower like Eric Rudolph (convicted in 2005 of killing an off-duty policeman in an attack against a Birmingham, Alabama, abortion clinic in 2000) will be inspired to carry out the mission. The advantage of this model is that it maximizes the resiliency of the organization and protects its leadership from capture or prosecution; its principal drawback is reduced capacity to order specific "desirable" actions (this is also a problem for law enforcement, since nobody but the individual, inspired terrorist knows in advance what he or she plans to do).

With the success of terrorist suppression after September 11, Al Qaeda and its affiliates have apparently adopted some of the characteristics of a virtual network. Leaders like bin Laden continue to organize some operations in the traditional commander-cadre manner, but increasingly, bin Laden is seen as a virtual leader whose principal role is to make pronouncements that inspire the membership and that of affiliated organizations to continue the *jihad* that bin Laden has declared and continues to champion.

Part of this shift has taken the form of a dispersion of terrorist organizations. During the 1980s and 1990s, bin Laden and his associates trained literally thousands of religious terrorists who have formed movements of their own in their home countries. Levels of affiliation and control of these "franchises"—as they are sometimes known—vary considerably, but they do change the nature of the terrorism problem. Cutting off one "head" (capturing or killing bin Laden, for instance) would not decapitate the movement he leads, because other heads exist and doubtless yet other leaders would arise to replace and play the role of the fallen leader.

The nature of the terrorist threat is thus changing. It is becoming more diffuse as terrorist organizations become more adaptable organizationally and otherwise (become more "protean," in Stern's term). This means that the nature of trying to control or dismantle the problem of terrorism is becoming more complex as well.

THE GWOT: DEALING WITH TERRORISM

Terrorism is a variant of the asymmetrical warfare problem already described as a—arguably *the*—prominent national security problem facing the United States, and the political reaction to the September 11 attacks has raised it to the highest priority for the country's security. Whether the rhetoric of the GWOT is more hyperbolic than factual is almost beside the point; the public commitment is that terrorism must and will be defeated: we are committed to "winning the global war on terrorism."

But what does that robust rhetoric mean? Exactly what (or who) is the opponent in this "war"? There are three possibilities. One is that the opponent is terrorism (which the official rhetoric suggests), but terrorism is a method, a way to do things. How do we defeat and subdue a method, and specifically a method that has endured for over two thousand years? A second possibility is that the opponent is terrorist purposes, but these are ideas that can only be "defeated" by being discredited, an intellectual process. The third possibility is that the contest is against terrorists, those who actually commit terrorist acts. Terrorists are at least a concrete opponent, but can terrorists be extinguished as long as their method works at least some of the time and there are adherents to their ideas?

All of these are valid questions for which definitive, consensually agreed-upon answers do not exist, but which must be dealt with if a coherent strategy for dealing with the problem is to be devised. Examine each possibility. It is frequently argued that it makes no sense to talk about war against an abstraction, and the idea of terrorism is the application of a method, a means to accomplish a goal. Can you "kill" an idea in some concrete or abstract manner? If so, how do know you have accomplished the task? Where, quite literally, are the bodies or the surrendering enemies? Wars, at any level, are contests between members of different groups to assert control. People and their ideas are not the same thing.

The war analogy suffers even if one switches emphasis and says the GWOT is a war on global terrorists. Switching the emphasis at least has the virtue of making a war of people against other people (a conceptual improvement), but it still retains two problems in the current context.

First, warfare against terrorists is war against asymmetrical warriors, as already noted. That means the countries seeking to defeat terrorism are militarily superior in conventional terms and that terrorism is the means by which terrorists seek to create a situation in which they have a chance to succeed. The problem here lies in the criteria for success for those seeking to snuff out terrorists and for the terrorists themselves. For the United States (or any other country engaged in terrorism suppression), the criterion is very exacting: the war cannot be won until terrorists everywhere specified by the war (the globe as currently defined) have been defeated. Those seeking to suppress terrorists must crush their opponents; in a phrase, they can only "win by winning."

The situation is different for the terrorists. Terrorists know that they cannot win in the traditional sense of crushing their enemies (win by winning), but equally, they know their enemies cannot validly claim victory as long as the terrorists can continue to operate. Thus, terrorists (much like guerrillas) realize that their criterion for success is to avoid being defeated and that the longer they remain a viable force, the more likely they are to become a sufficient enough irritant that their opponents conclude that acquiescence to their demands is preferable to continuing the frustrating struggle against them. The terrorists, in other words, can "win by not losing" or, at a minimum, prevent their opponent from declaring victory by avoiding losing.

The problem of defeating terrorists is made more difficult by a second problem associated with modern asymmetrical warfare: contemporary international terrorist organizations are nonstate actors. We know that most of the contemporary religious terrorists are Muslims who come from or have connections to parts of the Islamic Middle East. We also know that not all Muslims in the Middle East support the terrorists or what they do (although enough do to provide safe haven in which terrorists can hide), and that no state government has claimed association with major terrorist organizations since the overthrow of the Taliban in Afghanistan. To make matters worse, these nonstate actors generally imbed themselves within physical areas and among people sympathetic to them; they move around, including across international borders; and they rarely establish public physical symbols that can be identified with them (some Islamic charities that serve as fronts for terrorist activities such as recruitment and fund raising are partial exceptions).

The problem this creates for a "war" on terrorists is finding and specifying targets that can be attacked and defeated. When Al Qaeda was openly running training camps in Afghanistan, this was not so much of a problem, and occasionally a military attack would be made on one of these facilities (for instance, cruise missile attacks on Al Qaeda training camps in 1998 in retaliation for the bombings of American embassies in Africa). Since the fall of the Taliban and the dispersal of Al Qaeda into greater nonstate anonymity, military actions directly against Al Qaeda or its associates have essentially ceased. The problem, quite literally, is that we do not know what to attack, especially what we could attack that would move us measurably toward "victory." The most important military limitation is the inability to find and target the most vital parts of the terrorist existence—the so-called "centers of gravity" on which the terrorists rely for their continued viability. The result, according to Audrey Kurth Cronin, is "that it is virtually impossible to target the most vulnerable point in the organization." Until (or unless) these problems are surmounted, military efforts are likely to remain frustrating.

Then there is the more specific problem of the ultimate nonstate-based opponent, Al Qaeda. In one sense, Al Qaeda remains the major focus because it remains the center of the (increasingly virtual network) movement, but as it has morphed into many smaller groups with varying degrees of affiliation, the problem of rounding up and punishing the entirety becomes even more difficult, especially in a military sense. Al Qaeda is now as much an inspiration for others as it is a concrete opponent. Having said that, it has probably increased its resiliency at the expense of capacity to carry out devastating attacks. Ultimately, however, resiliency is more important to Al Qaeda than capacity, since resiliency is another way of saying survival and guaranteeing that they do not lose the war.

In some sense, the GWOT requires a continuing Al Qaeda presence. As former CIA official Paul R. Pillar explains, "The existence of a specific, recognized, hated terrorist enemy has helped the United States retain its focus. As long as Al Qaeda exists, even in its current, severely weakened form, it will serve that function." Were we to capture or kill bin Laden and his cohorts, we would destroy a terrorist focus, but we would not destroy terrorism; someone else would pick up the gauntlet. Al Qaeda and bin Laden help us keep our attention focused.

The continuing role of Al Qaeda is illustrated by a terrorist incident that occurred October 7, 2004, at seaside resorts on Egyptian soil in the Sinai peninsula. Bombs tore apart a series of resort hotels where many of the occupants were Israelis celebrating the end of the Yom Kippur holiday. The immediate question was who was responsible, and within a day's time, Al Qaeda had been identified as the likely culprit. While bin Laden has publicly condemned Israel for its suppression of the Palestinians, there are not publicly known instances of Al Qaeda attacks against Egyptian targets. So, was Al Qaeda really to blame directly (did, for instance, bin Laden order the attacks)? Or could the attacks have been carried out by an affiliate or franchise of Al Qaeda acting independently or simply deriving the inspiration to do so from bin Laden's general exhortations? For purposes of the GWOT, simply blaming Al Qaeda removed the need for such nuanced public judgments.

This introduction to dealing with terrorists is intended to convey that the problem is both physically and intellectually very difficult and that any simple, sweeping antidotes to the problem of terrorism are likely to be inadequate and to result in failure. That does not mean the task is hopeless or that things cannot be done to manage or mitigate the problem. In the paragraphs that follow, we explore dealing with terrorism through three lenses: conventional methods of suppressing terrorism (what we can do), levels of effort (who can do it), and a focus on undercutting terrorist appeal (how can we make terrorism less attractive).

Terrorism Suppression: Antiterrorism and Counterterrorism

In conventional terrorism suppression circles, two methods for dealing with the terrorist problem are most often invoked: antiterrorism and counterterrorism. The two terms are sometimes used interchangeably, although each refers to a distinct form of action with a specific purpose. Any program of terrorist suppression will necessarily contain elements of each of them, but failing to specify which is which generally or in specific applications only confuses the issue.

Antiterrorism refers to defensive efforts to reduce the vulnerability of targets to terrorist attacks and to lessen the effects of terrorist attacks that do occur. Antiterrorism efforts thus begin from the premise that some terrorist attacks will indeed occur (or at least be attempted) and that two forms of effort are necessary. First, antiterrorists seek to make it more difficult to mount terrorist attacks. Airport security to prevent potential terrorists from boarding airliners or the interception and detention of possible terrorists by border guards are examples, as is placing barriers around buildings so that terrorists cannot drive bomb-laden vehicles close enough to destroy the buildings. Second, antiterrorists try to mitigate the effects of terrorist attacks that do occur. This form of activity is also known as civil defense or crisis management and is largely the province of first responders such as police and firefighters.

At least three related difficulties hamper conducting an effective antiterrorist campaign. One is that antiterrorism is necessarily reactive; terrorists choose where attacks will occur and against what kinds of targets, and antiterrorists must respond to the terrorist initiative. A second problem is the sheer variety and number of targets to be protected. As suggested earlier, the potential list of targets is almost infinite, and one of the purposes of attacks is randomness so that potential victims are always off guard and antiterrorists will have trouble anticipating where attacks may occur. The third problem is, as noted, target substitution: if antiterrorist efforts are sufficiently successful that terrorists determine their likelihood of success against any particular target (or class of targets) is significantly diminished, they will simply go on to other, less well-defended targets. Given the variety of targets available, finding places and things that have not been protected is not impossible.

The other form of terrorist suppression is *counterterrorism*, offensive and military measures against terrorists or sponsoring agencies to prevent, deter, or respond to terrorist acts. As the definition suggests, counterterrorism consists of both preventive and retaliatory actions against terrorists. Preventive acts can include such things as penetration of terrorist cells and taking action—including apprehension and physical violence against terrorists—before they carry out their acts. Retaliation is more often military and paramilitary and includes attacks on terrorist camps or other facilities in response to terrorist attacks. The purposes of retaliation include both punishment, reducing terrorist capacity for future acts, and hopefully deterrence of future actions by instilling fear of the consequences. In addition, Special Operations Forces are sometimes used to penetrate terrorist staging areas for reconnaissance and intelligence purposes. The well-publicized June 2005 incident in which a Navy SEAL reconnaissance team was ambushed in Afghanistan is a tragic example.

Counterterrorism is inherently and intuitively attractive (which may be why there is a tendency to lump antiterrorist and other activities under the banner of counterterrorism). Preventive actions are proactive, taking the battle to the terrorists and punishing them in advance of creating harm. If effective, they prevent terrorist operations from being carried out and weaken the terrorist organization by capturing or killing its members. In its purest form, preventive counterterrorist actions reverse the tables in the relationship, effectively "terrorizing the terrorists." Pounding a terrorist facility as punishment from enduring a terrorist attack at least entails the satisfaction of knowing the enemy has suffered for the suffering it caused the victim.

The problem with counterterrorism, like antiterrorism, is that it is insufficient on its own as a way to quell terrorism. Preventing terrorist actions requires a level of intelligence about the structures of terrorist organizations that is quite difficult to obtain, and it has been a central purpose of terrorist reorganization into protean forms, discussed earlier, to increase that difficulty. If one does not know the terrorist organization in detail, it is, for instance, difficult to penetrate, learn of its nefarious intentions, and interrupt those activities. The absence of a state base that can be attacked means it is more difficult to identify terrorist targets whose retaliatory destruction will cripple the organization, punish its members, or frighten it into ceasing future actions. The difficulty of finding targets against which to retaliate is particularly frustrating for the military in its counterterrorism role because it denies them the kinds of targets associated with more conventional military operations.

Ideally, antiterrorism and counterterrorism efforts act in tandem. Counterterrorists reduce the number and quality of possible attacks through preventive actions, resulting in less frequent and thus more manageable antiterrorist efforts to ameliorate the effects of attacks that do succeed. Counterterrorists retaliation, then, can hopefully reduce the terrorists' capacity for future mayhem. In practice, however, these efforts sometimes come into operational conflict. The antiterrorist emphasis on lessening the effects of attacks may lead to publicizing the possibility of particular attacks as a way to alert citizens (the color-coded warning system, for instance), whereas counterterrorists prefer to keep operations as secret as possible to facilitate clandestine penetration and interruption. We return to this problem in the conclusion.

International versus National Efforts

There has been considerable discussion since September 11 about the appropriate level at which to conduct operations aimed at suppressing this current wave of international terrorist activity. In the immediate aftermath of the attacks, there was an enormous international outpouring of sympathy for the United States and willingness to join a vigorous international effort to deal with terrorists around the globe. That resolve resulted in a good amount of international cooperation among law enforcement and intelligence agencies in various countries, much of which continues quietly to this day. The more visible manifestations of that internationalization have faded as the United States has "militarized" the terrorist suppression effort (the GWOT as primarily "war") and moved toward actions opposed by the major allies in the law enforcement and intelligence efforts through unilateral actions in places like Iraq.

As already reported, the post–September 11 international effort has experienced apparent successes in reducing the size and potency of Al Qaeda as it existed at the time. The nature and extent of that reduction has been a matter of disagreement, as evidenced in disagreements in the 2004 American presidential debates (what percentage of leaders as opposed to followers have been killed, how many new members have replaced them in new organizations, etc.). The international problem has, however, clearly changed, and the question is how this change is and should be reflected in the degree to which ongoing terrorism should be treated as a national or international effort.

Within the United States, most of the visible activity on reforming the effort has been national. *The 9/11 Commission Report*, for instance, emphasized reform within the American government (principally in restructuring the intelligence community) as a way to respond to the evolving problem. One section in its recommendations chapter is titled "Unity of Effort Across the Foreign–Domestic Divide," but its primary function is to suggest improvements in the American ability to cooperate with foreign sources. Emphases on problems like border protection—port security, for instance—generally have a primarily national content.

Does the nature of the new threat suggest a greater inward or outward turning of efforts? Former CIA expert Pillar suggests that the evolving nature of the threat reinforces the need for greater internationalization. As he describes it, "In a more decentralized network, individuals will go unnoticed not because data on analysts' screens are misinterpreted but because they will never appear on those screens in the first place." Much of the added data on the successors to Al Qaeda can only be collected in the countries where they operate, but Pillar sees two barriers to sustained international cooperation. On the one hand, "an underlying limitation on foreign willingness to cooperate with the United States is the skepticism among foreign publics and even elites that the most powerful nation on the planet needs to be preoccupied with small bands of radicals." This leads to a second misgiving, which is the perceived "ability to sustain the country's own determination to fight" the terrorist threat.

There is also at least muted disagreement in the United States about proper emphases and relationships between parts and levels of government involved in the terrorism suppression effort. At the federal level, the emphasis tends to be on counterterrorism through intelligence and military actions aimed at foreign terrorists— defeating the terrorists overseas so they do not have to be defeated here, in President Bush's often asserted phrase. At the state and local levels, there is more emphasis on antiterrorism by the first responders. Those differences in perspective often result in failures to communicate between levels of government and in competition over priorities for federal funding.

Other Aspects of the Problem

A final problem of the conceptual nature of the GWOT is that it does not capture the entirety of the problem that it has been asked to solve. The GWOT, as suggested, is really an effort aimed at suppressing terrorists, as are the forms of dealing with terrorists discussed in the previous section. Somehow capturing or killing all the existing terrorists does not, however, destroy *terrorism*, which is the underlying purpose of the entire enterprise. As long as individuals and groups choose terrorism as the means to realize their ideas, terrorism cannot be wholly eradicated; only its current manifestations can be contained.

This other part of any effort to suppress terrorism is intellectual, a war of ideas that has two basic parts. The first is the intellectual competition between terrorists and their enemies—the underlying reasons terrorists emerge and the appeal they have among the populations that hide, nurture, sustain, and form the recruitment base for movements that employ terrorism as a method. In the current wave of religious terrorism, virulent anti-Americanism is the activator; the United States and the American way are portrayed as the major threat to Islam and the way of life that it promotes. As long as the United States (and the West generally) does not compete with this basic idea and assert and convince those in the Middle East that our ideas produce a superior existence *for them*, there will be an endless stream of recruits to the banner that no terrorist suppression efforts can even hope to overcome. The best chance of "defeating" these ideas may be that their millenarian goals will eventually be abandoned as unattainable—as has happened in the past.

The second part of the intellectual battle is over the use of terrorism as the method of those whose ideas we oppose. Not only must we compete in the forum of ideas that can lead to terrorism, we must also deal with what causes people to become terrorists. Regardless of what level of causation we begin at (societal, political, or psychological), we must persuade people that volunteering to be terrorists (in the most extreme case, agreeing to commit suicide to advance the terrorist cause) is not acceptable to them if we are to staunch the flow of recruits of terrorists intent on killing us. This problem, "draining the swamp" in which terrorists breed, is clearly a necessary part of any comprehensive strategy.

Conclusion: A Terrorism Strategy?

One thing has not changed since the terrorist attacks of September 11: the United States did not have a comprehensive, encompassing strategy for dealing with the risks associated with international terrorism then, and it does not have such a strategy today. What it does have is a series of catchphrases and partial approaches to the problem, some of which may actually contradict one another (Iraq and the war on terrorism, for instance). The same can be said of the world at large, but the problem is most poignant for the United States because it is the self-appointed world leader in the GWOT and because of the overwhelming preponderance of American power and resources that can and must be applied to reducing the risk of terrorism. Until the United States gets its act together, in other words, neither will the rest of the world.

The dilemma presented by confronting terrorism is twofold. First, it is a very complex problem of the kind with which political institutions are loathe to deal. Declaring a GWOT is a great deal simpler than dealing with the incredible complexities only broadly suggested in these pages. Individuals *within* governments can deal with these problems comprehensively, but large, cumbersome organizations with diverse purposes and agendas have a harder time. Second, the suppression of terrorism is not a conflict that can easily be won, if it can be "won" at all. Terrorism as an idea has been around for a long time, and it will likely continue to persist for a long time. The goal of terrorism strategy is to contain terrorism, to reduce the risks arising from it, not to exorcise it from national and international existence. That is not as high-flown a goal as obliterating terrorism, but it is more realistic.

What then are the goals and elements of a terrorism strategy? What we must do is raise questions, because there are no agreed-upon answers (if there were and they worked, there would not be the problem there is). Thus, the purpose of this conclusion is to help you organize and articulate questions about how a comprehensive strategy toward terrorism might be fashioned, not to provide the definitive answers to those questions.

The first and obvious step in devising a strategy is deciding what its goal should be. It is clearly not enough to say the goal is to "win" the struggle; we must specify what winning means. During the latter stages of the 2004 presidential campaign, the principal candidates effectively—if inadvertently—framed this question. Democratic nominee John Kerry, in a *New York Times Magazine* interview, argued the only realistic goal was to contain the problem, to reduce it to the status of a nuisance rather than a central, encompassing fixation; he drew an analogy with containing prostitution and gambling. George W. Bush replied fiercely that Kerry was wrong and that the goal of the GWOT had to be to hunt down and destroy terrorism everywhere it existed; winning means eradicating terrorism.

Which of these goals should we adopt as the bedrock of strategy? Eradication of terrorism is clearly more emotionally attractive, but is it a realistic or attainable goal for policy and strategy? As noted, terrorism has been around as a more-or-less permanent force for at least two thousand years (many scholars date it back to the first century A.D. to groups like the Sicarii and the Zealots), and although it has ebbed and flowed in its prominence across time, it has never disappeared altogether. Similarly, terrorist movements, such as the current religiously based terrorism, come and go, but they seem always to be replaced by something else. In that case, is a strategy based in destroying terrorism (more properly, terrorists) bound to fail and frustrate those who pursue it? Or is it more realistic (if less emotionally satisfying) to aim to minimize terrorism?

Then there is the question of how to implement the strategy. Clearly, any terrorism suppression strategy must begin with elements of both antiterrorism and counterterrorism, but in what balance? In the last section, it was noted that the two thrusts can be and sometimes are at odds with one another. An example shows this tension.

In August 2004, the American government announced it had seized computer diskettes from a suspected terrorist that contained blueprints for schools in New York City, New Jersey, the District of Columbia, and elsewhere. Coming on the heels of the school hostage-taking and murders in Beslan, Russia, earlier that summer, homeland security officials extrapolated that the diskettes might be evidence of a similar intent.

How should the situation have been handled? Through a quiet, behind-the-scenes counterterrorism effort whereby the potential terrorists were kept unaware the government had the diskette while counterterrorists observed, tried to penetrate, and then squelched any plans? Or through an antiterrorist approach that notified the public of the threat and urged them to take action that would make any attack less effective? The problem was that the two approaches contradicted one another. A counterterrorism approach meant the public would be uninformed and, if an attack occurred, would be comparatively unprepared to moderate the disaster. Should an attack succeed despite counterterrorism efforts, the government's actions would have been roundly condemned for not attempting to protect American lives by warning them of the peril. An antiterrorist approach meant any secrecy would be blown, making a counterterrorism effort much more difficult or impossible. It also meant that any terrorists plotting an attack would know the government was aware of their plans, would thus abort those plans, and would avoid arrest or worse. In the real case, of course, the antiterrorists won, and the potential plot was widely publicized. No attacks occurred, and no suspected terrorist were apprehended. Was that the right decision?

There is another structural concern in dealing with existing terrorists. How can we improve the effort to detect, penetrate, and frustrate terrorist activities? At the national level, for instance, the 9/11 Commission made some strong suggestions for reform and consolidation of governmental efforts, but all entail considerable change in how people go about their business. How much of the Commission's efforts will or should be implemented? In July 2005, there were leaked reports that the new Quadrennial Defense Review (QDR), released with the FY 2007 budget proposal in early 2006, would contain a reorientation of American forces toward a larger Special Operations Forces commitment to the GWOT (which it did). Would such a change simply add to the militarization of the problem?

Further, how much of the effort should be internationalized? Should the United States remain largely independent of others in efforts ranging from counterterrorism to cooperation with United Nations or other international efforts? Or should the United States encourage greater cooperation across borders, even if it disagrees with some of those efforts?

There is the further question of what else is to be done. At least two concerns can be raised in this regard. Clearly, one way to eliminate or lessen the problem of terrorism is to discourage or lessen its appeal to potential terrorists: fewer terrorists, by definition, would pose a smaller terrorism problem. Antiterrorism and counter-terrorism efforts may influence the actions of current terrorists, but they apparently do little to discourage, and may actually encourage, the recruitment of future terror-ists. Israeli destruction of the family homes of Palestinian suicide terrorists has rather clearly not discouraged others from signing up for that grisly mission, and it is at least arguable that the American military effort in Iraq—regardless of the merit of its stated aims—has the ancillary effect of increasing regional anti-Americanism and thus intensifying efforts to recruit terrorists to oppose Americans.

How can terrorism be made less attractive to potential recruits? One approach is to relieve the human conditions in which terrorism seems to prosper—to "drain the swamp" of terrorism-producing societal, psychological, and political conditions and thus make terrorism a less attractive alternative. Intuitively, such efforts appear to make sense, but they face objections. One is expense: uplifting societies to the point that terrorism is unappealing to the citizens would require extensive monetary and other resources (for instance, what would it cost to fund a Pakistani education system that would make the terrorist-producing *madrassa* system obsolete?). Are we willing to pay for such an effort? In addition, the results are uncertain: as many analysts point out, the September 11 terrorists came from Saudi Arabia, not some wretched back-water "swamp," and all the developmental assistance in the world presumably would not have had a positive impact on these people and what they did.

A second possible thrust of strategy might be to make terrorist targets less ap-pealing as targets. Current Middle Eastern religious terrorism is fueled by a virulent anti-Americanism that we find intellectually ludicrous and incorrect. Should the United States be mounting a much more comprehensive campaign to convince people in the region that the Western model is superior to the worldview that fanat-ical religious spokespersons are propounding? If we think, as we say we do, that the terrorist proponents are trying to drag the people of the region a thousand years back in time to some imagined caliphate that is more nightmare than dream, why do we not say so more loudly, convincingly, and consistently?

Finally, there is the question of exposure. One reason for the underlying anti-Americanism in parts of the Middle East is the level of supposedly corrupting American physical presence in the region (this has been a particular obsession of bin Laden for some time). The obvious reason for that presence is Middle East oil, and without that need, the reason for American presence is reduced greatly or disappears altogether. If that is the case, should national energy policy not be an important element in terrorism strategy? Some of the most vocal proponents of the GWOT in the United States simultaneously oppose higher fuel-efficiency standards

Challenge!

Terrorism and You

Terrorism is both a frightening and a confusing phenomenon. The attacks of September 11 established that all of us are potentially targets of terrorist actions, removing some part of our senses of safety and tranquility. Some of the resulting anxiety has abated as time has passed and renewed attacks have not occurred, but simultaneously we are warned of an ever-present, if virtually invisible, threat. The confusion is the result of trying to come to grips with this elusive, shadowy phenomenon. It makes reaching personal judgments all the more difficult.

What does the terrorism problem mean to *you*? Is it a "war," as it is advertised, or is it something else, something more or less frightening? Does it belong at the absolute top of the list of national security concerns, or is it somehow a lesser problem than that? Has the problem, in other words, been "hyped"?

And what about our efforts to deal with the problem? We are spending a large number of tax dollars on the problem, but are we getting our money's worth? Do we have a coherent approach to dealing with the problem? If you had the ability to change the policy, how would you do so? What do you think about terrorism and yourself?

for vehicles (the so-called Corporate Average Fuel Efficiency—CAFE—standards). Since oil revenue has clearly been linked to private support for terrorists in Saudi Arabia and elsewhere, is it not inconsistent to support strong terrorism suppression while driving a large, gas-guzzling sport utility vehicle? All these questions suggest difficult personal choices, as the accompanying *Challenge!* suggests.

This discussion, of course, only explores the tip of the iceberg of what a comprehensive terrorism strategy would include. The problem to date, reflected in the artificial designation of the effort as a war, has been to isolate terrorism and its suppression from other aspects of national and international concern. Terrorism, however, is a broader phenomenon that is part of a broader set of problems and international malaise. Until we start treating it for what it is, our efforts are bound to languish.

Selected Bibliography

Allison, Graham. *Nuclear Terrorism: The Ultimate Preventable Catastrophe*. New York: Times Books (Henry Holt & Company), 2004.

Atran, Scott. "Mishandling Suicide Terrorism." *Washington Quarterly* 27, 3 (Summer 2004), 67–90.

Burke, Jason. "Think Again, Al Qaeda." *Foreign Policy* (May/June 2004), 18–26.

Cronin, Audrey Kurth. "Sources of Contemporary Terrorism." In Audrey Kurth Cronin and James M. Ludes (Eds.), *Modern Terrorism: Elements of a Grand Strategy*. Washington: Georgetown University Press, 2004.

Dershowitz, Alan M. *Why Terrorism Works: Understanding the Threat, Responding to the Challenge.* New Haven: Yale University Press, 2002.

Gunaratna, Rohan. "The Post-Madrid Face of Al Qaeda." *Washington Quarterly* 27, 3 (Summer 2004), 91–100.

Gurr, Ted Robert. *Why Men Rebel.* Princeton, NJ: Princeton University Press, 1973.

Hoge, James F., Jr., and Gideon Rose (Eds.). *Understanding the War on Terrorism.* New York: Foreign Affairs Books, 2005.

Jenkins, Brian. "International Terrorism." In Robert J. Art and Kenneth N. Waltz (Eds.), *The Use of Force: Military Power and International Politics* (6th ed., pp. 77–84). New York: Rowman & Littlefield Publishers, 2004.

Krueger, Alan B., and David D. Laitin. " 'Misunderestimating' Terrorism: The State Department's Big Mistake." *Foreign Affairs* 83, 5 (September/October 2004), 8–13.

Pillar, Paul R. "Counterterrorism after Al Qaeda." *Washington Quarterly* 27, 3 (Summer 2004), 101–113.

Powell, Colin L. "No Country Left Behind." *Foreign Policy* (January–February 2005), 28–35.

Rapoport, David C. "The Four Waves of Terrorism." In Cronin and Ludes, *Modern Terrorism* (pp. 46–73).

Simon, Steve, and Jeff Martin. "Terrorism: Denying Al Qaeda Its Popular Support." *Washington Quarterly* 28, 1 (Winter 2004–05), 131–146.

Sloan, Stephen. *Beating International Terrorism: An Action Strategy for Preemption and Punishment.* Montgomery, AL: Air University Press, 2000.

Snow, Donald M. *September 11, 2001: The New Face of War?* New York: Longman, 2002.

Snow, Donald M., and Dennis M. Drew. *From Lexington to Desert Storm and Beyond: War and Politics in the American Experience.* Armonk, NY: M. E. Sharpe, 2000.

Stern, Jessica. *Terrorism in the Name of God: Why Religious Militants Kill.* New York: ECCO, 2003.

——— "The Protean Enemy." *Foreign Affairs* 82, 4 (July/August 2003), 27–40.

Whiteneck, Daniel. "Deterring Terrorists: Thoughts on a Framework." *Washington Quarterly* 28, 3 (Summer 2005), 187–199.

CHAPTER 11

Peacekeeping and State-Building: The New Dilemma

PREVIEW

Violence and instability leading to various forms of asymmetrical warfare such as terrorism and new internal war are concentrated in select parts of the developing world where the wretchedness of the human condition breeds the despair that leads to instability. In the 1990s, American involvement in these situations was justified on largely humanitarian grounds; today the rationale is suppressing terrorism. The question is what, if anything, can be done to alleviate those conditions and thus reduce the inclination to humanitarian atrocity or terrorist attractiveness. To address this problem, the chapter begins by identifying vulnerable societies, the so-called failed states. We then look at why and how we may intervene in the future. The possibilities for improving the situations, peacekeeping and state-building, are then examined, and the chapter concludes with likely effects of these actions for the future.

Contemporary, normally asymmetrical wars share three characteristics that endow them with their unique nature and that define the problems the United States and others must confront if they become involved in them. First, they share an important, sometimes exclusive, internal or civil component: at least part of the situation has elements within a state fighting one another, meaning that part of the military and political problem of ending the war and restoring the peace is reconciling formerly warring factions. This problem is exacerbated when the battleground is a failed state, as we shall see. Second, these wars occur essentially exclusively in the developing world, and so when outsiders like the United States involve themselves, there is inevitably some resentment about that involvement.

The third characteristic is the most consequential, most difficult, and least well understood: that these wars almost always have three distinct phases, all of which must be surmounted before success can occur. The first phase is the actual fighting phase—our normal concept of the totality of war—and the normal response is to bring that fighting to an end on some terms (what we will call *peace imposition*). The period after the fighting has ended is one of adjustment and unstable peace, and the problem is maintaining the peace and beginning to improve conditions in the target country (what we will call *peace enforcement*). Finally, the situation must be improved physically and politically (*state-building*) so that outsiders can prepare for their exit (what we will call *peacekeeping*).

This model of dealing with developing world environments has evolved through American involvement in a number of new internal wars in the 1990s, which was a decidedly mixed experience and one which was largely discarded after September 11. It is, however, virtually the identical structure of problems that we face in Afghanistan and Iraq. Although historical progressions are seldom linear, these dynamics, interrupted by September 11, are likely to continue into the foreseeable future.

The question of American involvement with force in the developing world was skewed by the events of September 11, 2001. Prior to the terrorist attacks, there was a lively, partisan political debate about the degree of American activism in the developing world. During the 2000 election campaign, then candidate George W. Bush and close advisors such as current Secretary of State Condoleeza Rice actively derided American intervention and continuing involvement in Second Tier locales like Kosovo and Bosnia, maintained the United States should cut back its involvement by scaling back or withdrawing American troops where they were present, and publicly promised that the United States would no longer be "the world's 911." More to the point, the commitment of American forces to missions such as peacekeeping and American resources to state-building was derided as a misapplication and overextension of scarce and valuable American assets.

During the 1990s, the United States became involved in a number of these developing-world conflicts and avoided others, with decidedly mixed results. In 1992, the United States joined the international response to suffering and atrocity in Somalia, which ended with American withdrawal after nineteen of its soldiers were slaughtered in an ambush in the country's capital, Mogadishu. In 1994, the United States launched an "intervasion" (part intervention, part invasion) to restore the elected government of Haiti but sat out the slaughter in Rwanda that same year. Operation Restore Democracy (the name of the Haitian operation) restored democracy only in the most generous sense of that term. Over a decade later, conditions remained nearly as wretched as they were before American involvement, and only the faintest hints of representative government exist. President Clinton deemed U.S. failure to act in Rwanda as one of the worst mistakes of his foreign policy. In 1995, the United States was a central player in negotiating and enforcing a ceasefire among the warring parties in Bosnia, an action it reprised in 1999 in Kosovo. The latter two involvements are notable because they required American military participation in ongoing, open-ended peacekeeping missions.

All these were low-priority operations that entailed relatively modest investments and risks for the United States. The United States, at least after Somalia, could indulge in the inclination to "do something" when faced with atrocity on national cable news, because the costs in blood and treasure was modest. In the Haitian, Bosnian, and Kosovar involvements, there have, for instance, been *no* American casualties from hostile action. That we cannot measure great benefit from these operations (how much difference does it make that Haitian democracy remains an elusive chimera?) has been less important than the absence of losses.

This whole question appeared to change fundamentally when the United States set its sights on Afghanistan in the fall of 2001. The United States had tolerated the repressive, virulently anti-American stance of the Taliban regime there since they came to power in 1996, on the grounds that no American interests were affected by their objectionable attitudes and actions. Their sanctioning of terrorism was, of course, regrettable, but until their refusal to hand over the terrorists dictated their removal from power, they were not very high on the American agenda.

The apparent need to change terrorist-prone societies altered the calculus of involvement in poor, unstable developing-world countries for the Bush administration. In the period between the fault lines, the motivation to become involved was primarily humanitarian, trying to alleviate great human suffering because it was, in President Clinton's justification for intervention in Bosnia, "the right thing to do." Terrorist-proofing similar societies became Bush's reason for involvement. Mohamed Zarea, an Egyptian human rights advocate quoted in the November 14, 2001, *New York Times*, captured the rationale: "This war on terrorism may eliminate a few terrorists. But without reform, it will be like killing a few mosquitoes and leaving the swamp."

It can be argued that the American mission to Afghanistan is totally unlike our involvement in, say, Bosnia, because of the emergence of truly vital American concerns associated with rooting out terrorism there. The United States, in other words, has had no choice but to do what it has done, making Afghanistan a deployment of necessity and thus unlike the Kosovar deployment of choice. Whether a similar judgment can be made about Iraq depends on the degree of the threat posed by the pre-invasion situation. In addition, in Iraq and Afghanistan the United States toppled existing governments and thus created many of the conditions that state-builders must rectify. Although that is true during the active military phase of involvement, the package of responses that the United States and its allies have suggested for the longer haul (phase three) includes the same imperatives as those in Bosnia, Kosovo, and other places: peacekeeping to restore order and a healthy amount of state-building to stabilize the situation so that Afghanistan joins the ranks of stable, antiterrorist states. We are committed to doing the same thing in Afghanistan we promised the Kosovars. Only the motivations and physical antecedents are different.

Are the Afghanistan and Iraq cases typical or atypical of what the future will hold? The answer largely depends on the lessons that other states take from the American response in Afghanistan and Iraq and its effects. Countries assessing likely future American responses may conclude that the United States will respond when obviously vital matters are involved (suppressing terrorists but not humanitarian motives). They may also conclude that American resolution to root out evil in the world is now sufficiently aroused that provocation of the United States is unwise in any circumstance. Whether the United States has become selectively or generally activist will be partially revealed by its actions against other states accused of harboring terrorists in the name of the Bush Doctrine. Whether responses to terrorism set a precedent that also applies to involvements in future new internal wars is something the U.S. government itself can probably not answer with any real certainty.

Assessing the likely future of American activism requires making two judgments, both of which are controversial and both of which apply equally to terrorist-suppressing and humanitarian motivations. The first is what the United States and its *developed* world allies seek to accomplish in the developing world. If we want to hold the troublesome parts of the world essentially at bay, that may suggest a fairly limited approach. If we adopt a more aggressive role, as the Bush administration has suggested, of promoting democracy and incorporating the developing world—and especially its more troublesome members—into the globalizing economy and general prosperity in the hopes that will remove their troublemaking, that suggests a much more activist course.

The other judgment is about how much we *can* accomplish. Our experience transforming developing states into modern or postmodern states is limited and spotty. We succeeded in South Korea but failed in Iran. Moreover, most of our experience has been in countries that were not among the most destitute; most of the candidates in the future will be in those difficult places. Afghanistan is almost a textbook case of the difficulties we will likely face more generally. Iraq magnifies the difficulties.

The simple answer to what we can accomplish is that we do not know. The activist path has only been attempted in Kosovo, and the effort is too embryonic to yield a judgment about whether it works (or what, if anything, does work). Afghanistan will be a follow-on experiment that we have not really started, over four years after the overthrow of the Taliban. If we succeed in helping transform Afghanistan and Iraq into exemplars in the region—more like Turkey than Iran—we will likely herald the experience and try it elsewhere. If we fail, we may not know exactly why. Was it the method that failed? Did we pick the wrong place to try that model? Is another model more applicable? Will *any* approach succeed? Should we try again, or abandon the effort?

All these questions apply equally well to potential terrorist-suppressing and humanitarian situations, because the West believes the same underlying set of circumstances breeds asymmetrical warriors in the form of terrorists and practitioners of new internal war. Those conditions are poverty, despair, and oppression that we believe constitutes the swamp that, once drained, will cease to be the breeding ground for future instability and violence.

To begin to come to grips with (if not conclusively to answer) some of these questions, we proceed in steps. First, we look at the kinds of places where intervention is likely to occur. In examining the failed states, we look at why they fail, what characteristics cause failure (and thus must be remedied), and how we might attempt to intervene. Second, we raise questions about intervention in terms of the purposes for which it may be undertaken and the forms that it may take in different situations. We then turn to the proposed solutions, notably peacekeeping and state-building, two different but interrelated approaches and goals. We conclude by speculating on how this complex of problems fits into the "new world order."

FAILED AND FAILING STATES: THE CONTEXT

Almost all the violence that currently plagues the developing world and boils over occasionally into the developed world, as the events of September 11 did, comes from parts of the developing world. For our purposes, the developing world can be divided into useful categories: those countries that are part of the globalizing economy and those that are not (for a more detailed discussion, see Snow and Brown, *International Relations*). Membership in the globalizing economy includes those countries that are part of the regional and global economic associations that became prominent during the 1990s: APEC, NAFTA, the EU, and the proposed Free Trade Area of the Americas. Geographically, this encompasses the Western Hemisphere (other than Cuba), most of Europe (including Russia, a member of APEC), and most of East Asia and the Pacific. The areas outside this network are principally found in Africa and parts of central and south (including southwest) Asia.

Using these categories to understand where violence is occurring, we find that it is overwhelmingly located in those parts of the developing world outside the globalizing economy. Other than Indonesia and the Philippines (both members of APEC), there are hardly any exceptions to this rule. While not all states outside the globalizing economy are violent and unstable, almost all the violent and unstable states are outside the global economy.

To understand why this pattern exists and persists, we must look at the kinds of states where violence is the norm. We begin by defining the failed states and the characteristics they tend to have, using my own distinctions to define failure and Ralph Peters's characteristics of that failure. While other characterizations may hold better or worse in some individual circumstances, these categories are generally useful for our purposes. We apply these distinctions to the kinds of conditions that must change for the emergence of stability and entrance into the globalizing economy, criteria for which we borrow from Thomas L. Friedman.

What Is a Failed State?

The term *failed state* was coined in the early 1990s to describe a phenomenon occurring in parts of the developing world. The prototype was Somalia, a state that had simply collapsed as a viable entity in 1991 following an overthrow of government and the inability of any other group to assume political control. Thus, Helman and

Ratner provide a definition of Somalia and states like it as failed: "a state utterly incapable of sustaining itself as a member of the international community."

In most cases, failed states have legacies of authoritarian rule but possess unstable regimes in which authoritarian rule has eroded but no viable alternative has emerged. These states thus slide from a condition of authoritarianism to one of anarchy from which they are incapable of extracting themselves on their own. In the most notable and troublesome cases, this anarchy is manifested in inconclusive, but often spectacular and bloody, internal wars.

State failure has both a political and an economic dimension. The political dimension may include anarchy, or it may be manifested by a weak, venal, and corrupt political system that has little control over its population, cannot allocate societal resources nor maintain a civil order, acts capriciously and oppressively toward its citizens, and thus is not accorded legitimacy by sizable parts of the population. In most cases, this ineffectiveness is structural as well as political in that important governmental institutions (law enforcement, courts, public services, etc.) are either nonexistent, hopelessly corrupt, or unable to operate effectively. Probably the most important shortfall is the absence of a criminal or civil judicial and law enforcement community that the public believes treats all citizens equitably and that those citizens are therefore willing to support.

These countries, generally but not exclusively located as they are outside the globalizing economy, are typically economically poor as well. In a number of cases, the reason is structural and endemic: there is little human or physical resource on which to build a viable economic condition. Haiti, for instance, is poor because there is essentially nothing in the country around which to build wealth, and it is hard to imagine how Bangladesh, which essentially is a flood plain of the Ganges River system, can ever develop a viable economic base. In other cases, whatever economic base exists is systematically misused (the looting of the diamond fields of Sierra Leone) or else maldistribution of wealth leaves a tiny elite in possession of fabulous wealth, while the masses toil in abject, crushing poverty. In some cases, the ravages of war add to the misery; twenty-four years of war in Afghanistan have left that country's modest prewar infrastructure in absolute ruin. The Iraqi economy has been at a standstill at least since 2003.

These two dimensions are interactive and reinforcing. Among the assets that weak or nonexistent governments fail to manage effectively is the economy, and their ineptitude or the resulting chaos their rule produces makes them especially unattractive to potential outside investors. Since living conditions are so poor and the government appears incapable of (or uninterested in) changing that situation, there is little reason for people to support a system from which they clearly do not benefit. If the government has enough coercive power to stifle dissent, there may be no practical alternative to sullen acquiescence. If the government is weak, the alternative may be active opposition either to overthrow and replace the regime or to benefit personally from the resulting chaos. Most basically, these countries are unable to provide basic security for their citizens, the sine qua non for all other forms of progress.

Not all states that show signs of failure fall into the same category. The worst cases, such as Somalia, Haiti, and arguably Afghanistan, have failed on all dimensions and have little prospect of changing their situation by themselves. Other states have not quite achieved the status of full-scale failure but are demonstrably showing signs of failure. The most prominent example of the potentially *failing* state is post-Suharto Indonesia, as depicted in Amplification 11.1. In addition, other states have shown signs of potential failure and thus can be designated as *failure-prone*. North Korea is an example.

Ralph Peters provides an interesting and valuable if unorthodox methodology for identifying what he calls "noncompetitive states." These noncompetitive states are not exactly the same as the failed states as defined already. What he develops is a set of criteria that can be applied to states in terms of looking at their potential for useful participation in the international system and in determining stability within states and the potential for state failure.

Peters's attributes are highlights of a generally failed condition. Three underlying factors in these societies underpin the list: they typically do not have a reliable

Amplification 11.1

INDONESIA AS A POTENTIALLY FAILING STATE

Indonesia, the world's largest archipelago and the fourth most populous state in the world, has experienced a downward political and economic spiral since it was one of the countries hit by the East Asian financial crisis in 1997. In Indonesia, the financial crisis triggered a political crisis that brought down the government in 1998 and left observers speculating whether Indonesia might move through the categories of state failure.

The financial crisis revealed great weaknesses in the Indonesian economy, as banks failed, savings were destroyed, economic expansion halted, and inflation ran rampant. The Suharto regime, which had been in power since 1966 and was widely regarded as one of the most corrupt regimes in the world, bore the brunt of the criticism and charges of cronyism and nepotism as the economy's weakness was revealed. Suharto was forced to resign, and between 1998 and 2001 two successors struggled in an atmosphere of recriminations regarding corruption. Some calm was restored when Megawati Sukarnoputri, the daughter of Achmed Sukarno, who led the Indonesian movement for independence from the Netherlands in the 1940s, was elected. She was defeated and replaced peacefully by Susilo Bambang Yudhoyono (known simply as SBY) in 2004.

Beyond political crisis, two factors cloud the future. One is the continuing economic crisis, which includes an active element that wants Indonesia to withdraw from the globalizing economy, a prospect most observers believe would further harm the economy. The other is a series of separatist movements in the far-flung archipelago that began publicly in East Timor and includes the Free Aceh movement in the province of Indonesia where there are large deposits of natural gas crucial to the economy.

Source: Donald M. Snow, "Debating Globalization: The Case of Indonesia," Chapter 9 in *Cases in International Relations: Portraits of the Future,* 2nd ed. New York: Longman, 2006.

and fair rule of law that applies to all citizens; they are generally rife with corruption (which is both a consequence of and reinforcement for a preference for the absence of law); and their economies are usually overly managed, particularly to favor those in power. They do not, in other words, produce a uniform sense of justice and security around which the population can gravitate.

Peters's list is also a warning guide of places to avoid. It contains seven indicators that individually and collectively demonstrate noncompetitiveness and in effect raise red flags about involvement with those societies. The first is a restriction on the flow of information within the society. As many others have also argued, control of the information available to a citizenry has historically been a major source of power, particularly restricting information that might indicate that other places have a better existence. Although the products of the information age such as computers and televisions make restriction more difficult, some states continue to try, and their effort is an indication of their backwardness. It has been argued that some of the distorted views held by some Middle Easterners about the United States—which result in virulent anti-Americanism that justifies terrorism—is the product of the manipulation of information by the government-controlled media of the region.

Second, noncompetitive states tend to subjugate women, restricting their rights in areas such as education and the workplace. This restriction may be a historic cultural artifact or it may be a means to ensure male control, but its practical impact is to remove half a country's talent from the productive process. Any society that creates such restrictions will, he argues, be uncompetitive with counterpart societies that do incorporate women. Resistance to such inclusion is in itself an indication of noncompetitiveness.

Third, noncompetitive states are unable to accept responsibility for their own failure to compete in the world. Rather than recognizing they are the problem, the leaders are more likely to project their ills onto hostile others outside, using these outside forces as scapegoats. A society unwilling to bear this responsibility is particularly unlikely to reform itself and make progress in the world. The United States has been a particularly useful "whipping boy."

Fourth, noncompetitive states typically either have the extended family, a clan, a tribe, or some similar entity as the basis of social organization. In many cases, this traditional social structure creates a crippling duality in terms of interpersonal dealings with societal consequences. In such settings, Peters argues, relations within the social unit may be very open and honest, but the structure creates an us-versus-them mindset that makes relations between groups much less forthcoming and honest. The upshot is that this traditional form of social organization encourages corruption within the society as a whole and impedes formation and development of the kinds of societal mechanisms necessary for progress into the contemporary globalizing world.

Fifth, the dominance of a restrictive religion is often a characteristic of a noncompetitive state. Such a creed helps to reinforce the us-versus-them mentality and the denial of responsibility for the shortcomings of state performance. Restriction of religious belief not only binds the group together against others but makes more plausible the claim that hostile outsiders (infidels) are responsible for the group's own fate. Sixth, this tradition-laden restriction tends to create and reinforce a low valuation of education, and especially education that goes beyond the transmission of orthodox, and often fundamentalist, theology. States that devalue education dilute the potential value of their intellectual talent pool and thereby render themselves less competitive. Restriction of educational access and inequality only adds to this crippling effect.

Finally, noncompetitive states tend also to place a low value on work. In these generally male-dominated societies, menial tasks are generally assigned to women and children, and men gain prestige not because of what they produce but on the basis somehow of who they are. As long as this condition persists, the incentives to excel through productivity are largely missing.

Is this checklist remarkable? In many ways, it is no more than a kind of quick visualization of the conventional wisdom about traditional, predeveloped societies. Most of these societies were, and are, authoritarian or at least patriarchal, with women subservient in an extended family–based society where few are educated and work is avoided. The justification for conditions was often based in a religious credo extolling the status quo, and information about the outside world was restricted to avoid contamination. Breaking the cycle that this circle represents is the essence of beginning the developmental process.

What do these largely socioeconomic conditions have to do with American national security? The short answer is that these conditions represent the swamp that may produce terrorists and human rights–abusing insurgents, and alleviating them is prerequisite to possible stabilization in those cases. Application of American force to crush terrorists or human rights abusers that does not take these problems into account will likely fail in the long run. These are the problems that must be surmounted if the third phase of contemporary warfare is to be successful.

In contemporary terms, these factors also reflect state failure. Societies exhibiting these characteristics are likely to be either authoritarian or, where the coercive veil has been lifted, anarchical, lacking reliable political institutions. The human wastage created by restricting the role of women or downgrading education is clearly a contributor to the economic misery that typically marks the failed states.

Peters's list also creates a checklist of things to change in moving away from failure, or at least a set of indicators that more basic deficiencies are being addressed. It is probably not productive to try to scale the deficiencies, arguing, for instance, that a truly failed state is one where all these characteristics are present, whereas a failing state only has three or four present. What the list does, however, is chronicle failure in a way that is fairly easily observable and suggestive (he argues, for instance, that a good way to tell about the status of women is to observe how, or whether, men and women interact in the terminal of the country's major airport).

Although Peters published *Fighting for the Future* in 1999, well before Afghanistan was catapulted onto the world's center stage, it is remarkable how well his categories illustrate the deficiencies of Taliban-ruled Afghanistan and how rapidly the provisional government of Hamid Karzai has tried to move to reverse these factors. While the early indications are positive, it is the longer-term implementation that is most important.

Information Flow Restriction. One of the major efforts of the Taliban was to shut the country off from the outside. A very visible symbol of Taliban rule was outlawing radios and televisions, often manifested in dramatic smashing of televisions and computers. One of the first images of Kabul and other cities after liberation was the marketing of replacements for those destroyed instruments of communication with the outside world.

Subjugation of Women. There was probably no country in the world that suppressed women as much as the Taliban. Women not only had to be fully covered (including wearing the most impenetrable head covering, or *burkas*, possible), they were systematically denied access to schools and the workplace. Within weeks of liberation, the *burkas* were virtually gone (although they have returned in modified form), and females were prominent in education and the workplace. On the other hand, when the first post-Taliban motion pictures were shown in Kabul after the liberation, only men were allowed to attend.

Inability to Accept Responsibility for Failure. This fairly common symptom of modern Middle Eastern Islamic states was especially pronounced in Afghanistan, where the fundamentalist rantings of Usama bin Laden and others were particularly filled with blaming the West, and especially the United States, for the region's ills. Bin Ladenism quickly faded as bin Laden and the Taliban were driven from power.

Social Organization on an Extended Family or Clan Basis. Afghan society has always been based on clan membership. The Taliban came principally from the Pashtun tribe, which is the country's largest ethnic group and comprises about 38 percent of the population, according to the CIA *Factbook.* Not all Pashtuns, of course, were Taliban, but the majority of the Taliban were Pashtun. Sorting out tribal concerns in the attempt to form a broadly based, multitribal form of governance is possibly the greatest challenge to establishing a legitimate government for Afghanistan and one that the history of tribal animosity and fighting suggests may not succeed for some time. The fact of recent Taliban military activity suggests that tribally based animosities remain a potent force.

Dominance of a Restrictive Religion. A particularly fundamentalist form of Islam underlay the attractiveness and purpose of both the Taliban and bin Laden. According to Michael Doran in a *Foreign Affairs* article, this view sees outsiders and even some Muslim state leaders as defilers of Islam. As he puts it, "In bin Laden's imagery, the leaders of the Arab and Islamic worlds today are Hypocrites (people who extol but do not adhere to the faith), idol worshippers cowering behind America, the Hubal (the symbol of pre-Muslim polytheistic idol worship) of the age." These views are highly restrictive and intolerant. Since many Muslims share this view of the West's negative influence but do not endorse bin Laden's actions, transforming these beliefs will be a difficult issue to handle even though the outward forms of repression claimed necessary by the Taliban are removed.

Low Valuation of Education. Clearly, the education system suffered under the restrictive attitudes of the Taliban against women (including female teachers), and the emphasis on the *madrassa* system in Pakistan is further evidence of devaluing the kind and quality of education that might be put toward making Afghan society more competitive. One of the first institutions to be revived in post-Taliban Afghanistan was the schools, but war-gutted school buildings and the absence of even rudimentary educational materials handicapped the effort.

Low Prestige for Work. During the days of Taliban rule, the economy essentially did not function, some indication that work and progress were less important than piety within the hierarchy of Taliban priorities. Reviving the economy, which necessarily includes making hard work a valued trait, is also a major challenge for the post-Taliban rulers.

What this discussion suggests is that removal of many of the outward symbols of noncompetitiveness has been a major emphasis of Afghanistan after the Taliban. Much of this change arises from a very grassroots appeal—from women shedding their coverings and men shaving their beards to street vendors selling boom boxes to schools resuming as teachers (including women) and students simply return to their old buildings—that at once symbolizes the absolute lack of appeal of the Taliban's creed and the desire to embrace modernity. Whether washing away these vestiges of noncompetitiveness will result in removing the causes of state failure partly depends on the will of the Afghans to embrace fundamental change and the willingness and perseverance of the United States to provide the necessary resources on which to build change. A similar exercise applied to Iraq is probably premature as long as the Iraqi resistance disrupts that country.

These symptoms of noncompetitiveness are especially evident in the failed states—those countries that have historically proven themselves incapable of successful self-governance and of providing adequately for their citizens. Most of these states are so far from the geopolitical mainstream that their problems are remote from and foreign to us; thus our tendency is to ignore them. Occasionally, however, their problems are thrust upon us. Very few Americans, for instance, could have conceived of an active military role for the United States in any of the countries in which we intervened in the 1990s, and before September 11, the same was true of Afghanistan and, to a lesser extent, Iraq.

Whether the causes are humanitarian (the 1990s) or traditionally geopolitical (the 2000s), the United States and other powers are and will continue to be drawn into developing world conflicts. In some cases, a sober assessment of vital interests impel interventions (thus deployments of necessity); in other cases, the geopolitical need for involvement is less apparently compelling (deployments of choice). For whatever reasons, involvement in developing-world conflicts—often internal, almost always asymmetrical in one way or another—has become the norm. Since there is little reason to believe this pattern will not continue, it behooves us to better understand these situations and what we can do about them.

Concepts and Forms of Intervention

The Afghanistan effort by the United States and the U.N. peacekeepers (the International Security Assistance Force or ISAF) attracted more attention than previous peacekeeping missions because of the association of the mission with international terrorism. The missions in which the United States was involved in the 1990s—Somalia, Haiti, Bosnia, and Kosovo—generated some initial publicity when the United States embarked on them, and in the case of Somalia, when the United States withdrew under less than ideal circumstances and with a less than favorable outcome. Interest, however, was never enormous, because these missions neither involved significant U.S. interests nor entailed significant costs in blood or treasure. In Afghanistan, interests were high and the costs moderate. In Iraq, interests seemed high initially and costs fairly low; as time has passed, the level of interests has become more controversial as costs have risen.

The 1990s missions had peacekeeping and, at least implicitly, state-building as objectives. In Haiti, the mission involved restoring Jean-Bertrand Aristide to the elected presidency from which he had been removed by a military coup and creating the conditions for future stability. The first objective was achieved during the four years the United States remained in the country as the lead party of the Operation Uphold Democracy coalition. The second objective is hard to label a success because Haiti still lacks the basis of a stable, prosperous state.

In Bosnia and Kosovo, the United States was part of a U.N.-sanctioned peace-keeping mission with the purpose of restoring order and preparing the countries for post-mission stability; in the case of Kosovo, the mission explicitly included state-building. The Stabilization Force (originally Implementation Force) entered Bosnia in 1995, and the Kosovo Force was formed in 1999. Both are still in place (if reduced in size), and no one thinks they can be withdrawn without an almost certain return to violence.

Although the same terms, peacekeeping and state-building, are used to describe Afghanistan, the situation is sufficiently different as virtually to defy comparison. The effort arises out of very different situations. In Kosovo and Haiti, repressive govern-ments were suppressing the population, and the first goal was to end the suppression. In Bosnia, the problem was to separate warring parties as the first step in implement-ing the Dayton peace accords calling for a separation of factions. In Afghanistan, there was a conventional civil war going on between the Taliban government and its opponents, which the United States pushed in favor of the insurgents (although prior to the stimulus of the terrorist attacks, we had essentially ignored the war).

The structure and purposes of intervention are also different. The United Nations initially authorized the ISAF to restore and enforce order in Kabul, but its mission be-yond that was not clear. The Afghans themselves expressed interest in a long deploy-ment providing security for more of the country while the situation stabilized. The United States, meanwhile, established its own longer-term presence both by establish-ing and maintaining control of airfields and the like in Afghanistan itself and by es-tablishing bases in adjacent former republics of the Soviet Union (e.g., Uzbekistan), while opposing the extension of the ISAF mission and declining to participate in it. Establishing bases outside Afghanistan were rather clearly hedges against outliving American welcome in Afghanistan itself. Meanwhile, international leaders were pledging support for rebuilding an Afghanistan ravaged by over two decades of war (in other words, state-building), without being very specific about what that entailed. By the late spring of 2002, hardly any developmental—or even relief—assistance had arrived, to the growing frustration of the Afghans. As of late 2005, the American presence remains significant (Karzai's personal bodyguards, for instance, are Americans). No one is referring to Iraq in these precise terms, but restoring order (peacekeeping) and rebuilding Iraq (state-building) remain basic needs.

Basic Distinctions

Outside interference in the affairs of other states is always problematic. While the motives underlying interference may be noble and pristine (they may also not be), they are never going to be viewed by those in whose countries interference occurs in the same way they are by the intervening parties. The initial motivation during the 1990s among interveners (usually under the flag of the United Nations) was publicly humanitarian, and helping the suppressed and suffering is always part of the honest motives that impel the actions. This is as true in American-dominated missions like Iraq as it is in U.N. operations. Such efforts will always likely meet some initial opposition, which will increase the longer the operation lasts and the intervening parties stay. This is true because intervention always has the effect—if not the intention—of providing advantage to some internal factions at the cost to others, and the losers will eventually not appreciate the effort or view it as benign. How many Sunnis welcomed the American intervention in Iraq, for instance? At the same time, lengthy interventions, especially in the formerly colonized world, will almost certainly begin to look like recolonization and create rumblings of imperialism.

This uncertainty of reception helps create the frame within which outside interference is contemplated. What outsiders propose to do really consists of two determinations. The first is what it will try to accomplish—its concept. To this end, the basic alternatives are between conflict suppression and state-building. The other question is how to accomplish the task—its form. Here we look at a continuum of actions with peace imposition and peacekeeping as its poles. We briefly define each of these and then examine them in some detail.

The first distinction is between conflict suppression and state-building. One of the frequent, recurring criticisms of American involvements in developing-world conflicts in the past has been the open-endedness of these missions. Part of this criticism is focused on the absence of establishing a clear initial objective to be accomplished. This criticism in turn leads to the more frequent alleged shortcoming, which is the lack of a clear point at which the mission is accomplished, sometimes called an end or exit strategy that tells us when we can go home. The absence of such criteria causes us to remain apparently endlessly and even aimlessly in places such as Bosnia and Kosovo and continues to afflict the deployment in Iraq and to a lesser extent Afghanistan. The longer the stay and the more seemingly ubiquitous the presence of the outsider, the greater the resentment of that presence will be among some groups, especially those which do not benefit from that presence, like the Iraqi Sunnis. This dynamic will occur regardless of how noble the outsider's personal intentions are.

When entering the chaos of a war-torn developing-world country that has been unable to terminate the violence itself (which is why a mission is called for in the first place), a state can have one of two missions. The first is conflict suppression, which involves either stopping the ongoing fighting (peace imposition) or making sure that a recently established but volatile ceasefire remains in place (peace enforcement). These actions do no more than cause the fighting and killing to stop; they do not in and of themselves assure postwar domestic tranquility. The simplest measure of success is whether the fighting is discontinued.

Conflict suppression does not, of course, address or solve the problems that led to fighting in the first place. A more ambitious definition of successful conflict suppression is that it results in continued peace after the force has been withdrawn. Unless the underlying causes of fighting are addressed, the reasons for fighting remain and are likely to be rekindled after the intervening parties leave. Conflict suppression deals, in other words, with the symptoms of violence, not the underlying disease. It is a bandage to staunch the wound, not a cure.

Since intervention usually occurs in failed or noncompetitive states, leaving behind a stable, nonviolent environment in which the return to violence will seem unappealing to the formerly warring parties is the clear requisite to success. As already noted, the societies that tend to collapse into violence generally require both political reform (institution-building, political reconciliation, etc.) and economic development to create a sense of present or future tranquility and prosperity that is clearly preferable to war and that thus commands the loyalty of the population (in other word, results in the conferral of legitimacy to the regime). The collective actions taken to accomplish this goal are what we call state-building.

Where both of these concepts are instituted, they are clearly sequential. A conflict must be terminated before any state-building can begin. A country can engage in conflict suppression without engaging in state-building, although the outcome is likely to be a reversion to war after the conflict-suppressing force withdraws. State-building cannot be undertaken unless successful conflict suppression has occurred; it would not be safe to try to do so.

This leads to distinctions about what the intervening state attempts to do—the forms of intervention. In common terms, interventions are known collectively as peacekeeping, although the term is misleading in its generally accepted form and describes only a part of what is undertaken when intervention occurs.

The forms of intervention encompass three distinct activities that form a continuum paralleling the three phases of contemporary asymmetrical war already introduced. At one end of the spectrum is peace imposition, which refers to actions taken to stop the violence in a war zone. In most but not all cases, peace imposition is undertaken for neutral purposes to stop the fighting and killing, what may be called neutrality of intent. The effect of stopping the fighting will never, however, be neutral in effect, if for no other reason than stopping the fighting halts the military success of whoever was winning and ensures the likely failure of whoever was losing. The result is that some will congratulate and embrace the interveners (the winners, like the Iraqi Shi'a) and some will not (the losers, like the Iraqi Sunni). This is even more dramatically the case when those imposing peace have created the situation in the first place, such as the United States did by overthrowing governments in Iraq and Afghanistan.

At the other end of the continuum is peacekeeping. In its classic sense, peacekeeping consists of monitoring and observing an established ceasefire between warring parties when the peacekeepers' intent and effect is to oversee a temporary condition of peace conducive to discussions intended to produce a lasting, stable peace. In the terms introduced above, a peacekeeping setting is one where state-building activities can be undertaken with the relative assurance that the peacekeepers will not be the victims of violence while they build or rebuild the economic and political infrastructure of the target country.

Lying between these two extreme forms of activity is peace enforcement. It is an activity undertaken when the physical fighting has been concluded but wherein it is uncertain that peace would be sustained in the absence of the outside force. Whereas peace imposition and peacekeeping represent responses to concrete, finite situations (states of war, peace desired by all parties), peace enforcement constitutes a wide range of situations, from a near state of war in which few of the participants prefer war to its alternative, to a situation in which almost, but not all, parties prefer peace. Most real situations into which outside forces are committed rightfully fall in the category of peace enforcement. Iraq, after "major combat" was declared ended in 2003, is a prime example.

Why are these basic distinctions necessary as a preface to a more detailed discussion of what we can and should do? The answer is that language is often used imprecisely when describing the options available, leading to confusion and misplaced actions and expectations. Afghanistan is a prime example.

Even before the last bombing run and the last organized shots were fired in Afghanistan in 2001, there was agreement about what the international community would help to undertake in that war-ravaged land—we would send in peacekeepers to make sure peace held (at least in urban areas such as Kabul), and we would rebuild the country and help its transition to stable rule (which roughly meant to create a government that opposes and will not harbor terrorists), or state-build

Is this language applicable to Afghanistan (or for that matter, was it applicable to Bosnia, or Kosovo)? Was the situation into which international peacekeepers were placed one of general tranquility, in which peace was the overwhelming desire of virtually everyone? Of course not. The fact that the United States felt the need for a continuing military presence in the country and surrounding countries clearly indicated the assessment that war could break out again, meaning the situation was a peace enforcement problem. The only question was where on the war–peace continuum the situation fell. Similarly, building the Afghan state in the state of chaos in which Afghanistan existed when the goal was articulated in late 2001 seemed fanciful in the short run. Although we use different language to describe what we seek to accomplish in Iraq, the needs are the same.

Peacekeeping

The term *peacekeeping* has its contemporary origins in a specific set of U.N. operations conducted during the Cold War that constituted one of the few notable successes of the world organization during that period. Those activities basically conform to the definition of peacekeeping described earlier and emphasize the observation and monitoring of ceasefires between formerly warring parties. In most cases, these peace-keeping forces were put in place between sovereign countries and had the passive pur-pose of making sure the terms of ceasefires were honored. Their success occurred when the parties truly preferred peace to war and thus preferred maintenance of the status quo to a return to violence. In those circumstances, peacekeepers could be neutral both in intent and in effect, thereby adding positively to the situation for all concerned. Peacekeeping works, in other words, when the parties want peace roughly in confor-mance with the conditions the peacekeepers are assigned to enforce.

That set of circumstances rarely holds in internal wars, as the United Nations learned in its two major Cold War intrusions into domestic fracases in the former Belgian Congo (later Zaire, now the Democratic Republic of Congo) and Cyprus. In the Congo in 1960, U.N. peacekeepers opposed the attempted secession of Katanga (now Shaba) province and found themselves in the position of partisans rather than neutrals, to the organization's discomfort and the mission's ineffectiveness. In Cyprus in 1967, the United Nations was so successful in imposing peace and a ceasefire line that the Greeks and Turks concluded there was no real need to settle their differences as long as UNFICYP (U.N. Forces in Cyprus) remained in place. The U.N. mission is still there, with no real prospect of being concluded and withdrawn.

When the Cold War ended, these distinctions and limitations were largely lost. In the euphoria of the U.N.-sponsored Desert Storm coalition, the security role of the world body seemed to have been enhanced, and it appeared likely the U.N. role would become central to international security. In 1991, the Security Council in-structed Secretary-General Boutros Boutros-Ghali of Egypt to draw up a blueprint for U.N. participation in the promotion of international peace in the post–Cold War world. In 1992, he produced *An Agenda for Peace*. Among other things, it la-beled almost any international intervention, regardless of whether it was in wars be-tween states (which have been virtually nonexistent since the Persian Gulf War) or internal (which virtually all wars have been), as peacekeeping. The confusion over roles and missions has been ongoing ever since.

The problem, of course, is that the wake of internal wars rarely resembles the tranquil situation for which traditional peacekeeping is designed. In most cases, missions are not contemplated until violence has been going on for some time and when the trigger for international action is the public revelation of hideous, often grotesque atrocity (such as in Rwanda). In those circumstances, the impulse for rec-onciliation will likely be overwhelmed by the desire for retribution, which peace-keepers can only interrupt (Albanian Kosovar reprisals against their Serbian former persecutors provides an example). The situation is normally tentatively one of peace enforcement—at best—wherein intervening forces must actively work to sustain the absence of violence rather than simply observe and monitor an established peace. The ability to remain neutral in effect, so crucial to successful peacekeeping, is nearly impossible to attain.

This situation has operational consequences as well. Classic, traditional peace-keepers are lightly armed forces (generally with only handheld weapons to be used only in personal self-defense) that require a minimum of physical or military support, since it is not anticipated they will be placed in harm's way. This also makes them relatively inexpensive, an attribute that makes them appealing to the United Nations, which must rely on the often fickle collection of member-state contributions to support its activities. Peacekeeping is cheaper than fighting a war, making the characterization of situations as peacekeeping appealing to a perpetually financially strapped organization like the United Nations.

The problem arises when a force designed for peacekeeping (and so conceptualized) is thrown into a war zone. This is exactly what happened in 1992 in Bosnia, when the UNPROFOR (United Nations Protection Force) was charged with monitoring a ceasefire between Serbs and Croats that almost immediately (and predictably) broke down, leaving the peacekeeping force at the mercy of more heavily armed oppositions. In the most embarrassing of situations, UNPROFOR soldiers were kidnapped and literally chained to military vehicles by Bosnian Serb forces to keep American and British bombers from attacking them.

The tasks and complexities surrounding generic peacekeeping take on added meaning if we add two other dimensions to the peace imposition–peace enforcement–peacekeeping continuum, as shown in Figure 11.1.

In the figure, the situation and missions are as already described, with the addition of the term *unstable peace* to describe the range of situations in which peace enforcement is needed. Clearly, the peace is increasingly stable as we move away from war and toward the consensus that peace is most desirable. The figure also shows the kinds of military skills required in various stages of the operation. When war is ongoing and peace must be imposed, the need is clearly for combat soldiers with all the equipment and other wherewithal necessary for self-protection and for imposing its will on a hostile enemy by brute force. When stable, self-sustaining peace is achieved, the monitoring function is largely a police function: the peacekeepers essentially make sure the "law" represented by the terms of the ceasefire are obeyed. The tools of their trade are light sidearms and aids to observation like binoculars. Combat soldiers may or may not be proficient at policing; police officers are typically not prepared for all-out combat.

The problem, of course, lies in the hybrid situation of unstable peace, which is the condition into which most outsider forces are in fact interposed (occasionally after imposing the peace in the first place) and where they are likely to be called upon to perform in the future. Clearly, when peace is fragile and fighting could resume, both combat and policing skills are needed, and in varying degrees of mixture as the situation changes. When the experience of war is still fresh, the combat soldier will still be needed to intimidate and coerce the parties not to begin fighting among themselves or to attack the peacekeepers. That role may provide a kind of shield behind which other,

Figure 11.1: Situations, Missions, and Force Requirements

Situation:	War -------------------	Unstable Peace	------------	Peace
Mission:	Peace Imposition -----	Peace Enforcement	--------	Peacekeeping
Force Required:	War Fighters -----------	War Fighters/Police	--------	Police

more positive and reconciling activities can take place, but in that role, soldiers do not contribute to the positive attainment of peace. The soldier, unlike the beat cop, does not befriend the neighbors where he patrols; doing so may get the soldier killed.

Ideally, the same people can fulfill both the combat and policing roles, adapting chameleon-like to changing conditions and adapting their behaviors accordingly. Unfortunately, the character and skills that make a good combat soldier generally are not the same as those for a good police officer, and developing the second set of skills may degrade the primary skill: the soldier-cop becomes a less lethal soldier, and the cop-soldier becomes a less compassionate, more ruthless cop. This dynamic is explored in the caricature contained in Amplification 11.2. The bottom line is

Amplification 11.2

THE TALK-SHOOT RELATIONSHIP IN PEACEKEEPING

The kinds of troops that should be employed in peacekeeping has been a matter of disagreement since the United States began participating in these enterprises and is an especially difficult matter in situations where duties go beyond simple observation and monitoring to actual or potential combat operations. Should peacekeepers be lightly and defensively armed observers on the model of military police? Should they be fully armed combat troops ready to respond to any situation? Or should the same peacekeepers be used to fill both functions?

The official position of the American military is that regular combat forces can be trained to be peacekeepers as well as combatants, and the frequent assertion by official military sources is that "any good soldier can do peacekeeping." But is that assertion true?

One way to look at the roles of passive peacekeeper/police officer and combat soldier/peace imposer or enforcer is what we can call the "talk-shoot relationship." For the policeman confronted with a potentially dangerous situation, the procedure is to try to resolve the situation peacefully and to fire only as a last resort in self-defense (talk first, then shoot). For a combat soldier, the failure to attack in a dangerous situation may be to put his or her life in peril, and the appropriate response is to defend one's self (shoot first, then ask questions). The peacekeeper who fires first may be a murderer; the soldier who fails to shoot first may be dead.

Can the same personnel perform both functions, making the right decision in stressful situations? What does the combat soldier on patrol do when he sees someone about to throw something at him, not knowing if the object is a rotten tomato or a grenade? The decision is particularly difficult if the assailant is a child, as is increasingly the case and for which the military has few developed procedures (see the Singer article, listed in the Selected Bibliography, for an assessment of this aspect of the problem). Also, can soldiers effectively make the transition back and forth from one role to another? If involvement in other people's internal conflicts is to become a common part of the future, answers to these kinds of questions must be found.

that real peacekeeping in the contemporary world includes a variety of roles that shift over time, suggesting the need to alter and fine-tune the composition of the force across time and as progress is attained.

The ongoing situation in Iraq illustrates this dynamic. The initial phase of peace imposition (if not in response to preexisting disorder and violence in the country) was a classic combat operation carried out by combat troops. The hope was that the new status quo would rapidly be accepted by the Iraqi people, producing a stable peace for which a shrinking peacekeeping force would be appropriate. Instead, the peace was rejected by the most disadvantaged group (the Sunnis), who instigated an armed resistance that has resulted in a peace enforcement situation closer to the war than the stable peace end of the continuum.

Even when the complexities of these situations are recognized and addressed, they only speak to part of the problem. Almost all the conditions that peacekeepers contribute to fall within the category of conflict suppression. As the situation moves toward the peace end of the continuum, the peacekeepers as police may make some positive contributions to restoring public confidence in the criminal justice system, but this will mostly occur when they are handing off their duties to natives recruited to replace them.

Moving the situation to one of stable peace requires restoring (or creating) confidence and loyalty to the existing order in the country itself. The changing roles assigned to peacekeepers may contribute to that goal and even be a necessary condition for success. Peacekeepers cannot create the conditions necessary to build a stable political system and economic prospects of prosperity. Doing those things is the province of individuals and organizations engaged in state-building.

State-Building

The rationale for state-building is a logical extension of the justification for conflict suppression. A state intervenes in the internal affairs of another for one of two reasons: either because the target state is engaged in a civil disagreement it seems incapable of solving itself and which manifests itself in great suffering (the humanitarian argument) or because the intervening state has some interest in a particular outcome (the realist argument). The first justification underlay American involvement in places like Bosnia, Kosovo, and earlier Somalia. The second justification formed the basis for American involvement in Afghanistan and may be extended to other places as part of the expanded "war" on global terrorism (as in the Philippines).

State-building is a logical part of these motives because simple conflict suppression will not by itself solve the root problems from which the violence has arisen in the first place—the conditions of the swamp. Somalia illustrates this problem. The roots of Somali anarchy lay in clan divisions that were deep-seated and historical and that had been magnified by several years of drought and starvation. The international effort there, however, was limited and short-sighted, at least partly because it was the first time the international community, with the United States in the lead, had tried to save a failed state. The initial effort was limited to conflict suppression designed to reinstate the flow of food supplies donated by the international community until the end of the drought began to result in crops being harvested.

The effort succeeded as far as it went, but it did not go far enough. Conflict suppression had eased the food crisis within weeks and had, by the estimates of American officials such as Chester Crocker, saved well over a hundred thousand lives that would otherwise have been lost to starvation. Unfortunately, staunching the wound did not address the real underlying problem—political chaos and structural economic misery—which the participants in UNISOM had no plans to address. Instead, they engaged in incremental acts of what we now call state-building, including trying to disarm competing warlords. The attempted disarmament of one clan leader's forces (those of Muhammed Farah Aideed) created such animosity that it produced the "Black Hawk Down" ambush in which nineteen Americans perished and which sent us scurrying away. The result has been that Somalia has largely remained in a state of desperately poor anarchy.

The idea of state-building went into disrepute after Somalia, enshrouded as a form of hated mission creep (incremental, unplanned expansion of the mission that distorts its original intent) that had led to American failure in that campaign. The charge was always misinformed. The United States failed to produce a stable situation in Somalia not because of what we did but because of what we did not do, which was attempt to engage in state-building. The effort might have failed had we done so, in which case we would *truly* have failed. It was not until the end of the decade of the 1990s that we decided to try again, declaring the building of a stable state the goal in Kosovo, a promise reiterated for Afghanistan in 2001 and, at least implicitly, in Iraq in 2003.

Can state-building turn a failed, noncompetitive state into a stable, contributing member of the international community? The answer is that we do not know because we have never systematically tried to do so before in the kinds of countries where attempts at state-building are likely to occur in the present and future. It is sometimes suggested that we engaged in state-building in Germany and Japan after World War II, but the problems were not the same. In the former Axis countries, the problem was clearing the rubble and rebuilding the physical infrastructure. The price we exacted was acceptance of democratic constitutions, the success of which we made highly likely with the generous influx of cash. If there is any parallel to the present, it may be the Republic of Korea, which became a priority after the Korean War, but we provided resources there proportionately far in excess of the amounts that will be available in contemporary failed states.

The inability confidently to predict success, combined with the frank admission that it will be a long, expensive, and difficult process, makes selling state-building difficult. Moreover, the places for which it is proposed—the failed and failing states—are simultaneously the most in need and, by definition, the most unprepared for the process. Just as the "great game" (Russo-British competition for influence) in nineteenth-century Afghanistan ultimately resulted in failure for both, American-led state-building may also fail.

Having said all that, the last two American presidents (Clinton in Kosovo, Bush in Afghanistan) have committed the United States to engage in state-building. To help assess what lies ahead for these efforts, I borrow three questions that I originally asked in *When America Fights* around which to organize the discussion: Where to go? What to do? And how to do it?

Where to Go? For the immediate future, that question has largely been answered. The United States is already part of the United Nations–led effort in Kosovo and is part of a similar, evolving effort in Afghanistan and Iraq. The "sample" has the virtue of representing the two motivations underlying intervention: humanitarianism in Kosovo, realism and geopolitics in Afghanistan. The countries also represent the various levels of desperation state-builders will encounter: Kosovo, as a province within European Yugoslavia, is much more developed than Afghanistan, whereas Iraq lies somewhere in between in developmental terms. At the same time, the outcome in Kosovo does not have the same urgency and thus priority that Afghanistan and Iraq have by virtue of being subsumed in the category of the war against terrorism.

The determination of places in which to intervene and engage in state-building is only partially our own choice. There may be some other places like Afghanistan where an apparent deployment of necessity leads to a state-building mission of equal necessity, and where American initiatives trigger the need, as in Iraq. More opportunities are likely to present themselves in states where failure and noncompetitiveness have their primary, even whole, negative impact on the citizens of the country itself and where involvement and subsequent state-building must be justified on humanitarian grounds, deployments and missions of choice. What they will all share is the enormous, even daunting, problems that state-builders will encounter.

Recognizing how difficult circumstances are likely to be is crucial to determining whether to engage in state-building. In most instances, there will be no functioning government (by design, in some cases, as in the criminal insurgencies) that has the loyalty of any sizable portion of the population. Instead, there are likely to be competing groups eager to ingratiate themselves with the state-builders to benefit themselves but unable to cooperate or uninterested in cooperating among themselves. Institutions are likely to be in ruin where they exist at all, and basic service providers are likely to be in short supply (during the Serb ethnic cleansing in Kosovo, public servants such as clerks and mail carriers were systematically targeted and killed to break down the Kosovars' ability to self-govern, for instance). Moreover, no regime or group is likely to have legitimacy in the eyes of the general population, a problem likely exacerbated by atrocities committed during the violent stage of the civil unrest. Sometimes these problems will be structural and historical, as in the tribal, clan-based warlord systems in Afghanistan and Somalia; sometimes they will be the result of the excesses of the civil conflict, as in Bosnia and Sierra Leone. Other problems, like those in Iraq, may be the result of regime change that threatens the established ethnic power order.

Economic travail is likely to be present as well. It is generally true that political peace and stability accompany prosperity and economic improvement and not poverty and misery, but the lack of peace and prosperity are major contributors to failed and noncompetitive status. Infrastructures are either nonexistent or destroyed by years of war (a central problem in Afghanistan) and must be built or rebuilt before other services can be addressed. In cold climates (Kosovo and Afghanistan) where winter is a problem and many homes have been destroyed, simply providing a warm space in which to live may be a top priority. In hot places like Iraq, turning the air conditioning back on is equally important.

What to Do? Although the generalized goals of state-building are easy to articulate, getting there is difficult and is made more difficult by two problems, one discussed in this section, the other in the next. The first is what exactly needs to be accomplished and is made more difficult by the absence of any comprehensive list of characteristics or plan for achieving them. The second is our general lack of detailed knowledge about local conditions and people, creating a difficulty in knowing with whom to deal and how.

Building or rebuilding an internal war–ravaged country requires action on at least four dimensions, all of which must be accompanied by and must reinforce efforts by peacekeepers. The first dimension is *political*, somehow bringing a sense of order and eventually legitimacy into a setting that probably lacks both. Within this category, the first and most vital task is the simple establishment of order, creating the condition where citizens can expect peace and the absence of crime in their daily lives. Initially, this role will likely be assigned to peacekeepers, but if the situation is one of peace enforcement and the peacekeepers are in fact combat soldiers, they need rapidly to be replaced by police when conditions allow. This process is a key element of the evolving American mission in Iraq.

A major first task is the recruitment of a police force, initially internationally and later from within the population. While this task seems obvious, it is not necessarily easy. Finding foreign police willing to serve in war zones is not easy; a force of thirteen thousand was authorized for Kosovo in 1999 and has never been achieved, even at premium salaries of over $90,000 for a one-year tour. Finding locals may also be hard; when the United States recruited a gendarmerie for Haiti in the mid-1990s, it turned out that many of the officers hired were former members of the terrorist *tonton macoutes* who wanted to be police so they could extract bribes from drug traffickers operating in the country. In Iraq, the resistance has targeted police recruits for assassination as a way to discourage volunteerism. At the same time, the criminal justice system must be revamped so that people view it as fair, and other governmental institutions must be created or restructured and personnel recruited to operate them. Simultaneously, preparations for turning governance over to citizens must be undertaken. In many cases, this entails helping to draft constitutional documents and finding the appropriate people to engage in a constitutional convention in a situation in which we know relatively little about the candidates and there is a long and well-established tradition of mistrust and noncooperation between groups in the political arena.

The second dimension of the problem is economic. When international interveners arrive on the scene, they are likely to encounter wretched economic conditions reflecting the destruction of the economy or the absence of developed economic structures. In some cases, what little economic activity does exist may be criminal, as in Afghan poppy and heroin production. In virtually all cases, conditions are likely to be sufficiently chaotic and unappealing that foreign investors are almost certain to be unwilling to come in, establish themselves, and create the kinds of jobs necessary for prosperity.

The first task is basic infrastructure development and rehabilitation. Where they exist at all, roads are in disrepair, bridges have been damaged or destroyed, railroad tracks are in disrepair, and airfields have been pockmarked or mined or both. All need attention for normal activities, including commerce, to resume. At the same time, electricity and water supplies have probably been disrupted; schools, hospitals, and other public buildings burned or bombed; stores looted; and private homes and apartments damaged. Until basic conditions of survival and living can be secured and the most basic services necessary for commerce and economic activity reinstated, little progress can be made on other fronts.

Military personnel attached to peacekeeping can be useful in alleviating some of these miseries. Just as soldiers (and especially military police) can help establish order and civic affairs units can aid in institution-building, so too can soldiers and military engineers repair and secure runways, roads, and bridges. These personnel are unlikely to be available in sufficient numbers or for long enough periods of time to make more than a dent in the problems (many of the American service personnel with the requisite skills are reservists whose long-term availability is controversial), but they can contribute to getting the process started. Private contractors represent one alternative, but protecting them has been an added burden in Iraq, and the lucrative nature of many of the contracts has led to charges of corruption and bribery in the awarding of some contracts.

Longer-term economic success almost certainly requires attracting outside capital in the forms of foreign direct investment, location of manufacturing facilities, and the like, in the target country. In order for this to occur, however, the target country must make itself attractive to investors. In addition to overcoming a likely unsavory reputation from the past, this means the development of policies and laws friendly to investors, the development of financial and educational institutions to support business, and a condition of tranquility and peace to reassure potential investors that their investments will not literally blow up in their faces.

The third dimension is social. In most of the failed states, there is a social cleavage within the population that may be racial (Haiti), ethnic (Iraq and Sri Lanka), clan or tribal (Afghanistan or Somalia), religious (Indonesia), or some combination of those (Bosnia, Kosovo), wherein identification with one group and targeting of one or more of the other groups has been the basis for violence. The result of violence, often aimed at innocent noncombatants, inflames hatreds already present, leaving a postwar condition of animosity, distrust, and desire for revenge that must be overcome. Doing so is usually easier said than done.

These emotions often run very deep, especially in countries where there was physical mixing of communities before the conflict. When the violence pits neighbor against neighbor, reconciliation after the fact can be especially difficult to accomplish. In Rwanda, for instance, Hutu tribal members identified their Tutsi neighbors for slaughter. In Bosnia, after marauding "militias" had driven particular ethnic groups out of villages, members of the offending group would occupy or destroy their homes.

The Bosnian government and international peacekeepers are still trying to return the dispossessed to their former homes. How Iraqi Sunnis, Shiites, and Kurds will finally reconcile is an ongoing question.

The residue of hatred and distrust in these communities will linger, in some cases for a generation or more. In some instances, it may be possible to partition the states in ways that leave ethnic or other groups together and secure. Cyprus is an example. In most cases, however, the partition solution is impossible or is more traumatic than not separating groups. In a country like Bosnia, or instance, commingling of population groups and the absence of natural physical boundaries (wide rivers, for instance) to create secure separation mean there are no easy ways to partition the country. At any rate, such solutions almost certainly involve uprooting and moving people to create ethnically pure communities. The history of such forced migrations does not commend partition as a method for broader application. The aftermath of partition of the Asian Subcontinent in 1947—when eight to ten million Muslims and Hindus were uprooted and forced to flee to countries where they were in the majority—is stark testimony to this problem.

The fourth dimension is psychological. Although many assessments of state-building ignore or play down this dimension, it is clear that the atrocious conduct of many of these wars scars many of the survivors, often for life. People, especially children, see acts of gruesome violence committed before their eyes. When it is personalized—a child watching the gory execution of a parent—the result can be deeply traumatizing and require considerable counseling to assimilate. Even hardened soldiers experience debilitating mental problems.

It is almost universally true that in the countries that experience these traumas, there is an absolutely inadequate supply of doctors and psychologists to deal with the problem. It is also usually the case that the health care system in these countries is one of the first victims of war. Since the health care systems typically were fairly primitive before the violence, the result is that a bad situation becomes even worse. An ABC television report on January 17, 2002, for instance, revealed there were only *eight* psychiatrists and three mental health wards in all of Afghanistan to treat the psychologically disabled there. The ward in Kandahar was little more than an open courtyard in which patients were chained so they could not harm others.

How to Do It? The preceding discussion has touched on only the tip of the iceberg of substantive problems with which state-builders must contend. This formidable list of tasks must be carried out in a situation in which multiple actors with very different perspectives and affiliations must cooperate with local officials in a place with which the state-builders are only generally familiar. The environment is likely to be competitive and chaotic, and not all of the groups providing services will trust either one another or the target groups whom they are trying to assist. To add to the problem, there is no "guidebook" on organizing such operations, and the international system lacks enough experience to suggest comprehensive useful precedents.

The first concerted state-building exercise identified as such was mounted for Kosovo. As Amplification 11.3 indicates, it is not a model one would necessarily impose on other situations, such as the efforts in Afghanistan and Iraq. Creating a

Amplification 11.3

KFOR AND UNMIK

At the end of the campaign to drive the Serbs out of Kosovo in 1999, the United Nations announced that the goal of the mission would be to build a stable, prosperous order in that province that could decide either to unite within a newly constituted Yugoslavia or become independent. The mission is thus state-building. The structure announced to implement the goal shows clearly the complexity and difficulty this kind of operation entails.

Although the entire effort is officially under U.N. control, this is not entirely the case in fact. Indeed, there are two separate entities operating in Kosovo, each part of a different command structure. The military peacekeeping element is the Kosovo Force (KFOR), which is a North Atlantic Treaty Organization (NATO) force commanded by a NATO general and reporting to NATO headquarters. The state-building element of the operation is the United Nations Interim Mission in Kosovo (UNMIK), which is headed by the Special Representative of the Secretary General (SRSG) of the United Nations, and he or she reports to the United Nations. The SRSG, in turn, oversees the operations of four activities that constitute the major emphases of the state-building enterprise. Designated the four pillars, each function is administered by a different international organization. Civil administration is the responsibility of the United Nations itself; the development of political institutions is handled by the Organization of Security and Cooperation in Europe (OSCE); economic development is the job of the European Union (EU); and refugees are dealt with by the United Nations High Commission on Refugees (UNHCR). Each of these organizations has somewhat different memberships and reporting requirements. The relationship between KFOR and UNMIK is informal, based upon the personal ability of the KFOR commander and the SRSG to cooperate.

monolithic effort wherein all helping groups are operating together in a spirit of cooperation working toward commonly accepted goals is the obvious purpose. Accomplishing these goals is far from easy.

At a minimum, state-building will have two different groups performing different tasks. On the one hand, there will be a military element engaged in peace enforcement or peacekeeping. The primary task of the military is, of course, keeping order and preventing the recurrence of violence, effectively acting as a shield behind which state-building can move forward. Their secondary mission, which is sometimes ignored by those planning or executing these missions, is self-protection, making sure their own members are not subject to lethal attacks from groups that suffer because of their presence.

The military component cannot be considered a single, monolithic entity, and it may have very different priorities than others. In most cases, the peacekeeping force will be a coalition of forces drawn from several countries under the auspices of either the United Nations or another organization, such as NATO. These countries will be present for a variety of reasons. Some have a philosophical commitment to this kind of mission (Canada and Norway as peacekeepers, for instance), while others will be there to collect the $100 per diem allowance provided by the United Nations (Ghana and Bangladesh, for example). While a commander will be identified for the mission, the individual country contingents generally report to their own governments, which instruct them on which orders from the command structure to carry out and which to ignore. When national and international orders contradict one another, national priorities prevail.

The United States has a unique position in these efforts. As the world's remaining superpower, the United States will almost certainly be involved at some level, usually including the provision of some troops. American presence is often at the insistence of the target government, and it may be the sine qua non for acceptance of a mission by the host country, as was the case in Bosnia. That participation will generally be somewhat reluctant and come with at least two conditions. One is a maximum participation by other states to demonstrate that the United States is not shouldering a disproportionate share of the burden. It will also insist that its forces remain under American command to avoid being placed in unnecessarily risky situations where casualties may occur. Often the Americans are called upon to provide logistical support such as getting supplies and personnel to the locale (which means, at a minimum, some American soldiers will be on the ground to protect airfields and ports) and to provide satellite and other signal intelligence that only the United States has the physical capability to provide.

National control of peacekeeping forces and the mandate to limit exposure to danger mean the military side of the operation will be difficult and also virtually guarantees some level of friction between the peacekeepers and the civilian state-builders. The civilian element will also be a hodgepodge of different groups with different priorities. Representatives of governments providing developmental assistance will be on the scene identifying projects and making sure that the private contractors with whom they do business are fulfilling their obligations. Representatives from whatever international body is in charge of the state-building enterprise must try to coordinate national efforts to be certain the process is orderly and that vital priorities are being addressed. In addition, a multitude of nongovernmental organizations (NGOs) will be on the scene, either caregivers such Medicins sans Frontieres/Doctors without Borders ministering to medical needs or monitors such as Amnesty International on the outlook for human rights violations. The media will also be present, at least in the early stages while the mission is still "news."

The ingredients for organizational chaos are clearly present and are made worse by two other factors. The first is dealing with the citizens of the country, who are the supposed beneficiaries of the effort. Who are their legitimate representatives? What do they want, and why? Will international efforts benefit one formerly warring group at the expense of others, thereby making things potentially worse rather than better? Do the state-builders know enough about the country and its people to make valid independent judgments on any of these problems? The answers to these questions are often less than absolutely clear to the state-builders.

There is also rivalry between the various groups that make up the state-builders. There is a general tendency for all groups to think their own part of the enterprise is most important and should receive the highest priority. At the same time, priorities may contradict one another. Doctors without Borders, for instance, believes that its mission to minister to health needs is paramount, especially in remote areas that may not be entirely pacified. They demand, as part of carrying out their mission, military protection that military commanders motivated by exposure of their troops to minimal danger may be reluctant to provide. The military will feel the same way about assisting the press or human rights monitors.

Challenge!

WHAT SHOULD WE DO IN AFGHANISTAN?

The removal of the Taliban government from power and its replacement by the Karzai government—supported by American and other foreign forces—represented the conflict-suppression phase of the international effort in Afghanistan (phase one). With the election of a permanent government in 2004 and the beginnings of international efforts to build and rebuild that war-torn country, an international state-building campaign has begun. The extent of that effort and its effects are not clear from the vantage point of 2006.

There has been clear rhetorical support for draining the Afghan "swamp" and building a stable country that will resist terrorist appeals and join the antiterrorism coalition in the future. As of the end of 2005, that rhetoric had not translated into the massive assistance program that most agreed was necessary to produce a stable and hopefully democratic Afghanistan.

All four dimensions of state-building need attention. Progress in the military dimension is most advanced, as an Afghan armed force and constabulary have been initiated; whether they will run afoul of traditional Afghan tribal rivalries remains to be seen. The Taliban, for instance, have been reconstituted as a military force and effectively rule a good deal of the countryside. The economic dimension has hardly been addressed at all. There is wide agreement that massive amounts of money are necessary to build the Afghan economic infrastructure and to rebuild the country after so many years of war. Beyond more or less vague promises of assistance, the flow of resources has been slow to come, and Afghan patience is being tested. The social and psychological dimensions likewise suffer from years of privation and violence. Exacerbating the situation is official government repression of the one major cash crop that could pump money into the economy: heroin-producing poppies. Prior to the Taliban regime, nearly 70 percent of the world's heroin was grown in Afghanistan from poppies, and after the Taliban were overthrown, peasant farmers planted new crops that had been forbidden by the Taliban. At the prodding of Western governments, those crops were destroyed (with compensation) in 2002, but a record crop was reportedly harvested in 2003. Efforts to control the situation have had mixed success.

What should we do for Afghanistan? How many American tax dollars should be spent on rebuilding the Afghan infrastructure and in building a prosperous society—especially since the results cannot be guaranteed? It is one thing to call for making an antiterrorist bulwark out of Afghanistan, but what budgetary sacrifices should Americans be forced to endure to produce such a state? Also, the degree to which we respond to Afghanistan's plight will create a precedent for what other states may expect from the United States in the future. How serious are we *in fact* to the continuing campaign against terrorism as it threatens to "attack" our own wallets? If we are not serious about state-building in Afghanistan (and there is little evidence we are serious about implementing the necessary steps), will anyone believe we are any more serious about neoconservative dreams to build a stable, democratic Iraq that will act as a regional role model? What do you think?

CONCLUSION: THE NEW WORLD ORDER?

The purpose of this chapter has been to present a particularly prevalent problem facing the international system—how to deal with the internally based violence that marks the principal challenge to a peaceful world—and what may be done about such problems. As the analysis has indicated, neither the problem nor the possible solutions is easy, and we are still learning how to approach and surmount these difficulties.

Prior to September 11, 2001, much of this analysis may have seemed obscure, even academic. The new internal wars happen in remote parts of the world where there are few American interests and thus where the United States can engage itself or not without great repercussions for the American people—deployments of choice where humanitarian concerns are central to the decision of whether to intervene and for what purposes.

The decision to take action against the Taliban government of Afghanistan *and* to engage in state-building afterward changes that calculation. The underlying assumptions in Afghanistan and Iraq were apparently twofold. First, the division of the world into those who oppose terrorism and those who visibly do not means that terrorism sponsors or sanctioners are fair game for military actions—intervention, in other words. The effect is to widen the range of places where we will contemplate military action. The second assumption, on which the determination to engage in state-building is based, is that converting these former terrorist states into the antiterrorist coalition requires "terrorist-proofing" their countries through improvements in their conditions—draining the swamp.

Both of these assumptions can be challenged, as can their implications for how the United States will use force in the world in the future. In the wake of the September 11 events, there was a consensus in much of the world that terrorism should be rooted out wherever it exists, but as the list of states condoning or protecting terrorism expands, that consensus may erode. How much of the world is likely to support attacking Iraq, Iran, Syria, Sudan, Somalia, or Libya, all states tainted by past or present association with terrorists? Many states may conclude that the assumption that the world is divided into those who support or oppose terrorism is little more than an American excuse to beat up on those with whom it has issue.

At the same time, it is not abundantly clear that the terrorism-proofing premise is valid either. The chief problem is whether successful state-building is possible, and if it is, whether it will accomplish the goal set out for it: Can we create countries that will resist terrorism? No one knows at this point.

The implications of these assumptions about how to fight terrorism are also controversial. As noted, the imperative of going after terrorists shifted the reasons for which the United States would contemplate intervention in civil disturbances from a humanitarian to a geopolitical, realist base. As if to reinforce this change, the Bush administration committed over six hundred Special Operations Forces (SOFs) to assist the Philippine government in early 2002 to suppress a terrorist organization with alleged connections to Al Qaeda but that was not directly linked to the attacks against the United States at all. It is one thing to justify military action after a direct military attack against the United States or Americans; a broader onslaught on terrorism expands the instances where American force may be contemplated in the internal affairs of other states.

These developments are particularly puzzling coming from an administration that campaigned on the pledge of reducing the number of American deployments around the world. In its first year in office, it authorized deployments in Afghanistan and the Philippines, sent agents into Somalia to assess the possibility of deploying there (on the assumption that the Somalis might provide bin Laden safe haven), forged a military arrangement with several former Soviet republics, and renewed saber-rattling against Iraq. In all of these places, the justification was that the United States acted as part of its "war" on terrorism.

Finally, there is a domestic element in this area that has two aspects. There was not great enthusiasm in the United States for our involvements on humanitarian grounds in Bosnia, Haiti, and Kosovo, but there was not a great deal of objection to President Clinton's justification of Bosnia that "it's the right thing to do." The reasons probably had to do with the relative inexpensiveness of the operations and the absence of casualties incurred in carrying them out. The Bush charge that these deployments overextended American forces did not have great impact on the election campaign and rings a bit hollow given his administration's willingness to deploy forces widely in the name of antiterrorism. The new deployments, on the other hand, are both more expensive and more dangerous than those in the 1990s. How much treasure and how many lives are we willing to expend to put alleged Filipino terrorists out of business?

The other domestic aspect is the competition for resources. A sustained American presence in Afghanistan and Iraq, especially participating in state-building, is going to be a great deal more expensive than American expenses in Bosnia or Kosovo, and those expenses (as well as alleged overextensions of Americans deployed) will increase as we attempt an earnest state-building program in Iraq. The American people clearly supported the expense and sacrifice in response to the direct assault against the country in the Afghan campaign. Will they be willing to bear as much when the direct connections are more tenuous? If we renege on our promise to state-build in Afghanistan (which we largely have as of summer 2006), will we truly honor our commitment to bring stable peace to Iraq?

Selected Bibliography

Boutros-Ghali, Boutros. *An Agenda for Peace: Preventive Diplomacy, Peacemaking, and Peace-Keeping.* New York: United Nations, 1992.

Doran, Michael Peter. "Somebody Else's Civil War." *Foreign Affairs* 81, 1 (January/February 2002), 23–40.

Durch, William (Ed.). *The Evolution of UN Peacekeeping: Case Studies and Comparative Analysis.* New York: St. Martin's Press, 1993.

Eizenstat, Stuart, John Edward Porter, and Jerry Weinstein. "Rebuilding Weak States." *Foreign Affairs* 84, 1 (January/February 2005), 134–146.

Foreign Policy and the Fund for Peace. "The Failed States Index." *Foreign Policy* (July/August 2005), 56–65.

Goldstone, Jack A., and Jay Ulfelder. "How to Construct Stable Democracies." *Washington Quarterly* 28, 1 (Winter 2004–05), 9–20.

Gurr, Ted Robert. *Why Men Rebel.* Princeton, NJ: Princeton University Press, 1973.

Helman, Gerald B., and Steven R. Ratner. "Saving Failed States." *Foreign Policy,* 89 (Winter 1992–93), 3–20.

Krasner, Stephen D., and Carlos Pascual. "Addressing State Failure." *Foreign Affairs* 84, 4 (July/August 2005), 153–163.

Peters, Ralph. *Fighting for the Future: Will America Triumph?* Harrisburg, PA: Stackpole Books, 1999.

Rotberg, Robert. "Strengthening Governance: Ranking Countries Would Help." *Washington Quarterly* 28, 1 (Winter 2004–05), 71–81.

Sachs, Jeffrey D. "The Development Challenge." *Foreign Affairs* 84, 2 (March/April 2005), 78–90.

Singer, P. W. "Caution: Children at War." *Parameters* XXXI, 4 (Winter 2001–02), 40–56.

Snow, Donald M. *When America Fights: The Uses of U.S. Military Force.* Washington, DC: CQ Press, 2000.

CHAPTER 12

The Geopolitics of Globalization

PREVIEW

Globalization, the predominant international dynamic of the 1990s, was given a severe geopolitical jolt by the terrorist attacks of 2001. In this chapter, we assess the strength and durability of those globalization dynamics in areas such as their impact on American predominance in the international system and how the outbreak of terrorism changes the realities of the international condition. We argue that despite initial apparent incompatibilities between globalization and terrorism-induced geopolitics, there is a growing possibility of their compatibility in the longer run. Finally, it is possible to assert a long-term national security strategy for the United Sates that combines both concepts to confront an international environment that is based neither on the geopolitics of the Cold War nor on the globalization of the 1990s.

The decline of significant international military confrontation and globalization dominated the international political landscape of the 1990s. The relative decline of international military and political confrontation was symbolized by the implosion of operational Communism and the end of the Cold War as well as a general decline in the frequency of international conflicts. The economic and political homogenization of much of the world, symbolized by the spread of political democracy and free trade–based economic capitalism, appeared ascendant.

Those trends are nowhere nearly as sharply evident early in a new century. The events of September 11, 2001, have jolted the system out of the bliss of apparent peacefulness and reminded us of the continuing relevance of the military instruments of traditional geopolitics. A number of factors, including the clear rejection of the ideals of globalization in parts of the Middle East and the rise of international terrorism and terrorism-driven geopolitics, make the linear ascendancy of globalization as the central feature of the global system much less certain than it was before the terrorist attacks.

Although it is hyperbolic to argue that "everything changed" on September 11, 2001, the events of that day have clearly served as a symbol to cast a shadow over the international system and helped raise questions about the direction in which the first decade of the 2000s will lead us. One question that quickly emerges is whether the attacks of September 11 and subsequent attacks against American allies Spain and Great Britain and elsewhere (e.g., Indonesia) and the resultant figurative declaration of war on terrorism means a return to the national security–oriented international politics of the Cold War (or something parallel to that), a retrenchment of the movement toward a reduced role and importance of globalization, or some new *modus vivendi* between globalization and traditional national security concerns. Almost no one suggests the possibility that the globalizing trend of the 1990s will survive (or return) in the way it existed during the heyday of the 1990s—the question is how much of globalization will survive.

GLOBALIZATION AS A GEOPOLITICAL PHENOMENON

Exactly how to consider globalization as a force shaping future international relations was an unresolved issue at the turn of the twenty-first century. There was, for instance, considerable disagreement on the extent to which the globalizing economy had in fact permeated the economic life of the countries that had embraced it and thus how deep and abiding it effects were. Advocates of globalization argued the influence was profound and growing and that positive trends such as democratization and economic interdependence would progressively render war less likely in the future. Moreover, the shape and pervasiveness of globalization have continued despite the loss of the spotlight. Critics pointed to statistics that showed far less change in international life than supporters argued. Thus, critics maintained that globalization in fact was much less pervasive than globalization in theory. A growing minority even pointed to the pernicious effects in matters such as environmental degradation, job loss and displacement, and underlying American imperialism that they said accompanied globalization.

This debate had both domestic and international elements. Domestically, the rise of globalism was tied inextricably if differentially to America's changing economic situation. Clearly, the dynamics of globalization had provided the fuel and direction of American reassertion as the preeminent global economic power and had contributed greatly to the enormous American prosperity of the 1990s. Not all Americans shared equally in this prosperity, as already noted: the same wind that blew fair over large segments of the American economy also moved to destroy those elements of the economy that could not meet the Ricardan dictate of comparative advantage. Thus, domestically, the globalization of the 1990s bred both staunch advocacy and just as strong opposition to globalization and its consequences at the domestic level. That polarization continues in the 2000s.

Internationally, the process of globalization and United States dominance in global affairs became virtually synonymous. As globalization spread, it was clear that the American model of economic organization was the victor in the competition with other alternatives (notably the so-called Asian model). Globalization was making those places in the world where it intruded look increasingly American; some countries such as India and China are also looking increasingly like competitors for the lead in globalization.

On the positive side, the fact that so many international students attended school in the United States meant there were, in most countries, young elites anxious to emulate the American way as a means to achieve the prosperity and wealth of the American system and the political freedoms attached to the American model. On the other hand, there were, in most of those same states, more traditional elements who opposed the spread of the American gospel. For some, it was evidence of what many viewed as a heavy-handed, arrogant imperialism seeking to reinforce the American position as a unilateralist hegemon. To others, the intrusion of the American system and American values was a direct threat either to their worldview or to their places in their respective societies. To many traditional elements in those societies, American cultural imperialism was as bad as its economic imperialism. Just as in the domestic debate, the rise of globalism sparked a negative and positive reaction within the system.

This debate had not nearly reached closure when the first airliner plowed into the north tower of the World Trade Center. The worldwide economic downturn triggered by the Asian crisis had dampened economic growth and prosperity worldwide and thus had stifled part of the enthusiasm for globalization. The antiglobalism movement of the late 1990s, which caught most officials initially unprepared, was having a major disruptive effect on world economic meetings extolling and solemnizing globalization. In the United States, the election of George W. Bush, a free trader who was less demonstrative in his advocacy of globalization than his predecessor had been, did little to rekindle the fires of globalization. It was not unfair to say that globalization had already lost some of the momentum it had gained during the previous decade. There was even growing suspicion that the apparent prosperity of the 1990s was an economic bubble of overinflation and overvaluation ready to burst.

Globalization and traditional geopolitics are not, of course, an either-or proposition. In the narrow sense, the term *geopolitics* has historically referred to the relationship between geography and politics, and even when it was expanded by the Nazis in the 1930s to include the notion that politics is dependent on geography, that "theory" included the assumption that economic success required geographic control of territory and that economic strength was key to political success. The concept of globalization represented the same dynamic from the other end of the spectrum, arguing that maximizing economic commerce required overcoming barriers to trade based both in political restrictions and geographic impediments to the movement of goods and services. The term geopolitics had, over time, been expanded to be nearly synonymous with national security, which was clearly germane to the Cold War period but not so obviously relevant to the postwar period. By 2000, the two concepts were thoroughly intertwined with one another.

The disagreement was not so much whether globalization had superceded geopolitics as the heart of international politics as it was over which paradigm was most relevant in an environment in which they coexisted. The traditional geopoliticians had suffered a bad decade during the 1990s, as the realist paradigm seemed decreasingly relevant to dealing with a generally tranquil international environment wherein cooperation between states in the economic realm seemed more important than rivalry among them in the area of national security. Traditional geopolitical symbols such as military force seemed increasingly applicable mainly for marginal concerns like peacekeeping.

The interaction between globalization and traditional national security concerns was muted during this period. Occasionally, the realms of global economic expansion and traditional security concerns would overlap and rub against one another. The case of China and Taiwan, discussed in Amplification 12.1, seemed an exception to the

Amplification 12.1

CHINA, TAIWAN, GUNS, AND BUTTER

The dispute between the People's Republic of China and Taiwan has been going on ever since the Nationalist Government of China was defeated by Mao Zedung's Communists in 1949 and forced to flee to the island off the Chinese coast. Although the threat of armed conflict is always present, the dispute has evolved into a classic instance of the relationship between traditional geopolitics and globalization.

The political basis of the dispute is the status of Taiwan. Both the mainland Chinese and the government of Taiwan agree in principle that Taiwan and China are a single country (in effect, Taiwan is a province of China). The only dissenters from this assessment are native Taiwanese who inhabited Taiwan before the Nationalists arrived and who favor Taiwanese independence. The disagreement is who constitutes the legal government of China-Taiwan: the Chinese on the mainland claim they are, and the Nationalists say they are. Resolving the issue only becomes a high priority when the Taiwanese threaten to formally dissolve their ties to the mainland and declare their independence. When this suggestion was made formally in July 1999, China mobilized forces, and there were hints of war.

The major problem with a forceful resolution was that it would have been extremely bad for business, the result of globalization extending itself to both Taiwan and mainland China. In particular, the decade of the 1990s witnessed considerable investment in enterprises on the mainland by Taiwanese businessmen, in the amount of a reported $39 billion by 2001. Moreover, war to put down Taiwanese independence would badly damage the advanced economy on the island, which China considers a future cornerstone of Chinese economic might. In the end, economic interests prevailed: advocacies of Taiwanese independence subsided, the People's Republic stopped rattling their swords, and business returned to normal.

general rule, as the Chinese rattled sabers over the prospect that Taiwan might opt for formal independence at the same time that Taiwanese investment on the Chinese mainland was increasingly vital to the economic well-being of both. In fact, there were, and are, points of compatibility and incompatibility between the two forces that were not explored fully when globalization seemed supreme and national security less obviously vital.

Because of the terrorist attacks on the United States, traditional national security concerns have once again risen to the top of the American foreign policy and world political agendas. In the process, the sources of potential inconsistency between the twin thrusts of national security (symbolized by the GWOT) and continuing global-ization have begun to emerge. At the core of that incompatibility is the question of the openness of American (and global) society, leaving Kurt M. Campbell to warn, "A U.S. crusade against global terrorism is likely to place the U.S. national agenda, featuring homeland defense, major military strikes, and heightened security, more squarely at odds with the powerful forces of globalization."

It is, of course, premature to judge how the clash between globalization and geopolitics will work out in the long, or even the short, run. Before even trying to es-tablish the parameters of that struggle, it is first necessary to review how globalization became the geopolitical force of the 1990s and the implications of that emergence for the international system and especially attitudes toward the United States. In that context, we can look at some of the major points of disagreement between the two approaches that have emerged in the aftermath of the terrorist attacks.

Globalization and the American Decade of the 1990s

It is tempting to equate the globalization decade of the 1990s and the emerging geopolitical decade of the 2000s with the presidents and parties that oversaw the development of American policy emphases in one direction or another. There is some merit in such a typecasting. President Clinton had economic matters clearly at the forefront of his political agenda from the moment he entered office and even before. President George W. Bush campaigned on a pledge of strengthening the United States' defense posture as well as promoting free trade, the latter a position he had advocated consistently as the governor of Texas. At the same time, each was the beneficiary or victim of events. Bill Clinton's emphasis on economics was rarely diverted toward matters of national security, and certainly not in any fundamental way that would force a reorientation back toward geopolitics. George W. Bush had his priorities thrust forcefully upon him by the events in New York and Washington. Preferences and events colored both leaders' priorities.

Clinton's preference for emphasizing international economics as the core of for-eign policy was apparent before he was elected president and entered office. The 1992 campaign was waged in the context of a global recession, the American part of which was rightly or wrongly blamed on the administration of George H. W. Bush and which the Clinton campaign promised to remedy. After Clinton's nomination, the rallying cry invented by Clinton aide James Carville—"It's the economy, stupid!"—became a major focus of the campaign.

When Clinton took office, globalization became the international bedrock of his economic policy. On January 25, 1993, only weeks after taking office, he announced the formation of the National Economic Council to assist him in forming economic policy. Although created by executive order rather than statute, the parallel to the National Security Council was apparent, and the clear signal was that the new council would have equal billing with the NSC in the Clinton White House. To emphasize the international component of his economic emphasis, Clinton made a very public appearance at the initial meeting of the Asia-Pacific Economic Cooperation (APEC) in Seattle where, among other things, he met with Chinese leader Deng Xiao-peng and began the process of building strong economic ties between the two countries.

Despite the fact that Clinton's own political party contained many of the most prominent and vociferous opponents of globalization on the American political scene, free trade became the centerpiece of his international policy. Clinton completed the process of getting Congressional approval of the North American Free Trade Agreement (NAFTA) in 1993 (which had been negotiated by his predecessor, George H. W. Bush), emerged as the leading force in promoting closer ties within APEC, and lent American leadership and prestige to the Free Trade Area of the Americas (FTAA) proposal. All were premised on the idea that greater economic interchange through trade was beneficial to both American and world prosperity and tranquility. In foreign policy terms, the posture was known as "engagement and enlargement," which emphasized support for countries sharing basic American political and economic values.

During most of the 1990s, there were few overt negative repercussions of the Clinton emphasis on economics. The Persian Gulf War had been decided before he came to office, and the only remaining loose end from that experience was the continued intransigence of the Saddam Hussein government, particularly in the area of international inspection of suspected production of weapons of mass destruction—an issue passed along to the current Bush administration and a consideration that helped lead to overthrowing the Iraqi regime. Otherwise, national security problems were muted, essentially limited to questions of intervention in internal wars in the developing world.

Domestic politics did not impede this emphasis either. Clinton never attained a widespread level of support within the national security community, most of whose members held him in some private disdain, but neither was there any concerted opposition to his leadership either. That he did not serve in the military during Vietnam and had apparently "dodged the draft" (by means of student deferments employed by many others, including Vice President Richard Cheney, during that period) raised some hackles, as did his administration's advocacy of gays in the ranks. There was also muted criticism of his inattention to things like military modernization and force morale, but in a generally peaceful atmosphere, these criticisms did not gain great weight.

By the end of the 1990s, things had changed. The great prosperity of the early and middle years of the decade had been dampened by a general international economic downturn, and the general prosperity that muted criticism on other fronts had given way to more general levels of criticism than before (emboldened, of course, by Clinton's personal problems). Suddenly, it became acceptable to criticize both the process and consequences of globalization and the United States.

Challenges to American Leadership from the 1990s

As long as the good times rolled, there was very little argument about the virtues of globalization or concern about its rules or other matters of potential disagreement. When the financial crisis in East Asia in 1997 first revealed serious flaws in the structure of the emerging system and cracks appeared in the prosperity of the go-go 1990s, the result was second-guessing and criticism of the United States and its stepchild, globalization.

The East Asian financial crisis was the first crack in the general prosperity of the 1990s, and an apparent harbinger of things to come at the time. It began in Thailand in 1997 when the national currency, the *baht*, collapsed on local and international markets. Triggered by a currency devaluation (a policy stating that the currency would be exchanged with other currencies at a lower value), the crisis rapidly spread to other countries in the region, causing collapse and dislocation in countries like Malaysia, Indonesia, South Korea, and even Japan.

The crisis contained both domestic and international elements. Panicked by the announcement of the devaluation, foreign and domestic investors descended on Thai banks and later on banks in other countries, demanding to withdraw their funds before their worth could erode even more. The banks had wildly insufficient funds to cover these demands, because their reserves had been largely depleted by bad—and often corrupt—lending practices. Many had lost money entrusted to them but had hidden that fact from investors by opaque, secretive banking practices. This revelation further dampened investor confidence, leading to further devaluation and the crisis spreading to other countries that held increasingly worthless Thai currency.

International investors added to the panic. Overly optimistic estimates of the strengths of East Asian economies had resulted in foreign direct investment well in excess of the ability of East Asian economies to responsibly absorb. The result was excess capital that could be diverted to economically unsound, often corrupt uses. Often these instances of "crony capitalism" involved collaboration between bankers, borrowers, and government officials nominally entrusted to protect investors' funds but instead hiding behind inadequate or nonexistent accounting regulations that allowed misuse of funds. Mesmerized by short-term profits, international investors largely overlooked these practices as cultural prices that had to be paid to do business in these countries. When the economic collapse began, these same investors extricated their funds as quickly as they could, adding to the general panic and disorder in the area.

When the crisis threatened to spread globally, the international financial community entered the situation, demanding change. In the United States, for instance, the value of stocks on the New York Stock Exchange plunged by a quarter in the Dow-Jones index before stabilizing and rebounding, and there was great demand to insure the experience was not repeated. That the effects of the crisis were temporary and that virtually all of the affected economies bounced back in the early 2000s was almost lost in the fixation with terrorism after September 11.

The East Asian crisis was not the first crisis the globalizing economy had undergone. The culprit in Asia was identified as the lack of accountability in financial transactions, and the cure was greater openness and visibility for the conditions of financial institutions and the business they do (what is known as *transparency*). The United States had experienced a similar situation in the middle 1980s in the S&L crisis. In that case, a number of savings and loan associations (banks providing savings and making loans, especially in real estate) had collapsed because they had made unsound loan decisions that had stripped away savings accounts of small investors who had traditionally found the S&Ls to be a good and safe place for their savings. Because the executives of some of the bankrupt S&Ls had made considerable financial contributions to elected officials, the crisis became a political scandal not unlike the corporate scandal of 2002. The result was a series of new regulations on financial institutions designed to insure transparency and thus honesty and responsibility within the American banking community.

The reaction to the financial crisis in East Asia was to demand that reforms similar to those enacted in the United States after the S&L scandal be applied to East Asian economies. This demand pitted the so-called American model of economic performance against the Asian (largely Japanese) model. Due to cultural and historical practices, the major difference between the two approaches was the degree of openness in financial activity. Based in traditions of deference to elders, different codes of ethical behavior, and the like, Asian practices were considerably more closed than those that had evolved in the West, especially the United States. A precondition for qualifying for funds from the International Monetary Fund (IMF) and other lenders to aid in recovery from the Asian crisis was the adoption of American financial practices. These requirements created resentment, particularly because the funds made available went first to compensate foreign investors rather than to the citizens in affected countries that had lost their savings.

Resentment was also increased by the fact that East Asian countries had no real choice but to accept the restrictions meted out by the IMF. Funds for recovery were not available elsewhere, and the IMF "seal of approval" of financial practices was necessary to attract direct investments into foreign economies. Moreover, the IMF was largely—and not entirely incorrectly—seen as little more than the agent of the United States government when it placed demands on countries, thereby increasing the sense of cultural imperialism on the part of the Americans.

The Asian crisis chilled some of the enthusiasm for globalization, as countries that had bought wholeheartedly into the process reassessed their situations in the wake of the crisis and the sacrifices of recovery. In places such as Indonesia (see Chapter 11, Amplification 11.1) the experience was particularly traumatic, and in addition to the political travails it entailed, it triggered a national debate over the extent and terms of its association with the globalizing economy. The crisis exposed an underlying structural economic vulnerability in places such as Japan, the strength of whose economy had not been publicly questioned or debated previously. Suddenly, globalization seemed neither as inevitable nor as necessarily desirable as it once had.

It also left a lingering bad taste in many Asian countries about the suitability of American and IMF "remedies" for the problems that led to the crises.

Questions about the globalizing economy also resulted in greater scrutiny and criticism of the United States. When globalization was producing increased prosperity for all participants, there was relatively little negative expression about the paramount role of the United States and its dominance of the world economy. The implicit sanctimony of American insistence on adopting its "superior" model privately rankled many who could not openly express their reservations while the system worked.

When the global economy slowed, such inhibitions dissolved. The forums in which the free trade motor of globalization was extolled suddenly became the objects of a wide-ranging coalition of rejectionists who saw globalization as exploitive, a threat to national sovereignty, and destructive of the environment, among other things (see Amplification 5.3 in Chapter 5). Public carping at American leadership rose globally over supposed American unilateralism and heavy-handed treatment of other countries. Predictions that the American Decade of the 1990s would be followed by an American Century became more subdued. Rejecting the Americans became an entirely more reputable position than it had previously been.

Globalization has continued to evolve outside the global spotlight focused on terrorism. Thanks to further technological refinements in telecommunications and the emergence of new entrepreneurial classes in both countries (much of which was educated in the United States), both China and India have emerged as global competitors of the United States in the delivery of globalization-based goods and services and, potentially, cutting-edge technology itself. The Chinese purchase of the International Business Machines (IBM) personal computer unit, and the increased "outsourcing" of jobs like telemarketing to India, have become powerful symbols of this phenomenon, discussed in Amplification 12.2.

Amplification 12.2

GLOBALIZED GEOPOLITICS IN A FLATTENED WORLD

New York Times political columnist Thomas L. Friedman has been a primary student and proponent of globalization. In 1999, he published The Lexus and the Olive Tree, which became a kind of "bible" of globalization. In 2005, he revisited globalization in The World Is Flat: A Brief History of the Twenty-First Century. He found that globalization had changed greatly "while I was sleeping" (the title of chapter one). Some of the change has definite geopolitical import.

Friedman's basic point is that the technology underlying globalization has become so diffuse, accessible, and affordable that people globally can become participants in the technology process that drives globalization. Instantaneous telecommunications, cheaper computers, and accessible information mean that almost anyone anywhere can become part of this process without great disadvantage. It is this democratization of globalization that has flattened the world by producing a level playing field for people globally to compete for leadership in the evolution of globalization.

Enter geopolitics. Much of American preeminence in the world has been its leadership in globalization, which has derived from its superior technological base and thus its advantage in setting the globalization agenda. That preeminence, however, is now being challenged by other powers, notably China and India, both of which have made sizable investments in educating a scientifically and technologically sophisticated class that, armed with the tools of the flattened world, could come to challenge American leadership. Friedman argues that unless the United States becomes mindful of this challenge and reasserts its technological leadership, the Chinese or the Indians could be setting the globalization agenda in another twenty years. That would be a geopolitically ominous turn for the United States.

THE IMPACT OF SEPTEMBER 11, 2001

The impact of the terrorist episode of 2001 on the globalizing economy remains ambivalent. International reaction has been decidedly mixed. All of the most developed countries roundly condemned the attacks and joined either in the overt campaign waged in Afghanistan against the Taliban and Al Qaeda or the much quieter international effort to improve detection and suppression of terrorists. No government has publicly condoned the efforts by Usama bin Laden and his associates; virtually all countries publicly condemned them.

Beneath the surface of official condemnation, however, was a growing expression in some quarters of feeling that the United States somehow deserved what happened to it, especially in light of increasingly unilateral American actions pursuant to the GWOT. This sentiment has been most widely expressed in the Middle East, on the so-called "Arab street." These expressions manifest themselves in ways as diverse as anti-American demonstrations to the sale of T-shirts bearing the image of bin Laden, and they carry the universal theme of an American comeuppance and satisfaction that the arrogant Americans have been brought to earth. To some extent, this sentiment reflects the kind of resentment felt toward whoever is the most powerful country; it also probably reflects a belief that it is appropriate for Americans to suffer some of the same kinds of indignities others routinely face.

Although the equation is rarely made, part of this sentiment may reflect a reaction to American economic dominance of the global economy, a kind of extension or even climax of the criticisms that have surrounded globalization since the Asian crisis and are manifested in the triumphal imposition of the American model. It is probably not coincidental that the support for anti-American terrorism comes from the Middle East, the region of the world that has been most resistant to globalization and whose leaders feel the most threatened by the economic and political changes entailed by membership in the globalizing economy. That the major target of the terrorist attacks were the World Trade Center towers in the heart of New York's financial district may also be less than coincidental, since they were important hubs and symbols of globalization. The fact that national citizens from eighty countries were killed in the attacks is only further evidence of how broadly the globalization and the pervasiveness of the global economy had spread. That the symbolism they evoked was part of the motive for the targets chosen has not been established, and other, more mundane explanations may have provided the reasons (for instance, the towers were the tallest buildings in New York and could be attacked without having to dodge through other structures, as an attack on the Empire State Building would have required). At any rate, the coincidence is there, and it is intriguing, to say the least.

Even as time passes, we are still assessing the general and specific impacts of the attacks and responses to them on international life. One of the more obvious policy areas where there is the potential for conflict is in the clash between responses to terrorism and the continuing globalization of the international economy.

Globalization and Terrorism

Globalization and responding to terrorism appear on the surface to pose two absolutely antithetical phenomena arousing very different impulses. A basic, underlying theme and requisite of globalization is openness and free, unimpeded movement of people, products, services, ideas, and financial resources across national borders. Indeed, most observers agree that globalization has been made possible by advances in telecommunications and transportation that have facilitated openness and movement. Before commodities, people, information, and ideas could be moved rapidly around the world, globalization as it now exists was basically impossible. For globalization to continue and expand, boundaries and other man-made restrictions on movement must continue to be progressively reduced, what Friedman would call the further "flattening" of the world.

Terrorism and particularly responses to terrorism, on the other hand, suggest closure and restriction of movement. Terrorist organizations are, by their very nature, clandestine and secretive, and it is not coincidental that they thrive in conditions of state sponsorship or sanction in the very closed societies that are outside the reaches of the globalization system. Terrorists prosper, however, when they can carry out their missions in open, unrestricted environments that they can penetrate easily with minimal danger of exposure or interference. A part of responding to terrorism requires making it more difficult to penetrate target societies.

The contemporary environment places international terrorists and globalizers at direct odds theoretically as well. For the globalizers, extension of the global system is at the heart of modernization, and its spread globally represents a value to be exploited and maximized. To terrorist organizations such as bin Laden's Al Qaeda, the intrusion of modernity, of which globalization is an important symbol, is the evil to be resisted. Because the United States is clearly identified as the major symbol of globalization and its system is at least a rough model of the societal changes that come with globalization, it quite naturally becomes the object of efforts to resist change.

In the roughest terms, this incompatibility frames the relationship between terrorism and globalization. Globalization requires openness and the unfettered ability to move about, and openness is a condition that terrorists find conducive to carrying out their nefarious actions. Responding to terrorism may require removing some of that openness as a means to prevent the success of terrorists by intercepting or monitoring their movement. Globalization needs openness to thrive, and responses to terrorism equally dictate restriction on that openness. The values of prosperity and security clash in ways that were unnecessary to contemplate during the 1990s.

The emphasis on incompatibilities, however, reflects a short-term rather than long-term view of the relationship between responding to terrorism and globalization. Short-term assessments are reactive, quite rightly concerned with responses to traumatic events and to the prevention of their recurrence. In the contemporary environment, this emphasis elevates responding to terrorism as the more immediate and important problem. In that circumstance in which the dictates of antiterrorism and counterterrorism and the promotion of globalization collide, dealing with terrorism has taken precedence.

But is an emphasis on closure and restriction a wise longer-term strategy? Are the concepts of globalization and response to terrorism locked in the equivalent of a zero-sum game in which one value can only be promoted at the expense of the other? Or is it possible to examine the problem and conclude that responding to terrorism and promoting globalization are both necessary tools in a strategy for "draining the swamp" in which terrorism thrives and thus contributing to the ultimate goal of defeating terrorism by removing the reasons for its existence?

The answer to the last question is overwhelmingly positive and is directly parallel to the relationship between conflict suppression and state-building elaborated in Chapter 11. The "war on terrorism" can be viewed as a problem similar to conflict suppression—making it impossible for combatants to fight one another or to engage in acts of terrorism. Just as conflict suppression does not get at the underlying reasons for internal war, neither will tactical responses to terrorism overcome the reasons people become terrorists. Rather, the state-building exercise designed to convince formerly warring parties that peace makes more sense than a reversion to war has its parallel in state-building efforts whose purpose is to make terrorism unattractive by economically and politically uplifting formerly terrorist states and drawing them into the globalization system. In this sense, the Bush administration's dual emphasis in the campaign against Al Qaeda, suppressing and destroying the terrorist network while simultaneously engaging in state-building in Afghanistan, makes perfect sense. How the campaign to reform and materially uplift Afghanistan works will thus be a strong indication of how well terrorism can be eliminated, just as earlier but ongoing efforts in Kosovo have represented a test of the ability to build states after ruinous internal wars. State-building is as much a part of the successful outcome of this war as the physical fighting, as Afghanistan attests. There are no guarantees this effort will succeed; there is not enough evidence to assert assuredly that state-building will drain the swamp and make terrorism unpalatable. It is, however, fairly certain that the absence of state-building and the continuation of terrorism will coincide.

The short-term incompatibility and longer-term compatibility between responses to terrorism and globalization occupy the remainder of the chapter, because that evolving and changing relationship may well represent one of the cornerstones of future national security politics—an important part of the way in which globalization and geopolitics blend together. We begin by looking at short-term incompatibilities and how they are likely to interact in the next few years. Following that discussion, we speculate on the longer term, on how state-building may help transform states that were formerly hotbeds of potential terrorism into members of the globalizing economy for which terrorism is an unappealing option.

Short-Term Incompatibilities

In the immediate future, attempts to insure or limit the recurrence of terrorist acts against the American homeland and of American interests overseas will almost certainly retain policy predominance. In that entirely understandable ordering of priorities, the relationship between open, nurturing globalization and restrictive responses to terrorism will likely emphasize the incompatibilities between the two aspects of policy. Where the two clash, the globalizers will be forced to yield or remain mute, to accommodate and adapt to the dictates of dealing with the geopolitics of the new century.

A small but growing literature is beginning to appear that deals with the short-term relationship. To date, this literature has suggested two specific areas of concern. The first reflects the vulnerability of the globalization system to disruption, a situation in which the efficiency of the globalizing system creates its own primary weakness. The second area of concern reflects the consequences of emphasizing policies that maximize responses to terrorism in terms of their dilatory impact on globalization. These analyses tend to emphasize the difficulty of reaching compromises favorable to both values.

Vulnerabilities. One of the major reasons for the success of globalization during the 1990s was its ability to establish greater efficiencies in the productive cycle. In large part, these improvements occurred, of course, as part of the privatization of economic activity that is one of the signal characteristics of globalization. This efficiency, however, has come with the cost of vulnerability. Flynn describes the problem: "The competitiveness of the U.S. economy and the quality of life of the American people rest on critical infrastructure that has become increasingly more concentrated, more interconnected, and more sophisticated. Almost entirely privately owned and operated, the system has very little redundancy."

There is a certain irony in this development, because the very forces that have improved the material lives of people have also created the conditions in which the underpinning of that prosperity can be undermined more effectively than in the past. Then, efficiency-compromising redundancies—multiple accounting and record-keeping systems, electronic and nonelectronic records, for instance—provided safeguards against the disruption of any one source of information. As Campbell puts it, "Many of the things that have left sophisticated Western societies vulnerable to terrorist attacks are the very efficiencies that have come as a consequence of persons', companies' and countries' relentless search for efficiency and maximum productivity." He cites examples of efficiencies such as curbside check-in at airports, e-tickets, and freer immigration policies that make the system more responsive and faster.

The public, including the national security community, has not been immune to this trend. Several years ago, for instance, the United States Air Force announced its goal to create a "paperless Air Force" in which all paper records would be eliminated and all information retained electronically. Beyond the Air Force's well-known obsession with technological gimmickry, the purpose was to enhance efficiency and save money by eliminating the need to produce, store, and maintain the mountains of paperwork the Air Force bureaucracy routinely generated. The problem was that instead of having several copies of information stored at several different places (inefficient redundancy), it was all in one computerized system that, if disrupted, could cause the information to be lost—irretrievably, in some cases. At the other end of the spectrum, the disaster of the World Trade Centers' destruction was partially mitigated by the fact that most of the firms located there had copies of records elsewhere to compensate for those lost in the attack.

A theme that recurs in discussions of globalization-related economic vulnerability is the concentrations of activity that globalization has induced. Homer-Dixon summarizes this aspect of the problem: "This additional vulnerability is the product of two key social and technological developments: first, the growing complexity and interconnectedness of our modern societies; and second, the growing geographic concentration of wealth, human capital, knowledge, and communication links." Modern society, physically shaped by a globalizing economy, makes an attractive target, and the attack on the World Trade Center was an almost perfect symbol of the consequence of that vulnerability.

The very openness of both the American and increasingly the global community also creates conditions in which terrorists can operate more easily. An irony of the problem is that closed, deprived social settings sometimes produce terrorists who could not possibly carry out terrorist acts in their own societies because of the preponderance of coercive, suppressive force that helps make conditions wretched. At the same time, they can flourish in the very kinds of societies that represent conditions in which terrorists would not arise.

The vulnerability of open societies has been the basis of much discussion about antiterrorist efforts in the United States and the degree to which attempts to shore up those vulnerabilities represent necessary or unwarranted infringements on civil and other rights. Openness has meant it has been relatively easy to enter and leave the United States, for instance. When those entering and leaving are businesspeople engaged in productive commerce, we view openness as a virtue and one of the reasons for the success of globalization. When that same permeability permits terrorists to enter and leave the country without detection, that is another matter. The same is true of communications. The ability to communicate instantly across the globe has been extolled as a major reason for the success of globalization, facilitating the flow and coordination of commerce, the movement of capital and ideas and the like at speeds and in ways unthinkable before the telecommunications revolution. Those same instruments of communication, however, also allow terrorist organizations like Al Qaeda to communicate with their far-flung cells and to coordinate their nefarious activities in ways heretofore impossible.

The globalization age is also an information and information-sharing age, facilitated by devices such as the enormous amount of material available on the Internet. While this aspect of the telecommunications revolution facilitates the sharing of a variety of useful information for legitimate purposes, it also allows access to information by terrorists to put to their own ends. As Homer-Dixon observes, "The September 11 bombers could have found there [the Internet] all the details they needed about the floor plans and design characteristics of the World Trade Center and about how demolition experts use progressive collapse to destroy large buildings." The same Internet that makes researching term papers easier can also help terrorists conduct their own "research."

Consequences. The short-term incompatibility between efforts to frustrate international terrorists and to promote the expansion of the globalization system of economic commerce has numerous consequences, from security and vulnerability to the movement of people and goods across borders. The problem is probably greater and receiving more attention in the area of border security than at any other place. Partly for historic reasons (friendship with Canada), practical and financial constraints (the difficulty of sealing the long border with Mexico), and policy decisions to facilitate the flow of goods and individuals into and out of the country (a direct result and purpose of globalization), the United States has extremely porous borders. This porosity has facilitated commerce and prosperity in the past. It has allowed an unimpeded flow of goods, the prices of which are not inflated by elaborate inspection requirements, to enter and leave the country, and it has permitted cheap (and often illegal) laborers to enter the country and produce goods at lower labor costs than would have been possible employing American citizens. At the same time, liberal immigration policies that, for instance, permit large numbers of foreign students into the country to study at American colleges and universities also enhance the talent pool for American private enterprise, especially in the areas of science and engineering where American students are in short supply.

That same porosity also facilitates the activities of terrorists. Terrorists have been able to move fairly easily across the borders between the United States and its neighbors, and it has also been relatively easy for them to move weapons (possibly including weapons of mass destruction) across those borders. As Flynn argues, the United States currently has no means to screen nefarious from legitimate entrants into the country: "The problem . . . is that the existing border-management architecture provides no credible means for denying foreign terrorists and their weapons entry into the United States." All the elaborate screening mechanisms at major airports cannot prevent an individual terrorist walking across an open field from Canada into the United States.

There are two subproblems here: who and what can get into the United States. Both aspects put terrorism suppression and globalization into direct conflict. Take the human part of the problem. As the investigation of the September 11 attacks reveals, a number of the terrorists originally entered the country on student visas, presumably to study at American universities. Surveys conducted after the terrorist attacks revealed that literally thousands of foreigners who entered the country under those pretenses were no longer enrolled in college (if they ever had been) and their whereabouts were unknown. Canvasses to find the missing were less than overwhelmingly successful, and many of these "students" remain unaccounted for.

What can be done about the problem? Hardly anyone disagrees with the proposition that real students who may become part of the skilled American workforce (or return to their native countries and improve conditions there) should be allowed entry to the United States, and no one disagrees with the proposition that potential terrorists should be denied. Were there some foolproof litmus test that would reveal into which group young foreigners belonged (and most of both the students and terrorists are young, unmarried men in their teens or twenties, as a recent study of suicide terrorists has concluded), there would be little problem. The difficulty, of course, is that such a test does not exist, and if it did, it would probably be only partially effective. Reconciliation between the dictates of countering terrorism and promoting globalization requires that some better form of discrimination be devised. Better screening of applicants before they leave their countries offers a partial, if expensive and time-consuming, solution, but it is a start.

The problem of monitoring *who* enters the United States pales beside the problem of knowing *what* enters the country. In addition to the 489 million people who passed through American border posts in 2000, Flynn reports that 127 million passenger vehicles, 11.6 million maritime containers, 2.2 million railroad cars, 629,000 airplanes, and 211,000 vessels went through American border checkpoints in that year. Most of the freight was not inspected for the simple reason that there are not nearly enough inspectors to monitor more than a tiny percentage of what comes across the border. This is particularly true at heavy usage entry points, such as the Ambassador Bridge between Windsor, Ontario, and Detroit, Michigan. According to Flynn, "nearly 5,000 trucks entered the United States each day in 2000. . . . U.S. Customs officers must average no more than two minutes per truck." He adds that a thorough inspection of a forty foot eighteen wheeler requires fifteen man-hours.

Aside from the problem of gridlock that would result if efforts to monitor goods and people were to increase enough to have reasonable assurance that contraband, including terrorist weapons, did not penetrate the country, there is also the disaster such an interruption would have on the American commercial system. Closing the bridge between Windsor and Detroit, to cite one example, would interrupt the flow of automobile parts from manufacturing to assembly plants on the other side of the border; in December 2001, such an interruption closed several American automobile assembly plants.

The permeability of America's borders both reflects the incompatibility of dealing with terrorism and globalization at the same time and highlights the difficulties associated with antiterrorism generally. In fact, most of the substantive points where the two forces of globalization and terrorism suppression collide will be in the area of antiterrorist operations. The transportation example shows the inherent difficulty of antiterrorist actions generally—it is essentially impossible to anticipate all forms that terrorism might take and all places where terrorism might be planned, and a strategy that relies wholly or even largely on antiterrorism will almost certainly fail some of the time. In terms of regulating boundaries, even the most draconian measures probably cannot succeed perfectly. As a result, decisions to improve their effectiveness that compromise the movement of goods, services, and people have to be balanced against the limits on how effective these measures can be.

Reconciliation. Efforts aimed at reducing terrorism have taken public precedence over the promotion of the global economy, an emphasis that suddenly appeared much less important than preventing a feared repeat of the awful attacks. At some point, however, it will be necessary to reconcile the contradictory interests of security and prosperity and to assess the degree to which American economic interests tied to globalization balance with those interests connected to homeland security.

Those who would promote the primacy of economic interests have clearly been on the defensive and have not loudly asserted a return to emphasizing and expanding globalization. The reasons for this quiescence undoubtedly are diverse but include a fear of being deemed unpatriotic by asserting a false return to the pre-attack normalcy. Arguing the case for renewed emphasis on globalization is tantamount to asserting it is time to get back to business. The popular mood, fanned by political leaders and the media, counter that we remain "at war," which is clearly not the normal environment for commerce.

When will the political atmosphere move back toward a more balanced view of the country's priorities? The answer to that question, ironically, lies largely in the hands of those who would do the United States harm through acts of terrorism, a point made earlier. The longer the lull between September 11 and the next serious terrorist incident in the United States, the more public attention will move away from terrorism and toward a return to pre-terrorist normalcy. Issuing warnings of threats that do not materialize, as the government did frequently in the months after the attacks, not only does not reinforce vigilance but probably undermines it and works to increase demand for change back to a normal life.

A period of some calm will almost certainly produce a calmer, more even-handed analysis of American priorities, one that will restore some, if not necessarily all, of the American enthusiasm for globalization. As the effort to deal comprehensively with the problem of terrorism evolves, it may also produce the realization that, in the longer run, dealing with terrorism and pursuing globalization are not only compatible elements of American strategy but are actually complementary pillars of such a strategy.

Long-Term Compatibilities

The idea that globalization and the campaign to end terrorism are positively related comes from extending notions about dealing with new internal war to the problem of dealing with terrorism. Such a comparison can be made on three bases: the environments in which the two problems arise; the comparability of the two approaches to solving the problem; and a comparison of the relative differences between the two.

Environment. It is striking that most of the states on the U.S. Department of State list of terrorist sponsors or sanctioners are also on or candidates for inclusion on the list of failed states. The two lists are not synonymous. Haiti and Sierra Leone, for instance, are clearly failed states but have not produced international terrorists, although in both cases, elements—including the government—engaged in domestic terrorism that is as reprehensible as its international counterpart. In each case where a failed state has become an international problem that the international system feels the need to remedy through something like state-building, indigenous movements have applied the same kind of fanaticism and terror against their own populations that international terrorists have applied toward foreign targets. The "fighters" of Sierra Leone's Revolutionary United Front, hacking off the limbs of innocent civilians, were certainly sending a terrorist warning to others who might consider not cooperating with them in the future. The narcoterrorists of Colombia use kidnappings and assassinations of Colombian officials and citizens to increase their power by frightening their opposition. Terrorism, whether directed domestically or internationally, is terrorism, after all, and the circumstances that produce either variety are likewise similar.

Without going into a detailed psychological or sociological profile of either terrorists or the fighters attracted to internal wars, there is a striking similarity in the countries in which both exist. Certainly there is a geographic distinction: most of the known international terrorists currently come from the Islamic Middle East, whereas most of the internal wars are in Africa and Asia. A kind of hybrid, where avowed revolutionaries engage in both civil war and terrorism, exists in places such as Sri Lanka (the Black Tigers of the Liberation Tigers of Tamil Eelam) and in the Philippines.

What all the places have in common is a sense of societal hopelessness and despair. The Palestinian refugee camps have for half a century been the recruiting grounds for a variety of terrorist organizations, including those involved in the recent suicide bombings, and the dynamic of attraction is simple enough. If one's life is sufficiently miserable, then there is little to lose in joining a terrorist movement, even if one may become a *shahid* (martyr) in the process. Springzak, citing an Israeli study on suicide terrorists, describes the typical Palestinian recruit as "a male, religious, unmarried and unemployed high school graduate" who may have had a relative killed in the struggle against Israel. The Tamil Tigers have a similar demographic profile. Recruits for Al Qaeda from the *madrassa* system are typically young male children who have been orphaned or abandoned.

Comparability of Approach. These similarities suggest that a similar approach to dealing with the problem may be advisable as well. Conflict suppression is the first step in "curing" failed states, but it is clearly not enough to produce post-conflict political systems that are stable and violence free. Similarly, antiterrorist and counterterrorist methods are necessary first steps in eliminating or containing the threat posed by a particular terrorist group or groups. In and of themselves, however, such actions cannot address the broader, underlying circumstances from which terrorism arises.

If the solution to new internal war is to produce stable societies through state-building, the same logic applies to reforming terrorist-sanctioning states, a conclusion apparently accepted by the Bush administration in its overall campaign in Afghanistan. Terrorist organizations thrived in Afghanistan because of the association of Al Qaeda and the government, but the underlying reality for the country was human misery that served as "the swamp" from which willing terrorists (many of whom were not Afghans but foreigners from more affluent countries such as Saudi Arabia) arose while others tolerated them in their midst. If a government is to succeed in Afghanistan that opposes and successfully suppresses terrorists, it will have to have the active political and economic support of a population that grants it support and legitimacy. Politics and misery as usual will only breed the next generation of terrorists; state-building aimed at improving the human lot is necessary to "drain" the swamp. It is somewhat curious in this regard that Israel, a country with more experience with terrorists than virtually anyplace else in the world, does not see that its harsh policy of retribution and economic deprivation against the Palestinians may be effectively creating the next generation of Palestinian terrorists (see Amplification 12.3).

Relative Differences. Just as in state-building for humanitarian purposes, a terrorism-reducing state-building ultimately will focus its economic component on making the target country attractive to the globalizing economy. Before this transformation can occur, target countries need to develop sufficient political stability and economic infrastructure to become attractive to private investors. International companies, the backbone of globalization, are not going to invest in places where the government cannot provide basic protection of their assets or where the government might be swept away by opposition forces at any moment. At the same time, a country with poor roads, ports, and airfields, an unreliable power supply, and a largely unskilled labor force will not attract foreign direct investment. Much of the basic infrastructure development necessary to reverse these conditions must come from public sources, since the projects they entail will not be self-liquidating (directly producing profits that can repay loans). Public funds have to do those things, and they must be aimed at making the target country attractive to the globalizers. Globalization thus becomes the handmaiden of counterterrorism.

The international community has not wholeheartedly embraced state-building for humanitarian purposes. When he entered office, President George W. Bush was one of the major skeptics of American involvement in humanitarian peacekeeping that had state-building as an element. Yet, within less than a year, he became a vocal proponent of doing in Afghanistan exactly what he was opposed to doing elsewhere. The reason, of course, is obvious: state-building in Afghanistan is part of the broader war on terrorism and thus a matter of American vital interests. It has a more important rationale there; making life more prosperous for Kosovars does not occupy the same level of priority.

The dynamics of state-building, however, are much the same in the two situations. If anything, state-building in the kinds of states that have traditionally harbored terrorists may be more difficult because those countries tend also to be the

Amplification 12.3

THE ISRAELI CAMPAIGN AGAINST PALESTINIAN TERRORISM

Relations between Israel and the Palestinians have deteriorated markedly since the failure of Camp David II. In December 2000, fighting broke out between the two sides that has continued well into 2005. That fighting between the Israeli army and bands of Palestinian youth (many of whom reflect the physical profile of suicide terrorists described in Chapter 10) has gradually expanded and become more bitter. Acts of violent terror (suicidal bombers) have resulted in recrimination and retaliation that are followed by counter-retaliation, and so on. Both sides blame the other for the violence and the failure to stop it, with good arguments on both sides.

The violence has hardened the political positions on both sides. The Sharon government insisted this *intifada* (uprising) is proof of Palestinian perfidy and especially the intransigence and ineffectiveness of the Palestinian political leadership. The Palestinians counter that the Israelis are slaughtering innocent Palestinians and intruding on territory ceded by Israel to the Palestinian Authority.

One can debate the merits of the case on either side and even sympathize with the spirit of vengeance the situation has engendered. A question increasingly asked as the violence dragged on is whether or not the policies are shortsighted. Particularly in the case of the Palestinians, is Israeli policy not virtually ensuring that the conditions in which terrorism arises will be present for the foreseeable future? Faced with economic desolation and physical and economic helplessness, will another generation of Palestinians emerge who are willing potential terrorists? If peace is the long-term goal of both sides, should either or both sides be nurturing the culture of continued violence—in effect assuring that the "swamp" that breeds terrorism remains fertile? At the same time, has Palestinian terrorism so alienated those Israelis who have favored accommodation that they have lost control to the hard-liners who oppose reconciliation? Has peace been made impossible by the actions on both sides? A decrease in *intifada* violence and the suspension of Israeli retaliatory strikes in 2005 offer an opportunity for hope; the Palestinian election of Hamas dims that hope.

kinds of states that have been most resistant to the incursion of the globalizing influences that are in turn key to terrorist-proofing them. Fundamentalism, in this case mostly Islamic, opposes the very changes that globalization brings with it.

State-building in states that have harbored terrorists is also terribly important if terrorism is to be eliminated or reduced to international inconsequence. The Afghan experiment is enormously important in this regard. It is inherently important because the country was the host of Al Qaeda, and their elimination is a necessary first step to restoring the integrity of North American security. Beyond that, the success of state-building in Afghanistan will have enormous importance as a precedent for future American national security and foreign policy, particularly if something like state-building will have to be undertaken in other places to which displaced terrorists flee to find safe haven. Afghanistan and Iraq, of course, are cases in point.

The Case of Afghanistan

Before 2001, Afghanistan was a country about which the average American knew very little. A landlocked country in the middle of central Asia, its historic importance has been that it sits astride some of the major trading routes between Asia and Europe, giving it a strategic importance that has brought legions of invaders to the land. During the nineteenth century, the British and the Russians played "the great game" for influence and control. In 1979, Soviet tanks rolled into the country, only to meet fierce resistance from the *mujahadeen* (freedom fighters), an experience from which both the Taliban and Al Qaeda claim their birth. In 1988, the Soviets limped out of Afghanistan in military disgrace, and the experience helped hasten the collapse of the Soviet Union three years later. In 1996, the Taliban, advertised as reformers who would root out legendary corruption in the Afghan government, captured Kabul and began their fundamentalist reign of terror. In December 2001, after their rout, an interim government under Hamid Karzai began the task of rebuilding the country in preparation for national elections. A major emphasis of his tenure was the forceful rejection of both the Taliban and terrorism. The American embassy in Kabul, abandoned in December 1989, reopened in December 2001; the Afghan embassy in Washington, closed in 1995, reopened on January 28, 2002, with Karzai in attendance and extolling a new and perpetual solidarity between his country and the United States.

Afghanistan is also one of the poorest, most desolate countries of the world, and its physical condition was made worse by over twenty years of warfare that has virtually physically destroyed Kabul and scarred the countryside. By any measure, the country's economy is a shambles. *The World Almanac and Book of Facts 2002* lists per capita gross domestic product at $800 and says that Afghanistan has three airports and eighteen miles of rails in a country the physical size of Texas with a population of 26 million. Life expectancy for males is 47 years; in an anomaly that demonstrates the fate of women under the Taliban, female life expectancy is 45.5 years.

By any measure, Afghanistan has been a failed state, and any efforts to raise standards to the level that the country will become attractive to outside investment are daunting at the very least. Despite a lull in intertribal political and military bickering attendant to the overthrow of the Taliban, the country remains deeply divided along ethnic lines, and ethnic disagreements have often been solved violently throughout Afghan history. Forming a government that reflects ethnic realities has been difficult, particularly since the deposed Taliban were mostly from the largest ethnic group, the Pashtun (who, as noted, constitute 38 percent of the population). Building and rebuilding the economy will be a very difficult and costly process.

Overcoming these obvious physical difficulties is not the only challenge facing efforts to stabilize Afghanistan and make it part of the terrorist-opposing coalition of states. As already suggested, the kinds of actions that will make Afghanistan a modern, stable member of the international community will be opposed by some in Afghanistan and others in the region on religious and cultural grounds. While the fanatical excesses of the Taliban were greatly hated by many, symbolically shedding the burkas did not mean that many Afghans lost their adherence to Islam. There remain fundamentalists in the country who find westernization and its attendant secularization of society offensive. Fundamentalism is still part of the Afghan equation, and fundamentalists are also active in the surrounding states, most notably Tajikistan (ethnic Tajiks are the second-largest ethnic group in Afghanistan) and Pakistan, where there are large numbers of Afghan refugees, including supporters of bin Laden and the Taliban.

Efforts to rebuild Afghanistan—and especially to try to transform it into something like a normal westernized state that can enter the globalization system—have to confront and be sensitive to the fact that this is exactly what many Afghans do not want to see happen. In the early relations between the United States and the post-Taliban rulers, the most prominent Afghans were also those who were most westernized and supportive of transforming their country. Karzai, for instance, speaks fluent and highly articulate English, and members of his family are prominent restaurant owners on the East Coast of the United States. His visions for Afghanistan seem to match our own and make the job at hand seem conceptually and physically easier than it almost certainly will be. Karzai may prove to have more support in the United States than he does in his native Afghanistan.

There is also considerable anti-Americanism in the Arab street. A prominent American presence in Afghanistan, especially the longer it lasts and the more transformation of Afghan society that it creates, is going to be watched very closely in the region by elements that do not want to see Americanization of the Middle East succeed. In fact, it is the prospect of that Americanization that fuels much of the hatred that many feel toward the United States. We have been down this road before in neighboring Iran—with disastrous results.

If Americans have any doubts about how carefully to tread to avoid creating more antipathy than sympathy and support, we need only look toward our closest ally in the region, Saudi Arabia. Since 1990, when the United States accepted the Saudi invitation to protect the regime from Iraq, there has been a continuous American military presence on Saudi soil that has recently been phased out. That presence was unpopular enough that bin Laden has considerable support in Saudi Arabia for his stated goal to force the Americans to leave and end the desecration of the Arabian peninsula, and Saudi millionaires are among the chief benefactors of the violently anti-American *madrassas* in Pakistan. To make the American presence less offensive, Americans were stationed in remote areas and not encouraged to interact with the natives. The Saudi royal family's support for the United States is unpopular in the country and causes them to treat the United States with less warmth than one might expect given the extent of the relationship across time. For them, embracing the United States—and especially American policy in matters such as Palestine—is the potential kiss of death.

The real danger against which any state-building effort in Afghanistan must guard is the American experience in support of the Shah of Iran from the end of

World War II until Reza Pahlevi was deposed in the Iranian Revolution of 1979 and replaced by a fanatically anti-American fundamentalist government that had Ayotollah Ruhollah Khomeini as its titular leader.

This is not the place for a detailed examination of the Iranian Revolution, but our experience there does serve as a warning to the United States as it seeks to help Afghanistan and possibly Iraq. The Shah of Iran, after he was returned to power in 1953 with the help of the CIA (he was briefly overthrown that year), sought to transform his country into a resurgent power in the region and the world—in effect, the restoration of the old Persian Empire. He calculated that the only way he could succeed was by embracing the ways of the West, and his White Revolution sought to transform Iran into a modern, Western power. The United States was the chief advisor in the process and helped direct the changes being instituted.

In retrospect, it is clear Iran was possibly the worst country in the world to try to westernize rapidly. The basis of Iranian society was a very conservative Shiite Muslim majority led by an activist clergy (a tradition within Shi'ism) who were deeply offended by the effects of westernization on traditional Islamic values, and the Shah and his partners, the "Great Satans," were blamed for the dilution of Islamic values that was occurring. The movement led by Ayotollah Khomeini was, in large measure, a fundamentalist reaction to the efforts to modernize the country, and it succeeded in toppling the Shah's regime and replacing it with a fanatically anti-American alternative that retains its position as a member of the "axis of evil" despite some moderation in its policies. In Iran, the United States attempted to aid in the westernization of an Islamic society into something the equivalent of a member of the globalizing economy today with results quite the opposite of those intended.

Could the same thing happen in Afghanistan? As the Taliban's period of rule proves, Afghan society is certainly capable of producing a Sunni fundamentalist regime that is equally anti-American and arguably more fanatically anti-modernist than the Iranian Revolution produced. Its recent resurgence and support among at least some Pashtuns suggest that its appeal has not disappeared altogether. While there was obvious popular relief at the lifting of Taliban restrictions and a visible embrace of some symbols of Western-style modernity, such as television, some of the fundamentalist instincts undoubtedly remain.

Afghanistan is not Iran. Activity like the shooting down of an American Special Forces Chinook helicopter in July 2003 provides evidence that the Taliban are in fact back. It still must be remembered that the Taliban had popular support when they came to power and only lost it as they imposed a much more puritanical, draconian rule than they had suggested before they achieved power. Clearly, it is in the American interest not to induce change that could reawaken the emotions that created the Taliban.

The key factor for state-building success in Afghanistan is likely to be a political and economic program that can overcome traditional ethnic differences. Politically, this effort requires nurturing institutions that all groups feel are fair and that cannot be distorted by one ethnic group at the expense of others or twisted to allow the traditional Afghan corruption the Taliban promised to overcome. That emphasis seems obvious enough, but it requires power sharing and cooperation that has long been absent in Afghan politics. Economically, the pace and structure of building and re-building must similarly be uniform countrywide so that regions dominated by some ethnic majorities do not prosper while others are ignored. Although sizable funds have been pledged by the United States for Afghan state-building, only a small portion has actually reached Afghanistan. Monitoring the progress of assistance programs as they presumably come on line will be important, as will insuring that the development that occurs does not have the unintended and untoward consequences that occurred in Iran a quarter-century ago. Progress in Afghanistan will be a measur-ing stick against which to evaluate similar efforts in Iraq. As of 2006, Afghanistan is not an unambiguously positive precedent.

CONCLUSION: RECONCILING GLOBALIZATION AND TERRORISM

The tranquil, go-go 1990s gave way to the troubled, insecure 2000s. The optimism that accompanied spiraling global prosperity through much of the 1990s was re-placed by a wary anxiety in an international environment where terrorism domi-nates our conversations, if less obviously the actual sequence of international events. Geopolitics, in the new clothing of terrorism responses, has overtaken the spreading of prosperity through globalization in the center of public consciousness about the world and our place in it.

It has become commonplace, virtually a cliché, to say that everything has changed since terrorism visited the American homeland on September 11, 2001. While the national and international dialogues have certainly come to focus much more clearly on the terrorist threat, the assertion seems inflated. If it is true, it is largely because we have said it is true so often that we believe it. The terrorist act on that fateful day was, after all, a single—if horrific—act that has not been repeated in any equivalent way on American soil. It may well be, and probably is, true that the lack of repetition has been because we are more vigilant and have thus thwarted other plans that might otherwise have succeeded. At a minimum, the Afghan cam-paign has made it more difficult for the current terrorists to operate their deadly net-works. How much harder it is for them, we do not know.

Has September 11, 2001, truly changed the environment? Or has it changed the way we *look* at the environment? There was a terrorist threat before the event, and as noted earlier, there were clarions who warned us of our vulnerability to that which befell us. Their warnings were generally not heeded then, and they are today. Is that a change of environment, or of how we view the environment? Has reality or our perception of reality changed the most? Do terrorist attacks in other places (London, Madrid) mean the problem is more intense or more diffuse?

The question of perspective applies as well to the more fundamental relation-ships explored in this chapter, notably the shifting relationship between globaliza-tion and geopolitics. Bill Clinton clearly was a globalizing president, although in the waning days of his second term, his personal and political difficulties drowned out much of the focus of his zeal. A sagging global economy added to a public defocusing on globalization issues. George W. Bush entered office with a known advocacy of globalization and an unknown preference regarding geopolitics. He campaigned as a free trader but also as an adherent of stronger defenses. The events of September 11 focused his emphasis for him.

The emphases on terrorism-driven geopolitics or expanding globalization continue to struggle for conceptual supremacy on the American and global stages. In the early going after the terrorist attacks, geopolitics rapidly came to the ascendancy in terms of domestic priorities and international dealings. The incompatibilities of the two concepts were emphasized in areas such as border control and the permeability of those borders, immigration restrictions, and the like. Those promoting openness and the free movement of goods and people were viewed as suspect, since freely moving people could be terrorists and weapons their cargo. Globalization issues became wrapped in the general discussion of security and the sacrifices necessary in terms of civil liberties and other freedoms needed to increase that security.

Will the advantage of geopolitics in the debate endure? As noted, the terrorists will have something to say about that question with their future activity or inactivity, but it is difficult to imagine the fervor will continue forever. The continued reference to the state of a war that palpably does not exist will almost certainly lose its magnetism unless some concrete entity emerges with whom to fight. Questions of economic well-being, which is certainly part of national security, will begin to compete with questions of the physical safety of the homeland. Globalization is, after all, a part of national security strategy, not an alternative to it.

The darker side of the debate over globalization and geopolitics is its equation with the debate over internationalism and unilateralism-neoisolationism. Globalization is a quintessentially internationalist idea. While globalization can be justified in terms of the unilateral, national advantages it produces rather than for its systemic virtues, the core and most of the rationalizations for globalization will necessarily be its contribution to economic and political global improvement. Terrorism-driven geopolitics can be promoted as either an international or a national movement, but its virtue ultimately will be judged on the contribution that antiterrorist measures make to the security of the country.

The two emphases are not, of course, mutually exclusive. The elimination of terrorism can probably be most efficiently accomplished through international efforts and collaboration in areas such as identifying terrorists and their movements. Since secret intelligence agencies will have to do the sharing and are, by their nature, interested in concealing rather than sharing what they know, there will always be limits on international cooperation, but it is clearly part of any strategy that is likely to succeed.

If the conceptual odds now favor an emphasis on geopolitics over globalization for the near term, what could cause that to change? The answer is one or both of two trends. The first would be a deemphasis on terrorism that returned terrorism to something like its pre–September 11, 2001, place in international and national priorities. The absence of major terrorist incidents over a period of time is probably the necessary condition for that to occur. The second would be an upturn in the global economy from which all countries would benefit but from which those most heavily invested in globalization could benefit the most. Both of these things almost certainly will happen sometime. The question is when and with what effects.

Challenge!

WILL GLOBALIZATION REALLY WORK?

An underlying assumption of those who favor the extension of globalization as a means to dampen violence and instability in the international system is that globalization will *in fact*, as well as in theory, have that desired effect. But is that assumption valid? Will globalization really work to achieve the goals its champions have for it?

Since globalization has not occurred everywhere, we cannot observe its effects to provide a definitive answer to our question. Something like globalization has been advocated for a long time, and there was a theoretical strand during the Cold War period that advocated something called *complex interdependence*, the gist of which was that as economies became more intertwined globally, the ability to make war would become physically impossible. The same sentiment had proven wrong at the turn of the twentieth century, when interdependence was supposed to render war highly unlikely, if not physically impossible. At the end of World War II, the functionalists hoped the United Nations system would so involve countries as to produce peace.

These experiences suggest that the success of globalization in producing a more tranquil environment cannot be accepted as a given. At the same time, that same experience does not provide conclusive evidence that globalization will not produce peace. The international system has, after all, undergone a "long peace" for over sixty years in which there has not been a major, systemic war since the conclusion of World War II, and the democratization and economic globalizing of the world has influenced that outcome. Moreover, no reputable observers look at the evolving international environment and prophesy the likelihood of fundamental, system-threatening conflict.

So, does globalization work? The evidence is clearly ambivalent, and the answer is a firm and unequivocal "maybe." Realizing that uncertainty should temper advocacy and opposition, what do you think?

SELECTED BIBLIOGRAPHY

Appleby, R. Scott, and Martin E. Marty. "Fundamentalism." *Foreign Policy* (January/February 2002), 16–22.

Bhagwati, Jagdish. "Coping with Antiglobalization." *Foreign Affairs* 81, 1 (January/February 2002), 2–7.

Campbell, Kurt M. "Globalization's First War." *Washington Quarterly* 25, 1 (Winter 2001–02), 7–14.

Ferguson, Niall. "Sinking Globalization." *Foreign Affairs* 84, 2 (March/April 2005), 64–77.

Flynn, Stephen E. "America the Vulnerable." *Foreign Affairs* 81, 1 (January/February 2002), 60–74.

Friedman, Thomas L. *The World Is Flat: A Brief History of the Twenty-First Century.* New York: Farrar, Straus, & Giroux, 2005.

Garten, Jeffrey E. "The Global Economic Challenge." *Foreign Affairs* 84, 1 (January/February 2005), 37–48.

Homer-Dixon, Thomas. "The Rise of Complex Terrorism." *Foreign Policy* (January/February 2002), 52–63.

"Measuring Globalization." *Foreign Policy* (May/June 2005), 52–61.

Nankivell, Kerry Lynn. "Troubled Waters." *Foreign Policy* (November/December 2004), 30–31.

Segal, Adam. "Is America Losing Its Edge?" *Foreign Affairs* 83, 6 (November/December 2004), 2–8.

PART

IV

THE FUTURE

This book ends with an attempt to bring together some of the observations about the past and present and to extrapolate them into the future of national security for the United States. Because the future, by definition, has not occurred and thus cannot be observed and described, this process is necessarily less precise and more suggestive than other discussions.

The major purpose of Chapter 13 is to assess the relative impact of the two major themes of the book, geopolitics and globalization, on the future. This discussion is developed around two major observations about the likely future, both of which were proposed in the introduction and represent recurrent themes. First, it argues that the events of September 11, 2001, while disastrous and horrific, may have been overly interpreted in terms of their profound effect on American national security in the future. American vulnerability to harm was demonstrated by the September 11 terrorist attacks, and dealing with terrorism will certainly continue to be an important concern, but one that has been overshadowed by the Iraq War as part of the geopolitical agenda. While traumatic, the physical integrity and survival of the United States were not and are not fundamentally threatened by either of those events. The second observation is that globalization and geopolitics are not an either-or proposition. Both concerns existed before the attacks of September 11, and both survived it. The question is what the balance between the two will be in the future national security equation.

CHAPTER 13

Globalization and Geopolitics

PREVIEW

The degree of trauma caused by the second fault line and the future balance between globalization and geopolitics are the principal foci of this concluding chapter. Organizationally, we look at the two major concepts sequentially, first raising the question of the future of geopolitics (largely through the lens of reactions to September 11 and the ongoing GWOT and war in Iraq) and then examining the future of globalization in light of the antiglobalization movement that emerged at the end of the 1990s. We then reexamine where geopolitics and globalization can come together as elements of national security policy. We conclude by repeating the age-old question, what makes us secure?

The pace of change in American national security has quickened and become more complicated in the past fifteen years. For most of the history of the American republic, national security was a fairly minor concern because American soil was only episodically threatened by outsiders—and infrequently at that—wishing to and capable of doing us harm. After the British finally abandoned the goal of recolonization at the end of the War of 1812, the United States was essentially physically invulnerable to serious attack for almost a century and a half until the Soviet Union gained the capacity to menace the American homeland with nuclear-tipped intercontinental ballistic missiles.

The great impact of the September 11, 2001, attacks was partly the result of the shocking loss of a sense of total safety or physical security. The danger posed by the terrorists who attacked us did not threaten the basic existence of the American republic; there could and would be no follow-up invasion that might topple the American system and enslave our citizens. American survival was not at stake; our sense of physical immunity from harm was. Superficial comparisons were drawn between the September 11 events and Pearl Harbor in 1941, but in retrospect, the principal analogy was the limited nature of the threat and the awakening it produced. Usama bin Laden had awakened the same sleeping giant that Admiral Yamamoto identified after Pearl Harbor, and like the events sixty years earlier, filled us with a "terrible resolve."

The last decade and a half have witnessed the quickening of the pace of changes in the environment in which national security questions are raised and dealt with. Before the fault lines were exposed, the preceding periods were long and, by current standards, fairly leisurely: the formative period lasted for over a century and a half, and the Cold War occupied our attention for about forty-five years. The two periods differed in intensity and how they ended. National security was a periodic concern for most of the time during the formative period ending in 1945, whereas the Cold War transformed our concerns and placed the national security state at the center of public policy.

Did a new and similar cycle begin on September 11? Certainly, there was change with which analogies could be drawn. The Cold War historian John Lewis Gaddis, for instance, drew a dramatic comparison in January 2002: "The post–cold war era . . . began with the collapse of one structure, the Berlin Wall, on November 9, 1989, and ended with the collapse of another, the World Trade Center's twin towers." Has time altered that judgment?

Could we be repeating the earlier cycle in the events since 1989? The formative period (1789–1945) and the post–Cold War period (1989–2001) share an environment featuring the relative absence of apparent serious threats and thus a lesser urgency and importance accorded to national security concerns. The Cold War and the post–September 11 environments share a greater sense of national security salience where dramatic threats have energized the public and policy elites.

But are emphases on the dramatic impact of change overdrawn? The factors that dominate our current concerns were also present between 1989 and 2001: militant, fundamentalist Islam was a rising factor in the Middle East, and terrorism was a force that was widely prophesied but largely ignored. There were precursors of the September 11 attacks on Americans overseas and at home that could have presaged the direct assaults on U.S. soil: the 1993 attack on the World Trade Center, the 1998 bombings of American embassies in Kenya and Tanzania, and the 2000 attack on the USS *Cole* in Yemen, for example. In fact, virtually the only things that changed after the attacks on New York and Washington were the facts of the attacks themselves and the heightened awareness of the preexisting problem of terrorism they created. Those changed perceptions, of course, spawned new policy emphases (the GWOT and the extension of that war to such states as Iran, Iraq, and North Korea, for instance). The war on terrorism became the umbrella under which a variety of policy initiatives and changes have been justified; the uncompleted war in Iraq is the continuing legacy of this dynamic.

These introductory remarks provide the context within which this concluding chapter proceeds. Because it reflects the current debate, we look sequentially at roles of geopolitics and globalization, and where they intersect, using the events of September 11, 2001, as the watershed between their past and future statuses. The first part of each discussion focuses broadly on established facts and interpretations of those facts, whereas the discussion after the watershed raises and examines questions and policy options.

THE FUTURE OF GEOPOLITICS
AND TRADITIONAL NATIONAL SECURITY

Those analysts and policymakers who are principally concerned with traditional geopolitical questions defined in national security terms have been on a roller-coaster ride since the fall of the Berlin Wall. Once it was clear that the crumbling of Communism was irrevocable and that the flame that had necessitated and fueled the Cold War had been extinguished, national security concerns faded into the policy background, muscled out of the way in large measure by the globalizers. In the wake of the Cold War, defense budgets shrunk globally, as did military forces virtually worldwide, although this contraction was less pronounced in the United States than elsewhere. Still, the prospects of continued peace made traditional military concerns increasingly far-fetched. Warnings about threats coming from rogue states like North Korea, Iran, and Iraq (President Bush's "axis of evil") and looming images of the pro-liferation of weapons of mass destruction and terrorism to those and other rogue states and organizations appeared to be desperate cries from a national security com-munity trying, not very successfully, to justify its continued relevance in a progres-sively less threatening world. Particularly within the military itself, the 1990s were a disheartening follow-on to the glory days of the Reagan buildup of the 1980s. Even the sumptuous accolades lavished on the military's success in the Persian Gulf War could provide only fleeting sustenance to the thin gruel of attention of the 1990s.

The terrorist watershed revived the national security community. President Bush (as well as then Vice President Gore) had campaigned on a promise of returned inter-est in and funding for defense, and after the election, Secretary of Defense Rumsfeld promised a thorough review and updating of American strategy and capabilities. In the months prior to September 2001, these rhetorical promises did not translate into concrete actions or generate grassroots support, causing some disquiet in the military and even muted criticisms of the new leadership. A return to center stage for the geopoliticians required some compelling event to recapture the public, including con-gressional, attention. September 11 provided that impetus; the threat had returned.

President Bush noticeably widened the mission for traditional national security instruments and promised to provide the tools for that expansion in mission and ca-pability in his 2002 State of the Union message and subsequent budget request. The expansion of mission was made most vividly with his axis of evil designation of Iran, Iraq, and North Korea. While not specifying what military action might be contem-plated against any of them at that time, he did promise there would be "conse-quences" if any of them planned to engage in acts of terrorism or provided the wherewithal—notably WMD and/or ballistic missiles—to terrorist causes. Most ominously, he did not rule out preemptive, unilateral action, presumably including the use of military force against them. "I will not wait on events while dangers gather," he said in his speech. "The United States of America will not permit the world's most dangerous regimes to threaten us with the world's most destructive weapons." In order to implement this ambitious and expanded geopolitical agenda, the President proposed an increase of $46 billion in defense spending over the previous year's projection. Some of this increase would go directly to the homeland security program, while the rest would be devoted to selective modernization of the force congruent with the administration's vision of the conflict environment (see Amplification 13.1). The warnings were a particularly poignant harbinger of the Iraq invasion to come in 2003.

Basic reforms proposed by Rumsfeld were put on hold by September 1, as the efforts of defense planners and implementers were redirected toward the evolving GWOT, and the reforms went into a deep freeze with the commitment of American

Amplification 13.1

THE SECDEF ON FUTURE FORCE

In an article in the May/June 2002 edition of *Foreign Affairs* (see Selected Bibliography for full citation), Secretary of Defense (SECDEF) Donald H. Rumsfeld lays out his vision of the future of American military force, both in terms of the kinds of conflicts in which we may become involved from now on (see *Challenge!* at the end of this chapter) and the kinds of challenges and problems we will encounter. His arguments are largely taken from the 2001 *Quadrennial Defense Review*, a document mandated by Congress and published over his name. Because the problems and challenges he presents will, among other things, presumably provide guidance to efforts to modernize the American military, they are worth noting. Following are the six challenges, although not in the order he presents them.

1. Flexibility and adaptation: "Preparing for the future will require new ways of thinking, and the development of forces and capabilities that can adapt quickly to new challenges and unexpected circumstances."
2. Environment of surprise: "In the years ahead, we will probably be surprised again by new adversaries who may also strike in unexpected ways."
3. Asymmetrical warfare: "Rather than building up conventional armies, navies, and air forces, they [our adversaries] will likely seek to challenge us asymmetrically by looking for vulnerabilities and trying to exploit them."
4. Terrorism: "Potential adversaries know that as an open society, the United States is vulnerable to new forms of terrorism."
5. Defense against the unknown: "Our challenge in this new century is a difficult one: to defend ourselves against the unknown, the uncertain, the unseen, and the unexpected."
6. As a result of the first five challenges, transformation: "The Department of Defense must focus on achieving six transformational goals: first, to protect the U.S. homeland and our bases overseas; second, to protect and sustain power in distant theaters; third, to deny our enemies sanctuary; fourth, to protect our information networks from attack; fifth, to use information technology to link up different kinds of U.S. forces so they can fight jointly; and sixth, to maintain unhindered access to space."

troops to Afghanistan in 2001 and especially to Iraq in 2003. These two ventures, which the Bush administration continued to argue are theaters in the struggle against terrorism as recently as his U.S. Naval Academy speech of November 30, 2005, have sufficiently occupied military energies and resources that there has been little time or energy for reform, and when Iraq becomes a "lessons learned" exercise (the eventual postwar assessment of our performance), those plans may require modification, as suggested in Chapter 8.

The commitment of American forces to the GWOT and Iraq in the way they have been used has caused international concern. Many American allies and friends see American actions as both excessively bellicose and unilateralist. Because the Bush administration emphasized what the United States will do with apparent disregard for the opinions of others and even over their strongly voiced objections, many American friends and allies who have otherwise supported the American effort against terrorism were given pause. Singling out North Korea and Iran as among the "world's most dangerous regimes" was particularly curious to some foreign leaders and analysts. The harsh denunciations made quiet North Korean overtures to South Korea more difficult to sustain while reinforcing the anti-Americanism of Iranian clergy opposed to moderating influences in that country. At the same time, administration officials, led by Rumsfeld, downplayed apparent North Korean compliance with demands to shut down their nuclear and missile programs and asserted Iran was still actively pursuing nuclear capability, disputes that continue to the present. Critics here and abroad openly came to question this bellicose approach to what seemed to them to be a political situation with diplomatic solutions. These criticisms were particularly intense as the administration publicly lobbied for support for invading Iraq and then went ahead with the attack despite nearly universal international opposition. These criticisms continue to reverberate into 2006.

The equation of geopolitics with terrorism through the extension of the antiterrorism campaign to Iraq guarantees that national security debates and advocacies will, for the foreseeable future, be tied to what is and is not the appropriate way to combat terrorism and threats to the United States more generally. Certainly, President Bush has made terrorism suppression the centerpiece of his administration in the international realm. Whether terrorism is a durable and adequate basis for the consideration of how the United States will face the world geopolitically is an open question. In the short run, periodic terrorist attacks—like those in July 2005 in London—fan the GWOT flame. The mid- and long-run prognosis is not so clear. At some level, terrorism will endure, as it always has; whether it will be the durable tether to ground national security policy is a more difficult projection. Sustaining waning support for Iraq exacerbates the problem.

Consciously or not, this adjustment of national security direction moves the military from its traditional mooring in Western-style, symmetrical warfare toward asymmetrical warfare as the new focus. This reemphasis got temporarily lost within national security circles in the general prosperity over the most sizable peacetime budget increase proposal since the administration of Ronald Reagan.

At some point, however, the hard question of what vision of future war the administration holds (a version of which is raised in this chapter's *Challenge!*) has to come to the forefront and be reflected in budgetary and other priorities. The traditional military role of "preparing for and fighting the nation's wars" requires an assessment of what kinds of wars those are likely to be and how (including with what) we might be prepared to fight them. Granting that any answer will encompass more than one narrow type of conflict, there inevitably has to be some sense of focus—one size military probably does not fit all wars.

Are asymmetrical wars the future for which the national security community can and will prepare? Fighting foes employing asymmetrical means is certainly nothing new for the United States, although it is a form of warfare at which the United States has not had great success. The Vietnam conflict was an asymmetrical war, Iraq has become an asymmetrical war, and most of the other American experiences in the developing world have contained asymmetrical warfare components. If most of the places where the United States will find cause to pursue opponents in the future are in the developing world—which they are—a robust asymmetrical capability may make sense, especially since none of these potential foes will willingly confront U.S. forces on our preferred terms. Only North Korea occasionally implies its willingness to engage in such a war, a boast that sounds more like a suicide threat than anything else.

It is not at all clear that the traditional military community that signed up with apparent enthusiasm for the war on terrorism truly accepts the implications of such a major reorientation of its priorities. The military aspect (phase one) of the campaign in Afghanistan had the effect of shielding the need to take harsh stock of what elevating terrorism to the center stage of our concerns and preparations implies; the more restrained success of rounding up Al Qaeda (phase two) may be the real future. The "shock and awe" invasion of Iraq, followed by the prolonged, persistent resistance, mirrors the Afghan sequence. How many more of these kinds of conflicts will we sustain?

If the real opponent in Afghanistan has always been Usama bin Laden and his Al Qaeda cohorts and if countering threats like those posed by bin Laden is the model of what the war on terrorism will be, then positive lessons of imposing symmetrical solutions with some asymmetrical embroidery is highly misleading. The Taliban was swept away fairly traditionally as the prelude to hunting down and destroying Al Qaeda, but the major quarry eluded the effort, and the Taliban have returned. Bin Laden remains at large, and the United States initially admitted in April 2002 that it had little idea where he might be; as Rumsfeld put it, the trail had gone "cold." It has gotten no warmer. Even Bush implicitly admitted the limited success of asymmetrical counterterrorism efforts to date in his 2002 State of the Union address when he declared "yet tens of thousands of trained terrorists are still at large. These enemies view the entire world as a battlefield, and we must pursue them wherever they are. So long as training camps operate, so long as nations harbor terrorists, freedom is at risk, and America and our allies must not, and will not, allow it." Over three years later, this assessment remains eerily poignant and relevant.

Is this how to focus American national security assets? Are the virtual moonscapes of parts of Afghanistan and the steamy jungles of the Philippine archipelago the battlefields where American forces will operate to track down and destroy terrorist cells? As posited in Chapter 11, international terrorism—including Al Qaeda—is no longer a monolithic, hierarchical organization (if it ever really was) that can be destroyed by lopping off its head (bin Laden). Rather, it has become a hydra-headed beast of loosely associated terrorist groups that act independently of those who inspire them. Increasingly, as in the 2005 London attacks, we speak of "Al Qaeda–like" terrorist actions committed by Al Qaeda "affiliates" without knowing exactly what that means. The problem is getting harder, not easier.

If the war on terrorism and its derivations like Iraq remain the focus of American national security policy, that clearly implies a reorientation of the national security structure, and it is not at all clear that the national security establishment embraces or is ever likely to embrace such a change. Traditional military force is likely to be deemphasized in such a strategy, as other assets such as intelligence and border security are enhanced to deal with different aspects of this semimilitary problem. Within the military and beyond, elements such as special forces, those "snake eaters"—who were the pariahs of the services but have gained considerable esteem for their positive roles in the Persian Gulf War in 1991, the Afghan campaign, and in Iraq—suddenly become central players while more traditional combat specialties are downgraded in importance. How many tanks, for instance, does the military need to pursue terrorists in Malaysia? How many Bradley fighting vehicles can meaningfully be employed in the jungles of some far-flung corner of the Indonesian archipelago? Does the use of nonmilitary personnel like CIA agents in special forces roles somehow further muddy the conceptual waters about war, as it appeared to when a CIA element assassinated a suspected Al Qaeda leader in Yemen in late 2002?

In the midst of the strong emotional response to the September 11 incidents, it has been easy to commit primary American assets and priorities to the war on terrorism and thereby appear to have created a focus for strategy that had been missing in the post–Cold War period. That effort creates an apparent base, much as the Soviet threat did during the Cold War, around which to orient national security. Terrorists become the geopolitical equivalent of the Red menace. If we still lack a peer competitor in the shadowy world of terrorism, at least we have a compelling opponent.

But does the amorphous face of terrorism provide a firm enough grounding for national security policy, or is it instead a prominent part of a more comprehensive policy? In the short term, the campaign against terrorism remains in the spotlight, sharing the glare with Iraq. But if terrorism suppression succeeds and we gradually lose our fear, so will our fervor for the effort fade back in the popular mind into the more traditional, limited role that countering terrorism has occupied in the past. There are several reasons for this likelihood.

The first is that a national strategy that has terrorism as its lynchpin will almost certainly meet growing domestic opposition if its implications are implemented with relish and enthusiasm. The most likely opponent will be the military itself, for several reasons. For one thing, a national security strategy based in countering terrorism relegates the military to a reduced stature in the national security universe. No less than Secretary Rumsfeld has admitted that in the overall campaign against terrorism, military force has a limited role, since terrorists are rarely organized and seldom fight in ways for which regular armed forces are appropriate. The dispatch of several Special Forces A-teams to assist the Philippine armed forces in tracking down jungle-based alleged terrorist insurgents is a much more likely model than the conventional effort early in Afghanistan. More Iraq-like actions are the only exception. But will our Iraq experience permit such actions in the future?

This effect on roles and missions is unlikely to be lost on the more traditional military specialties, especially when the budgetary implications of developing asymmetrical forces collide with plans to modernize traditional forces. Special forces are a lightning rod; their role has always been the stepchild of the armed forces since their conceptual formation in World War II in forms like the Marine Raiders (which the Marine command structure opposed) and in American Army assistance to the Greek government during the Greek Civil War. When Special Forces were formed in the 1950s and became the Green Berets, they were largely shunned within the Army, which preferred to think they were little more than fringe psychopaths performing minimally useful military tasks. In Vietnam, they reached their nadir when Special Forces became implicated in Operation Phoenix, a program of assassination of village figures who cooperated with the Viet Cong. Yet they are one of the centerpieces of the war on terror.

Moreover, the nature of the military role played by the armed forces in a terrorism-based strategy is likely to breed other opposition in the longer run. One source of opposition will come from the extensive activation of the National Guard and Reserves whenever a terrorist problem arises, and more dramatically in Iraq. In the immediate wake of the terrorist attacks of September 11, reservists were activated without complaint as part of the subsequent patriotic fervor. Reservists had hardly recovered from this kind of activation when they were recalled for longer, repeated deployments in Iraq that entailed considerable personal and family sacrifices and deprivations for the "weekend warriors." The question will almost certainly be raised whether this duty overly deploys both active duty and reserve forces, commits them to less than vital concerns, and erodes their effectiveness as combat soldiers—charges that have been levied against soldiers used as peacekeepers. It is ironic that President Bush campaigned on a pledge to end such "misuse" of armed forces and in less than a year had created the basis for the same problem. The hemorrhage of soldiers leaving the Guard and Reserves in 2005 enlivens this concern.

A terrorism-based strategy also has problems of coherence. Declaring "war" on a phenomenon (terrorism) provides ambiguous guidance in a way that focusing on a concrete opponent does not, and even supporters of the terrorism emphasis have admitted that one of their problems is specifying opponents. Since the military function in the campaign to suppress terrorism is not completely clear and may, in some cases, be decidedly marginal, it does not provide clear guidance about what to do and against whom for those who define military roles and missions and prepare service members to conduct hostilities.

Negative international reaction to such an emphasis is likely as well. While the United States' closest allies expressed sincere sympathy for the 2001 terrorist attacks and the resultant action in Afghanistan, the extension of the campaign to other places and for other purposes—overthrowing Saddam Hussein, for instance— has created a mounting level of dissent. In a March 2002 column, Steven Erlanger suggested the basis for allied concern about elevating terrorism to central status in American defense policy. The fear he attributed to NATO sources was that the United States was becoming so much more powerful physically (a trend accentuated by increased spending), especially technologically, than everyone else that we no longer needed the assistance of our allies but could, and do, increasingly act on our own, regardless of their sentiments. The way the United States operated essentially by itself in Afghanistan was simultaneously a compliment to the prowess of American forces and a fear that this ability only reinforces the American tendency toward unilateral, imprudent action. The deeper implication could be a negative impact on alliance cohesion at a time when it is universally conceded that greater international cooperation is necessary to deal with the threat posed by terrorism. Three years in Iraq only redoubles this concern.

Will the problem of terrorism provide a substitute for the Soviet threat of the Cold War, a mooring around which strategy can be developed? In the short run, the answer appears to be yes; especially if one includes Iraq in the terrorism net. Terrorism is, however, a fickle problem in the sense that a simple—even tactical—lull in the phenomenon by the forces of terror will almost certainly erode our resolve and cause us to defocus on terrorism and refocus on something else. Terrorism works conceptually better as part of a broader problem like developmental imbalances or poverty than it does as the central peg of strategy. A longer-term strategy, in other words, is probably better served by a more concrete and durable problem.

THE FUTURE OF GLOBALIZATION

There is an old saying that anything that appears too good to be true probably is. During the early and middle 1990s, it was a cliché that could easily have been applied to the globalizing economy. Accompanied by lavish predictions of continuing economic expansion, prosperity, and attendant political democratization, the progress of a revitalized global economy seemed inexorable. In some respectable economics publications, there was even speculation that the American-led new global economy was so robust that it might have surmounted the historical business cycle of boom and bust, as noted in Chapter 5. It all has indeed proven too good to be true.

Any assessment of the future of globalization must begin by asking why its promise was not fulfilled to the extent predicted by its most expansive advocates. The general conclusion is that globalization was oversold as a panacea for the troubles of the world. It was advertised as the solution to the world's economic and political ills, and that was almost certainly more than could be expected of it. The 1990s round of globalization foundered on overly inflated expectations. If globalization is to rebound in the current atmosphere of geopolitical dominance, its champions must learn from the past what is realistic and what is not. How much and what is the reasonable contribution of globalization to the international condition?

The overinflation of expectations had both economic and political dimensions. The triumph of the philosophy of free trade in the United States and elsewhere provided much of the fuel to pull the global economy (including the United States) out of the recession of the latter 1980s and early 1990s, and it combined with a wave of national legislation and enforced international practice in deregulation and privatization to help propel the go-go 1990s in the economic realm. Globalization was advertised as the high tide that raised all boats in the water, and the answer to any country's ills was adoption of something like Friedman's "golden straightjacket" (the applied version of the American model). Because the economy had become global and had gained such enormous size, it appeared to be insulated from the vicissitudes of economic downturn anywhere. Globalization was going to be a universal positive-sum game, a win-win situation for all who partook.

This optimism was captured in the Clinton administration's foreign policy of engagement and enlargement. That policy replaced traditional national security considerations with economic globalization as the centerpiece of foreign policy. The operative principle was free trade to promote economic growth and globalization; states engaged in the global economy could be added to the enlarged "circle of market democracies." Economics and political development were thus woven together as part of the emerging "democratic peace."

This assessment, of course, has proven overly optimistic, even romantic. Deregulation and privatization—the economic *and* political heart of Newt Gingrich's "contract with America" in 1994—coincided with and arguably aided the economic expansion, but it also created the atmosphere in which the infamous Enron Corporation could fashion and operate its financial deception until the Ponzi scheme collapsed in late 2001 and was followed by other revelations of corporate wrongdoing that had overly zealous deregulation as part of their causes. In the midst of the great expansion, the possibility that much of the good times was the result of bubble economies that would eventually burst was swept aside as old thinking in the "new economy." The expanding list of countries whose leaders reached office through the ballot box created a rarified atmosphere that suggested the triumph of political democracy (Francis Fukuyama's "end of history") as well. At the same time, the possibility that economic globalization might not lead to democratization, but instead might have, as Joseph S. Nye Jr. called it, a "democracy deficit," was underplayed.

Unfettered optimism belied history and even the views of its champions. A wave of economic interdependence and growing trade had washed through the international system at the beginning of the twentieth century, had produced the same kind of euphoric predictions, and had been given the lie in the human bloodbath of World War I. At the same time, even ardent supporters like Friedman warned there were countries that either would reject globalization or simply could not compete successfully. Middle Eastern fundamentalist regimes head the list of rejecters.

The storm clouds were lurking only slightly below the horizon. In 1997, the first warning sign appeared (however temporarily) in the economic downturn of the latter 1990s, and it was followed by a series of events that culminated in the terrorist attacks of September 2001 and the corporate scandals of 2001 and 2002 and beyond. These fissures represented warning signs about the expansive optimism of the early 1990s. Although one can quibble with the selections, I have chosen five "lessons" that arise from events and occurrences starting in 1997 that illustrate questions about the universal inevitability and desirability of globalization.

1. *The effects of globalization are not always positive.* This was the underlying message of the East Asian financial crisis. For half a decade or more, the secret to prosperity and progress for developing countries was adoption of the values of the globalizing economy and admission into its organizations like the APEC or the WTO. Prior to 1997, no country had ever been seriously "burned" by being part of globalization. As the crisis spread through eastern Asia and resulted not in instant remuneration to minimize the effects but instead in belt-tightening demands accompanied by painful structural reform, the possibility that there could be losers as well as winners in the globalizing economy had to be weighed. The unvarnished optimism of the 1990s lost some of its luster in the process. In its most extreme impact, the crisis produced political upheaval in Indonesia, resulting in the toppling of the thirty-two-year Suharto regime (in itself not an entirely bad thing) and leaving many Indonesians wondering if they wanted to rejoin the globalization system. That trauma has passed; the possibility of its return has not.

2. *The business cycle still exists.* This lesson was at least partially induced by the East Asian crisis and reactions to it. While markets in most places (notably the United States) did rebound worldwide from the impact of financial failure in Asia, the crisis contributed to a general increase in caution about the seemingly endless expansion of the global economy. Chastened by the effects of the crisis and the subsequent slowing of the global economy, there has been a growing realization that the most effusive promotions of globalization were hyperbole; nothing as fundamental as changing the basic nature of economic life (the business cycle) has occurred. Globalizing prosperity has returned (especially in Asia) since 2001, but it is a much quieter, lower-key phenomenon.

3. *Some people and groups do not like globalization.* During the heyday of globalization during the 1990s, there was virtually no organized dissent about whether globalization was a good idea or not and whether its spread should be opposed. Certainly there was discussion, largely academic in nature, about the compatibility of globalization with different people's values, but most of the criticism was isolated. H. Ross Perot's "great sucking sound" depiction of American jobs disappearing into Mexico after NAFTA was implemented in the midst of an apparently unstinting run of global expansion did not emerge at the time. By the end of the 1990s, however, the opponents became very public, demonstrating—sometimes violently—at meetings of the various forums that promoted globalization values, and they resurfaced as President Buch attended meetings of the FTRA and APEC in 2005. These *rejectionists* are a mixed collection of opponents in terms of their objections, and they have clearly put the defenders of globalization on the public relations defensive. The emergence of this opposition has further dampened the heat of advocacy. President Bush has always been a supporter of globalization (he is, for instance, a champion of the 2005 Central American Free Trade Agreement). Public opposition has made his advocacy much more subdued.

4. *Some places and groups violently oppose and resist the concept and application of globalization.* One of the underlying lessons of Usama bin Laden and Al Qaeda's

terrorist attacks had to do with why they launched them. Although these motives are widely vilified as not justifying the means, the underlying theme of bin Laden's hatred for the United States is its desecrating effect on the environment in which he wants to practice and enforce his own vision of Islam. Americans desecrate the holy lands of Arabia because they make it Western, a part of the globalization culture that the Americans personify. Bin Laden's assault on the United States may indeed be a single application of Samuel P. Huntington's "clash of civilization" thesis that future conflict will occur where different cultures with diverging values come into opposition. At a minimum, however, the fundamentalist Islam that bin Laden portrays himself as representing demonstrates that the values and aspirations of globalization are not universally held. While one can argue that the peculiar values bin Laden and his supporters adhere to are isolated and unique, they still demonstrate that the appeal of globalization is not universal. Bin Laden and others like him believe that traditional Islamic culture cannot survive if the Middle East globalizes, and so he opposes its entry into the region.

5. *The rules of globalization are not as well established as formerly advertised.* In the immediate wake of the East Asian crisis, the Western, essentially American model became the benchmark by which economic virtue has been measured, and the basis for that ascendancy is the transparency and supposed rectitude of American capitalism; what distinguished the American from the Asian model was the emphasis on honesty and trustworthiness that firms and governments demonstrated under the American model, which provided the transparency and openness in which investment and commerce could flourish and the return to robustness of Asian economics (notably China). That assumption was at least partially laid low by the 2002 corporate scandals. Among the apparent lessons that have emerged was that transparency failed; the extensive deregulation of the accounting industry allowed collusion and misrepresentation in ways and to extents not witnessed anywhere since the S&L crisis of the 1980s. That Enron and others could get away with their misdeeds for as long as they did punctured the sanctimony of American pronouncements of virtue in the management of its economy. The United States can no longer seek to impose its rules on the basis of rectitude with the same confidence it did before, because the scandals exposed another, darker side to the "new economy." The eventual resolution of the issues raised by the scandal may or may not result in useful reforms that can become part of global standards, as the S&L outcome did. Nonetheless, blind acceptance of the American vision of globalization took a clear shot.

Most of these dampening effects were in place or in the offing when the events of September 11, 2001, occurred, and only added fuel to the antiglobalization fire that had emerged by the end of the century. The terrorist attacks were clearly dramatic and influential: they certainly changed the nature and the character of the debate about the American place in the world and how to secure it. The national foreign policy agenda is now, and for the foreseeable future will remain, a national security agenda, not a globalization agenda. At the same time, the attacks on the

World Trade Center were directed against probably the most visible symbol of globalization in the world. People of eighty nationalities were killed in the attack and collapse of the two buildings; almost all were there doing the work of a globalizing economy in one way or another. The events dealt the global economy a blow, and it was reflected on stock exchanges—the lifelines of the globalization system—for the rest of 2001 and into 2002.

Depending on whether there are more instances like the 2002 scandals and how they play out in the public realm, the impact on globalization could be as profound as or more profound than the terrorist attacks. In many ways, the scandals personified the ultimate new, globalizing economy enterprise. Enron and the others proved bubble enterprises, elaborate shells with no substance built on dishonest accounting procedures that were a by-product of the deregulation and privatization provisions of the 1990s. Revelations of insider advantage, cronyism, and corruption sound remarkably like the kinds of charges leveled against Asian companies that compliance with American-inspired rules was supposed to cure. In light of these scandals, how could the next American-inspired IMF official confront the economics minister of a developing country and suggest the need to root out corruption in that country's system?

What do these experiences mean for the future of globalization? It is premature to assess in detail, but two points seem apparent. One is that the next, ongoing wave of globalization, as it unfolds, will be structurally different than the globalization of the 1990s. One of the principal differences will be that the United States will be less morally advantaged in shaping the evolving rules. The scandals robbed the United States of its virtue. That is bad news for Americans who aspire to and believe only we can provide global economic leadership; it is good news to foreigners looking for a more level intellectual and moral playing field on which to compete with the United States. At the same time, several years of large and growing deficits in the American budget since 2001, financed to a significant degree by foreign—notably Chinese—investment, means that American predominance may not be so overwhelming the next time around.

The other effect is that the next wave of globalization will have to be tied to, rather than distinct from, geopolitics and national security. Geopolitics is back and will remain important as long as two conditions hold: Americans must retain an interest in defeating terrorism, and terrorism must prove resilient, a problem worth our concentrated effort. Both are likely, and the geopolitical task will center on how to stretch and ultimately break that resilience.

WHERE GLOBALIZATION AND GEOPOLITICS MEET

President George W. Bush has committed himself, and thus much of the national agenda, to the primacy of the geopolitical pursuit of international terrorism and the promotion of democracy for the remainder of his second term. Iraq is its most visible symbol. His neoconservative version of *realpolitik* contends that terrorism is the most serious problem facing the United States and the world and that as long as this menace continues, other areas of foreign and national security policy must remain subservient to eradicating this scourge against mankind. The spread of democracy, it is reasoned, is a partial antidote, since Bush believes that free peoples will reject terrorism. Among the former emphases of policy subordinated in the determined pursuit of this foreign policy is the emphasis on expanded globalization, including the aggressive pursuit of market economics.

Given the sinister, ubiquitous nature of the terrorist problem, this emphasis is likely to be, or certainly can be construed to be, highly durable across time. Even if American and allied efforts are successful in corralling Usama bin Laden and dismantling his Al Qaeda network (goals that have remained elusive), doing so will not be the same thing as eradicating terrorism. As long as there are disaffected individuals and groups who focus the source of their misery on the United States, terrorism will be a worldwide problem, since some other states will likely be both targets and nurturers of terrorists. The question is how visible and threatening terrorism remains, and thus what priority can and should reasonably be assigned to fighting it. Amplification 13.2 raises the question of how terrorism and globalization may be related. When adventures like the war in Iraq are added to the agenda, the prospects get even murkier.

President Bush has an interest in retaining this focus. Prior to the attacks of September 11, 2001, his administration had no clear, overriding theme in the area of foreign and national security affairs. He had campaigned on revitalizing the military, but his first budget request offered a smaller increase in defense spending than Democratic nominee Al Gore had promised in his campaign. Although it is sometimes difficult to recall given the torrent of subsequent events, the early Bush foreign policy ship seemed to many to lack any semblance of a rudder.

Responding to terrorism brought a clarity to Bush administration national security policy that it had previously lacked. One can question whether the GWOT label is useful or helpful, but it certainly galvanized public opinion—including the support of a normally more critical print and electronic media—behind the effort. The focus had the virtues of being both plausible and enduring. The president clearly established the political high ground in the national security debate with this effort, and there seemed little danger he would relinquish it. The growing negative backlash as the Iraqi occupation lengthens and American and Iraqi casualties accumulate represents the greatest potential challenge to public support for this vision—support that had reached minority status by late 2005.

Is there any danger of overplaying the strong hand the President holds? The administration continues to pin its strategic vision on the GWOT, but is that grounding as enduring as it once seemed to be? Several factors could undermine the strategy. One is what might be called the "cry wolf" scenario. Since September 11, the White House has issued periodic, color-coded alerts about possible impending terrorist events that have not materialized, and it has engaged in highly complex, expensive efforts to insulate very public events like the Super Bowl and the Winter Olympics in Utah in 2002, to cite two early examples. In these cases, it could not be demonstrated that the efforts were responsible for preventing untoward occurrences, partly as a matter of logic (the fallacy of affirming the consequent: we did this to prevent X, X did not occur, therefore the reason was the effort) and partly because revealing

Amplification 13.2

TERRORISM AND GLOBALIZATION

The relationship between terrorism and globalization is complex and evolving, as previous discussions have suggested. The two are not an either-or proposition. There will be terrorism within a regime dominated by the values of globalization, and globalization continues in a world fixated on terrorism. The two are likely to compete with each other for our attention because they lead to different global outcomes.

Globalization clearly represents a threat to the purveyors of current religiously based international terrorism. A globalized world is a modernized, secular world, and as such, it is a world opposed by those who believe in fundamentalist Islam. Some of those opponents eventually radicalize and become terrorists (while others quietly support the terrorist goals), and the artifacts of globalization are inevitably targets for their ire. For the terrorists, the World Trade Center towers were a well-chosen target. At the same time, the very openness and fluidity of a globalized world provide opportunities for terrorists to operate more effectively than they could in the more closed society they appear to prefer. As Friedman puts it in a 2002 *Foreign Affairs* article, "We also saw the forces of globalization on September 11, 2001. Again, globalization goes both ways. It can threaten democracies as well as strengthen them. But on net, globalization will be a force for more openness, more rule of law, and more opportunities for people to enjoy personal freedoms and challenge authorities."

Globalization is one possible weapon in the GWOT, although its potential seems to be undervalued. If it is true that draining the swamp of the conditions that breed the despair that leads people to become terrorists will lead to a reduction in terrorism, then spreading the global prosperity to those places from which terrorists have emerged could clearly be part of the solution. If, for instance, economic conditions could be improved in places like Palestine and Pakistan to the point that teenaged boys who currently become suicide terrorists (profiled in Amplification 10.2 in Chapter 10) could find meaningful work, would they be less likely to submit to the appeals of terrorist recruiters? There are, of course, no guarantees that this would occur, but it would provide some indication of the strength of the two ideas.

how a plot was foiled would probably compromise future efforts. At some point, however, warnings followed by the absence of consequences may begin to look suspicious and result in an erosion of support. On the other hand, heightened security concerns in places such as New York in summer 2005 in reaction to the London bombings indicate a lingering apprehension about the future.

The second danger is in overextending the emphasis. In the months following the terrorist attacks, virtually all administration policy seemed to be justified as part of the war on terrorism. The need for budget deficits was rationalized on the basis that the war necessitated whatever efforts were necessary, including paying the country's bills with borrowed money. It was further argued that deficit spending is common during wartime. The fact that there was nothing resembling a war being fought to justify deficits after the Afghan military campaign ended in December 2001 did not seem troublesome to many Americans. Meanwhile, military budgets have soared to unprecedented levels since 2001; the United States, after all, spends more today on defense than the rest of the world combined.

A third possibility is that the GWOT will be perceived as ineffectual and its extension to places such as Iraq will come to be viewed as irrelevant or counterproductive. Will the essential unilateralism of the GWOT play effectively with the efforts of others (the British and Egyptians, for instance) who have become direct victims of international terrorism? Or will the increased internationalism of the problem dictate an international effort in which American predominance and individual action is viewed more as part of the problem than the solution?

As the occupation of Iraq continues and the rolls of American and Iraqi victims of the Iraqi resistance lengthens, larger parts of the American population (nearly 60 percent in late 2005) have come to believe that this theater of the GWOT is irrelevant at best and detrimental at worst to containing terrorism. Are we eradicating terrorism in Iraq against a resistance that Vice President Cheney declared in June 2005 was in its "last throes"? Or has the occupation become such a magnet for discontented Muslims that the country has been transformed into one huge recruiting and training base for additional terrorists? If the latter, is the GWOT really a coherent strategy for dealing with terrorism?

Where does the promotion of globalization fit into the policy equation? It has not disappeared altogether; in his 2002 State of the Union message, President Bush did repeat his plea to Congress to be granted the Trade Promotion Authority (that was subsequently granted). The President has formally endorsed the FTAA proposal in principle as recently as late 2005, but it is clear that he is unwilling to expend significant political capital on globalization issues that draw fire from some groups. Thus, globalization will remain on the periphery as long as the emphasis on the state of war is accepted by the people.

There is a glimmer of optimism about the resurgence of a policy emphasis on globalization within the American political system. The campaign against terrorism has pushed aside the emphasis of the Clinton administration and the United Nations on peacekeeping for humanitarian purposes. Peacekeeping missions to resuscitate failed states, the victims of bloody internal wars, remain in place (Kosovo, for instance) and continue to involve American forces where they had been committed prior to the shift in emphasis caused by the terrorist episode. The current administration has shown little interest in expanding that participation and continues to deride the idea when it arises. The commitment to the war on terrorism provides political cover to avoid future entanglements under the humanitarian banner. Military action against the states designated as the axis of evil in Iraq and possibly beyond further justifies avoiding committing U.S. forces to humanitarian-based peacekeeping, but the commitment of forces to Iraq has limited American military options in any case.

The glimmer comes in the form of state-building in the service of the campaign against terrorism rather than for purely humanitarian reasons. The prototype and test case, of course, is Afghanistan, since rebuilding the Afghan state was part of the original public American rationale for intervening and remaining in that country. The dynamics and effects of state-building in Afghanistan are likely to be essentially identical to those involved in humanitarian state-building, although obviously customized to differentiate between the political and economic conditions in Afghanistan and, say, Kosovo. Who participates will be different: European organizations such as the EU or OSCE are not present in Afghanistan in any sizable way, although some of the assistance will have to come from their members. The problems of state-building in Kosovo and Afghanistan are both similar and different: both share basic cleavages (called tribal in Afghanistan, ethnic in Kosovo) but different levels of development from which to build on. Having said that, the tasks of infrastructure development and the like will be similar in concept and design; the difference is that the effort in Afghanistan will have to begin from a more modest developmental base.

If these efforts are successful, the outcomes should also be similar, if for different reasons. Successful state-building in Afghanistan, as in Kosovo and elsewhere, is intended to produce stable, prosperous countries that become productive, reliable members of the international system. In the case of Kosovo, the reason for producing such a state is to increase the stability of the Balkans and thus reinforce the peace in Europe—in addition, of course, to humanitarian motives to improve the lot of the Kosovars. In Afghanistan, the purpose is less altruistic: to create a state and society whose members are resistant to terrorists (draining the swamp) in addition to a humanitarian concern for the Afghan people.

Part of the strategy of state-building for either reason is making target countries attractive to the private investors who are at the heart of the spread of globalization. A Taliban-dominated Afghanistan that forcefully removed half its human resources (women) from the workforce, destroyed the physical and intellectual infrastructure, and ruled through a system of random violence and repression was not going to attract foreign direct investment in the form of cash or imported industry. A democratizing, progressive, economically developing Afghanistan operating under the rule of law will presumably not only be resistant to the incursions of terrorist groups but also attract outside investors who can reinforce growing stability. Achieving this will not be easy. The limited lessons of humanitarian state-building apply, and the principal lesson may be the extreme difficulty and in some cases impossibility of getting from the prior condition of instability and despair to the subsequent one of peace and stability. In the case of state-building for humanitarian purposes, there are questions about international will to see the difficult course through to its uncertain conclusions. Whether state-building to destroy terrorism will prove a more durable motivation to confront the difficulties remains to be seen.

Afghanistan is, to repeat, the testing ground for similar efforts in Iraq. The plan for Afghanistan is the replica for implementing the neoconservative dream that an imposed democracy can take root in Iraq and become a model for the region that other Islamic states will emulate. The experience in Afghanistan through summer

2006 contains some caution about American willingness to follow through and actually engage in state-building. If the same thing happens in Iraq, what becomes of the neoconservative vision? How does the Hamas win in Palestine change things?

The idea of combining globalization and the geopolitical instinct to undermine terrorism demonstrates that the two forces are neither necessarily contradictory nor incompatible. Which is the dominant concern at any point in time will certainly reflect international realities and subsequent policy priorities. The 1990s offered no overarching security challenges that seemed to dictate the supremacy of traditional national security concerns, although one can argue that more concern earlier on with the growing terrorist threat represented by bin Laden would have been appropriate and might have prevented the events of September 2001. The reality of terrorism similarly dictated a concentration on more traditional geopolitical considerations. Although our preferences will influence the environment to some extent, events beyond our control will also help set the agenda. There is nothing profoundly new in that situation.

Conclusion: What Makes Us Secure? What Makes Us Prosperous?

The interests of states and their citizens are various and hierarchical. The most basic purpose of the state is to maintain its own survival and the physical security of its citizens from harm or death. A state that cannot perform that basic function has very little utility to anyone and clearly cannot pursue other, more mundane priorities. First things always come first.

The physical survival of the United States and the protection of its citizens from harm has hardly ever been a lively concern for the U.S. government. The United States has, for almost all its existence, been invulnerable to threats that imperil our existence and safety. The large reason for the trauma of the September 11 terrorist attacks was that they exposed to us that our sense of invulnerability to harm was mistaken; American soil could be attacked and American lives taken without the apparent American ability to prevent it. We quickly experienced what most citizens of other states had known for a long time: there is no such thing as absolute security in this world.

Security, of course, has both a physical and a psychological dimension. The physical sense has to do with the absolute, physical ability to provide safety from harm and destruction. For most of American history, broad oceans and friendly or weak neighbors meant there was little, if any, physical peril for the United States except when the country extended itself and thus placed itself at risk (the acquisition of Hawaii and the Philippines in the 1890s are primary examples). Physical security is, of course, the most basic, fundamental form of security. Technically, the United States' ability to guarantee its physical existence has been at risk since the then Soviet Union fielded nuclear-armed ballistic missiles capable of reaching the country with no means to intercept them. That prospect has become abstract for most Americans and has faded with the demise of the Soviet Union and the absence of plausible enmity between America and Russia. Usama bin Laden demonstrated that our absolute security could be breached and Americans could be subject to harm on our own soil.

Knowing we are vulnerable changes the way we look at the world, and we have just recently come to that realization. If Americans seem more obsessed with the consequences of the terrorist attacks than other peoples, it is largely because we have just recently lost part of our national innocence. Afghans, to cite one of our current focuses, learned a long time ago what the consequences of geography (occupying a major trade route) can be. The shocking loss of invulnerability to harm may have caused us to overreact about the extent of our vulnerability, to make us equate vulnerability to harm with more fundamental survival dangers.

The other form of security is psychological, what makes us *feel* secure or safe. In the absence of direct physical threats to security, the American debate over national security has historically concentrated, by and large, on the conditions that make us feel safe and allow us to prosper. The fact that since its establishment the United States has done almost all of its fighting overseas somewhere (the major exception being the Civil War, when we fought one another) is not a coincidence. Certainly there were important American interests involved, for instance, in American participation in the world wars, but it stretches credulity to maintain that the physical survival of the United States was one of them. Life would have certainly been more difficult for American commerce and security with a German-dominated Europe in 1918 or 1945 or a Japanese-ruled East Asia and the Pacific in the 1940s, but the country would have survived.

Most of our other uses of armed force have been deployments of choice rather than necessity, reflecting this distinction between the physical and psychological dimensions of security. The bulk of the national security debate since the end of World War II has revolved around questions about what makes us feel secure, once the necessities of dealing with the Soviet nuclear threat was removed by the establishment of the condition of mutual nuclear deterrence. In the post–Cold War world, the nuclear threat has faded in plausibility and partially in capability, and major threats to other U.S. interests did not emerge to dominate the agenda. In that atmosphere, the emphasis could move to those conditions that make life more commodious, to economic well-being through globalization as the major focus of concern. It was during the 1990s that notions such as economic and environmental *security* entered the public discourse, and we made war on drugs, not Communism or some other form of more traditional national security problem. The concern was clearly on the psychological dimension of security.

In intellectual terms, the great impact of the 2001 terrorist attacks was to move the center of the debate back in the direction of the physical realm of security. In our collective shock, the extent of the threat was probably overdrawn: Usama bin Laden and his cohorts could not destroy the United States or topple our government, terrorist threats that would be wildly beyond the capabilities and aspirations of any terrorist organization. Rather, the attacks demonstrated that our physical security was not absolute and that steps to minimize future breaches of our physical security were necessary and occupied the highest priority within the security realm.

As time has demonstrated, the national security debate is now defined in terms of homeland security, a term almost entirely missing from the dialogue on security prior to the terrorist events. Other security concerns have slowly returned as well. The Bush administration has led this trend, trying to maintain the focus on terrorism by progressively widening the range of concerns that fall under homeland security to encompass more conventional national security concerns such as force modernization.

So, what makes us secure? In 1989, before the Poles elected a non-Communist government and the Berlin Wall fell, the answer was the deterrence of the Soviet Union and the avoidance of World War III—keeping the Cold War cold. For the next dozen or so years, the absence of a peer competitor allowed us to relax our focus on military threats (except, of course, during the Persian Gulf War) and to turn our attentions to making ourselves prosperous—the ascendancy of the globalization system. The post–Cold War world allowed us to extend the "long peace" of

Challenge!

VISIONS OF THE VIOLENT FUTURE

In his *Foreign Affairs* article, Secretary of Defense Donald H. Rumsfeld also lists eight "lessons from recent experiences that apply to the future." They are:

First, wars in the twenty-first century will increasingly require all elements of national power: economic, diplomatic, financial, law enforcement, intelligence, and both overt and covert military operations.

Second, the ability of forces to communicate and operate seamlessly on the battlefield will be critical to success.

Third, our policy of accepting help from any country . . . is enabling us to maximize both other countries' cooperation and our effectiveness against the enemy.

Fourth, wars can benefit from coalitions of the willing, to be sure, but they should not be fought by committee.

Fifth, defending the United States requires prevention and sometimes preemption.

Sixth, rule nothing out—including ground forces.

Seventh, getting U.S. special forces on the ground early dramatically increases the effectiveness of an air campaign.

Eighth, and finally, be straight with the American people.'

What do you think of the SECDEF's list? How is it different from past formulations of the American posture? Is it more aggressive, more unilateralist? What are the implications for the kinds of forces the United States should develop for the future (in other words, what are its implications for force modernization)? Finally, based on your knowledge, do you agree with this vision of the future?

the Cold War; there has been no major war involving the largest powers fighting one another since World War II.

Did the terrorist attacks of September 11 end the long peace and usher in a fundamentally different set of concerns? Clearly, the tectonic shift of 2001 has moved the debate about safety and prosperity from the dominant role of prosperity to much more of an emphasis on the physical dimension of security. That is novel for Americans because it is a perspective with which we have not had to grapple very often in the past. What makes us secure now includes vigorously backed assurances that our physical safety against terrorists can be reasonably ensured and that our vulnerability to harm can be contained, if not eliminated altogether. Until that question is answered to the satisfaction of most Americans, we are reluctant to move back completely to an emphasis on what makes us feel prosperous. The evolving, increasingly negative disagreement over our involvement in Iraq is now a major element in the debate, arguably overriding terrorism per se.

The Cold War lasted roughly forty-five years. It took us seventeen years until the Cuban Missile Crisis of 1962 to understand that the principal objective of that competition had to be to avoid a system-threatening nuclear World War III that might destroy us all. It took another twenty-eight years to complete the job of defusing that problem. The post–Cold War world did not last as long, and the fact that we never found any name for it other than what it was not (it was not the Cold War) may suggest that we never entirely comprehended or adjusted to it.

And now the ground has shifted again. The shift has been dramatic, even traumatic, and it has caused us to react strongly. Like the end of World War II and the end of the Cold War, there will be a period of adjustment to new realities. The perspective of 2006 is probably too close to the fault line to see what has profoundly and fundamentally changed and what has not. The first answer to what will make us secure in the future is dealing with terrorism, but that is almost certainly not the total answer. The pendulum of central concern with physical and psychological security will continue to swing. We have not seen the last of geopolitics or of globalization.

SELECTED BIBLIOGRAPHY

Bhagwati, Jagdish. "Coping with Antiglobalization." *Foreign Affairs* 81, 1 (January/February 2002), 2–7.

Erlanger, Steven. "Europe's Military Gap." *New York Times* (national edition) (March 16, 2002), A1, A4.

Fukuyama, Francis. *The End of History and the Last Man.* New York: Free Press, 1992.

Gaddis, John Lewis. "Setting Right a Dangerous World." *The Chronicle Review* (electronic edition) 48, 18 (January 11, 2002).

Garrett, Geoffrey. "Globalization's Missing Middle." *Foreign Affairs* 83, 6 (November/December 2004), 84–96.

Hirsh, Michael. "Bush and the World." *Foreign Affairs* 81, 5 (September/October 2002), 18–43.

Huntington, Samuel P. *Clash of Civilizations: The Debate.* New York: Council on Foreign Relations Press, 1993.

————. *The Third Wave: Democratization in the Late Twentieth Century*. Norman, OK: University of Oklahoma Press, 1991.

Mandelbaum, Michael. "The Inadequacy of American Power." *Foreign Affairs* 81, 5 (September/October 2002), 61–73.

McFaul, Michael. "Democracy Promotion as a World Value." *Washington Quarterly* 28, 1 (Winter 2004–05), 147–164.

Nye, Joseph S., Jr. "Globalization's Democracy Deficit." *Foreign Affairs* 80, 4 (July/August 2001), 2–6.

Ottaway, Marina, and Thomas Carrothers. "Think Again: Middle East Democracy." *Foreign Policy* (November/December 2004), 22–29.

Quadrennial Defense Review. Washington, DC: United States Department of Defense, September 30, 2002.

Rumsfeld, Donald H. "Transforming the Military." *Foreign Affairs* 81, 3 (May/June 2002), 20–32.

Snow, Donald M. *September 11, 2001: The New Face of War?* New York: Longman, 2002.

Taylor, Terence. "The End of Imminence." *Washington Quarterly* 27, 4 (Autumn 2004), 57–72.

Index